# A FAITHFUL SPY

## The Life and Times of an MI6 and MI5 Officer

Based on the private papers of
Walter Bell, CMG and US Medal of Freedom

by

# Jimmy Burns

Chiselbury

With enduring love to

Kidge, Julia, Miriam, Nadia, Mila and James

# Contents

# Key Players & Organisations

## KEY PLAYERS

**Dean Acheson** US under secretary of state 1945–1949; secretary of state 1949–1953.

**Colonel John B. Ackerman** Assistant air attaché, US embassy London 1946–1949; air attaché 1949–1950.

**Julian Amery** British Conservative politician.

**James Angleton** CIA officer.

**Vincent Astor** American businessman.

**Oliver Baldwin** British socialist politician, son of Tory prime minister Stanley Baldwin.

**Roger Baldwin** American civil rights activist.

**John ('Jock') Balfour** British diplomat, Washington.

**Prem Bathia** Indian journalist.

**Cedric Belfrage** British journalist and spy.

**Isaiah Berlin** Russian-British philosopher.

**David Bruce** American diplomat and politician, head of the Office of Strategic Studies (OSS) London 1942–1945.

**John Buchan (Lord Tweedsmuir)** Author, politician and statesman.

**Patrick Buchan-Hepburn** Governor general of the West Indies Federation 1958–1962.

**Guy Burgess** British diplomat and Soviet agent.

**Tom Burns** Editor of *The Tablet.*

**Sir Gerald Campbell**

British consul general New York 1931–1938.

**Admiral Wilhelm Canaris** Head of Abwehr 1935–1944.

**Victor Cavendish-Bentinck** WW2 chairman Joint Intelligence Committee.

**Robert Cecil** British diplomat.

**General Jayanto Nath Chaudhuri** Chief of army staff India 1962–1966.

**Sir Warden Chilcott** Conservative MP.

**Sir Alexander Clutterbuck** British high commissioner India 1952–1955.

**George Conway** Honorary British consul Mexico 1939–1942.

**Duff Cooper** Minister of information 1940–1941.

**Brian Crozier** British journalist.

**Sir Smith-Mansfield Cumming** first chief of the Secret Intelligence Service (MI6).

**Constance Cummings** American actress.

**Allen Dulles** Director of the Office of Strategic Studies (OSS) Switzerland 1942–1945: director of the Central Intelligence Agency (CIA), 1953–1961.

**Herbert Dyce Murphy** Tonbridge alumnus, spy, gentleman explorer.

**Louis Einthoven** Dutch politician, lawyer and head of the Dutch security service.

**Charles ('Dick') Ellis** MI6 officer.

**Reginald Fletcher** Liberal, then Labour MP.

**Anne-Marie (Baroness) Franckenstein** Countess of Esterhazy-Galantha.

**Oliver Franks** British ambassador US 1948–1952.

**Hugh Fraser** Conservative MP.

**Monsignor Alfred Gilbey** Roman Catholic priest; chaplain of Cambridge University.

**Frank Giles** Deputy

editor of *The Sunday Times* 1967–1981; editor 1981–1983.

**Lord Halifax** British ambassador US 1940–1946.

**Michael Hanley** Director general MI5 1972–1978.

**William ('Bill') Hansberry** Pioneering African historian.

**Hugh Herbert-Jones** MI6 officer in Nairobi.

**Louis Heren** Correspondent for the London *Times*.

**Sir Samuel Hoare** Senior British Conservative politician.

**Sir Roger Hollis** Director general MI5 1956–1965.

**J. Edgar Hoover**, FBI director 1924–1962.

**Montgomery Hyde** MI6 officer.

**Lord Inverchapel** British ambassador US 1946–1948.

**Cheddi Jagan** Guyanese politician.

**C. L. R. James** Trinidadian politician and cricket expert.

**Thomas Kendrick** Head of the MI6 station Vienna 1925–1938.

**Bruce Kent** Campaign for Nuclear Disarmament (CND).

**Jomo Kenyatta** Kenyan independence leader.

**Margaret Kenyatta** Jomo Kenyatta's daughter.

**Gobal Das Khosla** Indian civil servant and high court judge.

**Daniel Milton Ladd** FBI special agent 1931–1949; assistant to the director Edward Allen Tamm 1949–1954.

**Thomas Lamont** American banker.

**Harold Laski** English Marxist theorist and economist.

**John le Carré** British author.

**Guy Liddell** MI5 officer.

**Lord Lothian** British ambassador US 1939–1940.

**Jay Lovestone** American activist, one-time communist leader.

**Reginald Lygon** (cousin of 8th Earl Beauchamp), husband of Mary Bell.

**William Lygon** 7th Earl Beauchamp.

**William Lygon** 8th Earl Beauchamp, also known as Viscount Elmley.

**Malcolm MacDonald** Son of Labour politician Ramsay MacDonald, governor of Kenya 1963–1964.

**Donald Maclean** British diplomat and Soviet agent.

**Melinda Maclean** Wife of Donald Maclean.

**Iain Macleod** Secretary of state for the colonies 1959–1961.

**Bill Magan** MI5 officer.

**Roger Makins** British diplomat Washington.

**Norman Washington Manley** Jamaican prime minister 1959–1962

**George C. Marshall** US secretary of state 1939–1945; 1950–1951.

Arthur Maundy Gregory Political fixer.

**Sir Stewart Menzies** Head of MI6 1939–1952.

**Sir Philip Mitchell** British diplomat, governor of Kenya 1944-1952.

**Henry Morgenthau Jr.** US Treasury secretary.

**Herbert Morrison** British Labour politician.

**Oswald Mosley** Founder of the British Union of Fascists.

**Bhola Nath Mullik** Indian civil servant and spymaster; director of the Intelligence Bureau of India 1950–1964.

**Jawaharlal Nehru** First prime minister of India 1947–1964.

**Oginga Odinga** Kenyan nationalist politician.

**Sir James Paget** MI6 station chief New York 1937–1940.

**Kim Philby** British intelligence officer and Soviet agent.

**Dusko Popov** Serbian double agent.

**Colonel Zarko Popović** Serbian spy.

**John Pringle** Jamaican businessman.

**Patrick Renison** British diplomat, governor of Kenya 1959–1962.

**Gunther Rumrich** Nazi spy.

**Sir George Sansom** British diplomat.

**William Sebold** FBI double agent.

**Sir Percy Sillitoe** Director general of MI5 1946–1953.

**Admiral Sir Hugh Sinclair** Smith-Cumming's successor as head of MI6 1923.

**Danylo Skoropadsky** Ukrainian dissident.

**General Carl ('Tooey') Spaatz** American World War Two general and father of Tattie Spatz,

Walter Bell's wife.

**Duncan Spencer** American banker.

**Harold Stanley** American banker.

**William ('Bill') Stephenson** Head of British Security Coordination (BSC) 1940–1945.

**Major Richard Stevens** head of MI6 The Hague 1939.

**John Strachey** British Labour politician and writer.

**Christopher Sykes** Author and Special Operations Executive (SOE).

**Edward Allen Tamm** FBI Deputy Associate Director, overseeing all FBI investigations nationwide 1951–1961.

**Captain Herbert Taylor** New York MI6 station chief 1929–1937.

**Norman Thwaites** British intelligence officer.

**Hugh Trevor-Roper**

British World War Two MI6 officer and historian.

**Sir Edward Twining** British diplomat, governor of Tanganyika 1949–1958.

**Cornelis van den Heuvel** Dutch intelligence officer.

**Valentine Vivian** MI6 officer counter-espionage unit.

**Christenze von Blixen** (aka Isaak Dinesen), Danish author.

**Adam von Trott** German foreign ministry official.

**Sir Dick White** Director general MI5 1953–1956; head of MI6 1956–1958.

**Eric Williams** Secretary of the West Indies Federal Party.

**Shirley Williams** MP.

**William ('Willie') Wiseman** New York MI6 officer and baker

**Elizabeth Wiskemann** World War Two intelligence officer.

**Robert Zaehner**

Tonbridge alumnus and academic.

## KEY ORGANISATIONS

**Abwehr** German military intelligence service.

**American Civil Liberties Union (ACLU)** An American non-profit organisation founded in 1920 to champion constitutional liberties in the USA.

**British Security Coordination (BSC)** A covert organisation set up in New York City by the British Secret Intelligence Service in May 1940 upon the authorisation of the prime minister, Winston Churchill.

**The British Union of Fascists** A British fascist political party formed in 1932 by Oswald Mosley. Mosley changed its name to the British Union of Fascists and National Socialists in 1936 and, in 1937, to the British Union.

**Combined Chiefs of**

**Staff** The supreme chiefs of military staff for the United States and Britain during World War Two.

**G-2** US military intelligence.

**Interdoc** Western intelligence network.

**Left Book Club** A publishing group pioneered by Victor Gollancz that exerted a strong left-wong influence on Britain from 1936 to 1948.

**British Joint Intelligence Committee** A central component of the British Government's secret machinery, liaising between agencies and advising on policy.

**KGB** Soviet secret intelligence agency.

**MI9** , British military intelligence escape & evasion section.

**National Joint Committee for Spanish Relief** (NJCSR) A British voluntary organisation founded at the end of 1936 to coordinate relief efforts for victims of the Spanish Civil War.

**Nationalist Socialist German Workers Party (NSPDG)** Official name of the Nazi Party.

**Office of Strategic Services (OSS)** US intelligence agency during World War Two.

**Section V** MI6 counter-espionage section.

**US Commission for the Care of European Children(USCOM)** A quasi-governmental American body established in June 1940, with the intent to try to save mainly Jewish refugee child ren who came from Continental Europe, and to evacuate them to the United States. However, most of the children were British refugees from the Blitz.

**X-2** OSS counter-espionage branch.

# Preface

When Walter Bell died in January 2004, aged ninety-four, the details of his life – not least of his professional career in the British secret services during a defining period in the history of modern espionage and security – remained a well-kept secret. He had been decorated with the US Medal of Freedom in 1947 for wartime services in support of the Allied cause and, close to his retirement in 1967, was appointed Companion to the Order of St Michael and St George (CMG), an honour reserved for those who make a significant contribution to the national interest. And yet, while providing some tantalising clues to an unusual and interesting career, an obituary in the London *Times* barely skimmed the surface of Bell's story.[1]

Descended from the founder of one of journalism's pioneering newspapers, the *News of the World*, Bell was the wayward child of an Anglican vicar and his artist wife, born into Edwardian England and spending his private school days in the run-up to World War One rebelling against his background.

His student and early adult years saw him embrace left-wing politics, while developing a network of influential mentors, thanks to whom he was recruited by MI6 in the mid-1930s.

Bell went on to inhabit the shadowlands of secret intelligence straddling the Atlantic during World War Two before serving in the UK embassy, Washington, during a critical period in the post-war Anglo-American relationship. There were subsequent postings in Kenya, India and the Caribbean, where he keenly observed the challenging politics of the twilight of the British Empire. Since these were largely covert assignments, his high-level contacts with key historic figures such as FBI director J. Edgar Hoover, UK wartime MI6 chief in the US, Bill Stephenson, the Russian spies Donald Maclean and Kim Philby, British spy chiefs Dick White and Roger Hollis, and post-colonial independence leaders Jomo Kenyatta and

Jawaharlal Nehru have remained both undiscovered and undisclosed. Until now.

Bell's story would have remained untold had his American widow, Katharine ('Tattie') Spaatz – daughter of Carl Spaatz, the World War Two US general and commander of Strategic Air Forces in Europe – not passed on to the author of this biography her late husband's extensive private papers.

At this point I should disclose a personal friendship with Tattie and Walter Bell. Tattie trusted me, and my credentials as an author and journalist, enough to believe I would use the material responsibly and constructively. By illuminating Walter Bell's life I would be adding to our understanding of the twentieth century and, with the passage of time (January 2024 marks the twentieth anniversary of Bell's death), provide posthumous recognition of his contribution to intelligence history. His unique access to a small number of key figures who were at the heart of the spy world constitutes a unique personal record of some of the failures and successes Bell gained intimate knowledge of when serving 'on His Majesty's secret service' (MI6) and 'in defence of the realm' (MI5). Among other things, Bell's papers reveal the strains between wartime British and US intelligence and the controversial nature and attitudes of key political, diplomatic and covert players over more than three decades that defined the geopolitics of the twentieth century.

It is Bell's extensive cache of papers – notes, memoirs, and correspondence with family, friends and sources, including revealing exchanges with controversial spies and leading government figures – that form the backbone of the narrative in the following pages. They provide a unique perspective of the key events that defined British international relations from the 1930s to the end of empire and the Cold War and the cast of characters involved as he experienced them at first hand. The personal detail and comment these papers contain bring to life a very human story, the fascinating less-than-ordinary story of a man who inhabited the world of discreet diplomacy and secret intelligence, his life and times.

The material informing the narrative that follows

provides an important addition to the existing bibliography of intelligence history. It shows how British spies could both shape government policy and also be ignored when it suited politicians, and lays bare the internal conflicts between the Allies and their vulnerability to penetration by Russian espionage and conspiracies linked to it.

Bell joined MI6 in the mid-1930s out of a sense of curiosity and ambition as well as patriotic duty, while coming to terms with the existential crisis of his generation, torn between loyalty to King and Country and the seductive appeal of communism when faced with the rise of fascism. His wartime experience was at the heart of the emerging special relationship between the UK and US intelligence services, the old empire giving way to a new global giant, with internal power struggles that he endeavoured to defuse.

Putting his faith in Churchill, Roosevelt and the transatlantic alliance, Bell served in the US during a critical period in the creation and development of the Anglo-American intelligence relationship leading up to World War Two and during the war itself. Post-war he was also involved in attempts to forge a special relationship with the Americans, serving in the British embassy, Washington, as private secretary to the ambassador Lord Inverchapel when, unknown to both of them at the time, the British Foreign Office and MI6 had fallen prey to unprecedented infiltration by Russian intelligence.

Then, as the Cold War set in and Britain's colonies pressed for independence, Bell moved to MI5, with further postings in Kenya, India and the West Indies. It was a politically volatile period when he was called upon to play a crucial role in the development of British security links with the newly independent governments.

A consummate networker, Bell's involvement with the world of intelligence continued during a long and active retirement, part of which was spent monitoring Soviet policy while defending the reputation of colleagues wrongly accused of being Russian moles.

The tension over the need to protect secrets and the public interest in exposing them would run and run and was destined to outlive Bell. Some intelligence files that might have helped put further flesh on his story remain unavailable for research or have been 'weeded out', as has been the fate of countless records destroyed by government order for reasons never explained, let alone justified.

In 2005, a year after Bell's death, when his personal papers were still gathering dust in dozens of cardboard boxes and folders undiscovered in the basement of his London home, the historian Peter Hennessy, in the prestigious annual Cambridge Hinsley Memorial Lecture series, lamented the challenges of writing British intelligence history given the resistance of the national security establishment to having its history written, either officially or by privateers.[2]

Fifteen years later the retired MI6 chief Sir Richard Dearlove, while demonstrating the advance to greater visibility with his presence as the speaker at the same public forum, justified the secret intelligence service's unique status within Whitehall as the only government agency claiming not just the power to decide for itself how much of its story could be told but the right to withhold countless records from public scrutiny.[3]

While this book would not have been possible without the substantial material of personal papers that I was lucky enough to have come into my possession, I have also drawn on additional testimonial and documentary sources, including recently declassified documents at the National Archives in Kew, and hitherto unpublished information held at the Churchill Archives in Cambridge, to test, provide context, substantiate and, where necessary, clarify or correct the assertions of its main protagonist. Spies, after all, are trained in duplicity as well as discovery. In researching Bell's life and times, I was conscious of the challenge of manoeuvring through the smokes and mirrors of the world of espionage and secret diplomacy. Despite the clarity shed by some historians accessing previously classified material, the diligent investigative work of some journalists and authors, and some other memoirs, it is a world that still serves to hide information across many areas behind official secrecy, when it is not obfuscated by misinformation and disinformation. During his lifetime Bell was determined to abide by the letter of the law and handle the official secrets to which he was party responsibly. He was protective of many of his agents and of information that, if aired, could risk lives. The personal correspondence and other papers he kept are testimony to the fact that he was never quite muzzled by his employers. They reveal a maverick who throughout maintained a critical attitude towards dogma, convention and the establishment.

While ever conscious of his privileged and clerical background, Bell trod his own, often anti-Tory and agnostic, path and was not always on the right side of authority. Rules were less important to him than his personal judgement of people and situations – he was the one who made the final decision on whether they were fair and just. Ultimately, it was in his conversion to Roman Catholicism mid-career that he showed himself to be a man driven more by faith in the common good than the atheistic ideology that drove some of his generation towards Moscow.

Walter Bell's legacy is that of an intelligence and security officer who remained a patriotic left-footer until the end, but never betrayed his country. He could have been tempted to become a communist spy, but remained a defender of Western ideals of democracy and justice and rediscovered his belief in a Christian God without feeling the need to be earnest about it. This is his inspiring story.

# 1
# Rites of Passage

On a late autumn afternoon in 1934, a tall young man with a slight stoop made his way along a cold and seemingly deserted residential road near Westminster, central London. Queen Anne's Gate was one of the capital's most elegant streets, lined with fine late eighteenth-century houses regarded by many architects as the best of their kind. He stopped for a moment in front of Number 21 and – no doubt with a sharp intake of breath – walked up to the front door and pressed the doorbell.

Walter Bell, aged twenty-four, had come to Queen Anne's Gate to attend an interview for a job he knew next to nothing about, other than the fact that it offered him a change from his hitherto rather dull life. As he stepped over the threshold, he could scarcely have imagined that the role he was about to take on would shape the course of world events and mark his performance in the unfolding drama.

These were politically turbulent times in which to make one's way in life. The year 1934 had the world convulsed and seemingly on the edge of worse calamities to come. With the Great Depression taking the global economy to rock bottom, people turned to whatever and whoever promised them a better life. In the fledgling power that was the US, President Franklin D. Roosevelt was under increasing political pressure from those who believed that certain aspects of the New Deal – mobilising the power and resources of the federal government to address the issues of poverty and inequality – were an unconstitutional overreach, and others who felt it did not go far enough.

With the US seemingly turning in on itself, elsewhere more extreme leaders were fuelling people's fears and prejudices to rally support and create a scapegoat for the world's problems. At the end of June 1934 Adolf Hitler, Germany's newly self-declared Führer, had carried out a brutal extra-judicial action against opponents, the so-called Night of the Long Knives – the latest evidence for those who did not wish to appease him that he stood outside civilised politics. In Russia Stalin was beginning his own massacres, while in China Mao Tse-Tung was spreading the communist doctrine. Closer to home Oswald Mosley's 'black shirts' were organising fascist rallies and clashed with communists and Jews on the streets of London, while radical students and some of their professors embraced Marxism as the only alternative to fascism.

A vicar's son with a generally conservative appearance, Bell seemed unlikely material for a political firebrand, but his politics were radically left wing, and he had a sense of adventure and confidence that made him feel ready to tackle the world. The interview came at a time when he wanted a new challenge, motivated as much by anger and a desire to change politics as by curiosity.[1] It marked a crossroads in his life and was a time for reflection.

* * *

Before his visit to Queen Anne's Gate, nothing very exciting had happened in Bell's life. He had had a relatively secure and comfortable upbringing, his very early years spent in in the vicarage of a quiet English village followed, after World War One, by the privilege of private if not entirely happy schooling, which planted the seeds of a rebellious youth. As he wrote many years later in a letter to his friend the journalist Anthony Hartley, he was enraged by the 'total indifference of the self-satisfied upper-class people who came to my father's Church, towards the unemployed, in particular the miners, who had only a miserable pittance to survive on'.[2]

As an adult he had taken on a few teaching jobs, but at the point where this story begins he was living in London in a house belonging to his mother's cousin and studying for the Intermediate Law Examination at the London School of Economics (LSE). His hopes of going up to Oxford had been frustrated by a temporary dip in his family's financial circumstances, but studying at the LSE, founded in 1895 by members of the Fabian Society who believed in the advance of democratic socialism, satisfied his youthful radicalism and ambition with excellent lecturers and key contacts (one of his contemporaries there was Richard Bissell, who had an official role in the post-war Marshall Plan, and later became a senior CIA officer).[3]

London University may have lacked the ancient spires, academic elitism and hedonism of Oxford and Cambridge, but LSE provided a very respectable undergraduate law degree in one of the world's leading law schools at the heart of a great capital city and was ideally placed to serve the legal profession. Its campus was adjacent to the Royal Courts of Justice and Inner Temple, the professional body that Bell joined as an aspiring barrister. It was also strategically placed between the other powers in the land, the nearby headquarters of the newspaper barons in Fleet Street, and a short bus ride away from Buckingham Palace, the main departments of government in Whitehall and the Houses of Parliament – a world of power and influence Bell was destined to become even more familiar with.

LSE had a vibrant political life reflecting the turbulent ideological and social atmosphere of the 1930s. Bell came to it having developed an early taste for politics in the 1929 general election when, between teaching jobs, he campaigned for Ramsay MacDonald's Labour Party. His law studies at LSE deepened his interest in left-wing politics. 'I was an increasingly "Our Age" disciple, which did me little good, except to introduce me to a lot of interesting and sympathetic people,' he later admitted.[4]

An important influence on Walter's developing world view were the lectures he attended on the British Constitution by the legendary political theorist and economist, the Marxist professor Harold Laski. Bell found much food for thought in Laski's disillusionment with capitalism, and a sense of urgency in the way the distinguished academic addressed the threat of fascism given the policies that were engulfing Europe in the 1930s. At the same time the marriage of Walter's older and only sister Mary to the aristocratic Reginald Lygon in 1930 had provided connections to influential elements of the political class and opened side doors that led, through politics, into the secret orbit of intelligence operatives.

Bell was invited to meetings of political and government contacts organised by Reginald's cousin, the Liberal MP William Lygon, who had the honorific title, bestowed at birth, of Viscount Elmley. (He would later succeed to the family title, as the 8th Earl of Beauchamp.) At one such meeting Bell was introduced to one of Elmley's friends, the former Liberal turned Labour politician Reginald Fletcher, who would be elected Labour MP for Nuneaton in 1935 and raised to the peerage in 1942 as Baron Minster before going on to serve as minister of civil aviation in Attlee's post-war administration.

Fletcher's politics and links with the intelligence services would have made an instant connection with Bell, who had an insatiable interest in world affairs. There is no record of how close the friendship was, or the content of their discussions, but Bell clearly felt relaxed enough in his company to talk to him about the dissatisfaction he felt about his life because Fletcher was soon to respond. One November morning in 1934, he rang Bell to inform him of a possible job opportunity. The Treasury had authorised the appointment of an assistant passport control officer (effectively vice consul) to New York on a salary of £1,000 per annum tax free, the equivalent of around £70,000 in 2021. Fletcher was quick to point out the bureaucratic and mundane aspects of the job, but, given Fletcher's connections with intelligence, and, no doubt, the tenor of their conversations, Walter would have almost certainly known that there was more to it than being a mere pen-pusher. He probably even realised it was some kind of intelligence posting – a seemingly mundane job that, behind its cover, offered a life that promised to be a great deal more exciting and challenging than anything he had experienced thus far.

But this was all still for the future. At the point when the offer was made any thoughts about the nature of the job, despite its potential significance, would have largely been overshadowed in Bell's mind by the dazzling generosity of the offer. The salary was far more than he had ever earned as a teacher, or than his father George Bell – Vicar of Riverhead – could ever have dreamed of. Walter reflected that George, in a good year, earned less than he himself was now being offered, and this included the fees for baptising, marrying and burying his parishioners while receiving modest donations to deal with the depletions of the vicarage, which faced an enduring problem of dry rot. The threat of poverty had been a constant theme of family conversations, with ominous references, somewhat exaggerated, that the workhouse hovered over Walter's future as a place of last resort.

Salary and tax-free perks aside, there was the location. The mere thought of a posting in New York, the first mega-city in human history and destined to be the City of Ambition that emerged from the Depression, was appealing after the staidness of London, offering an escape from his conventional family upbringing and religious discipline, and all the stultifying aspects of England's class-ridden society.

He was nevertheless conflicted. He knew nothing about the specifics of the job and questioned the wisdom of abandoning the chance of becoming a barrister for a future that might well be uncertain. While restless and rebellious by nature, in terms of his credentials for the career that was opening up to him, Bell was already showing signs of being a consummate networker. To help him make up his mind, he consulted with the wise men of the British judicial establishment in their historic citadels dating back to the Knights Templar of the Crusades.

Bell was invited to lunch to discuss his future at the ancient refectory known as the Inner Temple Hall, an imposing restored Gothic-style building with stained-glass windows featuring the coats of arms of noted treasurers from 1506 onwards. He would be in distinguished company. His host, as he would later recall, was his mentor Alexander Fachiri, secretary to the Master of the Rolls and an international lawyer. They were joined at the table by Cyril Asquith, the youngest son of Henry Asquith, prime minister from 1908 to 1916, and a number of barristers whose experience and wise counsel he respected. All were members of the Honourable Society of the Inner Temple, a professional association for barristers and judges in London and one of the capital's most influential and enduring clubs and networks.

Whatever advice Bell received at the lunch, he emerged from it having made up his mind to take up Commander Fletcher's offer without further delay. The next day at 4 p.m. he presented himself at 21 Queen Anne's Gate.

\* \* \*

Located in the heart of London, between St James's Park and Parliament Square, Queen Anne's Gate had a distinguished past. Many of its well-appointed houses were known to have been inhabited by eminent figures from English political history. The Victorian prime minister Lord Palmerston was born in the same quiet street in 1784 and other well-known erstwhile residents of this closely knit neighbourhood of privilege and influence included the World War One foreign secretary Sir Edward Grey and the early twentieth-century statesman, wartime minister, lawyer and philosopher Lord Haldane.

But the identity of the residents of Number 21 had been a closely guarded secret since 1926. For it was then that the building was turned over to the Secret Intelligence Service, MI6. In that same year the ever-expanding intelligence service had moved its first headquarters from West House, a Victorian villa on Melbury Road near Holland Park, west London, to a spot that took it closer to the heart of government and political life in Whitehall, Westminster.

The five floors at Number 21 included a flat belonging to the MI6 chief and related administrative offices. One floor was linked by an internal bridge to the nearby Broadway Buildings, at Number 54 Broadway, through which the chief could move, unobserved by the outside world, to an office he had in a block across the street from St James's Park underground station, built in 1924. MI6 staff occupied part of the six-storey stone building with its prominent mansard roof along with colleagues from the Government Code and Cypher School (GC&CS) (later renamed GCHQ).

When Bell went to Number 21 Queen Anne's Gate it was the head office of Britain's passport control, which in 1921 had been set up to manage several overseas MI6 posts under the same cover name by the first MI6 chief Mansfield Cumming, or C. Secret government financing of passport control channelled through its headquarters in London to offices overseas was an important component of classified British secret intelligence funding between the wars. [5]

Fletcher would have known that the UK passport offices abroad were run as 'cover' by MI6, but had kept up the fiction that the employment in government service that Bell was being offered was purely administrative and linked to control of immigration and visa applications. He told Bell that the job vacancy had arisen because there had been complaints of rudeness by the public to the staff of the consular office in New York. Several Americans had objected to being asked to pay the fee then required of all American visitors to Britain. A fresh, personable recruit with youthful energy, diplomatic tact and skills was needed.

Whatever Bell did or didn't know at this point, he would have needed no reminding that the true nature of his recruitment was to be kept secret, not just from the public but also from his family and friends. The limits of disclosure as to what government regarded as matters of extreme sensitivity had had a recent test case. Two years earlier the celebrated writer Compton Mackenzie, who had converted to Catholicism in 1914, had been prosecuted, not for his faith (although there were enduring residues of anti-Catholic prejudice in public life), but under the Official Secrets Act. He was fined and had a first edition of a book of memoirs about his World War One experiences as an intelligence officer withdrawn from publication. The book, *Greek Memories*, named wartime colleagues, mentioned that passport control and visa sections of UK missions abroad were often used as cover for secret work, disclosed that in its early years MI6 had operated as a section in the War Office known as 'M.I.i.c', and that its founding head Sir Mansfield Cumming, whom he named, was referred to as C.

Bell's appointment was with an MI6 officer who went by the name of Colonel Edward Peel RM. He turned out to be a simple conduit, who introduced him to a hierarchical chain of command with the words, 'Don't be afraid now, you are going to see the Admiral – just be yourself.'[6]

Bell followed Peel up a flight of stairs before being ushered into a comfortably furnished room heavily scented with cigar smoke. Standing before an open fireplace was the Admiral, a balding man of medium height. Admiral Hugh Sinclair had succeeded Mansfield Cumming as MI6 chief. Bell thought of Colonel Peel's advice about being himself, but struggled to make sense of the situation he found himself in.

His puzzlement was not helped when the Admiral barked his first question as to why on earth he was interested in such a miserable job. 'New York is a revolting place, the Americans object to having to pay for their visas, and are invariably rude, requiring tactful handling. The salary is not nearly enough to live comfortably in a city where life is expensive,' the Admiral told him. 'Are you really still interested in being considered for such an assignment?' he went on, drawing on his cigar.[7]

Unknown to Bell at the time, MI6 was in a phase of reorganisation and expansion after a long period between the wars during which it had run its skeleton operations abroad on a shoestring budget. The Secret Intelligence Service (SIS), while having its senior and middle management largely in the hands of World War One veteran naval and army officers, was reaching out to a new generation of university-educated public school boys in a period of recruitment that would accelerate with the advent of World War Two.

The MI6 chief Sinclair had recently secured an increase

in funding that would see the Secret Service budget (covering MI5 and MI6) more than double from 1935 to 1936 and 1937, with further sharp increases up to 1939 and beyond. In a Whitehall memorandum dated 9 October 1935 Sinclair complained that MI6's ability to anticipate and inform on Mussolini's imperial ambitions in Abyssinia and Germany's militarisation under Hitler had been hampered by lack of funds. He had drawn a characteristic naval analogy to note that his previous shoestring budget, which was meant to cover M16's surveillance of the whole world, was no more than that spent every year on the maintenance of one destroyer in home waters.[8]

The Admiral reassured Bell that he could count on his full support and that of his colleagues if he encountered any problems with the Americans. In the late inter-war years, the Federal Bureau of Investigation (FBI) (the new name given in 1935 to the Division of Investigation) had had some agents in South America, and the US army some attachés in Europe, North Africa and the Far East, but the US did not yet have a fully-fledged intelligence service of its own, which complicated MI6's own operational role on the other side of the Atlantic with no obvious partner sharing similar methods or philosophy.[9] As the lead US police agency, the FBI was jealously protective of its security and investigative role, including the monitoring of major criminals and suspect foreigners. Meanwhile MI6's official diplomatic interlocutor with the US government, the State Department, remained opposed to anything that might draw the country into another war in Europe.

But even if the British passport control office had to tread carefully not to be seen to violate US law or sovereignty, it still saw a role for itself. As Sinclair told Bell, his job would have an interesting if challenging aspect to it, involving 'making a few undercover enquiries from time to time'.[10] There were, the Admiral continued, some people who were willing to betray their country for money or the satisfaction of some other unspecified weakness. But the only betrayal Sinclair could imagine was one that went against the interests of the empire, so Bell was asked to keep a look out for subversive anti-colonialists among the imperial diaspora that lived in the US and to recruit any useful sources of information. 'If you have any moral scruples about taking advantage of such people in British interests, then better say so now,' the Admiral told Bell.[11] At the time Sinclair was not even thinking of the possibility of MI6 being betrayed from within its own ranks – as would later occur with the treachery of Kim Philby and George Blake – [12] but of foreigners who could be recruited as MI6 agents and double agents. The Admiral brought the meeting to a close and gave instructions to his secretary to take Bell to the paymaster, Commander Sykes, with the promise of an advance.

Bell could not help feeling a sense of anticipation at a major change coming to his life as he was led down the stairs and along the connecting internal bridge that led to the adjoining building and then taken by lift to an office on the fourth floor where Commander Sykes, a big burly man with white hair, handed him £50 to cover immediate expenses before taking him back to Colonel Peel. The complex layout of the MI6 headquarters – a jigsaw of anonymous rooms, corridors and staircases – seemed deliberately designed to lessen any chance of its detail being memorised by any as yet not fully trusted and uninitiated visitor unless they had abnormally sharp powers of observation and recall.

Bell was congratulated on his appointment but warned not to tell anyone about the secret side of his work. 'By this time my imagination was fired by thoughts of Bulldog Drummond and of course Colonel Hannay. I was clearly on the threshold of a great adventure, even though it was to be in New York and not in Germany,' Bell later recalled.[13]

Nevertheless, his initiation as an intelligence officer got off to a somewhat inauspicious start. During his first days in MI6 Bell was confined to sharing an office in Queen's Anne's Gate with Colonel Peel's' two secretaries – a Miss Franks and a Miss Cook (more cover names no doubt). The first struck him 'as a somewhat masculine type who chain smoked Craven "A" cigarettes and played hockey'. The second told him she had worked for Compton Mackenzie during World War One. Bell mentioned that he had been introduced to the service by Commander Fletcher, at which point Miss Franks remarked disapprovingly that he was a member of the Labour Party. It was his first encounter with the political tensions that lurked beneath the apparent esprit de corps of the British secret service.[14]

Bell later recalled: 'This gave me a jolt and started the process of undermining my romantic feelings about the Service. I had naturally assumed that Commander Fletcher's presence in the office was part of the Great Game. Not that I regarded Fletcher as being unconcerned, but as a Socialist myself I was comforted to think that we could all work for the same cause, and it made me feel safer and more respectable.'[15] He went on: 'It was only later that I realized that Fletcher was viewed with distrust by the Admiral, or rather the Chief as he was always known within the office, and so far as I could make out, by all the other officers. Still, it was a curious thing that Fletcher was able to work for the Secret Service and nurse a constituency for the Labour party at the same time.'[16]

Maintaining discretion about his own political leanings, Bell carried on with his training, which included a crash course on encoding and decoding telegrams, reading some relevant files on suspected security risks, and being lectured to by various officers, among them one who seemed to have a lot of interesting information about the growing strength of the German Luftwaffe.

One of the first senior officers whom Bell met was MI6's expert on the communists, Colonel Valentine Vivian, a former Indian police officer once stationed in Lahore and married to a bishop's daughter called Primrose. In 1931 Vivian, later deputy chief of MI6, had been relocated to London and put in charge of a new counter-intelligence section within the agency called Section V. Vivian told Bell that he was particularly interested in harvesting information about the US contacts of M.N. Roy, the

Indian communist who had broken with the Communist Party of India and organised his own pro-independence opposition group. In all, Bell's training took three weeks.

\* \* \*

On 12 January 1935, Bell sailed for New York aboard the Cunard liner RMS *Carinthia*. It was a cold, if relatively smooth, winter crossing. which allowed him to enjoy some of the glamour of the ship's elegant interior of American bars and smoking rooms, and its two-storeyed dining and dance venue, named after the Spanish Renaissance painter 'El Greco' and modelled in a palatial style. As the ship sailed up the Hudson and Bell stood on deck, he saw for the first time the totemic Statue of Liberty and the futuristic skyline of Manhattan. The 'land of opportunity' beckoned, open to new arrivals escaping the Old World, with its modernity and seemingly classless and invigorated democracy a striking contrast from what he perceived as the atrophy of the British political establishment, made up of certain Lords and other Conservatives who were destined to appease fascism between 1937 and 1939. As Bell wrote later: 'I had the good fortune to get my job in New York, where I experienced a great relief at escaping from the stuffy past and so being caught up in all those circles who chatted and drank their time away, while so many of the right people were applauding Mussolini and telling us how Hitler had pulled Germany together.'[17]

On 21 January 1935 a US immigration inspector stamped Bell's arrival papers, which gave his age as twenty-five, his nationality as British, his race as English, his tax status as 'diplomatic, government official', and his occupation as 'assistant passport control officer'. He had already travelled far from his childhood.

# 2
# A Family of Influence

Walter Fancourt Bell was born on 7 November 1909, in the small Kent village of Riverhead, his Holy Baptism duly recorded by his vicar father George in the parish church of St Mary's Book of Life.[1] Named after an eleventh-century saint, Walter of Pontoise, in deference to his father's Christian faith, he was the youngest of three siblings, with a brother St John aged nine, and a sister Mary aged six.

Walter was born at a high point in the fortunes of Great Britain. The death of Britain's then longest-serving monarch the Empress Queen Victoria, eight years earlier, is now seen to have marked the moment when national self-confidence peaked after a period of global commercial and military expansion had created the largest empire in history.

And Walter's family, the Bells, embodied this spirit of optimism and achievement, leaving their mark on society over several generations.

The Bells' extraordinary legacy can be traced back to John Bell (1745–1831), a well-regarded and well-connected figure in the London print trade. John was a bookseller, printer and publisher of several periodicals. Most importantly, he was a member of the syndicate behind London's *Morning Post* newspaper and the successful Sunday newspaper *Bell's Weekly Messenger*, launched in 1796.[2]

The newspaper was considered good value, and John Bell 'ensured its respectability, moderating its content and refusing to take advertisements to make it suitable for families'.[3] Over time it came to expand its market in the shires until 1896 when it became the *Country Sport and Messenger*. Bell's joint-stock organisation – of forty dominant publishing companies at one point – established a virtual monopoly of the sector.

Although John Bell became a popular publisher (his 109-

volume, 'literature-for-the masses' *The Poets of Great Britain Complete from Chaucer to Churchill* was among his best-known works), it was his son, John Browne Bell, who was to make modern newspaper history with his creation of one of the most famous titles in British journalism.

Priced at 3 pence, the weekly Sunday *News of the World (NoTW)* was launched in 1893 and 'carved out ... a remarkable place for itself in the mid nineteenth-century, becoming one of the largest newspapers of all time'.[4] Its first edition appeared in 1843 with an egalitarian declaration of intent that gave no inkling of the newspaper's later reputation for salacious reporting. At its foundation the *NoTW* aimed to give as much general news as possible, along with political commentary – broadly defined as generalised social radicalism. There was also some attention to literature, and a small section of sporting news. 'It was a cheap, respectable weekly aimed at the upper working and lower middle classes.'[5]

The *NoTW* originally thought of itself as a 'miscellaneous newspaper for family perusal, and enjoyment by the fireside'. In the words of the journalist and media analyst Roy Greenslade, 'By providing a mixture of news and entertainment, it was unashamedly populist. However, throughout the 19th century and into the early 20th century its content was not as sensationalist or titillating as some commentators have tended to suggest.'[6]

By the time John Browne Bell's younger sibling Adolphus had taken over the ownership and Browne Bell's son John William had become editor-in-chief (following his father's death in 1855), the *NoTW* had become the cheapest and biggest-selling Sunday newspaper in the world.

Under John William's editorship the paper was refined into a more upmarket and 'women friendly' Sunday newspaper, with the aim of attracting new advertising revenue. On his death in 1877 its ownership remained with his uncle Adolphus, a former solicitor and Walter Bell's grandfather.

On 5 August 1873 Adolphus had married Louise Clarisse Reynolds from Herne Bay, Kent, and readers were now offered a new addition to the newspaper's literary section in the form of a serialised novel penned by her. Louise's byline, given under her maiden name of Reynolds, showed her to be doubly well connected. For she was not only Mrs Adolphus Bell, wife of the proprietor of the *News of The World,* but also the daughter of a no less influential social actor – George W. M Reynolds, a committed Chartist and a republican, himself a well-known author and also founder of the notable contemporary and very popular penny paper *Reynolds News.*

The Bells' first child, George Fancourt Bell (Walter's father) was born in 1875. The only male of five children, he would be followed by Jessie, Dora, Winifred and Marie. Adolphus and Louise brought up their children at number 45 High Street, Islington, near the busy commercial junction of the Angel, with its tramways, pubs, and small corner shops and offices. The Bell residence was part of a neighbourhood of large well-built private houses and leafy squares that attracted clerks, artisans, and professionals well into the second half of the nineteenth century before the arrival of the working classes made the district more popular but less fashionable.

In 1891, with circulation hitting an all-time low of 30,000 readers, the *News of the World* was in financial trouble. The paper was dying because of its respectful dullness. A solution to the crisis came in the personality and wealth of the highly successful solicitor George Riddell, who understood the financial benefits of turning it into a popular newspaper that exploited the people's demand for titillation and scandal. When, in 1903, the family sold the business to Henry Lascelles Carr, who owned the Welsh *Western Mail,* Riddell – an astute operator who moved among the great and the good – took over the *News of the World'*s management. When raised to the peerage as Baron Riddell in 1918, he was dubbed the Pornographic Peer by his rival, Lord Beaverbrook of Express Newspapers.

Any hope that selling the newspaper would improve the family's circumstances was in vain, however, for the money from the sale was largely squandered by the Bells, and Adolphus's son

George, Walter's father, had to leave school in his teenage years
and work as an insurance clerk. He found the work soulless and
pedestrian, with any prospect of a career linked to the *News of the
World* ended after he saw the family sell their newspaper
holdings to someone he regarded as an aspiring pornographer.
[7]

In his late teens George decided to come out of the
patriarchal shadow, turning his back on the legal profession and
newspapers and choosing instead to prepare for Holy Orders.
His calling to God's service was influenced by the experience of
working for a while as a young volunteer among the poor in
south-east London with the Charterhouse Mission, a charity
founded in 1885 by the Old Carthusians at 40 Tabard Street in
the borough of Southwark. He worked as a layman under the
then curate of St Hugh's, Wilmot Vivyan, who later emigrated
and became a bishop in South Africa.

Gifted with a good singing voice, Bell had at one point
considered auditioning for the D'Oyly Carte Opera Company
but shied away from it, perceiving it as an unholy indulgence. [8]
He might well have inclined towards the artistic world, in fact,
but music converged with faith in his life when he embraced
Anglo-Catholicism, which had emerged in the nineteenth
century as an important, if not always appreciated, force within
the Church of England, not just working among the poor and
unchurched but stressing Catholic elements in the ritual of
worship.

He studied religion at Durham, one of only four
universities in the country at the time (the other three being
King's College London, and Oxford and Cambridge) from
where the bishops of the Church of England accepted degrees
for ordination in Victorian times. He then completed his further
training at Ely Theological College, which had a strong Anglo-
Catholic tradition.

George was ordained at the age of twenty-three and
started life as a curate in 1898, at St Mary's in Penzance, where
two years later he met and married Annie 'Muriel' Backhouse.
His future wife was the daughter and the fourth of eleven

children of Thomas Backhouse, a Yorkshireman from Redcar, and Ellen Croggon, a member of a well-known Cornish family that had owned a successful tannery in Grampound for centuries. Thomas Backhouse had chosen to live in Cornwall for health reasons (he is thought to have suffered from tuberculosis before he died aged forty-nine) as Penzance was believed to have an ideal climate for invalids. He was also artistic and was attracted, as his daughter Muriel would later be, by the early Newlyn and St Ives colonies of artists.

Muriel Backhouse, as she grew up being known, was six years older than George Bell when they got married. An accomplished if frustrated romantic painter and poet, her private wealth was drawn from her family's investments in residential properties in London and there was little in her early years to suggest that she was cut out to be the wife of a vicar. Her instincts from a young age were creative and free-spirited. Expelled from Cheltenham Girl's School for smoking, aged seventeen, she went on to pursue her love of art. She was a pupil of Norman Garston, one of the leading artists of the Newlyn School and also studied at the Slade School of Fine Art under William Opren.

After leaving college Muriel was overcome by an urge to find herself abroad (a love of travelling and adventure was one of the many traits her future son would inherit) and went to India, the jewel of the Imperial Crown. For a young woman in her late twenties of reputable social standing and private means, a passage to India was, in the later part of the nineteenth century, viewed less as an adventure than a 'fishing exercise', its usual purpose dictated by convention, that of finding a husband in the colonial service. In Muriel's case it inspired her to write some evocative verses about the vibrant nature of Indian culture and the physical enchantment of the Kashmir Valley, which would later resonate with her son's own post-war experience of India. However, she returned to the UK unmarried and unloved.

Muriel's opportunities for an emotional attachment were

now beginning to narrow. By the time she met George Bell, the young curate was in his mid-twenties, and she was an unmarried thirty-year old, quite a gifted artist without ever gaining recognition as a great one, at a time when the artistic world was still very much a male preserve.

Walter, her youngest and favoured son, would inherit two of her paintings, both by unknown artists, from her pre-married days. One was a watercolour of a rose garden, poorly imitative of the idealised rural scenes depicted by the most famous women artist of the period, Helen Allingham. It was considered for an exhibition at the Royal Academy but was turned down because the committee didn't like the inclusion of a human figure that was barely visible in the background.

The second unsigned painting was a striking portrait of Muriel in her mid-twenties. In shows her as an attractive young woman, her auburn locks cut boyishly short, dressed in a loose-fitting embroidered jacket with a white fur collar, the kind of artistic hair style and 'dress' that became fashionable in the last quarter of the nineteenth century, in contrast to the previous Pompadour haircut and restrictive corsetry. The jacket she is wearing is misty blue like her eyes, which look down from a delicately powdered face. While relaxed in her own presence, she seems to evade the painter, striking an enigmatic rather than shy pose, with a hint of complicity.

It's not hard to imagine that in his youth the virginal young curate of St Mary's Church Penzance, George Bell, would have found himself easily captivated by this attractive, mature young woman on the day he spotted her in his congregation, and would have been delighted to have her enter his life along with a family endowment that would be of support to his vicarage wherever it was destined to be.

A rather studiously posed photograph taken in the year of their marriage in 1900, shows the 26-year-old George Bell, well-groomed, bespectacled, and self-consciously pious, dressed in a clerical collar and cassock and reading a breviary, a strikingly similar pose struck in photographs by his early mentor at the Charterhouse mission and subsequent Bishop of Zululand

Wilmot Vyvyan.

Despite the rather stern-looking image in the photograph, George's personality was far from dour. He retained a good sense of humour, which came out in his sermons, and his parishioners would come to respect him as a good parish priest.[9] Yet from his early days as a vicar he considered himself a man of faith and with a mission. He offered Muriel's restless soul a moral compass without necessary stifling her creative impulses – or so she believed. With both families supporting the union, the marriage of George Bell and Muriel Blackhouse went ahead. St John was born within the year, and a second child Mary three years later.

After Penzance, George served for a short time as curate in the church of St John the Evangelist in Upper Norwood, South London, and in Folkestone. In 1905 he was appointed vicar of the small parish of Riverhead, a Kent village below the North Downs. Destined within eight decades to become an access route to the M25 and absorbed into the northern suburbs of Sevenoaks, Riverhead was then a peaceful hamlet of a few hundred inhabitants, bordering the River Darent.

Raised above the village on a hill and surviving well into the twenty-first century as its dominant landmark stood the church of St Mary the Virgin. Constructed in a pre-Puginian Early English Gothic style and with an innovative wide pillarless nave designed by Decimus Burton, it was consecrated in 1831 as a chapel of ease to Sevenoaks parish church. It subsequently became an ecclesiastical parish.

When George arrived in Riverhead he found the church in an advanced state of disrepair, its previous vicar (seemingly a man of poor conviction) unwilling to stem the rot. The nave was populated by bats and its altar was a partial ruin. The new vicar was determined to reinvigorate parish life and he got off to a good start.

George's appointment to the parish of Riverhead came accompanied by support from the Church of England in the form of a large home with ample grounds and financial assistance with his oldest child's education. The Bell budget was boosted by the substantial private income Muriel drew from the Backhouse family's property investments, in particular a number of Victorian houses on the Old Kent Road.

The vicarage where Walter would spend his childhood and early youth was approached from the church by a narrow path through scattered tombstones, the oldest covered by overgrown vegetation. It was built in the same ragged hard grey local limestone as St Mary's, which gave both buildings an air of timelessness and permanence.

With uncluttered and commanding views across the Downs, the vicarage had its own large garden and seven acres of additional 'glebe', church property land that was leased with a pastoral mission paying a vicar's stipend of £120 per annum. Together with Muriel's endowment this was more than enough, without ostensible extravagance, to support the family and private schooling of the children.

Supported further by donations from parishioners, George set about the church's restoration. He built a new high altar and installed new stained glass windows so that he was soon able to celebrate daily communion and engage in the rituals of his faith with due solemnity. George Bell became a respected member of the small local community as well as a spiritual figure, his clerical vestments and ritual  marking him out as a High Church Anglican.

In July 1910 the first summer holiday the Bell family took after the birth of their third child Walter was in Penzance. It was marked by the sight of the greatest fleet ever assembled entering St Mount's Bay. As George later reported in a letter to his parishioners from St Ives, he and his family watched a huge armada under the command of Admiral Sir William May – 200 warships, in eight lines each led by a flagship. The fleet, which included destroyers and submarines, had sailed to Penzance for a review by King George V, an event which had drawn large crowds. But before the king arrived, a turn in the weather with a strong gale forced the decision to up anchors and set off eastward to the more sheltered Torbay.[10]

Returning to Riverhead, Walter joined his siblings in the nursery under the charge of a middle-aged nanny, Emily Culbert, who came from the Bahamas. The Bells also employed a thirty-year-old local cook Ruth Taylor, and a young house maid from Essex Florence Carter, so Muriel was not short of domestic support.

But times were changing. The Edwardian period that drew to a close during Walter's childhood has sometimes been portrayed as a golden summer of long lazy afternoons and garden parties for the more privileged classes, where the sun never set on the British Empire. But it was also a time of increasing uncertainty, with a deterioration in international relations combined with domestic issues: the 1910 constitutional crisis of the House of Lords and the problems posed by Irish home rule, the women's suffrage movement and massive labour unrest. Most significantly of all, the shadow of war was looming.

George was seemingly untouched by these rapidly changing events. As a country vicar he was still working at a time when being a Church of England parish priest could be, as imagined by Anthony Trollope, a rewarding career for the sons of professional classes as wealthy beneficiaries of the state.[11] And with its secluded hilltop setting and walled gardens the vicarage too was guarded against the advance of modernisation, much in the same way as the vicarage the novelist Lorna Sage remembered from her childhood: 'an insular retreat and a refuge for the private self to read and hide and wallow in the resentment of others'.[12] Walter's childhood and adolescence were spent there, a feeling of insecurity lingering beneath the apparent rural idyll, imbuing its social life as well as its faith, not always in ways he would have wished had he had a choice. Visitors included eccentric archdeacons, who enjoyed Muriel's home cooking and the decent wine provided by her vicar husband.

As the youngest child, Walter grew up pampered by his mother, while having to submit himself to the mission and theology that his father pursued with unwavering pious rectitude. George Bell, as his son recalled years later, 'set to work with great energy to promote catholic teaching on the sacraments with appropriate devotions, ceremonies and decoration'. [13] The parish vicar was careful not to embrace the authority of the Pope, despite going as far as he could in replicating Catholic ritual while ensuring that his ministry was a focal point of community life with a focus on charitable work.

As an Edwardian paterfamilias, George continued to cling on to the old order as best he could, but on 4 August 1914 the Bells' idyll came to an end for ever.

On the day war was declared, the Bells were just another family looking out over the glorious rolling Kent countryside and preparing to visit the seaside. But soldiers were soon digging trenches in the greens overlooking the English Channel, followed by the arrival on English shores of the first Belgian refugees and the wounded British youth, shell-shocked and missing limbs.

# 3
# The Vicar's Son

One of the first photographs taken of Walter Bell as a young boy, aged four, dates from 1913. It shows him with his older sister Mary, both smiling, he clearly the youngest of the two, in a cotton frock and matching shorts, she in a white dress and matching long hairband in the brick-walled rose garden of the rectory. The scene is a picture of a magic garden of Edwardian childhood before the only world Walter had known until then was shattered. Walter was five years old when World War One broke out in 1914, bringing to an abrupt end those aspects of his existence that had made life seem a safe, sacral thing. A drawn-out innocence of childhood, framed by the seemingly undisturbed permanence of village life, was cut short.

With war came a tightening of the Bell domestic budget, which became increasingly stretched as Muriel's family income from property investments dried up. While the male members of the Bell family were saved from conscription because of their age, the war ended the sheltered existence that Walter had enjoyed as a child. 'The 1914 war put a swift end to nurseries and governesses so that I had my meals with grownups,' he later recalled.[1]

Part of him envied his financially assisted older brother St John, who spent the war years safely closeted, studying at a leading English private boarding school for boys. In 1915, while Walter was still a young preparatory schoolboy, St John was sent to Lancing College, Sussex. He spent the war years there – a period during which all the young masters ended up fighting at the front, and were replaced by elderly, and in some cases not very competent, teachers so that discipline, including corporal punishment, fell into the hands of the senior boys. St John became head of his house and captain of football. He retained good memories of Lancing, excelling in sport and as a chorister in the chapel, and enjoying the fact that the prefects were practically running the school.

As for the much younger Walter, he and his older sister Mary spent the war in the vicarage, in rather less idyllic circumstances than those suggested by the siblings' pre-war photograph. Walter, living at home with his parents, found himself in a household that seemed increasingly dominated by his father and the socially suffocating visits of fellow clerics.

The other parishes in the deanery were ministered by clergymen who differed among themselves as to belief, doctrine and religious practices generally. The Bells' visitors tended to be, for the most part, mild gentlemen but for an occasional representative of the extreme evangelical wing or low church clergy. As Walter later recalled of the fundamentalist puritans: 'I learnt to distinguish them from the more moderate ones because they tended to have walrus moustaches and to wear black straw boaters. These people were outrageous and their attitude towards the sacraments bordered on the blasphemous.'[2] They included one evangelical minister who during a week-long visit to the parish declaimed against popery with verbal violence.

Faced with such sectarianism George Bell stood his ground to prevent his church from 'being stripped of its crucifixes, statues, vestments and other objects of devotion in an orgy of Cromwellian sacrilege including evening communion without candles'.[3] George could show himself to be generous of spirit towards his fellow clergy, but also, if he felt the occasion and discussion warranted it, be outspoken and a bit pugnacious, very much like Vicar Fenwick in Anthony Trollope's *Vicar of Bulhampton*.

For young Walter, the pervading clericalism of his environment fuelled a youthful rebellion against institutionalised religion that mirrored his mother's emotional distress. Muriel struggled to adapt to the life expected of a vicar's wife, her early years of marriage and motherhood coinciding with a politically charged atmosphere over the issue of women's suffrage – although she did not become an active campaigner, her heart and politics were on the side of the ardent suffragettes. It was an instinctive radicalism that Walter would carry in his genes.

Having brought money to her marriage, Muriel tried as best she could to keep control of the family purse strings, while finding herself with little option but to partner her husband in parish affairs. Her life became tied up with fund-raising activities on behalf of the Christian Mothers' Union, all tea and cakes and discarded books, without finding an alternative outlet where she felt fulfilled as a woman in her own right.

George was absorbed by the affairs of the vicarage and felt responsible for the moral conduct of the village, while being emotionally distant from his children, as were many Edwardian fathers. Of the three siblings it was his older son St John, separated by some years from his sister and brother, who inherited the vicar's rectitude and conservatism, setting an example that his younger brother would show no inclination to follow.

As for Walter, the memory of his father would soften through the prism of time, forgiving of some of his eccentricities although never feeling any real intimacy towards him. George was, he would later recall, a 'delightful, understanding, tolerant and humorous man who attracted all and sundry to come to him with their troubles. While he was efficient and quite punctilious about ritual, he stressed that incense, candles, and such were appearances and not fundamental'. And yet, Walter went on, 'I grew up in this atmosphere and, no doubt due to some extent to my father's age, felt it difficult to engage his interest in my interests.' [4]

The rebellious streak that Walter developed owed much to the kindred spirit he found in his mother. Poetry and painting were her ways of bringing feelings and creativity into the emotionally silenced world of the patriarchal vicarage although her life as an artist receded once she got married, her creativity numbed by the insularity of parish life. Over time the extensive and intimate correspondence Walter maintained with her helped her fill something of the emotional void that opened up between she and her husband and their eldest son, making her feel connected with a far more adventurous world that beckoned beyond the insular English village life of St Mary's, Riverhead, Kent.

From early adulthood Walter shared his privately held and often controversial views about politics and faith, along with a record of his travels and the diverse individuals he met, in a regular exchange of letters with his mother, whom he evidently trusted as well as adored.

His transition from boyhood to adolescence, nonetheless, was not a happy one. At the age of nine he was sent to Beechmont Preparatory school in Sevenoaks. Its headmaster was an evangelical clergyman, the Revd. Clement Bode. As remembered by Walter, Bode bedevilled the young boys in his charge, much in the manner of the unpopular housemaster Mr Prout in Rudyard Kipling's novel, *Stalky & Co.* As Walter later recalled: 'He was a forbidding old man who induced a wickedness in one, particularly when he read out the Ten Commandments, looking at me at the end of each one and pausing. He seemed to imply that I had never intended to incline my mind to keep those laws.'[5]

In fact, there was the making of a maverick in the young Bell, who later reflected cheekily: 'I certainly coveted my neighbour's car but not his ass.'[6]

Bell's brother St John had attended Beechmont ten years earlier and been one of its star pupils. Walter, by contrast, was looked down upon by the uncompromisingly disciplinarian Mr Bode as a poor student and mischievous to boot. He felt hugely put out the day that Mr Bode offered him little cubes of white bread cut from a loaf like left-over crumbs from the kitchen table and taunted him with a challenge as to his true faith. 'What about the Real Presence?' Mr Bode asked him, referring to the belief held by Roman Catholics and some Anglicans that during the Eucharist the body and blood of Christ are wholly present under the appearances of bread and wine. As Bell reflected years later, 'It was the question that passed through my mind. I remember saying something about it to my mother who assured me that it was all right.' [7]

It wasn't until long after 1952, the year that George died, that Walter was to reveal another trauma suffered as a young boy. It was the day he was forced to have his first confession heard by his own parent, a clear abuse of George's priestly office. 'I was not frightened of him, but I was deeply embarrassed. I was given a little book with a long questionnaire setting out all the misdeeds of which the author could think without being too specific in certain directions...I took the questionnaire very seriously and in compiling my list of sins gave the prosecution full benefit of the doubt.'[8]

The incident (which would become a regular event), along with George's propensity to devote much of his preaching to the subject of sin and the need for abstinence and penitence, proved trickier still for Walter given that the congregation included girls and women from the parish who sat by the communion rail and talked interminably in hushed tones that fuelled Walter's early sexual fantasies.

On subsequent occasions Walter would scribble down his list of sins on a piece of paper in his bedroom before making his way through the kitchen garden, past the graves of vicars and parishioners, and slipping in through a side door of the church, there to share his inner thoughts with his father. Once the confessions were over, Bell would tear up his list of sins into very small pieces so that no one could read more than the shortest word, which was 'lie', and then scatter them on the asparagus bed, hoping that no one would ever find them. To his horror, one day his father came across the bits of paper on his way back to the house and accused him of being even more sinful.

'This was the last straw,' Bell later recalled. 'All the righteous glow was instantly extinguished, and what had originally been an embarrassing and humiliating experience was doubly compounded.'[9] He would also write:

I have Dad's death complex. I am told by

good authority that it is caused by too much
talk of sin in early childhood. A guilt
complex. I do hope those children [he was
referring to his nephews and nieces] will not
be inculcated with such error. What I
haven't suffered through the combined
effects of Dad's cassock (a terrifying garment
to a small child who can only see a black
mass) and the cane and Mrs Bode is nobody's
business! Mr JB [Bode] of course was a
disastrous experience.[10]

Despite the torments suffered at the hands of his
childhood schoolmaster Mr Bode, Bell was destined for less
traumatic experiences in his search for faith in adulthood, and
eventual conversion to Roman Catholicism.

# 4
# Lest We Forget...

Walter's post-war teenage years were spent overshadowed by his parents' financial problems and a family crisis provoked by his older brother St John. There had been a massive economic collapse in 1921, leading to a Depression. Very few businesses survived and had to be reconstructed or refinanced, often with existing shareholders losing everything.

Inflation, along with post-war economic recession and mass unemployment, destroyed much of the personal wealth that had been accumulated during the late Victorian and Edwardian eras. World War One was to impoverish many of those who survived it, regardless of class and privilege, and the Bell family proved no exception.

In 1921 whatever income that Muriel Bell had counted on from her family trust fund had dried up, with the value of property investments crippled by the war and its aftermath. In that same year St John left Corpus Christi College, Cambridge, where he had been a choral scholar with an annual scholarship award of £40, having no further funds available to support his university degree. The award, worth the equivalent of £2,800 today, had lost a quarter of its value at the outbreak of the war in 1914 because of inflation. [1]

St John became attached to a girl from the parish called Mildred Mead, three years older than him, who he had first met during a school holiday prior to going up to Cambridge. Like his father, he had fallen in love with someone his senior in age. Unlike his father, however, he had not taken Holy Orders. George insisted that before even contemplating marriage St John should first get a solid and well-paid job in the City of London.

George's eldest son secured employment at the Bank of Brazil in the City and within months was posted to its Argentine branch in Buenos Aires, where he married Mildred Mead on 12 December 1925. The formal church marriage service took place in the Anglican neo-classical Cathedral of St John the Baptist, the oldest non-Catholic church building in South America, dating from 1831. It had been built to cater for the large and influential Anglo-Argentine community that had built the country's railways and its wealth with trade and farming, not least in the meat business.

St John was not cut out to be a rebel and remained conservative by nature for the rest of his life, his wife Mildred no rebel either. She was the daughter of George Mead, a prominent figure in the insurance business who gifted his new son-in-law with a well-paid new job, setting him up in a lucrative, if dull, career for life. George Bell had declined a job in insurance when he chose to join the Church. But St John had few qualms about taking the opportunity to pursue his employment with Sun Insurance after the couple returned to London from South America in 1926.

By then his life and that of his much younger brother Walter had taken on quite different directions. Walter would grow up with no wish to emulate the way his brother had allowed himself to bend to his father's wishes and capitulate to conformity, both in his marital life and career. But first was the matter of his education, over which he had little control.

Instead of following his brother as a boarder to Lancing, Walter was sent by his parents as a day boy to Tonbridge School, just 10 miles away from Riverhead. While his father inclined on matters of faith towards the High Church as followed by Lancing College, where he had sent his eldest son, the stretched financial circumstances of the post-war period meant that he could neither afford to send Walter there nor pay for his full board.

Founded in 1553 as a free grammar school by Sir Andrew Judde, a merchant and mayor of London who was sympathetic to the cause of the Catholic Queen Mary, Tonbridge had an enduring reputation as one of the oldest of the country's private schools for boys that was very much in tune with the post-

Reformation state.

Focused on the upper orders of society and its military tradition during the height of empire and boasting one of the most beautiful cricket grounds in the south of England when the sport gained in popularity, Tonbridge had grown in size and stature in the second half of the nineteenth century. The school's large chapel and main school building in the redbrick of the Victorian Gothic revival were set back just off the town's main street, somewhat barrack-style. Behind its gates was a self-contained campus of 150 acres of playing fields and outbuildings, near enough to the centre of the town to make its presence known while still retaining its exclusivity. In the early twentieth century it became a prominent local landmark, along with the nearby Norman castle for visitors, a privileged enclosure that the young Bell felt a prisoner in.

Walter's sense of deliverance from the tyrannical Mr Bode at Beechmont was soon overtaken by resentment that he had been sent to a tougher school than his brother, and one that had retained a tradition for caning and bullying. No photographs of school sports or academic reports from Beechmont survive among Bell's personal papers, suggesting that it was not a particularly happy time for him. Nor, evidently, did the school consider him to have made any significant contribution to its reputation during his time there as he does not feature prominently in surviving school records.

Walter was nonetheless not alone among the Tonbridgians in feeling an outsider. One of the school's revered old boys, E.M. Forster, a posthumously declared homosexual, claimed he was unhappy at Tonbridge when he was a pupil there in the late 1890s. As the novelist would later record, public schools represented what he most hated in English life: philistinism, snobbery, the assumption of racial and class superiority, Englishmen going forth into the world with the sole purpose of asserting imperial dominance.[2]

Another of Walter's predecessors at the school, whom he would follow into the profession of spying, albeit in a less eccentric way, was the Australian-born late Victorian Antarctic explorer Herbert Dyce Murphy who, despite spending only two years at the school in 1895– 1897, gained notoriety in its records for outlandish exploits that earned him the title of 'Lady Spy, Gentleman Explorer' in a subsequent biography.[3] It was while at Oxford University and reprising one of his Tonbridge dramatic society roles that Murphy so convincingly played a woman on stage that he was recruited by British intelligence and carried out a secret assignment in drag in pre-war Belgium and France contributing to the intelligence knowledge of railway systems in northern Europe.

One of the few Tonbridgians that Walter would keep in touch with was Robert Zaehner, four years his junior. Both were destined to work in separate areas of secret intelligence during World War Two, and to maintain contact with each other over the years, after each converted to Roman Catholicism.[4] Zaehner blamed his school for the fact that he became an atheist during his undergraduate days studying classics at Christ Church, Oxford. Along with two other notable old boys, the writers Aleister Crowley and E. M. Forster, 'I had been brought up in Tonbridge School, a most undistinguished Anglican establishment at the time.' It was a mystical experience induced by reading a poem by Rimbaud that brought Zaehner to Catholicism at the start of World War Two when he worked for MI6 counter-intelligence in Iran.[5] Bell's religious conversion, as we shall see, proved a more protracted affair.

In striking contrast to the someone eclectic alumni mentioned hitherto, it is an establishment figure that stands out among Bell's contemporaries at Tonbridge. Leslie Rowan was also the son of a vicar who, also like Bell, chose a career in the civil service but was very different in every other way. Unlike Bell, Rowan is remembered as one of the school's eminent and exemplary old boys who excelled at cricket, rugby and hockey, and won a scholarship to Cambridge before pursuing a career that took him to the higher echelons of the civil service and a knighthood.

After university, Rowan joined the Colonial Service,

eventually moving to the Treasury, where he worked for Neville Chamberlain when he was chancellor. He was later promoted to the role of Churchill's wartime private secretary. While Bell may have subsequently respected Rowan's untarnished public service and his closeness to Churchill, he himself was never cut out to be part of the Whitehall machinery and was destined for a life less orderly, not without risk, and more suited to his non-conventional nature.

Far less successful despite a legendary heritage was another of Walter's contemporaries, Denis Percy Conan Doyle, the third child of Sir Arthur Conan Doyle, author and creator of Sherlock Holmes, the literary world's most famous detective. Sir Arthur chose to send his son to Tonbridge because it was close to the family home, and in preference to the Jesuit Stonyhurst College in Lancashire where he himself had been a pupil between 1868 and 1875.[6]

Walter and Denis never became friends at school. They shared fathers with strong personalities but with very different interests. Canon George the High Church vicar was quite unlike Sir Arthur, who was an ardent campaigner for divorce reform and a spiritualist, spending years exploring the paranormal despite creating the practical, scientific Holmes.

Tonbridge had the advantage for Denis of being closer to home in a school environment that, despite its chapel services, did not have religion at its core. His letters home suggest he enjoyed his time there.[7] Walter far less so, finding no advantage in being closer to home and, still less, nearer to his father's church. Denis moved to the US in the 1930s and spent World War Two there where he pursued his love of motor cars and high living, accumulating large debts. He was on the verge of bankruptcy at the time of his death in 1955.

Among the few surviving records of Bell's final year at Tonbridge, one shows the school registering his promotion to corporal in the cadet corps, although only just scraping through the Certificate A examination. Of the class of twenty-seven promoted, Bell came fourth from the bottom in terms of marks, a result that in a school like Tonbridge would have singled him out as a failure, given the school's proud military tradition.[8]

Bell had arrived at the school in 1923 as a 'day boy' (non-boarder) when the memory of the Great War that had ended five years earlier lay deeply embedded in the school's sense of patriotic mystique even if E.M. Forster's pacifism had long rejected it and was widely known. The conflict had cost the lives of 415 Old Tonbridgians and three masters, with one old boy, Major Eric Stuart Dougal, being posthumously awarded the Victoria Cross, the highest and most prestigious award for gallantry in the face of the enemy that can be awarded to a British soldier.

Bell was five years old when World War One began and nine when it ended. While his young age saved him from the tragic loss of life that wiped out many of the generation preceding him, he remained for ever mindful of its lessons and haunted by the experience of so many young men who were killed in the prime of their lives. As he wrote in a confessional letter penned to a friend long after his retirement, 'The First World War dealt a fatal blow to British self-confidence.' He grew up between the two wars 'much influenced by elders who had experienced the trenches, and told me about the horrors of that experience, and also the seemingly insensitive indifference which the top brass displayed towards the sufferings of the troops.'[9]

Bell was part of a generation of public school elites who were too young to fight in World War One and left school to find the world unshackled from its Victorian sheet-anchors, questioning everything from faith in God to the right of the social order to continue. Without a road map of certainty, many navigated the treacherous rapids of the post-war world by embracing ideological political extremes and, in Bell's case, also searching for God.

# 5
# Making a Living

On 3 January 1927 Bell wrote a letter to his mother from the Thomas Cook office in the Place de la Madeleine in Paris.[1]

Of the many Englishmen who would visit the same spot in the French capital in future years few would prove as notorious as Kim Philby. In the spring of 1940, while working as the accredited war correspondent of *The Times*, Philby waited for his Soviet intelligence contact there.[2]

In 1927, however, the two had yet to meet in their future roles as MI6 colleagues. While Philby was then a fifteen-year-old at Westminster School, from where he would win a scholarship to Trinity College, Cambridge, Bell, aged eighteen, was visiting France prior to starting another term as a teacher (a work experience post) at Oaklands School, on the Channel Island of Jersey.[3]

In his letter Bell told his mother not to worry so much on his account, as she had written to the headmaster at Oaklands the previous autumn expressing her concern that her beloved son seemed troubled, as much as she was, by a recurring flu bug. He then humoured her with a description of the youthful, if somewhat laid-back, headmaster Mr Crawshaw and his wife and the leisurely way in which the school's small population of pupils were managed with the support of himself and two other similarly young members of staff.

Walter shared a flat with one of the teachers by name of Brady, who had studied at Oxford with Crawshaw and served as an RAF pilot during World War One, surviving after his plane crash landed at Rottingdean, a favoured holiday destination for the Bell family in peacetime.

Walter's teacher's wage was supplemented by pocket money sent by his mother. He wrote her a letter thanking her for her latest *envoi*, reassuring her that he was 'doing well on £6 per term', while admitting that he had developed a penchant for smoking cigars and drinking 'good cheap champagne' at parties organised by the local Jersey militia while reading copies of the *Socialist Review*.[4]

After less than a year his enthusiasm for his job and life in Jersey generally was wearing thin. The winter on the Channel Islands, he wrote to his mother, was 'vile, worse than England, cold and damp especially damp'. The teaching job nonetheless gave Walter the time to pursue his legal studies for at that time he felt he might regain something of his ancestral links and follow the footsteps of his grandfather and great grandfather, who had both qualified as solicitors.

'Law is taking up a lot of my time,' he wrote to Muriel in a series of letters in the summer of 1928 revealing increasing dissatisfaction and restlessness. Confessing to no longer enjoying Jersey, he shared his hopes of returning to the UK and studying at Oxford, while doing some part-time teaching at the Cathedral Choir School, Christ Church, where he had heard there was a vacancy.[5] In his spare time he was studying criminal law, which he found 'awfully interesting' while toying with the idea, if he ever got to Oxford, of also taking a degree in geography, 'as geography contains modern history and all the modern international problems – very useful for political purposes I should imagine'.

He also longed to travel, which he did by taking the short ferry ride to mainland France. While back in Paris, he wrote to his mother from Claridge's Hotel, Champs Elysées, suggesting he was enjoying an escape from the parochial insularity of Jersey while visiting Versailles, Reims and Dieppe.[6]

That October he was back in Jersey and immersed in a deep depression, his Oxford plans stymied with no funds for his degree. He had decided he hated the soullessness of Jersey, where 'all is dead' as he told his mother while asking her to send him two books on UK politics – *Conservatism* by Lord Hugh Cecil and *Socialism* by Ramsay MacDonald. He continued his law readings again and was beginning to take an interest in politics.[7]

In a letter to his mother in November 1928 he gave the first hint that he was being drawn, unwittingly perhaps, into the world of secret intelligence. He told her, somewhat vaguely and giving no further details, that he had dined with someone with connections to the foreign service and had discussed a posting to the Levant consular service as a possibility. He had just turned twenty.[8]

By then Bell had moved back to the UK and, despite his Anglican upbringing, had taken up a temporary teaching post at the Roman Catholic Oratory Prep School in Reading where he spent his free time immersed in an active social life of dancing, dinners and parties while exploring the political landscape. At the start of an election year in 1929, he predicted the Tories were 'doomed'. 'Nobody with any common sense will vote for them,' he wrote to his mother.[9]

Days later he met the author and essayist Hilaire Belloc, a towering point of reference as well as controversy from his school days. Belloc, like Bell, had been born in south-east England, and waxed lyrical about Sussex, its culture and history, with great affection, turning him into an enduring legend in the county. His travel books about Europe, including his totemic *Road to Rome*, were viewed as a call to adventure by many of Walter's restless generation, along with his refusal to firmly back any one party or popular ideology.

By the late 1920s Belloc, by then in his late fifties, was more widely known as an ardent Roman Catholic and a polemicist, one of the Great Four of Edwardian letters along with H.G. Wells, George Bernard Shaw and G.K. Chesterton. When Bell met him the author was engaged in an ongoing attack on H.G. Wells's secularism, while defending Europe's Catholic heritage. He also advocated a socio-economic system based on distributism as opposed to capitalism and socialism, and the dissolution of parliament and its replacement with committees of representatives for the various sectors of society, an idea that was also popular among fascists. Somewhat unsurprisingly young Walter struggled to make sense of Belloc's eccentricity, describing him as a 'strange individual'.[10]

Bell chose instead to follow his socialist sympathies and volunteered his services to Henry Hamilton Fyfe, a veteran World War One left-wing journalist who had written a controversial anti-monarchist play in 1920 and was editor of both the *Daily Herald* and *Daily Mirror* before standing as the Labour candidate for Sevenoaks in the 1929 general election. On 23 April 1929 Bell spoke publicly for the first time in a political meeting in Sevenoaks, taking to the platform in support of Hamilton Fyfe's candidacy.[11]

Despite his lack of experience, Bell campaigned with youthful energy. His political activism seemed to respond more to a general restlessness about the complacency and sense of entitlement of certain Tories than any firm conversion to a cause. Unlike many of his generation he was much too much of a free agent to fall prey to doctrinal communism. 'I am becoming quite an artist (at electioneering). I have learnt to speak properly now, without notes, and can keep going as long as I like. Most gratifying ... Plenty of bounce. We are winning here...' he boasted.

His prediction of a landslide Labour victory proved over-optimistic, however. Labour emerged from the election with the most votes but without enough MPs to form a government of its own and the Tories won in Sevenoaks, with Bell receiving a gracious letter in defeat from Hamilton Fyfe thanking him for his support. [12]

Bell's early socialist leanings found some sympathy with his mother, who had declared herself hugely impressed by Hamilton Fyfe when he had spoken to her and other members of the Women's League in Sevenoaks a few weeks earlier.

Sensitive to the hardship and social discrimination, as well as the militancy of the Kent mining community, the prospective MP had inspired Bell with his denunciation of the growing poverty of those on low wages or unemployed – exemplified by the miners' plight in a county otherwise caricatured as the Garden of England because of its hops and orchards.

Bell's seeming disdain for the established class system was in striking contrast to the path that his sister Mary was now embarked upon. The day after Bell gave his maiden 'no to another Tory government' campaign speech on behalf of the Labour candidate for Sevenoaks, the aristocratic Reggie Lygon motored down from London to Riverhead, to ask its vicar the Reverend George Bell for permission to marry his only daughter.

Reginald Lygon was a young Eton- and Oxford-educated man who worked in the City and was a member of one of the best connected and better-known ruling families in the UK. His father was Lieutenant Colonel the Hon. Robert Lygon, himself the son of Frederick, the 6th Earl of Beauchamp through his second marriage to Lady Emily PierrePont, the daughter of the 3rd Early Manvers.

The Lygon family dynasty traced its aristocratic roots to a barony created in the fifteenth century, with a more contemporary alliance to the Tory political establishment and the army, and discreet links with MI5 and MI6. Reginald's aunt was Lady Maud who was married to the Conservative MP Sir Samuel Hoare, later Viscount Templewood, who had a long record of government service, not all of it in the public eye. Before serving as a government minister in the 1920s and 1930s, during World War One Hoare was recruited first by MI6 and then by MI5. He served in Russia and later in Italy, where his key intelligence officer based in Milan running agents and funnelling bribes to Mussolini and the nascent Italian fascists was Henry Lygon, the brother of his future wife Lady Maud Lygon and uncle of Reginald. [13]

The Lygon family, some of whom belonged to the bohemian young aristocrats and socialites in 1920s London known as the Bright Young Things, would gain literary notoriety thanks to Evelyn Waugh. The fact that Waugh and Walter's older brother St John Bell had been at Lancing together and that Mary Bell had married a Lygon were coincidences, but not without consequence.

While Waugh and St John Bell had little contact with each other during their boarding school days at Lancing, the author went on to befriend the Lygons and in the 1930s was often invited to stay, as were Mary and Reggie, at the Lygon family estate in Madresfield Court, an immense moated manor house at the foot of the Malvern Hills dating back to Jacobean times. Particular friends of Waugh's were two of Reginald's cousins – the heir to the title Viscount Elmley and his young brother Hugh – both of whom he had met during his undergraduate days at Oxford and used as source material for his best-selling novel *Brideshead Revisited*. (Lord Sebastian Flyte was based on Hugh, and the eldest of the Flytes, the Earl of Brideshead ('Bridey'), on Viscount Elmley, the son and heir of the 7th Earl of Beauchamp [14] who would become the politician William Lygon – one of Walter's political contacts in the House of Commons prior to his recruitment by MI6). [15] Waugh also befriended and corresponded with their three sisters, Lady Sibell, Lady Mary and Lady Dorothy Lygon.

Interestingly, by all accounts Mary Bell's husband Reggie Lygon moved in a different circle of friends to that of his cousins. Although he was at Oxford with Elmley and Hugh, he was less burdened by the family fortune. While a frequent visitor with his wife to Madresfield, he distanced himself from the controversial life of the immensely rich and grand holder of the family title, the 7th Earl of Beauchamp, whose homosexuality was notorious in high society and was destined to embroil him in a widely publicised scandal.

Although a family legend grew that Mary Bell was presented at court, she is believed to have met Reggie quite independently, and through some mutual friends of hers and Reggie's: a young Oxford-educated barrister and Tory, Gerald Thesiger, and his sister Oonagh. A diary kept by Mary at the time suggests that Reggie courted her over several months after the two met at New Year's Eve party at St Leonard's Terrace in Chelsea where the Thesiger siblings lived before Gerald got married to an American, Marjorie Ellen Guille, in 1932.

Her brother Walter, she noted, was among those who

came to 'dance the New Year in' and returned the next day for luncheon, suggesting that for all his socialist ideals, or in spite of them, he was happy to exploit his connection with high social circles to help further his career prospects.[16]

After the disappointing outcome of his active campaigning in the general election in June 1929, Bell had immersed himself temporarily in political science and theory, finding the libertarian socialist G.D.H. Cole's seminal work *The Next Ten Years of British Social Economic Policy* a 'most marvellous book, an absolute masterpiece'. [17] However, he had temporarily suspended his hopes of radical social change any time soon and had returned to the business of earning a living, with little enthusiasm, as a teacher, and studying law in his spare hours with the money he earned. In the autumn term of 1929 he moved from the Oratory School to a new teaching job he was offered by Robert Land, a friend of his father's and the headmaster at St Aubyn's Preparatory School for Boys in Rottingdean East Sussex.

Mary and Reginald Lygon married on 5 February 1930. The ceremony, attended by a guest list of the great and the good that included Tory politicians and eminent Lord and Ladies along with a rather more modest representation of the Bell family, took place at St George's, Hanover Square, the eighteenth-century Anglican church favoured as a venue for high society weddings until World War Two.

A surviving family photograph shows a large crowd of onlookers lining the route of the bride and groom as they walked out from the church towards a waiting car with Mary dressed in a fashionable Gatsby-style chiffon flapper gown with a flowing veil. Looking radiant, she is cradling a large bouquet of lilies with her right arm, her left arm entwined with her newlywed husband's. Reginald looks upright and dependable in traditional morning coat, evidently a prime catch for the vicar's daughter.

During the religious ceremony Mary was accompanied up the aisle by her father, who was dressed in morning coat and clerical collar – the very image of unity between State, Church and Establishment – holding a top hat. Her mother, seemingly afflicted by periodic hypochondria, was a notable absentee. She had written to the young couple beforehand, wishing them the very best but lamenting that she had fallen ill with a flu bug that prevented her from attending the wedding.

Ignoring Walter's professed disapproval of privilege and extravagance, Mary and Reggie went on to spend their wedding night at Walmer Castle in Kent, a former Tudor fortress that had evolved into a stately home for the Lord Wardens of the Cinque Ports, becoming the residence of famous names from the Duke of Wellington to Queen Elizabeth the Queen Mother. At the time the Lord Warden of the Cinque Ports was Reggie's uncle the 7th Earl of Beauchamp. The wedding celebrations went ahead seemingly without any whiff of the scandal that was to erupt some months later over the earl's homosexuality, forcing him to resign all his appointments and decamp to the continent.

Reggie and Mary's wedding was, in part at least, paid for by George and Muriel Bell from their limited savings as the parents of the bride. In a letter to his mother before the event, Walter rather ungraciously wrote that 'the wedding business is more expensive than I thought' and shared his concern that it might get in the way of a holiday he had planned with the family of a former pupil who had a house in Monte Carlo.[18]

Indeed, Bell distinguished himself at his sister's wedding by spending most of it scowling,[19] and later blamed the cost of Mary's dowry for the fact that he was unable to pursue his studies at Oxford, unlike the opportunity that had been taken by his older brother St John years earlier to study, even if only for one year, at Cambridge. Walter spent the rest of his life convinced that his parents couldn't afford to support him because they had spent any spare income on the Lygon marriage – and yet he made full use of the social networks that it opened out to him. Scandal or no scandal, Mary Bell's entrée into the Lygon family did Walter Bell's career prospects no harm.

# 6
# Political Networks

B ell's politics had become radicalised prior to his recruitment by MI6. During Ramsay MacDonald's short-lived Labour government (1929–1931) he joined the Socialist Labour Party (SLP), a small neo-Marxist splinter group, and befriended one of its allies, the journalist Oliver Baldwin, one of the more idiosyncratic of the left-wing Labour MPs elected to parliament in the 1929 election.

Educated at Eton, which he loathed, Oliver was the homosexual son of the Tory Stanley Baldwin, who served three times as prime minister during the inter-war years. But although father and son faced each other from opposite sides of the House of Commons, they avoided mutual personal attacks. Oliver's family did not discriminate against him on account of his sexuality, which he was open about, sharing an Oxfordshire cottage with his life-long partner Johnnie Boyle. The couple's domestic life was 'one of gentle, amicable, animal -loving primitive homosexual socialism'. [1]

As for Walter, he was evidently, at least for a short while, in awe of the free-spirited Baldwin, who not only embraced a sexuality that was not recognised by society but also fell out with the Labour leader MacDonald over his refusal as prime minister to embrace Keynesian spending on vast scale public works programmes while insisting instead on financial austerity.

Baldwin's overt homosexuality was not one that fitted easily with the politics of the day, nor with anyone wishing to pursue a career in public life, let alone in secret intelligence. Homosexual acts were outlawed, and homophobic bias was deeply engrained in government service, with the intrigue and betrayals of the Cold War destined to fuel an enduring prejudice. In later years one of the Cambridge spies, Guy Burgess, openly flaunted his homosexuality while serving as a civil servant and secretly spying for the Russians, while another, Anthony Blunt, was more discreetly homosexual, and a third, Donald Maclean, was allegedly bisexual. John Vassall, a British official posted to Moscow, was blackmailed by the KGB in the mid-1950s on account of being gay and spied for the Russians for seven years before being discovered.

A ban on homosexual staff in UK security and intelligence agencies, imposed because of the misguided view that they would be more susceptible to blackmail than heterosexual colleagues, and therefore a greater security risk, was maintained until 1991. Even though homosexuality was decriminalised in 1967 it was not until February 2021 that the head of MI6, Richard Moore, issued the first apology for the spy agency's historical ban on gay employees, denouncing the policy as 'wrong, unjust, and discriminatory'. [2]

Bell was as non-judgemental about Baldwin's homosexuality as the MP's own family were. Indeed, he looked up to Baldwin, and the way he was open about himself, as a refreshingly defiant stand against puritan tradition and the established order, surpassing in courage an alumnus of his old school whom Bell was proud of, the Old Tonbridgian E.M. Forster, whose most explicitly homosexual writings were published only after his death.[3]

A letter Bell wrote to his mother on 15 February 1930, when Baldwin was serving as Labour MP for Dudley, and within days of attending his sister Mary's high society marriage to the aristocratic Reginald Lygon in 1930, suggests that the friendship between the two men at the time occasionally verged on the frivolous, if not flirtatious, but nothing more. 'I had a most amazing time with Oliver, he says. 'My Clarion article has been quoted in the House! Rather Good! Oliver was furious at my wedding clothes! I told him I had joined the SLP so that made up for it.' [4]

That summer of 1930 Bell went travelling again, his curiosity in continental political developments on the continent stimulated during a visit to Strasbourg. As he wrote to his mother in mid-July, there he picked up much talk among the

'French upper classes' that there would be war within five years as Germany wished to regain lost territory while ensuring British neutrality.[5] Days later he visited a World War One cemetery and railed against 'the cynical and callous old men and women' he held responsible for sending so many young men to their deaths. 'I felt very Bolshevik,' he confessed, although he was far from being one.[6]

In the autumn he resumed teaching in Rottingdean, during which he claimed another of his more controversial entrants into his social and political network. He had received a message from a mysterious intermediary, Mr X, inviting him to meet Sir Warden Chilcott, the former Tory MP for Liverpool, who was urgently looking for someone to help write a political pamphlet. 'I said I would go and see him; he sounds a useful man and Mr X is very anxious I should meet him at any rate,' Bell wrote to his mother.[7]

Quite why Bell felt it necessary to protect Mr X's identity is a mystery. It suggests the source, who was acting as an intermediary, had some reason for not wanting his involvement to be known publicly. Bell might have had some reasons of his own for believing that his private correspondence was not secure. But then in the absence of independent verification it is unclear whether this was a serious proposition or was simply an attempt on Bell's part to humour his mother with an act of frivolity.

Whatever Bell's motives, Chilcott was no ordinary political figure to mention, let alone work with. He was at the time associated with the publisher Arthur Maundy Gregory, a well-known rogue and trickster. Gregory's claim to fame was as an intermediary in the cash for honours scandal of David Lloyd George's premiership (1916–1922), before being bought off by the Conservative Party and spending his declining years on the continent on a party-funded pension.[8]

As for Chilcott, he too swam in murky waters. His praise of the 'exemplary leadership' of Mussolini in contrast to what he saw as the corrupt nature of the parliamentary morass was a reminder that in the turbulent 1930s following the economic crash, even in Britain perfectly respectable figures could express weariness with democracy, and the same preoccupation with dictatorship. [9]

Chilcott's views were aired prior to publication as a collection entitled 'Political Salvation 1930–32', in the *Whitehall Gazette*, a monthly political magazine of dubious reputation whose offices were at 38 Parliament Street, opposite the Foreign Office and with Downing Street just a block away. The extent to which Bell lent himself to finessing the text is unclear and his papers give no further clue. But that he may have had a role in assisting the controversial Chilcott cannot easily be dismissed.

The *Whitehall Gazette* had been published since 1919 by Maundy Gregory, who shared one thing in common with Bell in that he was the second son of a High Anglican vicar and his well-born wife. He was nonetheless of a much older generation and had a history of falsehood and fantasy that had obscured the reality of his life. Gregory was something of a Walter Mitty character who had concocted a host of tall stories about himself that had only served to muddy the waters still further. [10]

Journalist and former MP Matthew Parris described how Gregory became 'Lloyd George's tout; he loved jewellery and smelled of brilliantine'. [11] For much of the time he merely sold information about people for money. The Foreign Office historian Gill Bennett could find no evidence that Gregory actually worked for British intelligence even though he claimed he did.[12]

When Bell was contacted with the offer of the Chilcott assignment, Gregory had successfully ridden out a decade mired in scandal and was reaching the pinnacle of a career as a political fixer with a network of clients and connections that provided him with a veneer of respectability.

Meanwhile Chilcott, as a Tory MP, had openly shared his view that Stanley Baldwin was much too flaccid a leader of the Conservative Party, and that the Labour leadership under MacDonald was out of touch with what workers felt and needed. By the time Chilcott's rantings were published in the *Whitehall*

*Gazette*, Gregory, who had never hidden his virulent anti-communism and had converted to Catholicism, had become disconnected with what he printed, hedging political opinion pieces with a disclaimer. Nonetheless he is thought not to have been averse to charging Chilcott a fee for the publicity.

It remains unclear why Bell, if indeed he did get involved, lent himself to such an assignment. He may have been an accessory to a conscious statement of political agitation, poorly defined and not really thought through but which, for a short time, satisfied a mischievous quest for excitement.

He certainly lacked a firm ideological motive, for he shared none of Chilcott's right-wing views. Nor is there any evidence that this was the ploy of a spy in the making, a convenient deep cover of the kind that would be used by Kim Philby and other communist spies at the bidding of their Russian recruiters. Russian intelligence's quest for long-term deep-cover ideological spies who could blend invisibly into the British establishment was still at an early planning stage in the early 1930s.[13]

In the third year of the Depression, the crisis of faith in the political establishment was certainly growing in and around the Houses of Parliament. It was a time when radicalism expressed itself in unexpected ways and Bell, trying to scrape a living as a prep school teacher, may have found himself temporarily drawn into a political maelstrom.

For a while in 1931, two of his political contacts – Chilcott (right-wing Tory) and the young Oliver Baldwin (left-wing socialist) – were sympathisers of Oswald Mosley's New Party. In March of that year, after hearing a speech by Baldwin expressing his deep disillusionment with Ramsay MacDonald's lack of political direction and conviction, Bell wrote to his mother and encouraged her to buy a pamphlet written by Mosley that was selling for 2s.6d. at W.H. Smith.[14]

Baldwin rejoined the Labour Party but refused, along with most Labour Party members, to join the National Government when Ramsay MacDonald took the decision to continue as its leader, and lost his seat in the election of October 1931, returning to journalism and writing anti-fascist articles during the 1930s.

While ideologically poles apart, both Chilcott and Baldwin's frontal attack on the established political system may have appealed to Bell, who was both impatient and insatiably curious. Nonetheless  his political activism during his youth never went further than canvassing for a Labour MP and possibly making some money from ghost- writing a polemical pamphlet from an eccentric right-wing Tory – neither of which would get in the way of the career in intelligence that was now beckoning.

In 1931 Bell prepared to further his law studies at the London School of Economics with an eye to eventually sitting for his bar exams. He had come to the conclusion that any real advancement in career terms might come down to who you knew – not least the well-connected Lygon family that his sister Mary had married into – rather than who you were, or what you believed in.

The late summer of 1931 had him travelling again. At the end of August he was in Budapest, where he spent two mornings in the parliament listening to a heated debate between left- and right-wing extremists on Gyula Karolyí's new right-wing government. Hungary had been thrown into economic and political turmoil when world grain prices plummeted after the 1929 New York Stock Exchange crash. 'Many of the inhabitants are dying of starvation while the wheat rots outside the city,' he wrote to his mother.[15]

Back in the UK, in the last week before the general election in October, Bell accompanied his friend Oliver Baldwin on the stumps. 'Oliver was awfully good and put his case admirably – he ought to get in,' Bell wrote.[16]

It proved to be wishful thinking. The vote resulted in a landslide victory for the National Government and a disaster for Labour with the young Baldwin among the casualties. Bell thought the Labour leadership had handled the situation in office 'deplorably'. As for the new government, he was no less scathing. As he wrote to his mother that November: 'the Cabinet is uninspiring, nothing original, a conglomerate of individuals who agree on next to nothing, badgered by a following of blind protectionists whose ignorance of the present world position seems to be deplorable. Trades Union riots would make a better display than they. Well, we shall see and pretty soon too.'[17]

Bell pursued his law studies at the LSE, a university founded in the late nineteenth century by members of the democratic socialist organisation The Fabian Society and which men of Christian faith like Bell's father regarded as Godless. The university appealed to Bell's rebelliousness and he certainly drew some theoretical inspiration from Professor Harold Laski, a towering academic presence at the LSE during that time.

Laski had a reputation as a brilliant lecturer as well as a radical ideologue. After gaining a degree in history at Oxford, he had travelled across the Atlantic after World War One, first to Canada, where he lectured at McGill University in Montreal, and then to the US, teaching at Harvard and Yale, where he cultivated friendships with progressive figures in journalism and the legal profession, wrote for the *New Republic* and edited the Yale law journal.

Laski's support for trade union rights during a controversial strike by Boston police made him a target of scurrilous attacks by anti-communist and anti-Semitic agitators. After Christmas 1919 a Yale university paper called on students to 'stamp out this spark of Bolshevik propaganda', urging that the next Soviet Ark that sailed (a reference to the deportation radicals on the SS *Buford*) 'transport this pseudo-instructor from the United States'. [18]

Laski returned to England the following year. After taking up a temporary post teaching at Cambridge, where he made an immediate impact on students, Laski moved to the LSE, where in 1926 he was made professor of political science. Laski turned to Marxism in his effort to interpret the conflicts inside capitalism and 'crisis of democracy' in the US and Britain during the economic depression of the 1930s. In 1934 he was embroiled in a dramatic, much publicised controversy when he gave a course of lectures in Moscow. Despite being attacked in the USSR for being critical of the communist system, a personal onslaught against him was launched by the *Daily Telegraph*, and right-wing MPs urged that his British passport be withdrawn along with government funding of the LSE, which was accused of being a 'hotbed of Communist teaching'. Although 'hardly a subversive' according to MI6's authorised historian, Laski featured in an MI6 list of suspected communist international links passed on to Scotland Yard in the mid-1930s.[19]

Bell's continuing interest in international politics had him visiting Berlin University and an unidentified English communist friend he knew there who he referred to as Robin, the son of a mysterious Mrs Z, as he told his own mother in April 1932. 'The place seems quite quiet, nothing exciting happens apparently in the political line, so there is no need for you to be awfully anxious if you do not hear from me very often ... Robin seems to have some nice friends here at the University. Don't suggest to Mrs Z that he is indulging in Communist activities as she will have a fit... One couldn't know there was an Election on today.'[20]

Many years later Bell's niece-in-law Ruth Thomas was introduced by Bell to an old Tonbridgian, the British academic and World War Two MI6 officer Professor Robert Zaehner at Oxford, months before he died in November 1974 on his way to mass. Thomas claimed that *he* was the mystery 'Robin', the 'son of Mrs Z' who Bell had met in Berlin in 1932.[21]

If such a meeting in Berlin did take place, Zaehner would have been nineteen years old at the time, a self-professed atheist destined to convert to Catholicism. His youthful enthusiasm for communism, and the somewhat far-fetched allegation against him that he might have doubled up as spy for the Soviet Union undermining post-war British intelligence operations in Iran and Albania, were investigated in the 1960s by Peter Wright, the MI5 counter-intelligence officer. But Wright wrote that Zaehner's humble demeanour and candid denial convinced him that the Oxford don had remained loyal to Britain.[22]

The politics of Germany from the early 1930s were certainly ideologically extreme on left and right. In the run-off of the 1932 German presidential election Bell witnessed, the independent incumbent Paul von Hindenburg won a second term against Hitler and his National Socialist German Workers Party (NSPDG). The NSPDG, whose members were known as Nazis, had risen from being a fringe group to becoming the second largest party in the Reichstag, the German parliament.

Bell was watching history in the making, venturing as close as he dared to a ring-side seat. His youthful quest for first-hand experience of politics in action and social networking skills continued apace over the next two years. Back in London, the end of the summer term of 1932 at LSE saw him hobnobbing with members of the Asquith family. He wrote to his mother Muriel reporting that one member of the family he referred to as General Asquith claimed that he was 'not in the least surprised that I am a Bolshevik'.[23] (The reference seems to have been to the Hon. Arthur M. Asquith, the third son of Herbert Henry Asquith, the 1st Earl of Oxford, the Liberal politician who served as prime minister of the UK from 1908 to 1916. )

Seemingly open to almost any opportunity that might come his way, Bell nonetheless drew a line when he was told there was a good opening in Nottingham as 'I would have to leave London, and this is a pretty beastly place'.[24]

Attending a house party in Warwick the following week, he enthused over his friend Oliver Baldwin's book on politics and spirituality.

> There can be few people who can claim to have worked out a philosophy of life for themselves which they can commit to paper. However, as I wrote to him yesterday, few of us have the advantage of a year's solitary confinement in prison on starvation diet coupled with extensive wandering in the East where religion lives and will

continue to live unless Capitalism gets its hold there too.[25]

He also expressed his disgust at the poverty he had encountered in the Black Country and the industrial Midlands:

Really it amazes me that we are as law abiding and humane as we are when we see abject squalor and ugliness in which millions dwell. It makes me boil that a country of wealth exploitation should produce such a mess – and on the very threshold are gigantic country houses occupied by opulent Foxhunters who are living on the wealth produced by such horrors.... It only shows how hopelessly wrong it all is and how radically it wants altering...[26]

# 7
# The Curious Traveller

In the early months of 1934 Bell, still without a fixed compass, went abroad again, in search of himself and a sense of where the world might be going. He wanted his encounters with different people and cultures to take him as far away as possible from the cosy parish life of his birthplace, Kent, and the social conformity of the vicarage. But however adventurous his chosen itinerary, it wasn't always easy to escape his background or his search for advancement. He was continually building up experiences, forging a character that was socially adaptable, politically more discreet in public, and inquisitive.

In February he sailed on the Orient Line's SS *Orsova*, between Crete and Port Said, having stopped off at Naples and visited Pompeii. Only days after boarding, however, he found himself in the Victoria Hospital in Cairo recovering from dysentery, with the support of a doctor recommended by friends in the American Legation. The hospital was 'full of loathsome English tourists', but for the modest sum of £5 he was well looked after by a group of German nuns for ten days.[1]

Once discharged, he found time to follow up his introductions to Sir Maurice Amos, the legal academic and judge who had served as a judicial adviser to the Egyptian government. He then travelled on to Alexandria, where he visited Rex Warner, an English classicist, writer and translator who was an old friend from his teaching days at the Oratory in Reading. Warner was the forgotten member of the Cecil Day-Lewis–W.H. Auden circle at Oxford in the 1920s, the dandyish vicar's son and disillusioned Marxist who led a life packed with colour, incident and, by his own admission, lechery. Returning to England during World War Two, he wrote novels about the devastating impact of totalitarianism and scripted propaganda films for the wartime Ministry of Information. While in

Alexandria, Bell continued to pursue a broad network of contacts, and lunched with Sir Thomas Wentworth Russell, better known as Russell Pasha, the famous head of police whose activities against drug traffickers were well known.[2]

The summer of 1934 was spent travelling by train through northern Europe, encountering its volatile politics at first hand. Bell visited Austria, where the far right had seized control, shutting down parliament and banning the Social Democratic Party. During the last days of the region's inter-war democracy, the rise of Nazism had continued its ruthless progress. With the end of the Weimar Republic and Hitler in power in neighbouring Germany in 1933, the chancellor of Austria, Engelbert Dollfuss, had shut down parliament and assumed dictatorial powers. Suppressing the socialist movement in February 1934 during the Austrian Civil War, he had then tried to cement his personal rule after banning the Austrian Nazi Party. Bell's visit coincided with political unrest provoked by Nazi agitators.

Just a year before Walter's visit to Austria, another future recruit of MI6, Kim Philby, had travelled to Vienna – ostensibly to improve his German before applying to join the Foreign Office, but with the aim of contacting the Austrian communist underground. It was in Vienna that Philby fell in love with a committed revolutionary, Litzi Friedmann, marrying her in February 1934 in Vienna Town Hall. The couple travelled to London weeks later where Philby made his first contact with Soviet intelligence.[3] The rest forms part of the well-documented history of the infamous Russian spy web known as the Cambridge Five.

Bell did not know Philby at that time. Both came from different family backgrounds, private schools (Bell went to Tonbridge, Philby to Westminster),[4] and universities (Bell to the LSE, Philby to Cambridge). But at these ideological crossroads, their different destinies may have been decided by their love life – or lack of it, in Bell's case – at the time.

Although Hitler's annexation of Austria was still four years away, Bell had picked a political hotspot to visit. That July he wrote to his mother from Innsbruck, giving little away other than that he was staying as the guest of a Baroness Franckenstein. Later correspondence reveals that she was Anne-Marie, the Countess of Esterhazy-Galantha of Hungarian noble descent, the wife of Baron Konrad von und zu Franckenstein. The Franckensteins were an ancient German–Austrian noble family who could trace their roots to medieval Germany.[5] They had been involved in politics for generations with Franckensteins who were known to be anti-Nazi. A cousin of Konrad's was Georg Freiherr von und zu Franckenstein, an Oxford-educated diplomat who served as the Austrian ambassador to London during the 1930s. In 1938 he refused to return home after the Anschluss, took British nationality, and was knighted by King George VI.

Anna-Marie and Konrad's son Joseph studied at St Andrew's University in Scotland and then taught at Eton College before campaigning throughout the Tyrol region against the Nazis' growing influence in the years leading up to the Anschluss, after which he fled to France. It was there that he met his future wife, the American writer Kay Boyle, before joining the US Army in World War Two and working with the OSS and the Austrian Resistance.

One can reasonably assume that the home of 'Baroness Franckenstein' in Innsbruck at the time Bell stayed there was a place where leading aristocrats who were against the Nazi regime would have met. International news from the extended family members who were in the know would have been exchanged. Many of the old Catholic families from the south of Germany and Austria, who were usually very conservative in their views, were vehemently against the Nazi regime – Nazis were often perceived as proletarian, anti-Church (particularly anti-Catholic) and simple criminals who wanted power.[6]

Bell rather vaguely wrote that while staying with 'Baroness Franckenstein' he was 'learning maths as well as taking French and German lessons'. He was less elusive about how he saw the general political situation in his correspondence with his parents, but only after first assuring himself that his letters home would not be intercepted. As he wrote to his father, the 'post is not interfered here [sic], the letters go via France, air mail letters come via Germany.'[7] It was as if he was working in secret intelligence already, reporting on what he believed to be worthy of note.

It is not inconceivable that Bell may have at some point during his time in Austria met Thomas Kendrick, the head of the MI6 station in Vienna, or perhaps become, even if informally, part of the network he ran. Although MI6 had sparse financial resources at the time, there is no evidence that the lack of funds hampered or compromised Kendrick's operations.[8]

In a consummate social networker like Bell, it is at least plausible that Kendrick would have spotted an opportunity for gaining any intelligence about political intrigues and loyalties from the contacts Walter had forged with members of the Austrian aristocracy. Bell's observations about the emerging Nazi threat would have been of interest to Kendrick, a veteran of the Boer War and World War One turned professional spy who, from the time of his posting to Vienna in 1925 to the early 1930s, had been mainly focused on suspect communist agents. 'Austria', Bell wrote to his father,

> is desperately poor, no one has any money, the War and inflation ruined everyone. The number of beggars is appalling...There was a mass arrival of Nazis here the day before yesterday. 23 were taken to Innsbruck. Dollfuss has decided to squash the bomb throwing. Not that the bombs do much harm when they are thrown! ... the Nazis threw a bomb into the garden of the Rome correspondent of the Neue Freie Press ... they also threw stones at one of the churches. Their behaviour causes little alarm, however, as their only object is to create disturbance.[9]

A few days later there was a failed coup attempt by Nazi

agents and Dollfuss was assassinated. In his continuing correspondence with his mother, Walter gloomily predicted that central Europe was entering 'an era of anarchy which will entail still more impoverishment, suffering, and violence. It would appear that we have come to witness the end of an epoch – a crisis such as the fall of the Roman Empire and the Reformation.'[10]

Bell's first-hand experience of Germany and Austria during the 1930s forged his view on Europe and would have made working for British intelligence an attractive career proposition, convincing him that northern Europe's turbulent ideological battles were a prologue to another war. Bell's letter to his parents had reflected growing despair about the gathering violence and repression in Europe and confirmed his anti-fascism. And yet a newfound optimism, however brief, was instilled in him thanks to an interest, not in communism – a cause that attracted many of his contemporaries – but (perhaps influenced by Austrian Catholics) in Christianity. As he noted in one of his letters home, there were many people in central Europe who were returning to the 'Great Catholic Church in response to the militant paganism of the Nazis and the atheism of the Communists'.[11]

Bell continued his travels through Austria and Germany, then crossed into Belgium, where he met with the military attaché at the British embassy in Brussels, having made up his mind that what he had witnessed was worth passing on. Conscious of the threat of Nazism, and wanting to do something about it, he seemed to be clear where his loyalties should be, and ready for an approach from MI6. Whatever information he shared with the military attaché, again it did his career prospects no harm.

Travel had certainly boosted Walter's self-confidence. As he later recalled, he felt 'something of an expert on Central Europe, and derived great satisfaction from arguing with complacent people about the dangers which I saw looming ahead'.[12] Now he faced a simple choice: whether to stay in

England and pursue a career in law or 'leave all this to go to a strange continent which had never called me'.

As the summer of 1934 drew to a close, Bell returned to the UK, his interest in international affairs and practice of engaging with a wide range of sources and situations enlivened by his foreign adventures.

Walter Bell was moving in a wide range of circles – the perfect background for a spy. Six months later, aged twenty-six and still unmarried, he would cross the Atlantic as a newly recruited MI6 officer.

# 8
# An Englishman in New York

MI6's new man in the US arrived in New York by ship in January 1935. Keen not to lose touch with his homeland Walter had asked his mother to send him weekly copies of *The Times*, later supplemented with copies of the left-leaning Manchester *Guardian* and the *New Statesman*, so he could keep in touch with British public life and its established elites along with the musings and machinations of Britain's political left. As yet without any emotional attachments, and with limited training but expected to learn on the job, the young bachelor was also determined to get to know a new culture while building up a network of local contacts.

Bell's cover post was vice consul, but his real job was as deputy to the New York MI6 station chief Captain Herbert Taylor (consul and head of the US passport office), who had joined the Secret Intelligence Service (SIS) from the Royal Navy and been in post since 1929.

Set in the heart of Manhattan's futuristic landscape, the New York MI6 station Bell was assigned to was a world away from the graceful and genteel early eighteenth-century house in London's St James's where he had been recruited. That said, it was one of the more discreet offices occupied by the different tenants at Number 26 Broadway, a 32-floor pentagonal skyscraper in the centre of Lower Manhattan's financial district.

Originally built for Standard Oil at the end of the nineteenth century, when the Renaissance Revival style became popular with rich Americans, the building had developed over various stages into a landmark of the city skyline, linked to the powerful business and politically influential Rockefeller family. By the 1930s it was an imposing red brick and limestone building, one of the largest structures in Manhattan, with a tower designed as a pyramid and a massive interior housing numerous offices that were served by eleven elevators – the kind of building that symbolised the power of oil at the heart of US capitalism. It offered an impressive address to its many different tenants, the most overt and senior British government presence being that of the consul general, Sir Gerald Campbell.

As Bell later recalled, 'British Consuls were expected to attend and speak at suitable gatherings such as the English-speaking Union meetings and to make suitable contributions to what seemed endless commemorations of Robert Burns by the numerous Scottish Societies. The Scots or the American descendants of Scots were tireless patriots. I remember little about the Welsh or Irish.'[1]

Bell's first New York home was a room in the Sutton Hotel, on East 56th Street, a semi-residential hotel between 2nd and 3rd Avenue 'with 'literary connections and a swimming pool' which in later years would count the Cambridge spy Guy Burgess among its clients. [2]

In the 1960s, long after World War Two was over, the building was destined to be redeveloped as a 21-storey luxury cooperative, located in one of the most coveted and sought-after neighbourhoods in Manhattan. In Bell's time it boasted unparalleled and breathtaking East River views, but back then had little else to recommend it other than that it offered the British consulate a special discount deal. 'No-one cleans shoes unless you give an order and make a fuss,' Bell complained. 'Likewise, laundry is a problem. Expensive and bad…They are also washed by rather inferior machines so that everything is slipshod.'

There had been sporadic British intelligence activities in the US from before World War One in targeting Irish and Indian nationalists. But it was only in 1915, six years after he had founded what became MI6, that MI6's first chief, Captain Sir Mansfield Cumming, also known as C, dispatched an agent to New York to gather commercial information related to suspect German activities.

This was followed in the same year by the appointment of MI6's first US station chief, Captain Sir William ('Willie')

Wiseman, who had worked as a partner in the New York investment bank Kuhn, Loeb & Co. prior to being commissioned into the Duke of Cornwall's Light Infantry.[3] In July 1915, Wiseman became incapacitated from further active military service after being gassed and temporarily blinded near Ypres, but despite his injuries the Winchester and Cambridge educated and titled baronet – highly rated by C – was recruited for general intelligence work.[4]

Wiseman and his deputy, Captain Norman Thwaites, a former journalist who had also been injured during the early years of World War One, established the MI6 station in New York. Thanks to a well-placed contact Thwaites had in The United States Department of State (DOS), Wiseman gained access to the highest levels of the US administration, making him one of the most successful 'agent of influence' in the first forty years of MI6's existence. [5]

In a role later replicated in the run-up to World War Two, MI6 played its part, along with the British Admiralty, in propaganda efforts to get American public opinion behind the Allies, as well as in securing intelligence on key policy makers and opinion formers. Famously, British intelligence was behind the dissemination of an intercepted and decrypted telegram from the German foreign minister Arthur Zimmerman to his ambassador in Mexico on 16 January 1917, containing information that Germany was planning unrestricted submarine warfare. The telegram included an offer of German assistance to help Mexico recover the states of Texas, New Mexico and Arizona, in return for a joint declaration of war on the US once it had ceased to be neutral.

After the US declared war on Germany on 6 April 1917 and during the subsequent remaining nineteen months prior to the Armistice, Wiseman's access to the higher echelons of the US administration had him playing an important role in developing Allied cooperation, articulating US views on such matters as war finance, deployment of troops in the battle zone, and foreign policy towards Russia. MI6 funds aimed at shoring up Alexander Kerensky's socialist regime and keeping Russia in the war were channelled via New York.[6]

Once World War One had ended, Wiseman was succeeded as head of the US passport control office by Maurice Jeffes, who in turn handed the baton in March 1922 to J.P. Maine prior to Captain Taylor's arrival in 1929. (By the mid-1930s Jeffes had returned to the UK and was heading up the passport control department in London.)[7]

The inter-war years saw MI6 involved in 'somewhat uneven reporting from New York on communist and radical groups in North America'.[8] Unlike his counterpart in the fellow agency MI5, who had warned about the rise of Nazism from the early 1930s, Admiral Hugh Sinclair, MI6's last head before World War Two (1929–1939), had supported a policy of appeasement in the lead-up to Munich. When examining Sinclair's papers many years later, intelligence historian Christopher Andrew found plenty of colourful details about his 'clubbability' among fellow public schoolboys, and his enjoyment of fine dining and good wines, but with intelligence material notably absent or removed.[9]

Bell's posting got off to a relatively inauspicious start professionally when his immediate superior Captain Taylor introduced him over lunch to a source in the US State Department. Topics discussed included the subject of the growing movement in support of Indian independence, which Captain Vivian remained obsessed by. Bell was appalled at the State Department official's description of Mahatma Gandhi as 'that guy who goes around with a pin and diaper',[10] but thought it diplomatic to keep his own counsel, as his task was to build an alliance with the Americans, not to fuel their distrust.

Through his posting on the other side of the Atlantic Bell had found a new life in a society that had broken free from the British Empire and consciously turned its back on tradition. As he later recalled, 'I had the good fortune to get my job in New York where I experienced a great relief escaping from the stuffy past and so being caught up in all those circles who chatted and drank their time away, whilst so many of the "right sort of people" were applauding.' He described the prevalent mood in the US in the mid-1930s:

> The minds of the American public were irrevocably made up. The US had been conned into the First World War, the Europeans including the British had borrowed vast sums of money which they had never repaid and had no intention of doing so…when the (British) Chancellor used to be asked in Parliament whether we might resume some payments – his answer was invariably 'No, sir'. This was in spite of pleas from our ambassador Sir Roland Lindsay that we should do something particularly when the clouds of war were gathering, and we looked like needing at least some friendly neutrality from the United States.[11]

From the outset of his posting Walter saw his main role as an 'influencer' of US attitudes towards the UK and vice versa, immersing himself in the life of New York – a city where outsiders, far from feeling isolated, could feel re-energised by its vibrant cultural life and unexpected meetings.

On viewing a Broadway production of Marc Connelly's *The Green Pastures*, with episodes from the Old Testament as seen through the eyes of a young African American child in the Depression-era Deep South, Bell told his mother: 'Negro idea of heaven and the development of the earth… Wonderful play, but forbidden in England, a great pity. They are so stupid in England about these things as it could do nothing but good…'[12] The play had won a Pulitzer Prize in 1930 with an all-Black cast, fuelling hopes that it would lead to more opportunities for Blacks on stage, and generating a cultural debate about the significance of Black migration to the urban north, the nature and importance of religion in Black communities, and the place of Blacks in the nation.

During his first summer in New York a depressed Bell –

he would suffer periodic bouts of the Black Dog, made legendary by Churchill, most of his adult life – had his spirits lifted by an unexpected meeting with Baroness Karen Christenze von Blixen-Finecke, a 'very amusing character'.[13]

The Danish writer had published her first book, *Seven Gothic Tales*, in 1934 under the name of Isaak Dinesen, which had won her popular acclaim on both sides of the Atlantic, and would come to be something of a legend with her soon-to-be-published best-selling autobiography *Out of Africa*, inspired by her life on her large estate near the Ngong Hills in British colonial Kenya. As Bell recalled, he met her during a visit she made to Coney Island and the seemingly casual encounter endured in his memory.

In both physique and accent, Walter bore a resemblance to Blixen's former lover, Denys Finch Hatton, the Eton- and Oxford-educated English aristocratic big game hunter and army officer who had been killed in a light aircraft crash four years earlier. On her arrival in the US, the divorced Blixen showed herself to be a vivacious and attractive woman. She had just turned fifty when she met Bell, who was half her age, and would have been open to flattery from an intelligent, well-spoken and handsome Englishman who was introduced to her as a British diplomat.

Unknown to Bell, as indeed to the New York society that greeted her, the Dane had been diagnosed with syphilis in 1915 during her marriage to the Swedish aristocratic game hunter Bror Blixen and had subsequently gone to Denmark for treatment. Although there was no cure at that time, the syphilis had gone into abeyance before she returned to Africa in 1921 and divorced Bror three years later. She had then started a love affair with Hatton, whom she had been friends with since 1918. According to a letter he wrote after their meeting, Bell was much taken by Blixen, who as well as being beautiful seemed to him to be 'fabulously wealthy and spends a lot of time big game shooting in Africa', and had seemed 'very bored by the long uneventful flight in the Zeppelin'.[14]

Following his brief flirtatious encounter with Blixen, Bell

travelled to Boston on a steamship, which took fourteen hours by sea each way. It was late August, high summer on the East Coast of the US. After the futuristic skyline of Manhattan, the plusher neighbourhoods of the New England capital (he did not visit the rougher south of the city) struck him as restrained and elegant by comparison. Its residential houses reminded him of the gracious MI6 building in Queen Anne's Gate, near London's Parliament Square, where he been recruited as an intelligence officer by Admiral Sinclair. 'Strange to be back in a real town laid out as though there was some thought of how people were to love rather than exist. Really quite an attractive place, full of houses looking like Queen Anne's Gate, only having green shutters colonial style,' he commented. 'All the communities are very rich and smug and talk in a super English accent...quite a different world from New York.'[15]

Bell found himself having to engage with the depressing realities of domestic and international politics. Late that autumn when back in New York he met up with one of his Labour Party contacts, an ex-MP called Rennie Smith who was on a visit with a delegation representing the anti-Nazi Friends of Europe. Smith told Bell of his fears about the war intentions of Nazi Germany and shared his concern that a Labour government would not take a strong enough line on the issue.[16]

Bell told Smith that he believed that Roosevelt's New Deal, which he admired, was losing much of its popularity and that the US president was facing a potentially serious challenge from the populist senator Huey Long, the former governor of Louisiana.[17] Long at the time was winning a lot of support in the south with his outspoken attack on the wealthy urban Baton Rouge and Washington DC elites for not doing enough to alleviate poverty and tackle other issues of the Depression, and proposed that every American should be paid $5,100 per annum. As a member of the Democrat Party, Long split with Roosevelt in June 1933 and was planning a bid for the presidency in 1936 in alliance with the influential right-wing Catholic priest Father Charles Coughlin. 'I imagine there is quite a chance of somebody like that getting in as there is no Socialist or Communist movement to speak of...the latter do much underground and only the intelligentsia are very left,' Bell wrote of Long.[18]

Weeks later, on 8 September 1935, Long was assassinated in the State Capitol by Carl Weiss, a doctor and son-in-law of one of his political opponents.

# 9
# Matters of Faith

From across the Atlantic Bell looked at political developments in Britain in the 1930s as part of Europe's doom-laden destiny of decline and disintegration.

The UK general election on 15 November 1935 resulted in a large majority for a National Government led by the Conservative Party's Stanley Baldwin, a huge disappointment for Bell who as a young student had enthusiastically canvassed for Labour.

Walter was critical of Baldwin − 'pipe in hand, an avuncular figure, the epitome of misplaced British middle-class moderation against a turbulent and menacing European New Age'[1] − and felt growing unease with the appeasement of Hitler along with, as Churchill warned, the government's failure to rearm sufficiently to prepare for World War Two. A particularly bad omen for Bell was the Anglo-German naval agreement of June 1935, signed by Baldwin after he had replaced Labour's Ramsay MacDonald as prime minister of the National Government. The pact allowed Germany a total fleet of up to 35 per cent of the size of the British fleet and, crucially, parity with Britain in its number of submarines. This went against the terms of the Treaty of Versailles, which prohibited Germany from carrying out any activities related to submarine development or construction.

Baldwin's justification for making the agreement was that it was better to have a limit on German rearmament than to have rearmament with no limit. However, it was Winston Churchill who resonated with Bell when he declared from the back benches in a speech to parliament:

> I do not believe that this isolated action by Great
> Britain will be found to work for the cause of

peace... I believe that if the figures of the
expenditure of Germany during the current
financial year could be ascertained the country
would be staggered and appalled by the enormous
expenditure upon war preparations which is being
poured out all over that country, converting the
whole mighty nation and empire of Germany into
an arsenal virtually on the threshold of
mobilisation.[2]

Towards the end of 1936 the New York MI6 station was
visited by the MI6 chief Admiral Sinclair during a Christmas
holiday trip across the Atlantic. Following his inspection Sinclair
reported that while the books and card index 'were well kept
and up to date', the office itself presented a 'somewhat dingy
appearance owing to the furniture and fittings being completely
worn having been in use for over twenty years'.[3] Drawing on an
increased MI6 allocation secured by Sinclair in the so called
'secret vote' of UK government spending, the New York station
was given carte blanche to arrange a complete refurbishing of
the office. And having interviewed Bell and members of his
small support admin staff – most of whom were 'elderly married
men who appeared to be rather down at heel' – Sinclair
approved a pay rise, which also helped boost morale.

Not that Bell himself was in the class of the disadvantaged.
During the first year of his posting to New York, in the autumn
of 1935, he was reminded of his family's ties with the higher
echelons of British society when his sister Mary and her husband
Reggie Lygon sailed first class across the Atlantic to holiday in
the US. The Lygons paid a visit to Bell's new comfortable living
quarters – an apartment on 340 East 57th Street – and the three
of them went off on a leisurely tourist expedition, taking in
Williamstown, Massachusetts and Cape Cod.

And yet Bell was a man of eclectic theological and
political tastes who resisted being hooked on any single doctrine
or fundamentalist cause. From his early twenties he had
developed an interest in the so-called Catholic Revival, a loosely

organised secular movement inspired by the writings of the French philosopher Jacques Maritain, who challenged materialism and ideological dogma. With his Christian humanism, Maritain's influence spread across Catholic and non-Catholic intellectual circles on both sides of the Atlantic as an alternative to the forces of fascism and communism.

Bell was much taken by a book written by one of Maritain's most fervent disciples, the English Catholic historian Christopher Dawson, analysing – prophetically, as it turned out – the way that the emerging fascist and communist ideologies were threatening the old complacency and self-confidence of the pre-World War civilisation. Having been born into High Anglicanism, Bell was now warming to the developing theology of Catholic social teaching. Catholicism also drew him away from the dogmatic Marxist-Leninism that led others of his generation and social class into the hands of Moscow. The sense of renewed spiritual faith in touch with the challenges of an emerging world disorder also seemed to provide an answer to Bell's existentialist concerns about the attitudes of appeasing upper crust British conservatives, and the unbridled capitalism he encountered in the US. Reflecting on Dawson's warnings of the emerging threat to a new world order of unforeseeable consequences, Bell noted: 'We seem to be in for an amazing race towards world dominance ... Meanwhile the capitalists will take a lot of money. There is a boom going on here and absolutely nothing has been learnt from past misfortunes.'[4]

Bell's interest in Catholicism was not without its trials, not least having to suffer the politically reactionary American bishops. Early on in his New York posting he tentatively took a short walk from his Manhattan office and attended a traditional mass at the Roman Catholic St Patrick's Cathedral. He was appalled by the hypocrisy he detected among some members of the Catholic hierarchy, who seemed to preach sanctity while propping up Mammon. The episode had him entering the cathedral and picking up on the tail end of a sermon in which the priest was speaking out against the materialistic solutions to the crisis of modern society. But, as he recalled later, 'there were money changers at the entrance to the cathedral who were crackling dollar bills...Cardinal Hayes benedicted us while the priest darted about...the Roman Catholics are assuming a fascist type of mind in this country. I came away vowing destruction to the whole hypocritical outfit...'[5]

His dislike of the excesses of American capitalism and the complicity of the Catholic bishops was matched by his pessimism about the English political establishment's inability to address the needs of the poorer classes. This was fuelled by the views of the man who had originally introduced him to MI6, the World War One Royal Navy veteran turned Labour MP, Reginald Fletcher, a future privy councillor, and minister for civil aviation in Attlee's post-war government before his appointment as governor of Cyprus.

Fletcher wrote to Bell, commenting gloomily about the 'pretty devastating political apathy of a government that is spending £250m on defence' but could not 'find even a million' for the economically depressed areas of the UK, nor money to raise the school age. 'Battleships are an iconic proposition while housing and human conditions deteriorate' wrote Fletcher.[6]

Meanwhile, among the books Bell read at that time was *The State and Theory in Practice*, a new Marxist opus written by his former lecturer from student days, Harold Laski. Bell caught up with Laski in April 1936, almost certainly more by design than coincidence, aboard the Cunard liner RMS *Aquitania* outbound from Southampton to New York. Walter was returning to his post after taking a short period of leave, while Laski, in the company of the less radical and non-Marxist Labour politician Herbert Morrison, was due to deliver a series of lectures organised by a group of German socialist exiles at New York's Columbia University.

Over breakfast Laski, seemingly trusting Bell as a political ally, told him he would keep him in mind for any 'suitable job' that came up if and when a Labour government was next elected. Perhaps sensing that such a shift on the British political landscape was a distant prospect, both men agreed that a 'few years' in New York might be more beneficial in terms of Bell's career prospects than cutting short his posting and returning to the UK. Laski suggested that a yearly visit would allow them to 'keep in touch'.[7]

'He (Laski) tells me that Morrison was pleased with my company coming over. I hope that with all these people taking an interest I should be able to get in somewhere eventually – if there is anywhere to get,' he told his mother.[8]

During their Atlantic crossing Bell managed to arrange to meet up with Morrison on his own and have him share information about the ideological tensions within Labour regarding its relationship with communism. Morrison was against such an alliance. Laski, together with the left-wing Labour frontbenchers the lawyer Stafford Cripps and George Strauss, who were visiting the US at the time, were, by contrast, advocates of cooperation with the communists in a popular front against fascism.[9]

In his informal conversations aboard the RMS *Aquitania*, Bell was interested in exploring the inner politics of the Labour Party and seemed to play devil's advocate, claiming to sympathise with the party's radical left, which supported the idea of a socialist alliance with international communism in a popular front.

While Morrison had made enemies as a politician, not least within the Labour Party, with a reputation for scheming and bullying, he evidently provided Bell with some useful political intelligence. Destined to be a prominent member of Churchill's World War Two coalition government and the post-war Labour governments, he seemed, for a while, to supplant the very different and far more radical Oliver Baldwin in the list of Labour politicians whom Bell thought worth singling out for praise. 'He really is a remarkably nice man, and he inspires more confidence in me than any other Labour man I have met, largely on account of his great administrative ability. He has been quite untouched too by the snobbery which is such a regrettable feature of many Socialists. His record in legislation is better than that of an ex-Minister.'[10]

Once back in New York, Walter caught up with Laski at a lecture he gave at the New School of Social Research. Among others in the audience was the young aspiring Russian American writer and virulently anti-communist Ayn Rand. She wanted to experience at first hand the legendary Laski, a prolific writer himself who had a reputation for finding fault with British and American politics, making him one of the bright and popular darlings of the left on both sides of the North Atlantic.

Rand emerged from the lecture confirmed in her instinctive ideological bias against Laski and would later use him as a 'spiritual source' for the character of the villainous art critic Ellsworth Toohey in *The Fountainhead*, her first major literary success published in 1943. She was irritated by Laski's 'mannerisms', his 'pseudo-intellectual snideness' and 'inappropriate sarcasm (his "only weapon")' and thought of him as a 'dining-room scholar' and a 'cheap comrade'. Rand sketched Laski while listening to him speak, in order to remind herself of his appearance (round face, black -rimmed glasses and black moustache).[11]

Bell seemed – or least pretended to be – undiminished in the sense of awe that Laski had provoked in him from his student days. He congratulated Laski on giving an excellent lecture when he met up with him privately afterwards to continue their discussion about the future of socialism and what US attitudes might be if war broke out in Europe again. He had by now developed a professional interest in Laski and wished to be trusted by the professor as a disciple.

By this point Walter would have been aware that Laski's movements in New York were of concern to a propaganda arm of the UK government, the British Library of Information (BLI). The department had been set up after World War One to support British interests in the US by providing reference information and documents on domestic, imperial and foreign affairs. Its role included briefing local media and advising visiting lecturers and other public figures on what they should say – or, more importantly, not say.

By the time of Laski's latest visit to the US, the BLI was one of various UK government departments trying to navigate policy between the needs of diplomacy on the one hand and propaganda and secret intelligence on the other, without undermining the trust of the US government (particularly the State Department) and agencies like the FBI. Bell thought the British were still held in respect by many Americans, who considered them 'a vastly superior race to other Europeans and with admirable institutions of state' – and yet he believed that Winston Churchill, the most vocal in his warnings about Hitler's rising threat to democracy, was relying on his personal friendship with the US President Franklin D. Roosevelt, whose 'popularity is declining and who is falling back on the capitalists for support'.[12]

In a prophetic private note that Bell penned at the time of his meeting with Laski, he wrote warning of the decline of liberal democracy and the rise of populism:

> It is quite evident to many people that European civilization, as we understand it, is about to disintegrate …It will presumably give way to some sort of anarchy with a tendency to communism which will become marked as the years go by. Liberalism is dying rapidly, it started years ago, but now is collapsing and even in England we must expect Fascist tendencies to become increasingly apparent. There will presumably be war fairly soon and then the two factions will have to fight it out.[13]

Although Herbert Morrison had warned him about the treachery of communists, Bell continued to meet with members of the radical left as part of his job. One of them was the former Labour MP John Strachey, who, like his friend Oliver Baldwin, had briefly joined Mosley's New Party, the precursor of the British Union of Fascists, in 1931 because of disillusionment with the collapse of Ramsay MacDonald's second Labour government.

Strachey, together with Laski, became a sponsor of the Left Book Club, which Victor Gollancz founded to canalise a Marxist and neo-Marxist movement of opinion, not least among Oxford and Cambridge undergraduates, through books and pamphlets. Among the most influential Marxist publications of the 1930s in the UK was Strachey's *The Coming Struggle for Power*,[14] which, from a theoretical point of view at least, was unhesitatingly revolutionary. As Laski's biographer Kingsley Martin put it: 'It urged that revolution was necessary and desirable, while Laski argued that it was undesirable and still possibly avoidable.'[15]

In the winter of 1939 Strachey visited New York to get material for a book about the New Deal and to lecture. He was, at the time, a declared supporter of the British Communist Party, although he was not a card-carrying member, so when he applied for his visa at the US embassy in London, he gave the US consulate plenty of time to refer his case to Washington. Somewhat to his surprise, the visa was granted and he sailed according to plan. Then, when he was halfway across the Atlantic, the State Department had second thoughts so that when Strachey arrived in New York he was declared a prohibited immigrant and sent to Ellis Island, where he was held for two weeks. He appealed against the order and was released on bail pending a hearing by the New York County of Appeals. While awaiting the hearing, Strachey went to stay with the banker Thomas ('Tommy') Lamont.[16]

These living arrangements appeared to have responded to covert interests in which Bell had some involvement. Lamont was a partner of J. P. Morgan Bank and one of the key movers and shakers on Wall Street. He was also part of a close circle of key British, US and Canadian friends in a network that brought banks into the world of diplomacy, journalism and secret intelligence inhabited by the likes of the British ambassador to the US, Lord Lothian, the lawyer and diplomat Lord Robert Cecil, the US newspaper editor William Allen White, and the author and member of parliament turned governor of Canada

John Buchan (Lord Tweedsmuir) who when in New York would secretly meet at Lamont's residence at 107 East 7th Street. Their common thread was that they were united in their support for the Allied cause and in their opposition to the isolationist America First campaign.[17]

One of those involved in tracking Strachey's US odyssey and helping, eventually, to legitimise his presence on American soil was Bell, himself a friend of Lamont's, who did not regard Strachey as a security threat but rather as someone worth meeting up with quite regularly at the time, and mixing with mutual friends, not least when Bell went skiing in Vermont.

On one such skiing trip Bell was accompanied by Strachey and another contact Bell had developed in New York, a leading figure in the Ukrainian diaspora opposed to Soviet rule, Danylo Skoropadsky. The skiing trip is mentioned in a letter Bell wrote to his father on 4 January 1939 without any details of what was discussed.

Of the two names mentioned, however, that of Skoropadsky was already part of a real-life story of espionage and intrigue involving Ukraine, Nazi Germany, and Russia.

When Bell made contact with Danylo Skoropadsky in the US, Danylo was of developing interest both to MI6 and MI5 because of his father's suspected links to Nazi Germany but also paradoxically because his professed pro-Britishness, virulent anti-communism, and support for the idea of a Ukrainian independence movement made him a potential source of intelligence and even military assistance not just against Nazism but also Russia if and when it ceased to be a wartime ally.[18]

While Skoropadsky was drawn into the shadowlands of spies, Bell's other friend Strachey had contacts of a more public nature, such as the widely respected New York lawyer, Norris Darrell, who represented Strachey and convinced the Court of Appeal to find in his client's favour.

As Bell and Norris Darrell knew and shared with the well-informed Lamont, Strachey was not popular with the American Communist Party and its newspaper *New Masses* because the

latter suspected, correctly as it turned out, that the Englishman's
Marxist convictions were weakening as a result of Keynes's
treatise on money and also his talks with New Deal economists.

'Strachey remained quite eloquent about such things as
judicial bias against political theories which might threaten the
established order, and that in turn would prejudice the position
before the courts of anyone holding left wing views', Bell wrote.
[19] And yet, as he recalled in a letter to Norris Darrell's daughter
when he caught up with Strachey immediately after he had been
cleared by the court: 'He [Strachey] was dumbfounded that a
high American court would treat a case of this kind purely on its
merits', and he reiterated over and over his profound
admiration for the legal team who had represented him, going
on to write:

> Strachey was a man who followed a theoretical case
> to its conclusion, hence his attraction to
> Communism. But he was never afraid or reluctant
> to be proved wrong, and whilst he obviously much
> admired your father [Norris Darrell] as an
> individual, he also, I think chalked up this
> experience as cogent evidence that the Democratic
> Society of which he had despaired was not so
> decadent after all.[20]

In other words, the suspect communist had been won
over, as Bell had been, to the cause of US democracy.

# 10
# Social Networks

In a letter to his mother in February 1936 from the Shelton Hotel, New York, Bell wrote: 'Dined with...., saw an adventurous film, had drinks in the Empire Room of the Rockefeller Center, Radio City. It has glass all around so you could look out on New York from the 67th story.'

Bell described New York as 'quite brusque, delightfully cosmopolitan, and full of amusing restaurants...but money goes quickly. Drinks 25 per cent more expensive (than in England) and I am tendering to drink more...alcohol is a snare here as no one has tea and an empty stomach quickly becomes intoxicated.'[1]

Thanks to his diplomatic status in the passport office as British vice consul Walter was given privileged access to mingle with celebrities, among them distinguished expatriates. In January 1937 he met Noël Coward, who was then in New York directing Gerald Savory's comedy play *George and Margaret*, and John Gielgud, who was starring in a Broadway production of *Hamlet* – 'a great experience', Bell recalled – and spent an evening at the Carnegie Hall on a night Stravinsky was conducting. He also met and befriended the American playwright Robert E. Sherwood, fresh from winning the Pulitzer Prize for *Idiot's Delight*, which had premiered at the Shubert Theatre.

Sherwood became a speech writer for President Franklin D. Roosevelt and was credited with having him describe the US as an 'arsenal of democracy' in his historic 'fireside' radio broadcast to the nation on 29 December 1940. [2] Britain was by then already in a death struggle with Hitler's Nazi Germany, which had occupied large swathes of Europe from France to the lowlands and Poland. Recently re-elected to an unprecedented third term in office, Roosevelt spoke to a still officially neutral nation about war mobilisation and the imperative of American engagement in the conflict. In Asia, Japan had occupied large parts of China and had its eyes on the central and south Pacific. While keeping to his campaign pledge that the US would not declare war unless attacked, Roosevelt made a forceful case for American military support for Britain. 'We must have more ships, more guns, more plans – more of everything. We must be the great arsenal of democracy.'

By then Sherwood had become a leading member of the Century Group, a powerful New York based pro-Allied interventionist lobby group active in the US before the American entry into World War Two that Bell kept in discreet contact with, using his social skills to engage with a wide network of opinion formers and informants.

A tall, good looking, self-confident young bachelor, with blue eyes, firm features, and an upper crust English accent that New Yorkers loved, Walter was socially in demand. He became a regular attendee at lavish cocktail parties, among those thrown by New York society hostesses such as Constance Cummings and Alex Abel Smith in their plush Manhattan apartments and country mansions in New Jersey. As he wrote to his sister Mary, 'You know I got off with Constance Cummings at Mrs B's cocktail party last week. Last night I went to see her play – *Accent on Youth* – where she is playing with Nicholas Hannen who was also at the party. I went and saw her afterwards and she has asked me to a supper party on Sunday night at her hotel and she is going to introduce me to her friends there. She is charming and very attractive, so with any luck the next few weeks will be quite amusing.[3]

Other star guests he found himself mingling with included Hollywood celebrities Merle Oberon and Leslie Howard, fresh from starring together in the box office success *The Scarlet Pimpernel* would in time become participants in the pro-Allied propaganda effort. (Howard went on to work for the Ministry of Information in Spain and Portugal and was killed in World War Two when the plane carrying him back to the UK from Lisbon was shot down by the Luftwaffe off the north coast of Spain.)

Contacts in Hollywood were to prove valuable assets as British intelligence enlisted US support in World War Two.[4]

Bell had been increasingly worried about a European war long before the Allies became embroiled in World War Two. For him, as for so many of his generation, World War Two was a story foretold on Spanish soil. In July 1936 the US and European media's attention had been caught by a right-wing military uprising against a democratically elected left-wing Popular Front government in Spain that plunged the country into a bloody civil war. The rebel military forces had military support from Hitler and Mussolini, while Russia provided some military assistance to Spain's Republican government loyalist forces. The Republic also received support from voluntary organisations such as the International Brigades, which included anti-fascist British and Americans among a variety of foreign volunteers, as well as the aid of the international communist Comintern and Moscow. The US and the rest of Europe kept out of the Spanish war, with Britain and France signing up to a non-intervention pact.

The Spanish Civil War stirred consciences and attracted a wave of donations on both sides of the Atlantic. Bell was clear which side he was on. 'The Spanish Affair is quite appalling,' he wrote to his mother on 18 August 1936.

I wish we had a Labour government in now in London so that we and the French could make a stand for the Spanish government. For that government is fighting our battle as much as their own. If Fascism wins in Spain it will follow in France and all Europe will be subject to the same reaction which can only lead to War.

I understand that the usual propaganda about 'Bolshevik' atrocities is appearing in the London press. Well, they will have a good time when Mussolini gets a base in the Balearics and Hitler gets a concession in Morocco in return for all the

help Franco has been given. However, there is a
chance that Socialism will win in spite of the
overwhelming odds.[5]

That September Bell felt drawn to the New York
bohemian neighbourhood of Greenwich Village, where, as he
put it, 'all the artists, anarchists and atheists live',[6] and described
himself as increasingly excited by the prospect of fascism being
defeated in Spain – a false dawn, as it turned out:

> It is magnificent the way in which these people are
> fighting their rights against those Clerico-Fascists.
> They are fighting for us too, I feel. ...How any
> decent minded person can have any idea of
> supporting that Franco with his Moors and Foreign
> Legion, beats me of course. RC [Roman Catholic]
> propaganda [in favour of Franco] is doing a lot of
> harm...
> Even if the people of Spain are beaten by this crowd
> of reactionaries, they will take their place in the
> ranks of the French and Russian Revolutionaries,
> as having made a magnificent fight alone, and
> betrayed by the cowardice of the neighbouring
> democracies. However, I am more optimistic than
> that, for I feel that a rebellion of this kind must be
> successful at the outset, and unless the Fascist
> powers intervene more than they are doing, the
> [Republican] Government will win out in the end.
> If they don't, France will go Fascist next, and as
> Laski puts it – Liberty in Europe will become a
> mere tradition.[7]

Bell's social contacts remained eclectic. Over that autumn
of 1936 he was happy to meet up again with, and be entertained
by, his aristocratic brother-in-law Reggie Lygon, who made a
business-related visit to New York, this time without his wife
Mary, who was pregnant with their second child.[8] He also

befriended Roger Baldwin, the controversial founder of the American Civil Liberties Union, almost certainly knowing that he was suspected of being a communist by the FBI. Walter spent an entire Sunday walking in New Jersey with him and listening to the activist's then sympathetic views about the Soviet Union, although he gave little away in a letter to his mother. 'Roger is a most delightful person, so refreshing after the ordinary run of Americans. He does a fine job with the Civil Liberties Union,' he wrote.[9]

Bell began taking Russian language lessons, although with what purpose is not clear, other than perhaps as a way of ingratiating himself with Baldwin, with whom he conducted further friendly encounters at his home 25 miles outside New York where they went skiing and skating together.

While continuing an active social life of theatre and concert attendance, Bell watched with increasing despair the gathering storm of a full-scale European war and the US's continuing refusal to become officially involved. He was horrified by the belated British reaction to German rearmament as well as what he saw as the lack of statesmanship of the political class in the British National Government and the weak moral compass of the Anglican Church as represented by its bishops in the House of Lords.

Walter's disenchantment with what he saw as the moral duplicity of some of those who waved the Christian banner extended to Hilaire Belloc, whose reputation as a poet, historian and essayist he had once admired, but who he now believed had been compromised by the sympathy for authoritarianism – not least Franco – and the anti-Semitism that the fervently doctrinal English Catholic showed in some of his writings. 'The fantastic nonsense to which Hilaire Belloc (gives) subscribes to ...really makes me despair of Catholicism,' Bell wrote to his mother on 6 April 1937.[10]

Bell's increasingly antagonistic perception of Belloc was fuelled by a meeting he had in New York that spring with Belloc's assistant, Jane Soames, to whom he was introduced by one of his American sources. A fellow Catholic, Soames was on a visit to the US after the publication by Leonard and Virginia Woolf at the Hogarth Press, London, of her translation of Mussolini's essay 'The Political and Social Doctrine of Fascism'. While intrigued by her, Walter was repelled by her politics, making him doubt the faith he had come close to embracing. 'I have met a rather interesting woman who lives in Paris,' he wrote home. 'She is rather Fascist, like all RCs [Roman Catholics].'[11]

He meanwhile continued with his periodical private rages against the British class system – 'there is nothing so safe and stuffy about England as its bourgeoisie' – and told Muriel he could think of 'nothing more awful' than spending the summer in Rottingdean on the Sussex south coast as she and his father were planning to do in the rooms of a school he had once taught in, which were rented as holiday accommodation.[12]

On 27 July 1937, a month after Stanley Baldwin had retired as prime minister and handed over to Neville Chamberlain, Bell wrote to his mother criticising the appeasers:

> We are going to pay dearly for this government and for so many years of Baldwinism. All the peace machinery has been thrown away, democracy has been destroyed in Spain, and we shall be left to defend our Empire alone and unaided in the distant future. The Spanish government has been treated shamefully and it's all because of the Tory party, 'All the damn good shots' and 'Good Fellows' are on Franco's side'.

The majority of the wealthy English middle class were philistines or, as Bell assessed, 'old school tie, chin-chin, Bingo, "spot of", nauseating...'

Meanwhile, by that summer a reshuffle of the MI6 team in the US was well under way with Captain Taylor relocated to London as an MI6 case officer supervising intelligence from the Americas. He was replaced as Bell's boss and head of station in

New York (head passport officer) by another naval captain, Sir James Paget. The succession to the top British intelligence post in the US followed a traditional pattern of selection based on social connections and hierarchy of individuals with a military rather than civilian background. Paget was not an intelligence specialist and had no particular qualifications for the job in New York.[13]

In 1938, Paget's father died, and he became the third baronet. He owed his baronetcy to his namesake grandfather who came from a Norfolk academic, business and ecclesiastical family. Sir James Paget, the first baronet, was an outstanding medical man of the nineteenth century, known best for his reports and studies of the progressive bone disorder known as Paget's Disease.

His brother was the Bishop of Chester, Luke Paget, who married the sister of Samuel Hoare[14], the British Conservative politician who served as foreign secretary during the latter stages of Bell's first year in his US post. However much Bell raged against the establishment, he could not escape his family's ties, which included his sister, and Samuel Hoare, each marrying into the Lygon dynasty, and his own connection to Paget.

Although only twenty-eight years old, Bell was actually senior in consular rank to Paget (who arrived without diplomatic status)[15], but seems to have been regarded as still too young and inexperienced, as well as potentially too restless and rebellious, to head up the office. Forty-nine-year-old Paget, like his predecessor, was nonetheless seemingly happy to delegate, with minimum oversight, much of the work to the well-educated and well-connected Bell, nearly half his age, who found it comfortable engaging with Americans, even if they made the job of influencing not an easy one to proceed with in an isolationist-minded America.

Unlike other head MI6 stations around the world, New York did not have a US national secret intelligence organisation with which to liaise in the 1930s. The days of the wartime Office of Strategic Services (OSS) and post-war CIA were yet to come.

The only American organisation that ran its own agents and engaged in undercover work, as well as carrying out intelligence operations in South America, was the FBI, which had been principally founded with a focus on major criminal investigations, developing the mission carried out by the previously named Bureau of Investigation (founded in 1908). Its director, J. Edgar Hoover, had a powerful and confrontational personality, a great deal of political influence, and, not surprisingly, saw the activities of any foreign spy agency on US soil as a threat to national sovereignty.

Bell had begun to wonder whether his New York experience might have run its course and whether it might be a good idea to put in a request for a reassignment. So he kept his lines open with his previous boss Captain Taylor, who had some influence within the MI6 hierarchy back in London. 'Captain Taylor has been fostering my interests in the proper quarter, so when I come home something might materialise,' Bell wrote in October 1937.[16]

While remaining loyal to the British secret service, Bell had become increasingly disillusioned with the government and the agency he was supposed to serve's pedestrian reaction to the growing German military threat – a reaction based on the advice it received from the higher echelons of MI6.

In contrast to the Security Service, MI5, senior MI6 officials in London, both before and during the Munich Crisis, tried to influence government policy, probably to a greater degree than ever before. They argued strongly that the Czechs should be pressed to accept 'the inevitable' and surrender the Sudetenland, the province in northern Czechoslovakia whose inhabitants were mainly of German origin, to Hitler. The high ranks of MI6 advised that Britain continue with a policy of calculated appeasement and not wait until German grievances boiled over and threatened the peace of Europe.[17]

Bell believed that fascism made war inevitable, and that the appeasers were both self-interested and wrong. 'The Tories are apparently prepared to let the Empire go by default, so we shall be spared a war perhaps. You just wait until they have built their armaments and have to pay for maintenance – there is going to be just one hell of a crisis. They will attack Social Services to pay for them and then there will be a row.'[18] To make matters worse, it was a British government that had 'apparently decided to let Franco win in Spain…. I am afraid we shall pay dearly for the actions of the last few years. With Spain in Fascist hands the balance of power will be well on the Italo German side.'[19]

His tirade extended to the hierarchy of the Catholic Church for its support of Franco, putting on hold any plans he had for an eventual conversion to Rome. 'To hell with that institution. It has become the rallying point of reactionaries the world over.'[20]

Excusing his absence from a planned Christmas family reunion back home at the vicarage, Walter told his father that he expected that his vicar parent would no doubt have his hands full of family without having his youngest son and daughter 'quarrelling over the fundamentals of Christianity as portrayed in the crib in the hall'.[21]

# 11
# The Gathering Storm

In early 1938 Bell crossed the Atlantic from New York to Southampton on the *Queen Mary* before spending a week on home leave in England. He had temporarily suspended his resistance to seeking some solace in a family reunion.

The picture in Europe was becoming increasingly grim. In Italy Mussolini's government had announced its first anti-Jewish legislation, banning foreign Jews from Italian schools. Following its annexation to Germany in the Anschluss, Austria saw the construction of its Mauthhausen-Gusen concentration camp and Switzerland decided to refuse entry to all refugees without a visa.

In Spain Franco's forces would move into Aragon, towards Catalonia and final victory in the Spanish Civil War. Forces loyal to the Spanish Republican government, supported by foreign volunteers – many of them British – fought a desperate rearguard action in the Battle of the Segre that cost hundreds of lives on both sides. This was followed by the withdrawal from Spain of the foreign volunteer International Brigades, which, at the height of their involvement, had been exalted by George Orwell and Ernest Hemingway, among others, as an example of selfless sacrifice in the fight against fascism.

On his return to the US, after his family visit, Bell flew to Cleveland, 'going through some thunderstorms which were somewhat alarming as the plane was thrown some hundred feet' and stayed with friends some 25 miles from the city. 'It was perfect for me as I really think New York makes people slightly insane after a while. The tension becomes quite unbearable.'[1]

In early August 1938 he wrote to his sister Mary from his hotel in Niagara Falls. He found the view from the Canadian side breathtaking, he said, and was surprised by the solicitousness of a 'vulgar taxi man' who wanted to take him to a brothel. 'Apparently this is the only prosperous industry around here. However, I kept my mercy.'[2]

Unmarried, and with no evidence of any emotional attachment to either men or women, Bell made light of any struggle he might have had with temptation to break with the orthodox Christian doctrine on sacred sexuality as espoused by his vicar father. But perhaps he was simply not in the mood. There is no evidence that brothels ever held any appeal for Bell, nor did this sort of *nostalgie de la boue*, or attraction to low-life culture, fire his imagination.

'I have at last been able to escape from New York and recover some modicum of sanity,' he told his sister Mary. 'The depression here is far reaching…the international situation is so awful that one wonders how long we shall be spared the war. It really is all quite nauseating,' he wrote. [3]

From Niagara Falls Bell flew back to New York via Toronto and Detroit, continuing to try and gauge North America's mood as Europe headed towards war. The Nazi take-over of Austria, the certainty that Franco would emerge victorious in the Spanish Civil War, and growing evidence of persecution of the Jews among those seeking refuge in the US via his consular office made Walter sink into his periodic Black Dog of depression as he hobbled around New York with one of his legs in a cast – the result of a skiing accident.

In Germany, August 1938, Hitler staged the grandest display of the German Navy since the end of World War One in the Bay of Kiel, and invited the Austro-Hungarian admiral and dictator Miklós Horthy to witness the sight, as the Rome–Berlin axis broadened to include Hungary. The two leaders then presided over a massive military parade in Berlin with foreign military observers noting the inclusion of an enormous new howitzer, a bigger and more lethal artillery weapon than anything seen before.

Growing activity by Nazi agents abroad extended to the US where, in December 1938, less than a year before war broke out in Europe, there was a much-publicised trial of three suspects forming part of a spy ring. The alleged ring was broken up after the arrest early in February of that year of Guenther Rumrich, a naturalised US citizen and army deserter recruited by German intelligence. Rumrich was arrested by the New York Police Department acting on behalf of the US Army and the State Department, following a tip by British intelligence that emanated from the British Security Service MI5 in the UK.[4] The case crossed Walter Bell's desk and required careful liaison and reporting, but it was badly handled by the Americans and caused friction between the two countries.

In January 1938, a month before Rumrich's arrest, MI5 had discovered that a Scottish hairdresser living in Dundee by the name of Mrs Jessie Jordan was being used by the German Abwehr (military intelligence) to forward correspondence to some of its foreign agents. One of the letters found at her address was from an Abwehr agent in the US codenamed Crown, who was later identified as Rumrich.

An important lead to the Rumrich case was provided by MI5's director of counter-espionage, Guy Liddell, who visited the US and Canada during that year to help develop closer intelligence and security cooperation between the UK and the US (and in particular with the FBI), in the run-up to a war with Germany that he, like Bell, had seen as inevitable.

Under its director Hoover, the FBI's crime-busting reputation had been rapidly growing in popularity during the 1930s when the case first 'struck' in February 1938. Liddell did not arrive in the US until April 1938 and by then the investigation was well advanced, only to go pear shaped. According to Raymond J. ('Ray') Batvinis, an FBI agent and historian, 'Hoover's men did a poor job of investigating the case due to a lack of experience in such matters. The Bureau was neither a counter-espionage nor counter-intelligence service at that that time. That was yet to come.' Sensitive details of the case were leaked to the US media so that most of the culprits fled to Germany under Hoover's nose. The main FBI investigator was fired, with the judge presiding over the remaining defendants publicly denouncing him and the FBI as incompetents.[5]

As Batvinis concedes, the highly publicised trial of Rumrich and his accomplices 'was hardly a roaring success for the FBI. Four times as many spies had escaped, including the biggest fishes. The FBI was roundly criticized in the press, and for good reason, as it was simply unprepared at that point in history to investigate such cases of espionage.'[6]

Among those who were appalled at the shenanigans in the US was MI5's Guy Liddell, who had provided the FBI with key sourcing and leads on suspect German agents only to see sensitive details of the case being leaked to the media.[7]

However, the FBI learnt 'some valuable lessons which were applied months later'. On the basis of information provided in February 1940 by a double agent, the German-born American William Sebold, it went on to successfully uncover a German spy ring leading to the conviction of thirty-three Nazi agents.[8]

Such spy dramas were keenly followed by Bell on his watch in New York. He was as dismayed as Liddell at seeing hopes of building an effective intelligence liaison based on mutual trust with the Americans suffering a set-back by the unravelling of the Rumrich case. Nonetheless Sebold's intelligence produced a seismic shift in the way the FBI did business.

As Batvinis puts it:

> From that point on the Bureau intensified investigation of foreign intelligence activities that included use of diplomatic officials on US soil, anonymous spies hiding in the fabric of American society, mail drops in neutral countries, and foreign funds passing through American banks destined for its spies.
>
> Advanced technical procedures were also developed involving shortwave radio

communications, large scale telephone and microphone surveillance and new photographic techniques. Hoover's investigators were soon on the move headed for South America and Asia to track down leads in what became known as the 'Ducase.' The three-fold goal: build a prosecutable case, lift the veil of secrecy shrouding German intelligence collection in the Western Hemisphere, and neutralize foreign espionage by controlling their agents in the US.[9]

In the run-up to and during World War Two, Bell was destined to be drawn into navigating through the turbulent British intelligence relationship with the US, while finding relief in occasional nights of innocent leisure. 'Mrs B. took me to a dance, lots of Viennese Waltzing and I danced till 5.30 am at one of the best parties I have attended in New York,' he wrote to his mother in April 1938.[10]

The bachelor life seemed to suit Bell, and he had developed a somewhat cynical attitude to anything that might engage him in any long-term emotional commitment other than finding a rich woman, much as his older brother and sister had done, and marrying into wealth. 'The only way to solve finance is to marry money, which should be possible!'[11] As he wrote to his sister Mary Lygon, who, in British terms, had married above her station: 'I envy all those people getting married, engaged, or otherwise involved. I never seem to meet these eligible women with money. Perhaps I don't look hard enough. No doubt I shall cut an attractive figure when I have been rejuvenated.'[12]

Before the year of 1938 was out, he received some home news from his brother-in-law Reggie Lygon and his sister Mary. The couple were now well established in their Chelsea family home in Embankment Gardens, and Mary had given birth to another daughter, their third child Barbara. 'It must be embarrassing to be landed with another infant just now. But still, if people won't take precautions – there is no excuse today… You never could have expected to have such a mob of grandchildren to brighten your life,' Bell wrote to his mother Muriel.[13]

From Bell's father came news of renewed financial problems haunting his family with the collapse of a trust linked to the Backhouse Estate from which Muriel had drawn her income over the years. Bell wrote back, enclosing a cheque with a small donation for his father's parish church in Riverhead: 'Your remarks about the Backhouse Estate are annoying. However, I doubt whether anyone will have an estate in a few years with the alternatives of war or inflation on the near horizon,' Walter wrote to his father. The storm clouds of war continued to gather over Europe, 'Everything is fearfully unsettled,' he added. 'Chamberlain seems bent on making alliances with the Fascists'.[14]

In 1938 Bell received a letter from the source who had originally introduced him to MI6, his old friend and mentor the Liberal turned Labour politician Reginald Fletcher. The Commander, as Fletcher liked to be called, suggested that the time might have come for Bell to ask for a transfer to Europe, closer to the front line of the European war that now seemed inevitable. Bell resisted. As he told his mother, he was still waiting for a 'new breed of leaders' to emerge in the UK capable of commanding his respect and loyalty.[15]

Bell's fear was that unless there was a change of government he would continue to be a 'tool of people I detest and despise until I am fortunate enough to die and have finished with it'. And yet he still believed that democracy was possible. The US was still 'comparatively a happy country where people still seemed inclined to build and fight for the sort of civilisation in which I believe.'[16]

Nonetheless the old class-ridden society he had escaped from caught up with him a few days later when his sister's cousin-in-law Lady Mary Lygon, together with her youngest sister Dorothy Lygon, arrived in New York accompanying their ailing father William Lygon, the 7th Earl Beauchamp, seemingly not knowing that he had been diagnosed with terminal cancer.

Within days of arriving in New York for the planned family reunion, William fell gravely ill. His oldest son and heir Elmley, whom Bell had first befriended prior to his recruitment by MI6, just managed to get to New York himself in time to see his father in his final hours. On 15 November, with his youngest child Dorothy also at his side, the 7th Earl Beauchamp died in his room at the Walford Astoria Hotel.[17]

A year earlier the controversial aristocrat had returned to England and his ancestral home at Madresfield after charges he faced for alleged homosexuality were dropped. But he died having lost the respect of some members of his family, including his wife and brother, and other members of his class, and ignored by the American public.

That autumn of November 1938, Bell attended the earl's funeral service in New York, as much in a personal capacity as with his diplomatic cover hat on as 'vice consul' – a belated gesture of solidarity aimed at his own sister Mary, husband Reggie and his friend Elmley, who inherited the title as the 8th Earl Beauchamp – and making up for the absence of any more senior representation by the British government. The low-key farewell to Beauchamp lacked the extended personal and religious drama of the final days of his literary model, Lord Marchmain in *Brideshead Revisited* who, as imagined by Evelyn Waugh, who knew the family well, returns to England and dies with dignity, surrounded by family love and absolved by a Catholic priest.

As Bell reported, the death in New York of William Lygon was 'a rather pathetic affair'. The new British consul general Sir Gerald Campbell 'did not seem to have heard of Lord B., and equally did not feel called upon either to be there or be represented, which did not impress me as being efficient or intelligent'. During the funeral Bell met up again with Elmley, who told him, seemingly referring as much to his family as to the fate of Europe, that 'everything is depressing.'[18]

By then German troops had crossed into Czechoslovakia, making a mockery of Chamberlain's 'peace in our time' Munich agreement with Hitler. A letter from Harold Laski urged Bell to come home as soon as possible, presumably to prepare for war and Chamberlain's downfall, but Bell resisted. He had invested some of his savings in the New York stock market – or so he told his mother. 'I am enjoying life here as much as anyone with a guilty conscience can. I feel very much like that young man in the bible who refused to follow Christ because he was too deeply interested in the stock market.'[19] Such apparent frivolity masked his deep sense of foreboding after Chamberlain had allowed himself to be duped by Hitler.

In times of crisis Bell pursued ways of personal escape, however short-lasting they might prove. In January 1939, recovered from his accident on the same slopes the previous year, he enjoyed another skiing holiday in Mount Mansfield, Vermont and New Hampshire. 'Skiing is very good for one's peace of mind, in addition to making me very healthy', he reflected.[20]

Bell belonged to a generation of young, privately educated Englishmen who owed their enthusiasm for the privileged sport to the memorable performance of the British skiing team in the 1936 German Olympics held in Garmisch-Partenkirchen, Bavaria.

The captain of the English Olympic skiing team was the twenty-year-old future MI6 officer Peter Lunn – six years younger than Bell – whose father Arnold, himself a former champion skier, refereed the slalom race. The English team finished twelfth in the alpine skiing combined event – the highest British placing and a source of great celebration among compatriots, along with the much-publicised refusal by the Lunns to attend the opening procession and a lavish banquet laid on for participants by the Nazi organisers, such was their detestation of totalitarianism which they owed to their Catholic faith.

At the outbreak of World War Two, Peter Lunn followed Walter Bell and others of his age group into secret government work, joining MI6 in 1941, and became one of its leading officers during the Cold War years and later in Northern Ireland.[21]

# 12
# Seeking Allies

By early 1939 the reality of Nazi expansionism had fully embroiled the New York MI6 office. With the US remaining officially opposed to any military involvement of its own against Hitler, the results of racial persecution and territorial annexation forced increasing numbers of Jewish refugees to escape continental Europe and seek new lives across the Atlantic.

British government policy and bureaucracy had not made things easy for German and Austrian refugees entering the United Kingdom – on 2 May 1938 visa restrictions were imposed on those who wished to do so. As a result the head passport officer and MI6 station chief in Vienna, Thomas Kendrick, became increasingly frustrated and fired off letters to any country that might take in Jewish refugees.[1] He was not alone in feeling the pressure. As Bell wrote, 'My days mostly were taken up by trying to give advice to refugees. Very difficult as nobody seems to have made up their minds what they want to do about them. There will be many more shortly from Prague and Budapest which are rapidly becoming indistinguishable from other areas of appeasement'.[2]

From London two of Bell's mentors in MI6 – Captain Taylor and Reginald Fletcher – privately shared their frustration at Neville Chamberlain's premiership with Bell. Late that June Fletcher wrote to Bell confirming his worst fears, that Chamberlain was still obsessed with pursuing a policy of appeasement, 'so I suppose we shall see him fixing Poland up in a manner to suit the Fuhrer.'[3]

Bell continued to take what breaks he could afford away from the pressures of New York, still an Englishman abroad, bachelor at large, forever extending his social network. In contrast with earlier times, when no evidence emerges of emotional attachments, some pre-war photographs have survived suggesting occasional dalliances in his bachelor days including one with the wife of a European diplomat. Two holiday snaps were taken in 1938 and 1939 of Bell looking very relaxed and intimate in the company of an unidentified attractive young woman with a precariously drooping blouse. Bell left no record of any relationship with her in his papers and none have come to light, but, according to Ruth Thomas (the niece of Walter's future wife, Tattie Spaatz) the photograph of them both conveys an image of the light, mischievous, charming side of his personality.

During his time working for MI6 in New York, Bell met and befriended the author and critic Marya Mannes, who worked for *Vogue* magazine in the 1930s and later for *The New Yorker*. During World War Two she was recruited as an intelligence analyst by the Office of Strategic Services (OSS).[4] Bell, perhaps only half-heartedly, proposed to her at some point between husbands – she married three times (in 1926, 1937 and 1948), each marriage ending in divorce. She was five years older than Walter – not quite the age gap he had in his brief platonic infatuation with middle-aged Karen Blixen, but it suggests he may have been drawn to older women, or perhaps suffered from a mother complex. (As it turned out Katharine Spaatz, the woman he was to meet, marry, and stay married to for the rest of his life, was ten years younger than him).

Meanwhile, in pursuit of a growing network of friendly sources, Bell also visited Palm Springs, where he met up with a senior executive of Morgan Stanley Bank, Harold Stanley, who had come out for a short break from New York. Stanley would go on to launch a fund-raising campaign in 1940 on behalf of the US Commission for the Care of European Children, a private organisation providing relief to young refugees escaping Nazism. Bell and Stanley discussed the war news from Europe while staying in a palatial hotel. Further skiing trips followed, including one to Albany in March 1939 – 'skiing wonderful, powder most of the day, downhill trails of 4-5 miles, I have never skied so well in all my life. I have also made so many good friends through it…'[5]

The situation in Europe looked ever more dangerous. On 6 April Bell read the transcript of Churchill's speech during a debate in the House of Commons. Although the main subject of the debate was the ineffectual impact of sanctions against Italy, Churchill used it to remind members of parliament of the real and present danger to security and peace in Europe posed by Nazi Germany.[6]

Bell had warmed to Churchill as a belligerent anti-Nazi, also valuing the fact that he was one of the few British politicians who Americans had heard about and respected – the archetypal British aristocratic bulldog whose mother had been a rich US-born heiress.

'Mr C's speech was admirable. It does seem a pity that we had to wait so long and get into such a desperately dangerous position before this…. It has been clear for so long, what was going to take place…' Bell wrote.[7]

War nerves now contributed to the health issues that were to bedevil Bell for most of his adult life – less the product of any life-threatening illness than of a hypochondria he had experienced from school days. He developed problems with his digestive system, which were almost certainly aggravated by heavy drinking. While in New York he underwent an irrigation course by a Swedish masseuse, who pumped 36 gallons of water through his rectum in an hour to deal with 'an obstruction that was accumulating poison'. The treatment cost him $5, which he thought money well spent. It left his liver re-energized and made him feel '100 per cent better'.[8]

Late that September of 1939, Bell's concern with his personal health dissipated in the face of an unfolding drama of much greater consequence! Hitler invaded Poland, leaving Chamberlain with no option but to declare war. It was an event that Bell had long expected but which nonetheless forced him to reflect with a generosity of patriotic spirit and faith that had not characterised him until then. He now saw war as potentially transformative, ushering in the possibility of a more just and democratic world order.

After hearing Chamberlain's declaration he wrote: 'The only thing to do now is to get on with it and be as optimistic as possible. The so-called peace has been so grossly unpleasant that the new situation is almost a relief, and at any rate enables one to look to the future once again. It is bleak indeed for people who can only think in terms of the old order, but if you regard it as part of the evolution of society into a better future, then it has a different future.'[9]

Bell thought Chamberlain struck a tragic figure in his speech to the House admitting just how mistaken he had been, although, as he wrote on 26 September 1939, the greater tragedy had been brought about by the 'inability of England to find a government since the last war which could have guided Europe into a new and better era'.[10]

The new reality forced a major rethink in London about the UK diplomatic and intelligence presence across the Atlantic, with the new UK ambassador to the US, Lord Lothian, and the head of the British propaganda effort – the minister of information Duff Cooper – competing to direct the best strategy for breaking down US isolationism in favour of intervention.[11]

Securing US official interventionism in World War Two proved a protracted affair. Two months after the British had declared war on Germany, Walter wrote to his mother describing himself as 'very busy and likely to remain so'.

Bell was finding the task of influencing the US to offer full support as an ally a continuing challenge even if the impact of British influence and friendships within the US media, which was fed regular items of anti-Nazi propaganda, was soon bearing fruit. 'The American press is having a wonderful time writing about battles and things. The Stock Market is jumping all over the place. The sentiment here is overwhelmingly pro-British, but also very much averse to getting mixed up in it all,' he wrote.[12]

Showing signs of greater sensitivity to local opinion, and seeing the need to win hearts and minds rather than squander the chance of an alliance with too bullish pressure, he was not totally unsympathetic about US caution when it came to committing American lives to a war that still seemed very distant and not of direct consequence for national interests: 'I hope English people are not being too rude about American isolationism; it is very natural, and when we were an island we were none too anxious to get involved in distant quarrels,' he went on, before adding. 'We are far more likely to get help from Americans if we understand their attitude. They are not being self-righteous about it at all – at least none of my friends are.'[13]

In trying to understand US public opinion and how best to get it on side, Bell found himself very much on message with Lord Lothian. In September 1939 the politician and newspaper magnate was appointed British ambassador and no sooner had he arrived in Washington than Bell predicted enthusiastically that he was 'going to be a great success' pursuing British interests.[14]

Despite his aristocratic background, Lothian had an open, unsnobbish personality that had him warming to American values, and Americans warming to him. Bell would later remember him with grudging respect. Despite his reputation as an appeaser, 'his friendly personality appealed to many influential Americans, and he was more popular than his predecessor Sir Ronald Lindsay who was regarded locally as arrogant'.[15] Lothian was known on the lecture circuit, in which he built up a reputation for simplicity. 'This appealed to Americans who tended to think of the British ruling elite as being surrounded by servants and being incapable of doing anything for themselves,' wrote Bell.[16]

The ambassador set up the new British Press Service (BPS), with a focus on circulating solid information on the war effort, and to try and defuse the impression that the British were engaged in a whispering campaign of falsehoods. Lothian helped enlist US economic aid for the war effort and initiated the joint Anglo-American military organisation of the Combined Chiefs of Staff.

For Bell, wartime brought not only an intensifying

workload but also financial pressures on the personal front. In March 1940 he heard from his brother St John that his mother was without an income and asking whether he might help. Bell wrote to his sister Mary saying he was strapped for cash himself, living on roughly $US300 per month, 'having been caught by both Exchange depreciation and Income Tax'.[17] The claim was not entirely factual as one of the perks of his MI6 assignment overseas, was that it was secretly funded and tax free.

The Bell family's financial troubles were nonetheless symptomatic of a national crisis. It was Lord Lothian who on his arrival at New York's La Guardia Airport on 23 November 1940, told a press conference, 'Well, boys, Britain's broke; it's your money we want.' The remark, widely reported by the American news media, caused a sudden drop of confidence in sterling and was exploited by German propaganda.

Lothian had expressed an uncomfortable reality of Britain's situation. The cost of its military effort against Hitler had nearly drained Britain's reserves of currency and gold. In early December 1940, Churchill wrote to President Franklin D. Roosevelt warning that the moment was fast approaching when Britain would no longer be able to pay cash for shipping and other supplies. Already well aware of the dangers posed by Nazi Germany's expansion, Roosevelt was determined to answer Britain's needs. That answer would come a few months later in the form of the Lend-Lease programme, whereby the US could lend or lease war supplies to any nation deemed vital to the 'defence of the United States'.[18]

Unsurprisingly, Bell had come around to not only admiring Americans but seeing them as holding the key to a better future. 'The contention that the Americans are a lot of Shylocks is so utterly unfair,' he wrote in April 1940. 'You will never get a democracy to face up to a fight until you have convinced its average citizen that his own life and security is menaced. They [the Americans] will do nothing unless they feel under threat. Meanwhile we shall need them still more when the time comes to make peace, therefore do not let us in any way lose our dignity or our tempers because we have to bear the brunt of this misery.'

He went on:

> I react instinctively from chauvinism, and I still
> dream occasionally of a world where this miserable
> nationalism has been relegated to its proper
> function, and where some of the principles which I
> believe in are allowed to flourish. America is still
> able to live normally, and life here stands out in
> such contrast to that of Europe. Given the
> opportunity, and the necessary encouragement, the
> inspiration for a better world will yet come from this
> side of the Atlantic.[19]

# 13
# The East River Club

On 3 September 1939, the day Britain declared war on Nazi Germany, Bell lunched alone at New York's East River Club, one of Manhattan's most exclusive social venues. Built on the site of an old cigar factory, it had been inaugurated in 1931, four years before Bell was posted to the US – 'after the Great Depression had begun but before despair had set in' as the *New York Times*'s Jacob Bernstein would much later report.[1]

The club was on a cul-de-sac at the edge of East 52nd Street with a commanding view and access to the East River, the main attraction for the tycoons that numbered its founding members being that they could moor their yachts just outside the building. Those drawn to its facilities from its early days included some of New York's most prominent family tribes including the Astors, Roosevelts and Vanderbilts. It later marketed itself as a family club by design, with equality between men and women, and full-service sporting and social club facilities in the heart of the city – a good place to relax and develop good contacts.

But on that autumn day of 1939, Walter Bell's mood was dark. From the East River Club he wrote to his mother, reflecting 'what an awful day' it must have turned out for his family back home and so many people they knew. While he had long foreseen a second world war starting in Europe, Bell took no comfort in its coming to pass. He wanted to make sense of the unfolding events without being overwhelmed by them. His hopes rested with the US coming to Britain's aid sooner rather than later. He wrote on:

> Even I, who have been saying all along that this
> fiend (Hitler) should have been killed at the start,
> did not expect this sudden outbreak… As I write we

have not started yet, but I cannot see what can come of delay, so long as that crowd is in power in Britain there will be no peace.

I do hope you will not go through too bad a time. It seems here to be just as unreal as the Spanish nightmare was, except that all the shipping is dislocated. It is a comfort that we are much better prepared now than in 1914 – and I cannot help thinking that a halt will be called before anything too dreadful takes place. All these remarks seem futile and stupid. I am thankful to be here for the start, anyway – everyone is on our side, and we shall get a great deal of help from the United States...[2]

Among the East River Club's most distinguished members known by Bell was the wealthy and well-connected Vincent Astor, a long-term friend of Roosevelt's who had become one of the president's key advisers on intelligence matters. Both Astor and Roosevelt had courted British royalty in April 1935 aboard Astor's palatial 263-foot yacht *Nourmahal* where, during one of their leisure cruises together, the two friends had a much-publicised lunch in Nassau with Their Royal Highnesses the Duke and Duchess of Kent, and Lord and Lady Clifford of the Bahamas.

Astor later went on to use his position as one of New York's most powerful and best-informed businessmen to help the FBI successfully intercept and break up a network of German agents planning a major sabotage operation in 1938.

The FBI used a room in the *Newsweek* Building, the 43-storey skyscraper Astor owned at 444 Madison Avenue, to monitor the offices of its double agent William Sebold's Diesel Research Company, a front used by the Abwehr to distribute funds to secret agents in America.

Astor and Bell would have shared their delight with the success of the FBI operation, which used state of the art listening devices and hidden cameras to record the meetings between

Sebold and thirty-three Axis spies, including Fritz Duquesne, the Nazis' head operative in North America. As a result, a crippling blow was dealt to the Axis's fifth column in America.[3]

In April 1940, Astor wrote a two-page letter to Roosevelt detailing the formation of The Club – as he called the private residence where he had secret meetings with Bell and James Paget, Walter's immediate superior in the MI6 station in New York . Their aim was to continue to obtain 'unofficial British co-operation' or, as he also put it, 'leads useful to us'.[4]

The Club, also sometimes referred to as The Room, was also used as a meeting point between British intelligence and other pro-British prominent New Yorkers including the publisher Nelson Doubleday, the president's son Teddy Roosevelt Jr, and David Bruce, the future head of the London-based wartime European operations of the US intelligence and special operations, the Office of Strategic Services (OSS), and post-war ambassador to Britain, France, Germany and China.

The Club was, in fact, located in Vincent Astor's townhouse on New York's East 82nd Street just off Park Avenue. Astor owned the entire building. The FBI's historian Ray Batvinis visited it long after it had been vacated by the Astors after the end of World War Two, and before its latest owner, a chubby Hungarian-born dentist from Long Island, blew it up, killing himself over a domestic dispute with his ex-wife. The Room was the first-floor parlour that fronted on the street. It was located to the right of the foyer as you entered the front door. Modest in size, with a marble floor and a fireplace, it comfortably sat five or six.[5]

The Club had run into diplomatic difficulties in February 1940 when the US State department in Washington issued MI6 with a formal if unpublicised complaint,[6] as in its view such unofficial intelligence activities by a foreign power on US soil was a breach of trust and unlawful, seemingly encroaching on sovereign rights when it came to espionage activities in the US. The contact between Astor and British intelligence was briefly suspended, then resumed, with Roosevelt's blessing – part of a growing cooperation that was officialised once the US had formally entered the war.

In late June 1940, two weeks after Nazi troops had entered Paris, David Bruce, one of the well-connected and wealthy American anglophile members of the intelligence-based Club or Room, arrived in London as the newly appointed special delegate of the American Red Cross. Prior to the US officially entering the war, Bruce's efficient and dedicated oversight of liaison with British relief agencies and his witnessing of the way Churchill's loyal patriots were resisting and suffering the early offensive by the German Luftwaffe did much to advance the Allied cause, along with the American journalist Edward Murrow's graphic reports of the London Blitz for CBS Europe,

Bruce's official work provided cover for developing his close relationship with British intelligence, his reaction to the world crisis endearing him to chroniclers of the 'special relationship' that England and America forged in adversity.[7] Bruce and Bell focused on strengthening the same mission of Anglo-American cooperation from both sides of the Atlantic.[8]

In New York Walter Bell kept up with other American sources to further the Allied cause. It was at the East River Club, in fact, that Bell, in the run-up to World War Two, began what became an enduring friendship with Duncan Spencer, a World War One veteran, banker and wartime intelligence operative of Scottish descent.[9]

Spencer was himself an intimate friend of John Buchan, the novelist who became Lord Tweedsmuir when he was appointed to a high post in British imperial government service and whose own background in intelligence and wide social network became an invaluable asset with the outbreak of World War Two before he died in February 1940.[10]

The novelist, in his role as Canada's governor general, suppressed his anti-war feelings and felt it his patriotic duty to do what he could to help the British Empire in its fight against Nazism, including working round the fringes of diplomacy with other agents of influence generating US support.[11]

Spencer himself seemed a character out of a Buchan novel although his role was far from fictitious. Buchan saw him as a key figure in a confidential network he formed to help inform US decision makers and swing public opinion behind Britain.

Spencer was born into a shipbuilding family near Glasgow in 1897 and was a child when his parents divorced. Although his full name was Duncan McGlashan Spencer, he was better known by family and friends as 'Pat'. Lore has it that he was separated from a pet donkey called Pat when he was a very young boy and insisted on taking the name. 'Loss of family attachment punctuated his youth, so this perhaps was his way of dealing with loss,' recalled one of his daughters, Leslie Spencer.[12]

Escaping from domestic turmoil, 'Pat' emigrated, aged ten, with his mother to the US. Among the more eccentric relatives from whom Spencer seemed to have inherited a taste for risk-taking was his great uncle Alex, a mathematician who had taught at Oxford and volunteered as an adviser to Pancho Villa before the Mexican revolutionary had him shot as a suspected spy.

When World War One broke out, Spencer enlisted for active service in Europe as second lieutenant in the Canadian Royal Flying Corps – in the same regiment as Bill Stephenson, who was to become Walter's Bell's main employer as head of MI6's lead wartime intelligence organisation, the British Security Coordination (BSC) in New York. It is likely that Spencer's World War Two involvement with British intelligence drew from this earlier shared experience with Stephenson in World War One. As his daughter Leslie told me: 'Dad very much wanted to fly again in World War Two but was deemed too old. So, he may have been in touch again with Stephenson, who then encouraged him to serve in intelligence.'[13] After World War One Spencer and Stephenson went their separate ways into the corporate sector before getting involved with government service and intelligence.

Spencer studied business before graduating from the

University of Pennsylvania's Wharton School and embarking on a career in Wall Street. By the late 1930s he was working as an executive banker with the Fiduciary Trust Company International (FTCI) managing sensitive foreign accounts. While not among the highest profile or biggest banks on Wall Street, Fiduciary Trust had a particular niche, which was managing individual wealth. It had influential founders and clients but was not a commercial bank and thus had a lower profile. According to Spencer's account of his own secret activities, this made it easier for the FTCI to be a quiet conduit for financial support for British intelligence operations in the inter-war years .[14]

The founding directors of the FTCI were Grenville Clark, a Harvard-educated lawyer and Elihu Root Jr of the anglophile Wall Street law firm, Root, Clark, and Buckner.

Clark was a close friend of Roosevelt's and both he and Root were influential figures in the inter-war period. They helped lobby the drafting of a law of universal military training for all young Americans, and Root headed a committee in 1940 entitled 'Immediate Aid to Allies Short of War' before joining the Army Air Forces' Strategic Target Board during World War Two. Clark also became a leading interventionist with the Fight for Freedom campaign in support of direct US military intervention in the war. He encouraged Spencer as a young promising executive whom he trusted with some of the bank's deepest secrets. Clark became his father-in-law in 1955 after Spencer's first wife Josephine Choate died in 1951 and he married Louisa Clark.

By the outbreak of World War Two, Spencer had become the latest American banker to develop links with British intelligence. In his unpublished memoir, dictated to and typed by his secretary in later life when he was apparently still in full control of his faculties (he would later suffer a stroke), Spencer cryptically covers his wartime role, using codenames for some but not all the characters he names.

An example of how useful informal, non-diplomatic

channels of communication and operation could be, when exploited the right way, was the plan Spencer helped bring to fruition early on in World War Two, with Buchan's support as governor, to have Canada as a location to help train pilots to serve in the RAF, since British aerodromes would be vulnerable to German bombers.

Buchan was a very discreet man (there is precious little about his early World War Two involvement in his memoirs) and would not have openly written to correspondents about any intelligence connections he had made. However, because of his experiences in World War One, when World War Two broke out in 1939 he was extremely keen to make connections with businessmen, opinion formers, journalists, politicians and, embryonic intelligence and intelligence propaganda operations in the US.

Spencer claimed that before his posting to the UK he was handling covert funds deposited in the Fiduciary Trust on behalf of British intelligence destined for agents in Europe and that his friend the novelist John Buchan was involved in the early stages of World War Two, prior to his death in February 1940. If true, Fiduciary's support for the Allied cause was more discreet and less ambitious than the widely publicised funding in World War One provided by another major US institution. J.P. Morgan, which arranged for the largest foreign loan in Wall Street history – a $500 million-dollar Anglo-French loan – and acted as purchasing agent in the United States for the Allies. On behalf of Britain, J.P. Morgan placed over $3 billion worth of contracts with American suppliers,[15] a role criticised by anti-war groups who claimed that US lives in World War One had been unnecessarily sacrificed to serve the speculative interests of bankers. Walter Bell nonetheless included both J.P. Morgan and Fiduciary Trust in the web of friendly sources he developed during his MI6 posting in New York.

Spencer and another influential Wall Street banker, J.P. Morgan's Thomas Lamont, were among the contacts John Buchan shared in common in New York with Walter Bell. All four were friends of Lord Lothian, the UK ambassador in

Washington. Buchan advised Lothian when the latter first arrived in Washington as ambassador. The two attended secret meetings at Lamont's house in New York in October 1939, when Buchan spun a story that he was in town, consulting American doctors about his recurring stomach problems.

As his granddaughter Ursula Buchan put it:

> I have always thought that the medical trip was a feint; my grandfather had brilliant doctors in Montreal already and the New York doctors didn't suggest any different treatment. He went to New York for other reasons, meeting bankers like Lamont and 'Pat' Spencer, as well as his old press colleagues from First World War days, and British diplomats. He was bent on 'influencing', but that's not necessarily the same as encouraging spies.[16]

The only extant private diary of Buchan's for World War Two is dated 1939, prior to his death in February 1940, so that the precise extent of his role in the early critical months may never be known unless further light is shed by the declassification of intelligence files. However, on the basis of her own research, Ursula Buchan subscribes to the view that her grandfather's contribution to the wartime cooperation between the US, Canada and Britain proved its worth.

Spencer, referred to as 'Pat', appears several times in Buchan's 1939 diary entries. The diary records that Buchan met Spencer in New York on 14 January, then in Ottawa on 9 September, in New York again on 20 and 23 October, and then finally back in Ottawa on 11 December. That's quite a lot of meetings in the course of one year with one New York banker![17]

Given that Buchan died in February 1940, before the transatlantic military and intelligence cooperation really got organised, his wartime role should not be exaggerated. Apart from anything else, as governor general of Canada he was the representative of the head of state and was not supposed to get involved with politics or high-level intelligence contacts. Nevertheless, his friend Spencer gives some tantalising clues that Buchan's covert diplomacy may have included work with the British intelligence services.

In his unpublished memoir, in which he describes Buchan as a 'truly brilliant man', Spencer recalled someone coming to 'Tweedy' (as Buchan was nicknamed), and telling him that he had been approached by a German spy who wanted to buy information about Canadian, American and British plans for an invasion of Germany. 'Since at that time there were no such plans, Tweedy said "Let's make up some plans for them – utterly false, of course, and sell them to the Germans." He proceeded to do just this, and the fake plans were sold to the German spy. Tweedy had a great imagination.'[18]

According to another episode recalled by Spencer, an emissary from London called 'Baby Face' was sent by John Buchan with money to finance an agent with the name of Dicky Scott in neutral Spain and Portugal. Spencer relates how he met 'Baby Face' when he came to New York to help track suspect Nazis, an area that came under Bell's MI6 remit. One episode described by Spencer has him accompanying 'Baby Face' to the River Club where they met a 'German acquaintance of mine of German ancestry and another man who I had never met.'[19]

Then a spy drama worthy of a Buchan novel unfolded.

> Baby Face asked me if I knew the men. I told him I barely knew one, and the other not at all. He asked me for an introduction, and I introduced him. Then when I was getting drinks for all of them, I saw them walking out – Baby Face on one side of the German and another man on the other side. He was a spy. Later when I saw Baby Face again, I asked him what he had done with the man. He said he first shipped him to Mexico and then on to England. Baby Face was the best of intelligence agents.[20]

Neither the identity of Baby Face or the other man is

revealed, but Bell at the time is believed to have already met Spencer, who was to become an enduring friend, and indeed may have been present that day in the East River Club, another mere player in a game of spies.

It seems likely that Spencer met Bell in New York in the early part of World War Two, when their shared hopes of Britain countering the Nazi threat ultimately rested on US interventionism on behalf of the Allied cause. Both men were separately subsequently posted to the UK. Spencer was enlisted with MI19, a sector of the War Office's British military intelligence branch responsible for enemy prisoners of war intelligence matters, and Bell with MI6, liaising with the nascent US intelligence agency, the OSS.

# 14
# To War

In January 1940, four months after the Nazi invasion of Poland led to Britain's declaration of war, Bell wrote that he felt lucky to still be relatively safe and in post in the US, even if part of him longed to be on the home front.

> I am certain that it is really a great stroke of good luck to be spared the misery and lunacy which is going on. For a while this is a clear-cut issue in one sense, in another it is not. As I have seen things over the past years, we have no one to blame but ourselves for this predicament. We refused to face reality – we relied on others to do our dirty work and all reeks of hypocrisy, smugness, and stupidity. I don't know what to think about the future…By Spring all may be shambles. I am not defeatist in the least – I am sure we will win, but God preserve us from these old mug monsters…What an awful place Poland must be now if the things we read are true.[1]

On 10 May 1940, Bell got the bitter-sweet news he had longed, hoped and prepared for. As Nazi troops advanced through Europe, Winston Churchill became Britain's wartime prime minister. Cometh the hour cometh the man.

While Bell held Churchill in great esteem he had little time for the foreign secretary Lord Halifax, whose suggestion of engagement with an Italian offer of mediation with Hitler was stopped in its tracks by Churchill in a tense cabinet meeting held in a committee room in the House of Commons heavy with cigar smoke. Halifax was to last another six months as the only surviving appeaser in Churchill's first wartime cabinet and his only potential rival before, much to Bell's regret, he was sent to Washington.

'His lordship (Halifax) stands on nothing that claims my interest,' wrote Bell.

> He was associated for too long with these people who enjoyed drinking and appeasing the Nazis. He and his class have got England into the worst jam in its history, and she will only be rescued by the energy of WSC (Winston Spencer Churchill) and the instincts of self-preservation aroused by the woefully and damnably betrayed working class. As far as I am concerned, they are the only ones who are likely to retrieve the situation and get us off to a new start.'[2]

The advent of war saw a major upgrade of the entire overt and covert organisation used by the British to win over US public opinion. It would pave the way for an unprecedented period of close cooperation on wartime intelligence and security between the two countries.

What soon became clear was that the MI6 operation in the US was in for a much overdue expansion with the aim of giving it a central role to the Allied war effort. Of the new arrivals in the US tasked with this mission, and among those to gain notoriety, was the Canadian-born businessman turned spy chief, William ('Bill') Stephenson.

Few of the key players in World War Two history straddle fact and fiction as much as Stephenson, making the truth in terms of his story, as related by himself and others who drew on information he provided – in Ian Fleming's case as inspiration for his James Bond books – a subject of dispute to this day.

Two biographies of Stephenson – *The Quiet Canadian* by a wartime member of the BSC, the author and MP Montgomery Hyde, published in 1962 with the claim 'the truth can now be told',[3] and *A Man called Intrepid* (Stephenson's alleged wartime code-name) by the Canadian author and journalist William Stevenson (no relation), which also claimed to be a true story of World War Two espionage – have both been challenged in terms of historical accuracy.[4]

Both books were published after Stephenson suffered a very severe stroke in about 1960 and became the victim of delusions, so that any claims made by him since this episode should be accepted with extreme caution, as Bell wrote in 1982.

According to Bell, *The Quiet Canadian*, which made Hyde 'a lot of money', was based on the 'laborious' earlier drafting by Stephenson's wartime deputy Dick Ellis, whose own reputation was later tarnished by allegations that he may have spied for both the Germans and the Soviets before World War Two – Ellis admitted having sold secrets to the Germans.

'Stephenson was one of those people who enjoyed a personality cult and assembled around him people who would do his bidding,' wrote Bell. 'They received some reward, but it was at the cost of their independence. This applied particularly to Dick Ellis,[5] whom Stephenson treated shabbily. Stephenson with all his money should have seen that Dick was spared acute financial worry.'

Bell shared his thoughts in a letter to an MI6 colleague, which also made clear his view that Stephenson was not a fraud, while noting that his wartime boss's officially acknowledged contribution to the World War Two Allied effort 'should have been written up by a serious scholar, who would have been left up to make up his own enquiries and assessments'.[6]

Bell's instinct that Stephenson merited a proper study was correct, but the task was not made easy by Stephenson's determination to control his own legacy. Like the FBI chief J. Edgar Hoover, he was a narcissist and their 'ambition and control-freakery makes it very difficult to get to the truth of things.'[7]

It was not until 1998 that Nigel West (the pen name of the former MP turned intelligence historian Rupert Allason), published *The Secret History of British Intelligence in the Americas, 1940-45*, which purported to be the first complete and unexpurgated version of the official report of the British Security Coordination's wartime activities assembled under the direction of Stephenson in 1945, immediately after World War Two.

The main drafting of the official report was done in different stages by the Scottish American academic writer, Gilbert Highet, and Tom Hill, another of Stephenson's wartime subordinates, while Roald Dahl, the later best-selling writer of children's books, contributed for a short period. Dahl served as a Royal Air Force assistant air attaché assigned to the British embassy in Washington between 1942 and 1945. During his posting Dahl had a passionate affair with Congresswoman Clare Boothe Luce, wife of the owner of *Time* magazine, helping diminish her anti-imperialism and dislike of Churchill.[8]

According to West, twenty copies of the British Security Coordination report were printed before Hill and his wife, the US writer Helen MacInnes, were instructed by Stephenson to collect the archive of documents on which it was based and burn it. Up to ten copies of the report were distributed to Churchill, MI6, and the Special Operations Executive, although according to West, 'none of these emerged'.[9]

The book on Stephenson by the author William Stevenson, *A Man called Intrepid*, is, according to West, 'largely a work of fiction' and the publishers in fact reclassified the work as fiction.[10]

As far as MI6's historian Keith Jeffery is concerned, 'Beyond the BSC (British Security Coordination) Official History of 1945, clearly designed to show the organisation in the best possible light and based on records that were subsequently destroyed, no comprehensive record exists of its work. Although a sizeable proportion of the many thousands of telegrams between New York and London were retained, very few of the more substantive letters and reports that went by diplomatic bag appear to have survived'.[11]

What has come before and what follows in this book is an attempt to see through the smoke and mirrors with a narrative that is as factual as the available evidence permits.

Stephenson was recommended to MI6 in the summer of 1939 by Desmond Morton, Churchill's key intelligence adviser.[12] MI6's chief, Sir Stewart Menzies, subsequently agreed to have Stephenson head up the MI6 representation in New York, to try and establish good communications with the FBI's J. Edgar Hoover and – through William Donovan, the founding chief of the wartime Office of Strategic Services (OSS) – the White House.

Stephenson arrived in New York in June 1940, his mission turning into something that became a great deal more ambitious than simply developing MI6's links with US departments. BSC expanded into an organisation which straddled intelligence, security, propaganda, and covert diplomacy and with a territorial remit that included Latin America and the Caribbean, as well as North America.

Among the many friends Stephenson made in the US was the lawyer William Donovan, a World War One veteran who was entrusted by President Franklin Roosevelt to set up a US intelligence service that would support the Allied war effort. But for all that, Stephenson was always under direct orders from MI6's chief, C, not an independent agent.[13]

Stephenson was an unusual addition to the higher echelons of MI6. The most verified aspects of his controversial and deceptive life have him born in a red-light district of Winnipeg and raised by adoptive parents.[14] He was a World War veteran who at the age of twenty joined the Canadian Expeditionary Force in 1917, before securing a transfer to the Royal Flying Corps, where he earned military medals for his gallantry and courage as a pilot.

Stephenson's upbringing set him apart from the public school educated English naval officers that came to lead MI6 between the wars. Nonetheless Captain W.S Stephenson MC (Military Cross) DFC (Distinguished Flying Cross) came to consider himself a loyal member of the empire who had fought for king and country and made this known to all who met him.

After World War One, Stephenson married an American heiress and ventured into business, making an early fortune in manufacturing, and selling radio sets before setting up his own investment fund, the British Pacific Trust, which owned shares in a number of companies operating in northern Europe in the 1930s. Such business interests involved Stephenson developing well-informed contacts in Scandinavia and Germany which morphed into the informal Z network that fed intelligence about Hitler's industrial militarisation to Churchill in the run-up to World War Two. In the summer of 1939 Stephenson had his first meeting with senior MI6 officials in London to discuss his industrial spy network with the support of Desmond Morton. Then, following the appointment of Stewart Menzies as the new wartime head of MI6 in late 1939, Stephenson was enlisted to lead the British intelligence wartime effort in the US.

Stephenson's appointment was received as a breath of fresh air by Walter Bell who felt that the MI6 operation in the US on the outbreak of World War Two was under-resourced and in urgent need of a clear and well managed operational remit. He was also relieved to hear that his immediate boss in New York, James Paget – nicknamed 'the Bart' because of his honourable status – was not being sent back to the US after his extended recall to home base. The news of Paget's departure liberated Bell from any vestige of loyalty or respect he felt he owed to his senior colleague and opened up the opportunity of pursuing his MI6 role as part of Stephenson's wartime operation.

Prior to Stephenson's appointment, Bell had formally applied to be relocated to the UK in February 1940, but his request was ignored by a head office that saw Paget's transfer away from the US as being a greater priority and evidently considered Bell an officer worth keeping in a post that was set to take on a much greater importance.

No sooner had Stephenson arrived with his assistant Major Dick Ellis, a World War One veteran and experienced MI6 officer who counted on the personal support of the head of service, C, Sir Stewart Menzies, than Paget was sent back to the UK on indefinite leave.

That same June of 1940, when Stephenson was posted to New York, saw the collapse of the British Expeditionary Force in France with the loss of over 11,000 lives and 57,000 captured, and the evacuation from Dunkirk of nearly 560,00 troops (340,000 British; 220,000 French and Belgian). The US public was stirred by the heroism they glimpsed behind the military disaster, and Churchill's defiant rallying call to the British people to be prepared for a long fight against the scourge of Nazism by land, sea and air, and 'never surrender'.

Bell wrote to his mother recognising the 'trial' she and the British people were being put through by 'Mr. C [Churchill]' but reporting that 'the performance of the BEF [British Expeditionary Force] has made a tremendous impression here [in the US] and has gone a long way to wipe out the very earthy contempt they [the Americans] have had for us until now.'[15]

The fact that Churchill had formed a wartime coalition with Labour on 10 May 1940, Bell believed, augured well for the future, improving Britain's chances of defeating Hitler and opening up the prospect of a long overdue transformation of British society once the war was won:

> I do hope now that Labour is in a key position, there will be a real effort to get the country up to date – it is the last chance we have got – otherwise Hitler will kick us into obscurity, misery, and poverty which will be richly deserved…. There's a great chance now to have a reorganization – not revolution – which is the intelligent way to do things. There has to be an end to snobbery which has grown worse in England instead of better. If it is not done by ourselves, it will be readily done for us by people who actively hate titles, hyphenated names, and all that bunk. I feel optimistic about England now for the first time. We have a real chance to go forward now instead of stagnating the way we were doing…[16]

The early months of World War Two were certainly challenging for Bell and all who worked for Stephenson's BSC as the organisation focused on ending American neutrality. As well as coordinating Anglo-American HUMINT (human intelligence collaboration), the BSC intensified efforts to persuade the US to enter the war. The scale of the challenge was underlined by a Gallup poll published in July 1940, the month after Stephenson's arrival in New York, in which less than 13 per cent of Americans surveyed said they would vote in support of entering the war. The isolationist America First lobby spread its influence across the country, with labour leaders, clergymen, scientists and businessmen including Henry Ford adhering to the campaign. Perhaps the most notorious celebrity of the isolationist cause was the legendary pilot Charles Lindbergh, an anti-war activist who became the subject of numerous complaints from members of the public who suspected him of being a German spy or part of a Nazi propaganda unit.[17]

The reorganisation of MI6 in the US under Stephenson restored Bell's sense of mission along with his faith in the importance of the US as a major ally that would reinvigorate Churchill's fight against Nazism. He hoped that a new Britain would emerge after an Allied victory, liberated from its past: 'I don't know what to think about the future...By Spring all may be a shambles. I am not defeatist in the least – I am sure we shall win, but God preserve us in our victory from these old mug monsters .... anachronisms who messed up the last choir. This time the settlement has got to be made by the generation most vitally affected, and there must be no more thought of going back to Queen Victoria's Diamond Jubilee...'[18]

Bell was told that Stephenson was moving the MI6 offices in New York from Number 26 Broadway to the thirty-fifth and thirty-sixth floors of the International Building in the Rockefeller Center, 630 Fifth Avenue and was counting on his services. He was happy to have Stephenson as his boss, believing that he had the measure of how to deal with the Americans. As he later recalled:

We had no idea about how to approach the Americans. The most valuable thing he [Stephenson] did was talk sense about the Americans. The British feeling was the Americans were a bunch of salesmen. The disquieting thing was that they were all rich. Stephenson cut all that out. He said, 'That's all bullshit. They're our friends. They'll help us. And we need them if we are going to win. Which is what Churchill thought. Of course, he was right. Absolutely...he was an invaluable person. In many ways Stephenson was very uncouth. He knocked the establishment and the rules and pretty much did what he wanted. He wasn't paid or anything. So, if he didn't like what you were doing, he'd tell you to bugger right off.[19]

The small MI6 station that Bell had got used to working in since his arrival in the mid-1930s was transformed, with new recruits from different agencies brought in from the UK and admin hired locally and from Canada. Among the latter were dozens of young Canadian women from Winnipeg, Stephenson's hometown, who had answered a discreetly worded small ad in the local newspaper looking for secretaries with an interest in 'British government war work'. Interviews in the town's Fort Gary Hotel followed along with security checks by the Royal Canadian Mounted Police before those cleared were enlisted. Their travel was paid, and they were housed in screened hotel accommodation in New York, their movements carefully monitored and controlled to avoid contact with any suspect enemy agents.

Recruits were spread out across strictly compartmentalised jobs, which limited the scope of any detailed knowledge of the organisation to only an internally approved 'need to know basis' while they were made to sign forms committing themselves to secrecy about details of their activities. There was no ostensible uniformed security around the tall skyscraper they worked from in the Rockefeller Center's International Building, and they entered their workplace, across the street from St Patrick's Cathedral, through unmarked doors.

The still unmarried Bell found his flirtatious if chaste encounters with the Canadian admin assistants and cypher girls employed by the BSC in 1940 a welcome respite from the secrets and tensions of war. As he let slip many years later in a letter to Leslie Spencer, the daughter of his friend, the wartime US intelligence officer 'Pat' Spencer: 'When I was working in British Security Coordination in New York in 1940, the Canadian women staff complained bitterly that no one made a pass at them, and I became rather popular for being an exception.'[20]

The surviving testimonies of several secretaries who worked at the BSC show they enjoyed their work, and found it exciting, full of intrigue and colourful bosses who all seemed to be part of a mission believed to be critical to defeating the Axis powers.

Grace Old was typical of the secretaries recruited in New York for the Allied war effort. Born in Wales, her father ran a tobacconist shop before emigrating with her as a young child to the US between the wars. In 1939 she was nineteen years old and had graduated from high school in Cranford, New York, when she got a part-time job with the British consulate before being transferred to the administrative offices of the UK government's propaganda arm, The British Information Services in Rockefeller Center. The BIS, part of Churchill's Ministry of Information, liaised closely with the British Security Coordination.

Her section included a cousin of the Queen Consort's, David Bowes-Lyon, and the historian John Wheeler Bennett, who, together with Bell and other members of Stephenson's team, led efforts to persuade the United States to enter the war on the Allied side by presenting the British case to the US press, and liaising with relevant US and UK agencies. She was then transferred, along with Bell and others, to Stephenson's higher powered and secretive BSC. 'Once the US had entered World

War Two, I helped in the liaison work with the US OSS handling classified documents. We never knew what each was doing in the building, but I remember those who came through the office I worked in included Otto von Hapsburg, Aldous and Julian Huxley, and Theodore Roosevelt's grandsons Kermit and Quentin...' recalled Old.[21] She described the diminutive Stephenson as 'very quiet, not very flamboyant, he would take the lift to one floor but then he would walk down and meet people so as to throw people off the trail...Everyone seemed to be in awe of him[Stephenson] because of his links with the special operations training facility in Canada known as Camp X and the fact that he'd fought for the British Empire in WW1.'[22]

One meeting that Stephenson chaired stuck in her memory when interviewed many years later. Those around the table were discussing a report that an American merchant seaman had been passing information to the Nazis and someone suggested he should be dealt with. 'Stephenson took a pistol out, laid it purposely on the table and said, "I just did". Next, we read in the papers that the sailor had been found shot dead. We assumed that Stephenson had done it, but we never heard anything more about it.'[23] Myth or reality, the suggestion that Stephenson had a special 'licence to kill' endured in this and other former BSC employee accounts, forming part of his legend, along with the shaken but not stirred and very strong dry martinis he allegedly mixed.

# 15
# South of the Border

In late 1940 Bell was posted as an MI6 officer working for Bill Stephenson's British Security Coordination (BSC) organisation on a short-term assignment under cover to the British consulate in Mexico City. During World War Two MI6 would dramatically expand its operations in both North and South America to counter German threats to Allied interests. His posting coincided with the arrival of the first special agents to be deployed by the FBI in Latin America as part of its newly created Special Intelligence Service (SIS). The British and American operations were connected in terms of sharing the common aim of countering German surface and submarine maritime activities, identifying enemy agents and assessing threats to Allied political and economic interests including oil supplies.

The development of closer ties between British intelligence and the FBI would prove protracted. The FBI agents were trained as criminal investigators or law-men, not counter-intelligence officers or spies. South of the Rio Grande they were soon floundering, finding it difficult to assume cover roles as businessmen, develop local sources and provide accurate reports to New York.[1]

While there was much publicity about possible Nazi activities in South America, there was no specific or accurate information, at least none that the FBI agents could get their hands on. And yet within days of Bell's arrival, on 15 November 1940, information that four German ships planned to run the British blockade near Tampico in the Gulf of Mexico proved correct and led to the ships being intercepted and stopped by the US Navy.

Although later claimed by Stephenson as a major reporting coup for the MI6 Mexico station, the situation would not have been resolved without the operational support of the US Navy. The well-sourced information led to four German ships steaming out of port into the Gulf of Mexico to be met by US destroyers, which trained the full battery of searchlights on them.

While the German presence was not in itself a bellicose act, given that the US had not yet declared war and its destroyers were on Neutrality Patrol, it nonetheless had the effect of an all-out attack. In the 'ensuing panic' one of the German ships, the *Phrygia*, either caught fire or was deliberately scuttled. While her crew took to their boats, the others returned to port.[2]

In a subsequently published official chronology of US Navy operations, the historian Robert J. Cressman writes that it was the USS *Plunkett*, a Greaves-type destroyer, that prevented the German ships *Orinoco* and *Phrygia* from leaving Tampico. The oil-exporting city and port was located in the south-eastern part of the state of Tamaulipas, on the north bank of the Pánuco river, about 6 miles inland from the Gulf of Mexico, and about 500 miles north of the capital, Mexico City.[3]

In early 1941, just a few months into his posting, Bell was felled by a combination of the tropical summer of humid heat and heavy rainfall and the unfamiliar diet of heavy spiced food and highly intoxicating local tequila. He was hospitalised suffering from severe hepatitis and amoebic dysentery and subsequently spent weeks convalescing in a colonial mansion in Cuernavaca as the guest of the honorary British consul in Lerma, an old colonial town about 30 miles west of Mexico City.

The consul's name was George Conway. A one-time Fabian Socialist like the founders of Bell's old university the LSE, Conway came from a penniless background and made a fortune. When Bell met him he was the chairman of the Light and Power Company as well as an expert on Spanish colonial history, around which he had built up a private library and archive. He was, in Bell's words, 'a perfectly delightful man'.[4]

A great admirer of William Morris, the Victorian textile designer, poet, novelist, translator and socialist who pioneered the Arts and Crafts movement, Conway was a man of eclectic tastes with a multitude of cover roles, who was a helpful source of intelligence on suspect Nazi activity.

Bell found Conway a genial host, and Cuernavaca close to paradise after the chaotic urban architecture and violence of Mexico City. It was one of Mexico's most loved colonial towns, a haven of tranquillity and natural beauty known as the City of Eternal Spring because of its all-year-round temperate climate and stunning vegetation and landscape. Walter spent his convalescence driving out to the surrounding country of volcanoes, prairies and rivers and taking leisurely walks through gardens filled with a variety of flowering trees and plants including bougainvillea, jacarandas, African tulips, lilies, jasmine, tabachines and daisies. He also read a lot, taking advantage of Conway's 'very remarkable library' to delve into Mexico's history and customs and the accounts left by earlier foreign visitors.

The Mexico Bell came to know as an intelligence officer posed a different kind of threat to that found by Graham Greene and Evelyn Waugh during their separate trips to the country in the 1930s. The brutal anti-clerical purges of the 1920s had ceased to be a central part of the political landscape and were instead replaced by Nazi designs on the US's southern neighbour, requiring good Anglo-American intelligence cooperation and robust diplomatic action in response.

Bell's assignment coincided with a new rapprochement between Mexico and the US, leading eventually to a general agreement signed in November 1941 that resolved most of their outstanding disputes. The old problem of US agrarian claims was settled, a reciprocal-trade treaty was outlined, and the Mexican peso was stabilised and supported to maintain a constant dollar ratio. The United States agreed to continue silver purchases at world prices and to provide long-term loans to buttress Mexico's economy. Alongside Allied intelligence operations against Nazi Germany, agreements were reached by the US on military aid, primarily to professionalise the Mexican army and its small air force.

Further south of the Rio Grande, the Latin American continent was not short of military officers and politicians sympathetic to the Nazi cause, nor of German secret agents prepared to operate against the Allies. The threat had its propaganda value for those seeking an end to US neutrality.

German meddling in Latin America had been viewed with concern by the Roosevelt administration from the outset of World War Two with a Gallup survey in May 1941 showing that 81 per cent of Americans polled were prepared to support US military intervention if Germany or any other European power were to attack a country in Latin America, the US's 'backyard'.[5]

The continent certainly provided fertile ground for intrigue and dirty tricks when the BSC's operational agenda grew to encompass news manipulation and black propaganda. Anti-German stories were fed to the US media to counter and denigrate organisations perceived to be pro-Nazi or virulently isolationist such as the America First Committee. One of the most notorious stories spun by the BSC was a report in October 1941 about an alleged map of Latin America showing the continent divided into five new states that were controlled by Hitler and linked by extensive German air routes from Europe extending into Panama and Mexico.

The map was cited by Roosevelt in a pro-war anti-Nazi speech on 27 October 1941. 'This map makes clear the Nazi design not only against South America but against the United States as well,' he warned.[6] There were, allegedly, two copies of the map – one was in Hitler's possession, the other with the German embassy in Buenos Aires. It was the latter that a British agent had reportedly got his hands on after stealing it from a German embassy courier in the confused aftermath of a car crash in the Argentine capital, no casual accident but one that had been deliberately planned.

For all its drama, the report of the document's discovery was almost certainly fabricated and the map a forgery, with the story of its provenance 'just too pat to be wholly believable' as author William Boyd discovered while researching the BSC's Latin American conspiracies for a novel. 'How come a German courier, who was involved in a car crash in Buenos Aires, happened to have a copy on him? Conveniently, this courier was being followed by a British agent who in the confusion of the incident somehow managed to snaffle the map from his bag and it duly made its way to Washington,' wrote Boyd.[7]

And yet the BSC's black arts continued to target South America. In May 1941 Stephenson sent another of his MI6 recruits, Bell's colleague Harford Montgomery Hyde, to Bolivia to investigate a rumour that the Nazis might be planning a coup there. The assignment turned into a duplicitous exercise by British intelligence, with Stephenson authorising Hyde to exaggerate the threat by forging letters allegedly written by German officials planning a coup that were passed on to the Bolivian government and to the White House.

On 19 July 1941 the Bolivian president Enrique Peñaranda declared a nationwide state of siege in response to alleged plans involving 'foreign political interests of a totalitarian character' with the plot widely reported by the US media, seemingly unaware that the story was part of the MI6 campaign to draw Roosevelt into the war effort.[8] The use of misinformation mixed in with propaganda formed part of what Bell's wartime boss Stephenson justified as 'political warfare'. The controversial influence campaign aimed at winning over the US public away from America First and towards intervention in World War Two had never been used by the British on such a wide scale.

Bolivia was known for its mines, some of which produced tungsten, a material used in machine tools of military application, and also for its legends. Until then its most famous American visitors had been Robert LeRoy Parker, better known as Butch Cassidy, and his fellow outlaw the no less mythical Harry Alonzo Longabaugh, known as the Sundance Kid, who disappeared there in 1908, the precise circumstances and location of their death the subject of enduring conjecture.

The FBI had a presence in Mexico that it did not have in Bolivia. This meant Bell having to cooperate with his American FBI colleagues in tracking the German military and intelligence presence in the region while also helping to encourage Mexico to become an active pro-Ally belligerent in World War Two.

On 22 May 1942, after Germany sank two of its tankers, Mexico declared war on Germany and Japan, its strongly anti-Nazi foreign secretary, Ezequiel Padilla Peñaloza taking the lead in urging other Latin American countries to follow suit and support the Allies too.

Mexico's major contribution to the war effort was the steady supply of raw materials for the US industry. It also contributed hundreds of thousands of temporary farmworkers (*braceros*) and railroad men under the Bracero Agreement, negotiated by the United States in 1942 to alleviate labour shortages occasioned by the military draft.

'Having seen something of Latin America,' Bell wrote on his return from Mexico to the US to be reassigned to further wartime MI6 duties, 'I have no belief in its future except as developed by the USA and the odds are on the US doing it.'[9]

Stephenson's BSC made early progress in helping Churchill secure initially clandestine US military assistance in the form of rifles and ammunition, and Flying Fortresses, although the key was the ancient US warships the UK received in exchange for US naval bases in the Bahamas. The US also provided heavier wartime material such as naval destroyers.

At the same time the BSC drew on the development of a transatlantic intelligence relationship to strengthen a black arts campaign of anti-Nazi propaganda and exposure of fifth column enemy agents. The campaign gathered strength in the summer of 1941 when Stephenson's friend Bill Donovan was tasked by Roosevelt to lay the foundations of the US's first foreign intelligence service with the establishment of the office of Coordinator of Information, the forerunner of the Office of Strategic Services (OSS), modelled on MI6.

Bell regarded his boss Stephenson as a business tycoon, a promoter in the western hemisphere style with imagination and style. Stephenson realised that in Donovan he had the ear of the president and could press for the destroyer deal and other matters that the British government considered urgent and important. He believed that an external US intelligence service (hitherto non-existent), both for straight intelligence and for special operations, had to be built up as rapidly as possible, and that the BSC was the only organisation equipped in any way to promote this.[10]

While in Mexico the excitement Bell felt about his new assignment in what for him was unchartered territory, was initially overshadowed by his concern for the security and safety of his family in the UK, which he had much time to reflect on during his extended convalescence.

At the outbreak of war, Bell's brother-in-law Reggie Lygon signed up for military service, while his sister Mary and her three daughters were evacuated from London and joined Walter's parents in the vicarage in Riverhead. When the Luftwaffe began its bombing raids on the British mainland that September following the Battle of Britain, Bell wrote to his family warning them that they should move again as their lives were at risk given the proximity of the village to a munitions factory, the RAF airfield of Biggin Hill and Churchill's country residence of Chartwell, along with its vulnerability to any German land invasion across the channel.

Worried by the increasing intensity of German bombing raids on UK soil, Bell urged his parents to leave the vicarage in Riverhead and join Mary and her three daughters, who, following his advice, had left for Madresfield Court, the Lygon family estate in Worcestershire beneath the Malvern hills. As Mary and Reggie's daughter Barbara recalled many years later: 'Walter sent my mother a warning that her life and that of the family would be in danger if they stayed in Kent. He seemed to have intelligence about the threat posed by the German raids.'[11]

Despite its large size, Madresfield, where Mary and her three daughters were evacuated to in 1940 was relatively safe from attack. Set in a remote, almost secret part of the country,[12] and half-hidden by trees, it was far less exposed to stray Luftwaffe bombs than the Kent village of Riverhead, near the English Channel, where George and Muriel Bell resolved to remain, caring for their church and parish. At one point the village had an army company based in its grounds and hosted secret meetings of the Danish Resistance as arranged with the mistress of the house and estate, the Danish-born Else Schiwe, Countess of Beauchamp. Her first husband, Peter Dornonville De La Cour had died in 1924, and in 1936 she married William Lygon, Viscount Elmley, who had taken the title 8th Earl Beauchamp on the death of his father in 1938.

Madresfield was also, early on in World War Two, earmarked as a safe haven for the princess royals, the future Queen Elizabeth and her sister Margaret. To make way for them Mary Lygon and her daughters, along with their nanny, were temporarily moved from the main quarters and nursery to Beauchamp Court, a large cottage on the estate, although the planned arrival of the princesses never materialised.

Royalty or no royalty, German bombs or no bombs, Walter was unable to convince his father to move from his parish in Riverhead. George saw his duty as the vicar to stay with his community, and his wife Muriel stayed loyally by his side.

Only the younger residents in Riverhead lived the aerial dogfights of the Battle of Britain in the sky over Kent like a great adventure, with one boy, Brian Price, later recalling the excitement he felt collecting spent cartridge cases, shrapnel, incendiary bomb fins, ammunition clips and other junk. A large time-bomb fell in gardens near the church but miraculously failed to detonate.[13]

One morning, the inhabitants of Riverhead woke to the sound of machine gun fire. A Henschel biplane had dipped out of the low clouds and fired on a military convoy on a road just beyond the village. The local sports ground was commandeered by the army, and George Bell would often come across some of the billeted soldiers in exercises with the local Home Guard acting as 'the enemy'. After his Sunday service, some of the

Home Guard volunteers would exercise by blocking some of the local roads dressed in military fatigues, armed with basic rifles and with their faces blackened.

In the early days of World War Two, George Bell struck some village residents as a somewhat aloof and forbidding figure, not least to some of the younger generation who felt terrified in his midst. 'He had a very bad temper' recalled his granddaughter, Barbara Lygon, of her time in the vicarage before moving to Madresfield Court. 'We had to tiptoe around not least when grandfather was writing his sermons in his study. So unlike grannie Muriel who was terribly kind and read me stories like the Owl and the Pussycat.'[14]

In 1940 George Bell was fifty-five years old and the outbreak of war in his hitherto peaceful and self-contained village parish put him under the severe strain of moral responsibility. He was a tired and much older man compared to the young curate that had first taken over in his late twenties, full of fresh ideas and missionary zeal. Lacking his former youthful vigour, he struggled to face up to all the tragedy and anxiety that came with the war, although he never failed his community. Few of his parishioners at the time realised the strain on him of carrying on, generally single-handed, the daily and Sunday services, often to the noise of guns and enemy aircraft. After broken nights, when bombs were falling, he would be up and about to watch over his beloved church or be at the beck and call of anyone who needed help and courage.[15]

George Bell remained a formidable and much respected figure, his looming presence in church services when not attending personally to parishioners, very much in evidence as the war encroached on the rural idyll of his small parish. The village had two public air raid shelters built on either side of the church, one in the northwest side of Chipstead Common, the second under the railway arch near the River Darent. There were two 'overflow' classes at the Parish Rooms and the pupils there took shelter in the crypt of St Mary's Church during air raids. Canon Bell always seemed to be in the midst of it all.

Among those left with an enduring memory of George Bell in wartime was Margaret Nicholas, who arrived, aged five, at Riverhead with her mother in 1941 as a young evacuee from London and stayed there for the rest of the war before becoming parish secretary many years later:

> Canon Bell would walk through the village in his long black coat and a biretta, forbidding, and a bit frightening. He kept the High Church services going, insisting that his servers change his robes for communion. My schoolteacher would take me to the Church. I just loved the service. I thought it was magic...the music, the candles, the incense. It helped us forget about the war although once we were out of the Church, it was with us again. The old Vicarage had a coach house which we used for Sunday School meetings. We had a Morrison Air Raid shelter in our sitting room in the Old Cottage in Chipstead Lane and the whole family slept in it together.'[16]

It was a great shock to the inhabitants of Riverhead when the V-1s (doodlebugs) and V-2 rockets arrived later in the war. The guided rockets were Hitler's last desperate throw of the dice – an attempt to dent Allied complacency that the war was won, by serving notice of Germany's enduring military potential.

As Margaret Nicholas recalled: 'We were taught that when these V1's came over we were quite safe while their engines were running. But if the engine cut out, you knew a VI was going to fall...Then we would get down on our knees with our hands over our ears...the nearest one to us just missed Marley Tiles Company factory in the village and fell into a pond.'[17]

One afternoon a large RAF convoy came and parked in an area of open parkland on the outskirts of the village called Chipstead Common to form the tented local HQ for barrage balloons. One local balloon brought down a V-1, but its severed cable snagged the telephone wires in Chipstead Lane. On another day a balloon brought down a V-1 in a nearby cabbage field with the shredded plants radiating from the small crater.

On VE Day in 1945 George Bell was not alone when he hung some old Christmas lights in the front of his house in the shape of a 'V'. And he joined his fellow villagers when they gathered around a large bonfire on the common and celebrated as an effigy of Hitler was set alight.

Back in 1941, if the errant youngest son shared one thing in common with his father the vicar it was the patriotic fervour stirred by Churchill's leadership and faith in a future that would offer a positive alternative to fascism and communism. As Bell wrote to his mother:

> The Prime Minister has caught the imagination of everyone, and they like the way Labour is coming to the fore.... Something has happened in England which I had given up hope of seeing – the working classes producing a great leader from their own group.... We have regained and I believe shall retain our greatness as a result of this. We were decaying under the leadership of those bloodless Conservatives. I disagree with Dad when he says that Labour could have gone into Chamberlain's government. If they had, England would now be ruled by Mosley and Pollitt[18] with orders from Berlin. We have to thank the greatness of Churchill, surely the greatest leader we have yet produced, combined with the great force of Labour, which up to now has been stuffed by our class system. The British Revolution, a fine orderly movement in accordance with our tradition is beating the despicable cruel and mean Revolution of Germany. It will expose the hollowness of Communism, and thus as its forbears, the Liberal Revolution a century ago, it will lead the world into new age

where everyman gets an equal education, an equal status in the nation and an equal share in the good things of life.[19]

In Mexico Bell could barely imagine what his parents were going through in wartime Kent. It seemed more than a continent away, a very different kind of war experience even if it was against the same enemy. He had been thrown into a tropical climate and largely covert war. There were no bombings of civilian targets or full-scale engagement between armies. But the energy resource rich Mexico's proximity to the US and to the rest of Latin America made it strategically important, and vulnerable to infiltration by German agents intent on breaking the economic blockade, and smuggling thousands of tons of oil through Mexican ports.

# 16
# Pearl Harbor

In March 1941 Walter Bell broke an unusually long period of silence in the extended correspondence he had engaged in with his family since first being posted to the US six years earlier. He had received a letter from his parents expressing concern as to his whereabouts since writing his last letter from Mexico, months earlier. 'You seem somewhat mystified as to where I live,' Bell wrote back, giving as his new address 42 Scott Circle Washington DC, a new apartment 'complete with air conditioning and near the office'. It was within a short walk from the British embassy chancery.[1]

Following Roosevelt's successful re-election and after discussions regarding lend lease were under way, Bell had relocated from the MI6 station in Mexico back to the centre of operations of the British Security Coordination (BSC) which Stephenson had set up on the 36th Floor of the Rockefeller Center on New York's 630 Fifth Avenue and with offices also attached to the chancery of the British embassy in Washington.

Although the BSC's existence had been formally registered and welcomed by the US government at the end of January, its activities raised suspicions, not least among a key member of the US administration, Adolf Berle – the anglophobe assistant secretary of state.[2] Berle was concerned that Stephenson had every intention of widening the Anglo-American relationship to develop 'a full-size secret police and intelligence service' that encroached on territory which the FBI considered its preserve.

Within months of Stephenson's arrival in June 1940, the BSC had expanded its organisation to act as a hub and effective clearing-house for a range of covert and propaganda activities with MI6 at its core along with other key agencies such as MI5, the Special Operations Executive (SOE), the British Information Services (BIS), the Imperial Censorship station based in Bermuda, Naval Intelligence, and the British

Purchasing Commission (BPC).[3]

On his return from Mexico Bell found himself involved in the UK operations aimed at seeking US military assistance for supplies via the BPC while also caught up in propaganda and intelligence operations against Nazi Germany. His work meant spending time in Washington, where a close colleague was Anthony Rumbold, whose cover post as third secretary in the British embassy made him a key liaison with the MI6 team in New York. 'If only we can get the use of this country's aeroplane factories, that is all we want so far as I am concerned...' Bell noted in the early stages of the British lobbying for US military assistance.[4]

Bell had returned to the US from his first overseas posting beyond its borders to find himself working under one of his least favourite politicians, Lord Halifax, the new British ambassador. Halifax had been appointed in January 1941, after the death of Lord Lothian, who had died in Washington after refusing medical treatment for a kidney infection because of his Christian Science beliefs.

Halifax's appointment was controversial. Although commentators on both sides of the Atlantic had suggested the post should go to someone with sound anti-appeasement credentials and a flair for publicity, Halifax was one of the 1930s appeasers. A fox-hunting aristocrat who had an ill-disguised contempt for the media, he had a reputation for being aloof, and was Churchill's last potential rival to leave the wartime cabinet.[5]

Churchill 'tended to use foreign vacancies as a means of removing troublesome politicians'[6] and the new ambassador had accepted the post reluctantly. Nonetheless Halifax's tenure got off to a dramatic beginning on Friday, 24 January 1941 when he steamed into Chesapeake Bay aboard the newest, largest and fastest battleship in the Royal Navy, the 35,000-ton *HMS King George V*. He was met by President Roosevelt who had sailed out on his yacht, *Potomac*, to personally greet him before entertaining the ambassador and his wife, Dorothy, to tea on board.

However, within two weeks of his landing in the US,

Halifax had run roughshod over the secret channels and more subtle propaganda efforts to win over American public opinion in support of the Allied cause. He made a highly publicised visit to the Senate and House of Representatives, fuelling an angry report in the isolationist media accusing the ambassador of meddling in internal American affairs. The resulting uproar was such that the US administration convinced Halifax that he should postpone the traditional inaugural address of a new British ambassador to the influential anglophile Pilgrims Society in New York, much to the fury of one of its key members, Thomas Lamont, the Wall Street banker.

Lamont was among the influential anglophile Americans that Walter Bell had befriended since before the outbreak of war. Another was David Bruce, who after seven months in London heading up the American Red Cross in the UK, was back in Washington, looking for a more discreet role in wartime secret intelligence that would have him returning to London.[7]

Seeing his friends Lamont and Bruce let down by the new British ambassador was bad enough, but Bell had other reasons for distrusting Halifax professionally and disliking him as a person. In later years he would recall two episodes that he felt illustrated both Halifax's sense of self-entitlement (the trait Walter most despised in the British ruling classes), and his failings as a senior diplomat when engaging with a key ally at a critical time in world politics.

The first story had Halifax's reputation as a keen foxhunter bringing him an invitation to join a very 'snobbish, and almost unique hunt in Valley Forge Pennsylvania'. Halifax accepted but, it being war time, he thought that he should dress simply in jodhpurs and a tweed jacket. As Bell commented: 'This achieved what must have been 100 per cent disapproval because it insulted the snobbish Hunt which only operated with total finery, and the general public who heard about it and who thought that the British ambassador ought to have no time for such frivolities in time of war.'[8]

The second episode Bell recalled was a conversation he

was party to in the British embassy canteen with the legal attaché John Foster and their mutual friend Isaiah Berlin, the Oxford-educated philosopher and historian of ideas. Berlin had been recruited by the propaganda arm of the Allied cause, the British Information Service (BIS), the successor of the British Press Service, in New York, and was also working for the British embassy in Washington, from where he wrote his weekly telegrams on the state of opinion in the United States. Foster remarked: 'I think Halifax is beginning to do some good.' Berlin replied: 'No, no, he has reached zero. He has stopped doing harm, but he is not doing any good.'[9]

The British presence in Washington in 1939 had only had a couple of hundred Britons attached to the embassy. Before the end of 1941, there were thousands of British people working in Washington, at least under the nominal control of the ambassador. Bell recalled: 'He [Halifax] was perforce a remote figure overseeing it all. But he did try to make himself known as widely as possible and began to attract respect and loyalty.'[10]

After the fall of France, Britain had become the last bastion of democracy in Europe. There was no more room for old pro-British versus pro-French controversies and it was reluctantly admitted by some in Washington that the British were entitled to project a favourable image of themselves in the hope of breaking down at least some of the innate prejudice stemming all the way back to George III's redcoats that most Americans entertained. Britain was not short of American friends with the Fight for Freedom interventionism campaign providing a solid American constituency on which to build.

By the spring of 1941 the British embassy in Washington was not just a key centre of British wartime diplomacy but also a den of intrigue, as it became embroiled in Churchill's plans to develop a strong transatlantic military and intelligence alliance, greatly facilitated by his direct and warm personal relationship with President Franklin Delano Roosevelt. The personal Churchill-Roosevelt correspondence excluded Halifax from the high-level decision-making process and reduced his role, as Halifax told a friend, to 'not much more than a Post Office...

for the rest I'm a public relations fellow, making speeches and showing them a nice ambassador' – at least when he didn't manage to alienate Americans and some of his staff.[11] On 11 March, Roosevelt tilted towards the Allied cause by signing, after its approval by Congress, the Lend Lease Act allowing Britain, China, and other Allied nations to purchase military equipment and to defer payment until after the war.

A letter Bell wrote to his father on 29 May 1941 showed that he had lost none of his ability to network and develop key contacts. Bell knew that an unnamed friend of Fowler Hamilton, the former Rhodes scholar turned legal adviser to the US Board of Economic Warfare, was on a visit to England with 'updated news'. Walter told his father that Hamilton was 'showing a growing interest in Japan', and that he had been with him recently at a meeting with a recognised British expert on Japan, the historian and diplomat Sir George Sansom. 'Sansom is about here (in Washington) now after some hair-raising experiences with the Japanese,' Bell wrote.[12]

Sansom was well informed on Japan, a country where he had served as a resident diplomat attached to the British consulate from 1904 to 1938, the year when the Foreign Office had appointed him 'adviser at large', with a broad remit to develop useful intelligence from key sources – no longer, as he had been until then, tied to his office but now acting, as he thought, in a way that was 'desirable and useful.'[13]

While Sansom obtained uniquely sourced information about Japan's preparations for war, he did not feel listened to. 'Some of the British community here are saying I ought not to be allowed to retire; but of course, I can't explain that after 35 years of service I am simply not being used!' he diarised during his last pre-war days in Tokyo on 13 August 1940.[14]

Two weeks later, on the verge of his departure to the United States to take up an academic post in Columbia University, and as the local situation became critical, Sansom received a belated plea to stay in post from the British ambassador to Japan Sir Robert Craigie, who until then had consistently ignored his advice.

Sansom's mind was made up, although he had not lost his sense of patriotic duty and felt his expertise would be put better use in the US. That autumn he left Japan and travelled to New York and from there to Washington where the ambassador Lord Halifax offered him an advisery role on the Far East. The following spring Halifax told him that he had received a telegram from the Foreign Office saying that they wanted Sansom posted to Singapore as adviser to the Far Eastern Mission of Economic Warfare. His 'special operations' mission was to collect intelligence on Japanese encroachments on Malaya, South China, Thailand, Burma and Singapore Island itself.

Sansom was sent to Singapore and was there with his wife as war with Japan approached in the last months of 1941. In early November he shared intelligence with top officials of the British Royal Navy and – through secret backchannels in Washington – with the US President Roosevelt that the Japanese planned to establish themselves in Singapore so as to make a swoop south to Siam and Malaya. As it happened, Bell was not in Washington. After a year of suffering the lingering consequences of the hepatitis and amoebic dysentery he had contracted during his posting in Mexico, Bell was given leave to restore his health and took time off, away from the embassy, on an Arizona ranch.

He was still recovering on health leave a month later, 7 December, when Pearl Harbor, the US naval base near Honolulu, Hawaii, was attacked. The next day the US Congress declared war on Japan, as did the UK government after the Japanese attacked Hong Kong, Singapore and Malaya, marking the beginning of the Pacific War.

The question of who was to blame for the way the US got taken so badly by surprise on those grim days of infamy when its defences of the Philippines and Hawaii were overwhelmed, as later the British were forced to abandon Singapore, was destined to be explored and debated by numerous historians and writers.

The US military commander in Pearl Harbor initially

shouldered the blame for the debacle. The US military SIGINT capability failed to identify and disseminate an accurate advanced warning of the Japanese attack.[15] It was arguably one of the biggest intelligence failures in twentieth-century history, even if it did have the benefit of ending US isolationism. The catastrophic defeats of 1941–1942 led to a period of recrimination and backbiting during which MI6, as the key secret intelligence service of the Allies at the time, also got its share of the blame.

A major study based on declassified documents published more than fifty years later by the military historian John Costello suggests that the chain of defeats that overwhelmed US forces and drew their country into the war against Japan and Germany in December 1941 was a direct consequence of a major failure of military strategy and foreign policy by the Roosevelt administration.[16]

The same study details the signals and human intelligence on Japanese war plans, which Churchill was party to and which he shared with the US administration, including specific information about the Japanese intention to wage war against Great Britain which, the US Army Pearl Harbor Enquiry Board concluded, reached Roosevelt on 26 November 1941.

Despite many records of MI6 reports and its agents during this period still remaining classified, the British Secret Intelligence Service's authorised history by Keith Jeffery claims that although information gathered from Japan itself was 'clearly pretty poor', there was some evidence of accurate reporting on forward Japanese dispositions in the latter half of 1941.

As many as twenty-one reports on Japan's 'preparations for Southward move' were issued to the War Office and Far East Combined Bureau between 30 November and 7 December 1941. These focused on a steady build-up of Japanese army and air force units in Indochina, although there was no apparent specific mention of Pearl Harbor.[17]

According to one of Bell's wartime colleagues,

Montgomery Hyde, it was their boss, the New York based head of the MI6 wartime network, Bill Stephenson, that was a conduit for relevant intelligence on Japan's military intentions between Washington and London.[18]

That Sansom's reports were ignored as part of a breakdown in intelligence process, strategic errors, and diplomatic and military failure in the lead-up to the attacks on Pearl Harbor and, in its immediate aftermath, the subsequent Japanese offensive in Southeast Asia, was suggested by Bell in a letter he wrote after British troops surrendered Singapore to the Japanese in February 1942.

Bell privately wrote of Sir George Sansom in a way suggesting that his value and importance as an intelligence source was only belatedly recognised by the US and UK governments. Sansom was 'a very remarkable little man with a stupendous knowledge of his subject', who was 'a week ahead of the Japanese all along'. Bell described the way intelligence was mishandled as a 'story of blindness and stupidity',[19] a view Sansom expressed when he returned to Washington after he evacuated from Singapore, in a belatedly upgraded intelligence role attached to the British embassy.

Sansom was strongly critical of General Arthur Percival, commander of the British Empire forces during the Malayan campaign and subsequent Battle for Singapore, describing him as a 'staff officer' who should never have been promoted.[20] Percival's surrender to the invading Imperial Japanese Army force was the largest surrender in British military history and undermined Britain's prestige as an imperial power. Churchill called it 'the worst disaster and largest capitulation in British history'. It was blamed on Percival's poor organisation and weak command.[21]

The Japanese attack on Pearl Harbor involved a back story of failure in the intelligence process, which Bell, while not directly involved with, or responsible for, knew about.

The story began in August 1941 when a double agent recruited by British intelligence, the Yugoslav-born Dusko Popov, codenamed Scout by MI6 and Tricycle by MI5, arrived in New York from London. With the agreement of MI6, Popov had met up with John Pepper, a colleague of Bell's in the British Security Coordination (BSC), who went on to escort the Yugoslav to New York.

Popov was introduced by Pepper to FBI special agent Charles Lanman and also met the head of the FBI New York Office Percy Foxworth, who had been put in charge by his director Edgar G. Hoover of the agency's Special Intelligence Service. Popov showed the British and American interlocutors a microdot questionnaire that he had been given by the Abwehr, showing interest in obtaining detailed military information about Pearl Harbor's military defences four months before the attack. The information was shared at the highest level within the BSC and passed on to Hoover.[22]

Of the eight formal subsequent investigations into the Pearl Harbor attack, however, not one mentions either Popov or the intelligence he claimed to have provided British intelligence and the FBI with. Popov claimed in his own autobiography that he had told the FBI he had received a secret ten-page Abwehr list of instructions, which included a section containing a request for details about Pearl Harbor.[23]

According to FBI historian Raymond Batvinis, the controversy was laid to rest long after World War Two was over when the FBI's Popov file was declassified showing that Arthur Thurston, the Bureau's officer assigned to the newly created National Defence Division in Washington had informed the US Navy about Popov's orders on 25 September 1941, three months before the attack.[24]

Former CIA officer turned intelligence historian Thomas E. Troy, having reviewed the FBI files on the Popov case released in 1982, stated that they contained 'no hint of an attack warning'. In Troy's view 'the accusation against Hoover of his alleged responsibility for the Pearl Harbor disaster is not the truth but a canard.'[25]

And yet the conclusion that declassified FBI documents vindicate Hoover and refute Popov is based on a false premise

– namely the idea that if something is not reported to the public in heavily censored FBI documents, it did not happen.[26] Even if Popov did not give an explicit warning, the point remains that the FBI did not treat the Pearl Harbor queries seriously as strategic intelligence.

In his account of Popov and Pearl Harbor, the former US corporate attorney turned writer Larry Loftis alleged that Hoover actively withheld the information provided by the Yugoslav spy from President Roosevelt. Later, during the eight Pearl Harbor investigations, Hoover 'buried the information in classified FBI files, never to see the light of day... the countless MI5, MI6, and British Secret Service officers who knew of the document were gagged by Britain's Official Secrets Act. They could say nothing.'[27]

Walter Bell told the FBI's director Hoover's biographer Anthony Summers that he was in Washington when Popov was in New York and knew that he was being run as an agent. According to Bell he was personally not made aware at the time of the Pearl Harbor allegation as he had had a recurrence of the ailments he had picked up in Mexico and had only got back to operational duties 'in late January or early February 1942'. He was nevertheless close enough to the case to know that British intelligence and the FBI had had serious disagreements about Popov's credibility as a source:

> While I never had anything to do with Popov, I used to hear gossip about him both from British colleagues and the two or three senior officers I knew in the FBI. The latter were very sceptical about Popov on account of his raffish private life and were undoubtedly reflecting the views of Hoover himself. I think I would have heard if Popov had had a personal encounter with Hoover. Hoover was not given to seeing people like that and with his very puritanical values would have been very reluctant to receive him.[28]

In his biography of Hoover, Summers states that the fact that FBI files contain no record of a meeting between Hoover and Popov proves nothing. Hoover 'made an art form' of concealing information in alternative filing systems or simply not recording it at all. He would quote other British intelligence sources that Popov had met Hoover.

Other historians have argued that even if the warning had been passed to the right person or persons, it is unlikely to have made a difference. There was no mechanism for evaluating and disseminating it, and the recipients were not conditioned/trained/accustomed to receiving and acting on such reports. In addition there was an American perception that the Japanese were inferior, and not able to mount a sophisticated operation. Even if a warning had reached the desk of the commander-in-chief of the US Pacific Fleet, Admiral Husband E. Kimmel, he might well have done nothing different.[29] As it was, it was Kimmel who bore the brunt of the blame for America's lack of preparedness.

Bell's own correspondence in the days leading up to Pearl Harbor sheds light on the extent to which both British intelligence and the US administration were caught by surprise by the Japanese attack. A letter Bell wrote to his mother on 5 December 1941 – two days before the attack – was penned while staying at a ranch in Arizona in the company of an eclectic group of American friends, Elliott and Carleton Ward Cheyne, the actress Florence Auer and her husband. The VIP guest was Henry Morgenthau Jr., as Treasury secretary the second most powerful US administration official after President Roosevelt, rivalled only by the FBI director Hoover. Earlier that spring Morgenthau was one of the pro-British members of the Roosevelt administration, along with Harold Ickes the interior secretary and the secretary of war Henry Stimson, who favoured reinforcing the Philippines as a demonstration of the US's intent to stand firm against Japan.

The content of Bell's letter suggests that it was Germany not Japan that was on his mind and that of his guests as they took their pre-Christmas break in the seclusion of the ranch. As Bell wrote:

> Few seem to realise what a terrific job it is going to be to beat the Nazis. The country is not aroused for a really great effort. There is comparative indifference to the ship sinking... I wish we could produce some war aims... The trouble is that this country and Great Britain have been without direction during the past 20 years. Hence, they cannot define objectives. It is not too bad for us as we have the simple choice of fight or go under, but the Americans do not see it that way for themselves. They are not immediately and physically threatened, so they are apt to be apathetic like we were over Czechoslovakia. It is a disintegrating state to be in and puts us all at a disadvantage vis a vis the Nazis who have a real goal they feel they are chasing.[30]

By the time Bell's letter from Arizona reached his mother at the vicarage in Riverhead, everything had changed. Following the attack on Pearl Harbor, on 8 December 1941 the US declared war on Japan, and a similar declaration of war against German and Italy came three days later.

# 17
# Making Friends with the FBI

'The rapid growth of OSS into a large and formidable agency, which owed much to the help and advice provided by Stephenson and his people, and its impact on SIS (MI6), reflected the positive, as well as the ambivalent and difficult sides of the Anglo-American special relationship during the Second World War and after.'

Keith Jeffery,
*MI6, The History of the Secret Intelligence Service 1909-1949*

B ell's correspondence, and other documents he kept in his personal file, attest to the high regard in which he was separately held by two towering figures of Anglo-American intelligence and security history, the mutually antagonistic FBI chief J. Edgar Hoover and the head of the British wartime intelligence operation based in the US, Bill Stephenson. As detailed in a later chapter, after World War Two ended in 1945 Bell was awarded the US Medal of Freedom, a decoration established by President Harry S. Truman to honour civilians whose action had been of particular benefit to the war efforts of the US and its allies.

Hoover wrote to Bell in November 1942 to express his appreciation of Bell's 'personal cooperation in all matters of mutual interest', and his hope that their 'close relationship' would continue through the 28-year-old Special Agent Arthur ('Art') Thurston, who had been tasked with opening the FBI's first office in wartime London.[1]

A separate Certificate of Service or citation that Bell kept among his papers was one honouring the fact that between 1940 and 1945 he had 'performed valuable service of a confidential nature' as a member of the British Security Coordination (BSC). The signatory, the BSC chief Stephenson, wrote to Bell in May 1945, after the BSC was disbanded following the end of the war in Europe, with an even more effusive letter than Hoover's.

Noting how he had drawn on Bell's working experience and contacts built up in the pre-war years as an MI6 officer in New York, Stephenson wrote that 'in terms of our own history you were here, of course, considerably before the beginning of time.'[2]

As well as bringing his proven experience as an MI6 officer to the BSC, Bell, according to Stephenson, was also a 'pioneer of new and important activities', most of which were considered of too sensitive a nature by MI6 to be included in any declassified account of its wartime activities. In his letter of appreciation, Stephenson states that in the early stages of World War Two Bell helped reorganise the Allied intelligence presence in Mexico, producing 'results of immediate value and lasting worth'.[3]

He also goes on to state that after returning to the US and working for the BSC in New York and in Washington, Bell was entrusted with 'various essential tasks'. In his citation, Stephenson makes special mention of 'the very cordial relations' that Bell developed with an unnamed agency 'upon whose cooperation and good the success of our efforts' has been largely dependent.[4] The agency appears to have been a veiled reference to the Office of Strategic Services (OSS), the wartime intelligence agency run by Stephenson's close friend William Donovan.

Early on in World War Two the FBI chief Hoover initially embraced Stephenson's appointment as MI6's head of the wartime BSC and the setting up of a new operational Anglo-American intelligence hub at New York's Rockefeller Center. For his part, Stephenson arranged for a team of FBI team of agents to visit London, where they spent months studying the organisation and procedures of the British Security Service (MI5) and MI6. But as America entered the war the relationship between the two men descended into bitter acrimony.[5]

Rather than act in the capacity of wartime intelligence liaison partner, Stephenson tried to assert his hegemony, much to Hoover's chagrin. Hoover accused Stephenson of not sharing information he felt he was entitled to and that was useful for FBI operations. The discord was fuelled by operational guidelines agreed between London and Washington that assigned MI6 the role of acting as MI5's representative to the FBI – a situation that Hoover soon found untenable as he felt that the FBI, with its experience of surveillance and investigation linked to domestic security, had more in common with MI5 than it had with MI6, which Hoover regarded as an external intelligence service.

Notes that Bell wrote and buried among his private papers about his wartime work shed light on the challenges he faced when trying to deal with both Stephenson and Hoover, caught, as he was, in the crossfire between two mega-egos.

In early 1942 Bell was summoned to the BSC headquarters in New York by Bill Stephenson and tasked with improving relations with the FBI. Days earlier, one of MI6's senior wartime recruits with increasing influence in key operational matters such as the security of signals intelligence material, the former Special Branch Indian police officer Colonel Felix Cowgill had visited Stephenson. With Stephenson's blessing, Cowgill appointed Walter ('Freckles') Wren, the MI6 station chief in Trinidad, to head up MI6's Section V counter-intelligence section in the US. For British counter-intelligence in the US to be allowed to do its work it needed a close liaison with the FBI headquarters in Washington and Stephenson suggested that Bell should take charge of this.

This was easier said than done. In mid-1941 Stephenson's relationship with Hoover had deteriorated when the head of the BSC became deeply involved in helping Bill Donovan set up his foreign intelligence service. Hoover was intensely jealous and suspicious of this development. Hitherto, he had been the big Man of Intelligence[6] in Washington, overshadowing the offices of US army and navy intelligence, which were small and did not impinge on his preserve. As Bell later recalled: 'In mid 1941 Stephenson had lost his warm relationship with Hoover when the Canadian head of the BSC had become deeply involved with Donovan in starting up the Office of Strategic Services, as the WW2 precursor of the CIA came to be known.'[7]

Turf wars were played out with a US presidency – most of it Roosevelt's – that, according to former CIA officer and historian Nicholas Reynolds, never really had an interest in or grasp of how espionage could be effectively used.[8] Alongside a clash of egos, Hoover's distrust of the BSC was the result of what his staff were experiencing and reporting to him, namely Stephenson's freewheeling-style operationally, recruiting agents and tapping foreign embassies behind the FBI chief's back and in a way that appeared to breach US sovereignty and established diplomatic rules.[9] Hoover saw the Stephenson/MI6/Donovan/OSS liaison as an unwelcome encroachment on his turf, and an unnecessary and disruptive duplication of effort. So he set out to harry Stephenson and his organisation, stirring up a key US administration official, Adolf Berle, to promote legislation to curtail BSC's activities[10].

Undeterred, Stephenson believed that an external US intelligence service for both straight intelligence gathering and special operations had to be built up as rapidly as possible once the US joined in the war effort. Given its mushroom-like growth since his arrival in the US in the summer of 1940, Stephenson felt that his was the only organisation that was in any way equipped to recruit, train and promote a new US intelligence capability. And he saw the pursuit of this objective as a priority. It was a tough challenge. One of the ironies of the US declaring war on Japan and Germany in December 1941 was that the consequent determination of the State Department, US military service department and the FBI to be the controlling influence in clandestine activities came close at one point to threatening the BSC's very existence.

As Stephenson warned MI6's chief Stewart Menzies in January 1942, less than a month after the attack on Pearl Harbor and just as Bell was tasked with liaising with the FBI, the

McKellar Bill came before the US Congress, requiring the registration of all foreign agents, whether friend or suspected foe, along with detailed disclosure of their appointments and activity. Stephenson feared that the bill might in effect render the BSC inoperable. Menzies was less concerned, pointing out that money received by MI6 need not necessarily pass through any bank, as had occurred in the past, and could come directly from the British embassy, while MI6 agents were secret men unknown to anyone outside the organisation.[11] However, Stephenson felt he had little choice than to defuse the controversy over the BSC's role by trying to mend his bridges with Hoover and trusted Bell, with his accumulated US experience as well as pro-American sympathies, as the man for the formidable job.

Bell's new duties involved a daily meeting with Milton Ladd, the FBI's national director, who dealt with counter-intelligence in the US and Latin America. 'This relationship developed more happily than I expected, but all the time I sensed that there was a barrier beyond which I was unable to penetrate,' Bell recalled. 'Allegations were made to me about Stephenson's misdoings which personally I didn't always understand but I did my best to clear up.'[12]

In his efforts to build up a closer relationship between the British and the FBI, Bell accompanied and advised Guy Liddell, at the time MI5's director of the security agency's counter-intelligence B Division, when he visited Washington and New York in June 1942 for meetings with various senior FBI agents. The ten-day visit was the first Liddell had made to the US since the FBI's mishandling of the Rumrich case in 1938. But with the US now a major ally in the war, and the increasing presence of American military and intelligence personnel in the UK, he had little option than to seek to heal old wounds and embrace a new spirit of cooperation.

A twenty-year veteran of the Security Service, Liddell was then considered by many to be Britain's finest counter-intelligence officer. Bell developed a close and lasting friendship with him, feeling he was a person that he could confide in and talk to freely about both official and personal matters. He briefed Liddell on his arrival in New York and later accompanied him in Washington to all the meetings with the FBI. In contrast to Hoover's distrust of Stephenson and Donovan, Bell found the FBI 'intensely interested in all that he [Liddell] had to say – and they were disarmed by his personality.'[13]

Liddell's US trip began with a meeting in Washington with Hoover's second-in-command Edward Allen Tamm. The MI5 officer found Tamm rather too full of himself as he laid out a large map of the United States with pins and bits of cotton. Tamm confessed to the difficulties of using internment against German citizens in the US as it involved a process of denaturalisation that was 'cumbersome', in contrast to the UK where, under the wartime Aliens Order approved by Churchill in 1940, MI5 had been given draconian powers to deal with anyone who could be a fifth columnist.[14] Tamm told Liddell and Bell that he was frankly amazed that there had been no act of sabotage committed in the United States, and that espionage cases that had come to the agency's attention had been of a 'crude variety'.[15]

Nothing that Tamm had to say dissuaded Liddell from his view that the Americans had yet to reach the efficiency of the British when it came to dealing with suspect German agents. The large map on Tamm's wall, showing clusters of 'alien population' corresponding almost exactly with the country's industrial centres, did not impress Liddell, who noted that the 'Americans seem to have a mania for diagrams, many of which I fear are meaningless or misleading.'[16] As for Tamm, 'all this vast mise-en-scène was not so much to impress the visitor as to impress the gentleman who occupied the room of his own importance.'[17]

Bell and Liddell next saw the FBI's C.H ('Kit') Carson, who was responsible for counter-espionage activities south of the Rio Grande and who Bell would have had some dealings with when he was in Mexico. Carson was keen on engaging British help in countering attempts by the US State Department to take the lead role in policy regarding alleged German spies deported from South America. The US State Department had agreed with South American governments to have the arrested Germans sent back to Europe in exchange for nationals from the countries from which they came. The FBI wanted to keep the deportees in the US, and Carson asked his visitors whether they could do something through the British embassy in Washington to strengthen FBI's hand.

However, other meetings that Bell and Liddell attended not only underlined the problems that MI5 faced in winning the trust of Hoover, but the tensions that existed between the FBI chief and the head of the BSC, Bill Stephenson, over the handling of espionage activities on US soil.[18] While in Washington, Liddell lunched with assistant commissioner Wyndham Bruce, the Royal Canadian Mounted Police's liaison officer with the FBI who, when asked to frankly share his information as to what the US agency thought of MI5, replied: 'If you really want to know, they think you are too cagey and that you are holding up on them.'[19] As Liddell went on to recall in his diary: 'I told him that in many ways they were quite right and one of my preoccupations would be to get things loosened up.'[20]

And yet there were evidently several egos still at play, as well as departmental rivalries with the BSC and MI6 over which Liddell did not have jurisdiction. Emerging a few days later from a meeting with Hoover, at which Bell and Edward Allen Tamm were present, Liddell jotted down in his diary that the FBI chief was 'obviously the prima donna type', and 'it was obviously no good discussing with him such matters as double-cross agents' as his mind was 'working on political relations with other departments'.[21]

Hoover remained obsessed with retaining FBI control over security and espionage activities in the US and was strongly resistant to the expanding activities of the BSC under Bill Stephenson, who had allied himself with the nascent US wartime intelligence agency the OSS under his friend Donovan. As Liddell noted bluntly in his diary: 'Hoover hates Donovan's guts.'[22]

At their meeting in early June 1942 Hoover and Liddell, accompanied by Bell, agreed that British intelligence and security cooperation with the FBI should improve. As a token of good will, Liddell offered Hoover the opportunity to send Harry Kimball, the Bureau's espionage section chief, to London for detailed briefings on MI5's emerging initiative 'in the use of human sources for strategic deception', in other words the Double-Cross counter-espionage and deception operation involving double agents run by the British Security Service.[23]

That August Liddell, in London, noted in his diary that he had received a teleprinter message from MI6 to say that Kimball – accompanied by another senior FBI officer Clarence Hince, and Walter Bell – was on his way to London for meetings with British security and intelligence officials, 'at the invitation of MI5'.[24]

Bell arrived in London that summer of 1942, as MI6's go-between between the FBI and his friend MI5's head of counter-intelligence Guy Liddell in a follow-up meeting to that involving representatives of all three agencies held weeks earlier in Washington and New York. He was also authorised by MI6's chief Stewart Menzies to accompany Kimball to a further meeting in late August 1942 with Liddell. It was there that Kimball made clear Hoover's continuing concern about the BSC. Liddell recalled: 'Harry Kimball of the FBI...told me that before leaving America he had spent two hours with J. Edgar Hoover and Edward Allen Tamm [FBI assistant director] and was given a mandate to discuss the affairs of his department with me and to explain Mr Hoover's grievances.'[25]

As Liddell later documented in his diary, the 'real cause of the trouble' was that the BSC's head man Bill Stephenson had opted to cooperate with Bill Donovan's fledgling intelligence service rather than Hoover's long-established FBI, running agents and surveillance operations involving foreign embassies in Washington without clearing this with the FBI or asking for its assistance.

While these methods were judged by Stephenson to be successful in securing intelligence on German activities that were useful to British war aims, Hoover felt that such methods violated long established diplomatic rules and failed to recognise that the BSC and those who formed part of its organisation were guests of the United States and vital wartime liaison partners. Hoover seemed particularly piqued that what was reported to him by his own people as BSC's shenanigans, including the recruitment of secret sources in the US, was being done behind the FBI's back.[26]

Bell reflected on the secret tensions affecting the BSC's dealings with the FBI in a private memorandum that provided valuable insight into one of the major controversies affecting US–UK wartime intelligence relations.[27] He described the challenge that he faced in undertaking his World War Two assignment of 'cultivating' the FBI while in the US in 1941 and during the early weeks in London in the summer of 1942. Bell mentions that during 1941, the BSC set up an espionage section aimed at the Vichy, Italian and Spanish embassies in Washington which employed its own agents and recording devices and the staff who knew how to work them.

> That Hoover was aware of this and disliked it all was inevitable. After Pearl Harbor these operations were supposed to have stopped. But, throughout the time of my liaison with the FBI, which lasted until the autumn of 1942, the impression lingered that they had not. There was much speculation within BSC itself about this, apart from the FBI misgivings. Certainly, when I returned to London, I was sure that some such activities had continued and I felt unhappy about it, because I had my heart in the FBI liaison and was anxious to further mutual trust. I never succeeded in re-establishing the credibility of Stephenson, or his chief associates.[28]

While Bell appears to have sympathised with Hoover's mistrust of the BSC, he also recognised the importance of Stephenson's wartime role and knew him well enough to define his personality, suggesting that behind a power struggle between agencies lay two rival chiefs and a clash of egos. Hoover had a reputation for being protective of his organisation, and was, in the words of an FBI agent, 'at anyone one time...egotistical, a dandy, vain, generous, thick-skinned, thoughtful, mean-spirited, and cruel'.[29]

By contrast Stephenson, wrote Bell, while heading up a major Allied wartime intelligence coordination effort, had the values of a western hemisphere tycoon – 'self-acquired money, dealing with and manipulating people and power for its own sake...generous to his friends, kind in unobtrusive ways, approachable and devoid of pompousness and hypocrisy'.

According to Bell, Stephenson 'sincerely believed that he made a unique and immensely important contribution to the mobilization of American power on the British side...He disliked the British establishment, and they mistrusted him for good reasons. But I think it is fair to say that had he not turned up and functioned as he did, the loss to British interests would have been formidable.'

As Bell went on to record in a private memorandum he wrote after he retired from government service in the late 1960s, if the British had not had any early cooperation with the new American external intelligence service, the OSS led by Bill Donovan, as Stephenson encouraged, the OSS's initially challenging efforts to set itself up as an effective organisation in its own right without British help would have created far greater setbacks for the Allied cause as well as undermined the post-war relationship between the CIA and MI6. Mindful of the treachery of his MI6 colleague Kim Philby, Bell concluded: 'Would this close relationship have survived Philby, had the foundations been less deep? Philby cannot be blamed on Stephenson.'[30]

In November 1942, Bell was, under orders from the MI6

chief Stewart Menzies, moved away from the BSC operation in the US and to a new role, working with American intelligence OSS officers in London. The fact that by his own admission Bell's discreet mediation role between agencies 'never succeeded in re-establishing the credibility of Stephenson, or his chief associates in his dealings with the FBI' suggests that he may have burned his BSC bridges before ending his first posting in the US. Had he spoken too candidly to Stephenson about his calamitous failure when it came to getting Hoover on side? Did Stephenson happily rid himself of a loyalty problem?

Hoover refused to meet with Stephenson after their rupture in the autumn of 1942. However, he did extend Bell the honour of an audience in his office to personally thank him for his service to the FBI. On 7 November 1942, Hoover wrote to Bell regretting that due to a bad cold that had him confined to his home for a week, he was unable to get to the office for the planned meeting on the eve of the Englishman's departure to London. But he took the opportunity to effusively thank Bell and to say that it was 'with regret' that he had learnt that he was leaving the US.

Hoover ended his letter by expressing his hope that their separation would be 'but a physical one' and their close official relationship would continue through agent Thurston, the new FBI representative who was due shortly to arrive in London on attachment to the US embassy.[31]

There is no evidence that Stephenson might have accelerated Bell's departure thinking that perhaps he could no longer trust in his continuing loyalty to the BSC.

The reason that Bell was relocated to London was that the MI6 chief Stewart Menzies believed that by the autumn of 1942 the BSC's operations in the US had passed their zenith, and that London needed reinforcement after becoming the main base for intelligence and security cooperation as the Allies began to push back Nazi Germany's occupation in Europe. There was a job ready to be filled by Bell, drawing on his diplomatic as well intelligence skills and US experience, integrated in top secret joint teams with the Americans.

While the Anglo-American Alliance after the Pearl Harbor attack was as close as any alliance had ever been in the extensive common endeavour to defeat the Axis powers neither party completely abandoned its national sovereignty.[32] The OSS increasingly asserted its role in intelligence work in the US and also developed independent sources of information and organisation in Europe, sending its own officers to London to liaise with MI6 and SOE, while in November 1942 Hoover had an experienced officer 'Art' Thurston open up the first FBI office in the US embassy with a brief to liaise with British counter-intelligence.[33]

The opening of the FBI's first London office was celebrated officially as an important milestone in the history of the FBI's relationship with British law enforcement and secret and security services. Thurston's mission as Hoover's permanent representative was to establish direct relations with Sir David Petrie, the director general of MI5 and Menzies, the MI6 chief. It was in Thurston's interest, as it was in Bell's, to defuse personal tensions that threatened to undermine the professional transatlantic cooperation on intelligence and security in World War Two.

At Menzies's invitation, Thurston met the MI6 boss in London, at his 54 Broadway (St James's) office on the evening of 7 December 1942. After some light banter, Menzies began putting out feelers about Hoover's attitude toward BSC and Stephenson. Wasting no time Thurston launched into a review of the latter's transgressions along with a catalogue of Hoover's complaints that finally led to the decision for a direct liaison with MI5.[34]

Menzies learned that, despite Bell's best efforts to liaise, Hoover considered that Stephenson's perceived tendency to play fast and loose operationally, with scant regard for US sovereignty on intelligence matters, let alone adequate sharing of information or consultation with the FBI, had fostered an 'exceedingly poor impression'. This caused Stephenson to damage 'himself irreparably' and never enjoy 'the Bureau's confidence again'. Thurston told Menzies that the FBI was aware that the British had broken German codes and were reading Abwehr messages. The FBI agent insisted that any future Bureau cooperation with MI6 hinged on FBI access to these messages, as they affected espionage in the western hemisphere.[35]

Many years later, when a historian of the FBI and former agent Ray Batvinis asked Thurston who his principal liaison contacts were during his time in London, Thurston identified Kim Philby as his contact man at MI6 and Anthony Blunt at MI5, both later exposed as Soviet spies.

Philby, after his January 1963 defection to the Soviet Union, wrote his propogandist and self-promotional memoir vetted by the KGB entitled *My Silent War* in which he confirmed his contact with Thurston, characterising the young FBI agent, with more than a touch of irony, given that the most successful Soviet double agent of the Cold War had managed to dupe him as he had countless other colleagues, as a 'thoroughly competent operator with whom it was a pleasure to work.' As Philby wrote: 'I had every reason to cultivate him, and he happily reciprocated the bootleg intelligence I passed him.'[36]

Much as Philby may have suggested that he had exclusive access to FBI intelligence and thus ability to influence matters, and inflated his personal role in the US–UK intelligence relationship, his was not the only line of communication between allies.

Bell was among the MI6 colleagues who continued to navigate the stormy relationship between the BSC and the FBI and preserve the essentials of the transatlantic intelligence alliance, working closely with OSS officers posted in London and without sharing secrets with Moscow.

An MI6 report written during the time Bell liaised with the FBI asserted that among the 'tangible' results of cooperation in countering enemy and subversive activity was the 'arrest and/or prosecution and conviction' by the US authorities of 'seven key enemy agents' and some twenty associates.[37]

And yet one area in which MI6 had had a longstanding interest in the US, the activities of Indian nationalists opposed to British imperial rule – and which Bell had been given responsibility for while in New York – proved contentious. Any cooperation that US government agencies may have offered in this area ceased at the end of June 1944, after Bell had been redeployed to London. The reason, according to MI6, was due to 'the latent American dislike of the popular conception of British imperialist suppression of Indian nationalist aspirations', rather than 'any officially inspired policy'. Nonetheless MI6 and the FBI started jointly investigating communist activities, especially in South America, from October 1943.[38]

There was some evidence of communist agents working within the BSC, but its discovery proved protracted. The left-wing English journalist based in Hollywood, Cedric Belfrage,[39] codenamed Benjamin by the Russians, was employed by BSC between 1941 and 1943 during which time he passed on documents to Jacob Golos, a Russian spy in New York. To this day the true nature of Belfrage's activities remains far from clear. Despite claims by some intelligence historians that he was an important spy for the Soviets, declassified National Archives files reveal that MI5 was not able to establish much about his activities and never interrogated him.

The files contain no evidence that Belfrage had direct access to Stephenson or worked closely with him, or with Bell in his role as the main BSC liaison with the FBI, and later with the OSS, despite the claim by Christopher Andrew, MI5's official historian, that 'Moscow valued him (Belfrage) higher than Kim Philby and the other Cambridge spies'.[40] What is known is that Belfrage never hid his left-wing views and links with the Communist Party during the 1930s and after World War Two, thus arguably making him far too obvious a candidate for recruitment as a Soviet agent.[41]

The case against Belfrage nonetheless was built on the testimony of Golos's lover Elizabeth Bentley, an American spy and member of the Communist Party USA (CPUSA) who became a paid informer of the FBI. In November 1945 Bentley contacted the Bureau saying she had been part of a Soviet spy ring operating in the US in which Belfrage had also been involved. She told the FBI that in late 1942 or early 1943, Belfrage was introduced to Golos by the general secretary of the CPUSA Earl Browder or V.J. Jerome (a senior CPUSA official) and subsequently met Golos on a number of occasions. Bentley recalled, 'Belfrage turned over to Golos a variety of items that came to him at the British Security Coordination New York headquarters, both material on British concerns and American material that had been given to the British.'[42]

When the war ended Belfrage took a position with the Allied Occupation government in Germany before returning to the US as a founder of the *National Guardian*, which for a number of years was the most influential popular front leftist magazine in the US.

By then the top counter-intelligence programme, known as the Venona Project – initiated during World War Two by the US Army's Signal Intelligence Service – had decrypted cables from the New York Office of the KGB to Moscow between June 1943 and September 1943, which implicated Belfrage, designated by 'an unknown cover name Number 9'. Belfrage is among 349 names, including US citizens, non-citizen immigrants, and permanent residents of the US whose covert relationship with Soviet intelligence was confirmed in the deciphered cables of the Venona Project, according to research carried out by historians John Earl Haynes and Harvey Klehr.

The cables showed Belfrage giving the KGB an OSS report that British intelligence had received on many topics: the anti-communist Yugoslav Resistance; reporting to the Soviets what the BSC head William Stephenson had said about British policy on the second front after meeting Churchill; describing the tense relationship between BSC and FBI; offering to establish covert contact with the Soviets if he were assigned to permanent duty in the UK; and delivering to Ukrainian-born spy Jacob Golos, who was the head of the CPUSA's liaison with Soviet intelligence, documents he had obtained during a visit to

London.[43] In 1947 when the FBI questioned Belfrage, he admitted having met Browder and Jerome separately and a man whose name he did not know but, in his words, 'looked a great deal like the FBI's photo of Golos'.

Belfrage said he had met Jerome 'with a view to finding out what I could about Communist and Russian politics'. He had supplied him with information about Scotland Yard surveillance tactics back in the UK and also with some documents relating to the Vichy government in France, which were of a 'highly confidential nature with respect to their origin but which contained information of no value whatsoever'.

'My thought was to tell him [Jerome] certain things of a really trifling nature from the point of view of British and American interest, hoping in this way to get from him some more valuable information from the Communist side,' Belfrage told the FBI.[44]

Belfrage was deported to the UK by the US Immigration and Naturalisation Service but was never prosecuted because of lack of evidence even if it was claimed by the FBI that Venona showed that he had lied.

Belfrage fought publicly to defend himself, insisting that he was innocent of any crime and that he had fallen foul of political persecution. In 1955, following the vociferous campaign against alleged communists in the US government and other institutions carried out under Senator Joseph McCarthy, he voluntarily returned to the US where no charges were brought against him. He later wrote two books about his US ordeal, claiming that he had been one of many victims of baseless paranoia about Soviet espionage.[45]

Historians to this day dispute the extent to which BSC was infiltrated by Soviet intelligence in World War Two, if at all. The two other wartime employees with links to the BSC, suspected of leaking documents to Moscow, the Russian- born lawyer Alexander Halpern and his one-time secretary the Czech-born Gertrude Rient, who for a short period was also Belfrage's girlfriend, were never incriminated by the Venona decrypts and relevant investigations by the FBI and MI5.[46]

The Bell papers certainly provide no evidence of any links Bell might have had with any of the three, and there is no mention of Bell in any of the files that have been released on the alleged Soviet penetration of BSC. What we do know is that while both Belfrage and Bell shared left-wing views in common and befriended radical Americans with links to the Communist Party, only Belfrage acted in a way that had the FBI informing US immigration authorities of their view that he had a compromising relationship with Soviet intelligence.

Bell was in Mexico when Belfrage first joined the BSC in New York. By the time Belfrage is alleged to have started passing information to the Russians, whatever its relative value, Bell been posted back to work with MI6 in London.

# 18
# Plotting Against Hitler

Following Bill Donovan's appointment as head of the newly formed Office of Strategic Services (OSS) in June 1942, his officers began to increase their numbers in Europe, with a headquarters also being set up in London. Walter Bell knew several of the senior OSS officers well. Information shared between him and the Americans included intelligence obtained from captured German prisoners of war and anti-Nazi Germans planning to kill Hitler.

In the period leading up to the outbreak of war in September 1939, Hitler had survived at least thirty assassination plots of varying degrees of sophistication. Once war had been declared, the oath of personal loyalty demanded by Hitler of his military officers and senior officials, along with the tightening of the security and repressive apparatus to counter the enemy without and within, heightened the risks for any resistance, not least home-grown. Even so, in the last half of 1943, there were six separate attempts by disaffected German officers to murder Hitler.[1]

So, what did British intelligence contribute to this narrative? On 14 July 1944, just six days before the most serious attempt on Hitler's life, the UK government's advisory Joint Intelligence Committee (JIC) reported that there was no intelligence that a coup against Hitler was in the offing. In other words, there was no change from the assessment by the 'high table' of Britain's intelligence community six months earlier that no convincing evidence had been received of any conspiracy to overthrow the Nazi regime any time soon.[2]

And yet just because the JIC reported as it did, it did not mean that intelligence had not been gathered and disseminated. In fact it had, but the intelligence had simply fallen on deaf ears. Since the autumn of 1943, around the time that Bell was relocated to London, details of an organised and determined internal conspiracy against Hitler – the most serious thus far with names of the protagonists – was known to MI6, thanks to human intelligence (HUMINT) drawn from contacts with some of the conspirators and the debriefing of German officers captured by the Allies as prisoners of war.

The intelligence was reaching the Allies despite MI6 and other British government agencies being officially prohibited from contacting German opposition, as per the orders given by Churchill to Anthony Eden in September 1941. In the minuted command, Churchill stated: 'We should not depart from our policy of absolute silence. Nothing would be more disturbing to our friends in the United States or more dangerous with our new ally, Russia, than the suggestion that we are entertaining such ideas. I am absolutely opposed to the slightest contact.'[3]

Perhaps, as suggested by the historian Max Hastings, Churchill recognised that democracies diminish themselves by resorting to the targeted killing of heads of state, even the monsters. Stalin by contrast, having no such moral scruples, devised a plot to kill Hitler in the winter of 1941 involving a former boxing champion Igor Miklashevsky posing as a defector, but then withdrew his orders, fearing this might lead the Western allies to make a separate peace with a successor regime.[4]

Churchill's policy regarding anti-Hitler conspiracies had been decided on pragmatic grounds in the aftermath of a controversial MI6 operation to establish links with the German opposition to Hitler and stop the war, which went badly wrong. On 9 November 1939, two MI6 officers, Captain Sigismund Payne Best and Major Richard Stevens, the head of the MI6 station at The Hague, arranged to meet a German general who was supposedly leading the conspiracy against Hitler. However, they were kidnapped by the Gestapo on their way to the meeting at Venlo on the Dutch-German frontier and taken into Germany. Hitler and Himmler suspected that the British officers were the 'wire pullers' of an attempted bomb attack on Hitler days earlier although in fact that attack was the work of a lone would-be assassin, a German carpenter and watchmaker called Georg Elser, who was opposed to Hitler's militarism and totalitarianism. Following the arrest of the British officers, the British became even more careful in their contacts with German anti-Nazis and the channels of communication were reduced still further.[5]

The two British MI6 officers disappeared until April 1945 when the Allies found them in a small German village in the Tyrol. They were alive but their kidnapping was a humiliating disaster for MI6. Tim Milne, an MI6 colleague of Bell's in World War Two, wrote that the Venlo incident was one reason why the general attitude in London to anti-Hitler conspiracies was cautious.[6]

There was no shortage of attempts to enlist Allied support by anti-Hitler German conspirators during World War Two. As the historian P.R.J. Winter points out: 'The contention that British intelligence and the prime minister knew nothing of any consequence about the German opposition and that this constitutes an intelligence failure is mistaken.'[7]

Bell's wartime work involved forwarding information about the assassination plots against Hitler to Americans in Britain such as David Bruce, the OSS head in London.[8] Bruce's appointment in December 1942 brought about a notable stepping-up of the OSS–London operation, and a strengthening in its relations with the British. In Bell, Bruce had a friend and colleague.

Bruce had replaced the experienced diplomat William Phillips, whose short posting in London was notable more for its caretaking of OSS–British relations than for any innovation in establishing actual operations. Phillips had had a distinguished record in public service, serving twice as under secretary of state and also as US ambassador to Italy in the inter-war years. After London, he served as special US envoy to India before being appointed General Eisenhower's special adviser on political affairs in Europe.

It was during Phillips's time with the OSS in wartime London that Bell is thought to have befriended his daughter Beatrice – an attractive 28-year-old, five years younger than him, and, like him, unmarried. The two met up again in post-war Washington before Bell's marriage in 1948 to Katharine ('Tattie') Spaatz (see Chapter 21, The General's Daughter). Beatrice eventually married the divorced wartime veteran Rear Admiral Elliott Strauss in 1951. A signed photo of her was one of a handful of photographs of old girlfriends from his bachelor days kept by Bell among his private papers.[9]

Bruce in his diary was critical of a 'William Phillips', curiously an individual of the same name, but not Beatrice's father, the head of the OSS in wartime London he replaced in 1942. The 'William Phillips' Bruce refers to bluntly as being 'stubborn, opinionated...a loner', and in intelligence terms, an 'amateur who knew nothing' and who had been running 'two useless agents'. He was a a rather shady intelligence operative who showed up in the early days of the London OSS office with only vague connections to Washington and was mistrusted by the British.[10]

Bruce was both rich and well connected. From a wealthy Virginian family background, he had gone on to marry the daughter of Andrew William Mellon, the banker, businessman, industrialist, philanthropist, art collector and politician who had served as one of the longest serving US Treasury secretaries. His family ties (not least being Mellon's son-in-law) combined with personal affability and ambition brought him onto various corporate and museum boards, among them the prestigious and cultural powerhouse National Gallery in Washington.[11]

Bruce had just turned twenty when he was sent to France in World War One in 1918, but never saw action as the Armistice came before he was engaged in battle. World War Two, by contrast, was destined to anchor him with a purpose in life: the experience of running the OSS's most important overseas operation, which confirmed a lifelong interest in foreign service.

When the UK declared war on Germany in World War Two, and before the US intervened, Bruce went to London to work for the American Red Cross. After Pearl Harbor, he joined

Bill Donovan's Office of the Coordinator of Information (OCI), the predecessor of the OSS in Washington, where he met and began his long enduring friendship with Bell as OCI, followed by the OSS, and developed links with MI6. Once Bruce had moved back to London to take up his executive OSS post, his patrician and cosmopolitan background helped him build up his network of key contacts. As documented in his wartime diary,[12] during his time as head of OSS in Europe (1943–1945), Bruce was very much at home in the private clubs and other privileged venues frequented by MI6 officers.

Bell was authorised by MI6 chief Stewart Menzies to share with Bruce intelligence the British had gathered about anti-Hitler German conspirators. The intelligence did not deter Allied plans, which were to proceed with their final military offensive on the German Army and secure Hitler's military defeat after the Normandy landings.

The July plot of 1944, codenamed Operation Valkyrie, involved a bomb attack on a meeting Hitler attended at his Wolf's Lair headquarters near Rastenburg, East Prussia. The three military leaders of the conspiracy were central figures in the German Resistance movement: the aristocratic army officer Claus Schenk Graf von Stauffenberg along with General Friedrich Olbricht and General Ludwig Beck of the German general staff. The bomb destroyed the conference room and killed three officers and a stenographer. But, shielded from the blast by the solid-oak conference table leg, Hitler survived, with a perforated eardrum and his trousers in tatters. Following the failure of a subsequent military coup, Hitler exacted a ruthless retribution, with the ringleaders and dozens of other army officers and civilians suspected of involvement being rounded up and executed.

Bell's important contacts with the German conspirators was first identified by the late Antony Cave Brown while researching his biography of the wartime MI6 chief Menzies. His research papers in Georgetown University include wartime intelligence documents full of details about German anti-Hitler conspirators which drew on information provided by MI6. The documents are largely drawn from US SCI – Special Counter-Intelligence Detachment – units manned by OSS officers with whom Bell is thought to have worked, drawing information from captured German intelligence staff and agents after the Normandy landings and General Patton's breakthrough of August–September 1944.

While Bruce gained a reputation for getting on well with his British wartime intelligence counterparts and ministers, Bell recalled that his friend's engagement with Lord Beaverbrook, one of the towering personalities in Churchill's wartime government with a reputation for brashness, proved challenging.

Bell related how, while he was posted in London in World War Two (the precise date is unclear but was likely to have been during the autumn of 1943 after Beaverbrook had taken two key appointments which developed his reputation as a key political ally and personal friend of Churchill's) his wartime boss in New York, Bill Stephenson, for whom Bruce had 'tremendous regard', accompanied the OSS officer to meet the newspaper publisher and politician at his palatial country estate in Cherkley Court in Surrey.

Beaverbrook was Lord Privy Seal at the time, and responsible for the organisation of the House of Lords. He was also head of the Anglo-American Combined Materials Board, a World War Two government agency that allocated the combined economic resources of the United States and Britain. The board had been set up by Roosevelt and Churchill on 26 January 1942.

At their meeting with Beaverbrook, the BSC chief Stephenson, accompanied by Bruce and Bell, were joined by two Labour ministers of Churchill's coalition government, Ernest Bevin and Hugh Dalton. As Bell recalled, at one point Beaverbrook made a disparaging remark about the Americans that was of such tactlessness that Stephenson and Bruce nearly walked out in protest. 'Our guest is a distinguished American and I didn't bring him here to be insulted. We're leaving,'

Stephenson was reported as saying. Beaverbrook apologised. As Bell told the Canadian historian, Bill Macdonald: 'You don't do that in Beaverbrook's house without knowing him very well.'[13]

Whatever Stephenson's influence on Churchill and his advisers as well as on US intelligence officers might have been – and this remains a subject of dispute – Bruce and Bell's challenges in wartime London were of a different nature and played out at a more discreet and less official level. They had to contend with the underlying conflicts of interest that existed between different sections of British intelligence and the related strains with US intelligence when dealing with anti-Hitler conspiracies.

Bruce wrote in his diary that his experience was that British proactive espionage – as opposed to reactive or counter-espionage – was 'lamentably weak', especially regarding Nazi Germany, and tended to duplicate what the Americans had obtained through their own sources.[14] He was not about to shoot the messenger, however. Bell's sharing of intelligence with Bruce was restricted from MI6's HQ Broadway, near St James's, under orders from the agency wartime chief Stewart Menzies. This was because Bruce was not cleared to read the top-secret ULTRA signals intercepts drawn from the breaking of German codes.[15]

Bruce's command suite at the OSS European headquarters was housed in a bland, grey nondescript five-storey brick building at 70 Grosvenor Street, Mayfair. But in a mirror of MI6's organisation, the OSS's main operational headquarters became physically separate from the offices of its counter-espionage X2 division by 1943.

Such a system of parallel, subdivided and potentially competitive operations had the potential to create more distrust than harmony. The tension between MI6 head office and its counter-intelligence Section V mirrored that between different sections of OSS and, more broadly, between British and American intelligence. The wartime friendship between Bruce and Bell contrasted with this dysfunctionality and rivalry, which surfaced now and then within Allied intelligence cooperation without ever fully undermining it.

The suspicion within the OSS that MI6 was withholding intelligence on the German conspirators was sufficient to have one of its senior officers, Colonel John Haskell, confront the MI6 chief Menzies at one point and demand that Broadway (MI6 HQ) give him any information on the subject in return for valuable Breakers material.[16] (Breakers was the code name for the anti-Hitler conspiracy used by Allen Dulles, the wartime director of the OSS based in Switzerland.)

Dulles was tasked with tracking German plans and activities, and had established wide contacts with German émigrés, Resistance figures and anti-Nazi intelligence officers.

One of his cases had him running a German agent who supplied him with texts of telegrams between German embassies and Berlin, most of which were not available through the code-breaking machinery at Bletchley Park. Code-named Wood, the agent was Fritz Kolbe, a German Foreign Ministry official. Kolbe had first gone to MI6, who rebuffed his approach, and then went to the Americans who judged him of the highest quality. Dulles, who went on to head up the CIA during the Cold War, described Kolbe as 'not only our best source on Germany, but undoubtedly one of the best secret agents our intelligence service has ever had'.[17]

MI6, for all its protectiveness about ULTRA, knew that it had no option on occasion but to rely more on human sources than signals intelligence on decoded communications. This was because the conspirators, for their safety, deliberately did not contact or communicate with each other via Enigma or any form of encrypted system used by the Nazi regime. Nevertheless, the MI6 chief Menzies kept a tight British control on the intercepted signals information, which gave British intelligence an important insight into Hitler's strategy, strengths and vulnerabilities with which to judge the chances of any conspiracy succeeding and how such an outcome would impact on the war.

Menzies and some of his officers in MI6, including Bell,

were not as intransigent in their dealings with the German anti-Hitler conspirators as were Churchill and the Foreign Office after Halifax was replaced by Eden as foreign secretary.

In November 1942 a group of MI6 officers deliberated over a four-page intelligence report on the growing rift between German military intelligence led by Admiral Wilhelm Canaris, the head of Abwehr, and the Nazi Party as personified by Himmler.[18] The thrust of the report was its suggestion that the war in Europe could be brought to a swift end if the British government were to encourage a military coup against Hitler, supporting its planning and helping to consolidate the end of the Nazi regime once the Fuhrer had been toppled and preferably killed.

According to the historian and wartime MI6 intelligence officer Hugh Trevor-Roper, the report's wider circulation within Whitehall was vetoed by the team's immediate superior and line manager, the deputy head of MI6's Section V, Kim Philby. Initially it left the other MI6 officers involved 'baffled'. Trevor-Roper, with the evidence of hindsight, would later suggest that Philby, already secretly a Russian mole, was acting in the interests of the Soviet Union.[19]

Certainly Stalin, whose soldiers were then battling to expel the German army from Russia, had no wish to have Britain striking deals with senior German military officers, however disgruntled they were with Hitler. Stalin was looking to the post-war settlement in a way that played to Russia's interests. Thus he wanted Germany not only militarily crushed but incapable of stemming the consolidation of communist rule in a post-war Eastern Europe, an outcome to which the conservative Catholic military conspirators against Hitler – anti-Nazi but also anti-communist – were opposed.

And yet, while the Philby conspiracy theory remains compelling, since Trevor-Roper's death in January 2003 evidence has surfaced that intelligence handled by some MI6 officers was, in the words of one historian, 'simply too hot' for Britain's political leaders, wedded as they were to a rigid policy of 'absolute silence' regarding the anti-Hitler resistance.[20]

Trevor-Roper short-circuited the usual chain of command in MI6 and passed the report to Churchill's scientific adviser Lord Cherwell, who is believed to have shown it to the prime minister.

The report was eventually shared in June 1943 with MI5, where Guy Liddell noted in his diary that Trevor-Roper had written 'an extremely interesting memo' suggesting that the anti-Hitler conspiracy had stirred internal rivalries at the heart of Nazi intelligence.[21]

The extent to which the report impacted directly on policy remains unclear to this day as do many of the details surrounding MI6's relations with German conspirators, since the relevant agency's files remain closed to historians. What is known is that six months before the attempted assassination of Hitler in July 1944, MI6's counter-espionage Section V had pulled off a major coup when it recruited Erich Vermehren, a member of the Abwehr based in Istanbul.[22]

Significantly, one of Vermehren's friends was Adam von Trott zu Solz, a German Foreign Office official and fellow Oxford Rhodes scholar who would become a key player in the plot to oust Hitler that Bell monitored. Von Trott's mother was half-American, which gave him many links with the United States, while his Oxford days in the 1930s forged enduring friendships with members of the English establishment including David Astor.[23]

And yet von Trott was a complex character with a troubled 'sense of loyalty', the title of a biography by Bell's close friend and World War Two veteran, the Catholic author Christopher Sykes.[24] It was published in the late 1960s long after the German's execution – hanging by a piano wire cord – ordered by Hitler following the July 1944 plot.

Like many German patriots, von Trott initially welcomed Hitler's coming to power after the humiliation of the Versailles Treaty. Influenced by Hegel's writings, von Trott saw parallels between the rise of Nazism and the French Revolution and argued that to oppose Hitler was to oppose the natural process of history. As Christopher Sykes wrote of his subject: 'The constructive response [he favoured]...was not rearmament and guarantees, but an imaginative and authentic persistence in a Europeanisation of the entire problem until a genuinely tranquillized Germany would move with her fellow European states to the next stage. The programme might be vague but so, often, was Hegel.'[25]

Sykes served in the Special Operations Executive (SOE) during World War Two. A mutual friend and wartime colleague of both Sykes and Bell was Elizabeth Wiskemann, who had befriended von Trott while serving as the assistant press attaché to the British legation in Bern, a cover post for her real work gathering intelligence from inside Germany and the occupied territories. Wiskemann also worked for the British Political Warfare Executive, the government's clandestine propaganda organisation.'Often clumsy and confused as he was, von Trott with his enormous charm had succeeded in forming a chain of friendships, but also of suspicion, in Britain and the United States', she recalled when reviewing Sykes's biography of the German.[26]

In late 1943, with the help of von Trott, Erich Vermehren was assigned to the Abwehr, given two weeks' training in the use of wireless codes and secret links, and then deployed to Istanbul, where he arrived in early November 1943. Two weeks later he made contact with British intelligence and his name was passed on to Nicholas Elliott, the MI6 officer based in Istanbul, and to his friend Kim Philby in Section V. Philby is thought to have later betrayed the names of an unknown number of Catholic anti-Nazi Germans who subsequently disappeared after World War Two when they are believed to have perished at the hands of the Russians because they were considered anti-communist.[27]

On 14 February 1944, Hitler sacked Admiral Canaris and decreed the setting up of a unified German intelligence service, which merged the Abwehr with the domestic security organisation, the SD (Sicherheitsdienst) under the control of the head of the SS, Heinrich Himmler. The decision pushed the baby out with the bath water. 'SD officers with the haziest notions of military intelligence procedures and techniques took over positions where networks of agents, painstakingly built up over years, were "burnt" in weeks. As the intelligence war reached its climax ahead of the Normandy landings, the Abwehr was literally hors de combat,' writes Canaris's biographer Richard Bassett.[28]

By the early summer of 1944 ahead of the assassination attempt in July, the entire German intelligence service was, in the words of Michael Howard, 'thrown into a state of confusion just at the moment… when its efficient functioning was vital to the survival of the Third Reich'.[29]

Himmler's move to absorb the Abwehr was strongly resisted by Canaris, but the admiral came under the spotlight during the crackdown on clandestine anti-Hitler opposition following the assassination attempt. Admiral Canaris was eventually executed for high treason in the Flossenbürg concentration camp in April 1945 as the Nazi regime was collapsing.

Long before that, ULTRA, the signals intelligence based on intercepts of German encrypted secret messages, along with intelligence from MI6's key human assets, provided the British with information about the scope and scale of the purge that Hitler had carried out among his suspected enemies in the Third Reich, especially in the higher echelons of the German command in Paris following the July bomb attack. The scale of the purge, which included the arrest of the chiefs of operations, signals and supply services of the German army in the West debilitated Hitler's chances of winning the decisive battle of the war in Western Europe.

Despite Hitler being initially convinced that the bomb on 20 July 1944 was planted by MI6, he soon found out that this was not the case. The bomb, fitted with a British chemical-delayed-action fuse and an explosive from SOE captured stock, was furnished by General Hans Oster, the chief of staff of the Abwehr, who approved of the conspiracy and was kept constantly informed on its developments but never lent active assistance.[30] MI6 played no direct part in the attempt to kill

Hitler.

Certainly, the nature of the Operation Valkyrie plot, involving close access to Hitler's headquarters, meant that a non-German military outsider bluffing his way into the compound with the bomb would have been hugely risky if not impossible. Which is not say that British intelligence did not have prior information about the plot. Indeed, it may have decided to let it run, calculating that it had nothing to lose and everything to gain as, even if it failed, as it did, the result would be a major purge of Hitler's high command that would weaken Nazi Germany operationally.

Among those involved in spying on the Germans were three key figures in British intelligence. Bell had formed a close professional relationship with two of them: Guy Liddell, the head of MI5's counter-intelligence B Division and his wartime number Two and future spy chief Dick White. He would meet the third during his wartime post in London, his MI6 colleague Kim Philby.

Of the three, it was with White that Bell was destined to develop the most enduring personal ties. Born geographically and socially into similar social backgrounds – Kent and middle-class – they both shared an understanding for and certain admiration of the United States, having lived and worked there between the two world wars in their formative professional years as young recruits to the spy game. White was, uniquely, to become chief first of MI5 and then MI6 during the Cold War years. Before first joining MI5 pre-World War Two, he had travelled extensively in the US after graduating from Oxford and gaining a Commonwealth Fund Fellowship to study American history at a US university. Like Bell, he had also travelled in Germany during the 1930s, witnessing the rising power of Hitler.

Although White was born three years earlier than Bell, they both entered the world of intelligence during the mid-1930s, the first recruited by MI5, the second by MI6. When Bell was posted to New York by MI6, White, with the blessing of both MI5 and MI6, went to Germany to gather intelligence on opposition to the Hitler regime, and how far, if at all, this extended up the hierarchy of the Third Reich. Two Germans whom White befriended were Adam von Trott and the Lutheran priest and theologian Dietrich Bonhoeffer, both of whom were arrested, tortured and killed in July 1944, after the unsuccessful attempt on Hitler's life.[31]

White contributed to a counter-intelligence blueprint for the detection of any Nazi resistance after Germany's surrender, but he was limited, as Bell was, in his ability to assist anti-Hitler conspirators. By and large, Great Britain and the United States insisted on the unconditional surrender of the German Reich as the only way to ensure post-war peace in accordance with Roosevelt's proclamation at the end of the conference held in Casablanca, Morocco, 14–24 January 1943. The Soviet premier Joseph Stalin, who was invited, was unable to attend because the Red Army was engaged in a major offensive against the German Army at the time.

The Casablanca Conference took place just two months after the Anglo-American landings in French North Africa in November 1942 launched from Gibraltar after the British had secured the complicity of Franco's Spain behind its official neutrality. [32]

Roosevelt and Churchill resolved to concentrate their efforts against Germany in the hopes of drawing German forces away from the Eastern Front, and to increase shipments of supplies to the Soviet Union.

While they would begin building up forces in England in preparation for an eventual Normandy landing, they agreed to launch an invasion of Sicily and the Italian mainland to knock the pro-Axis Italy out of the war. Churchill and Roosevelt also planned to strengthen their strategic bombing campaign against Germany. [33]

The view that came to prevail within Allied intelligence was that the anti-Hitler conspirators had no unity of aims beyond a general plan that, simultaneously with a peace offer, the German armies in the West were to withdraw and let the

Western allies in. Positions in the East were to be held to prevent occupation of German territory by the Russians. The aim was to open the West and to close the East.

The anti-Hitler conspirators cannot be blamed for their failure given that the internal and external cards were stacked up against them. As the historian Danny Orback writes:

> The main opposition groups ...were not close-knit entities, nor was the 20 July coalition one body. Contact between people who were opposed in varying degrees to the dictator was too difficult and dangerous....it is hard to comprehend the totalitarian omnipresence of Hitler's spies, the thoroughness of Nazi control, and the mistrust which prevailed among all Germans.[34]

British suspicion of the anti-Nazis responded to a political imperative – not just Churchill's orders but also Russian interests. Those who were prepared and willing to engage with conspirators on a basis of personal trust were limited to a very small group of individuals. The extent of their involvement varied, as did their motives. One of the sources handled by British spies was Wolfgang Gans zu Pulitz, later exposed as a communist agent, who cautioned Dick White against trusting the German Social Democrats. Another was Admiral Canaris, whom Kim Philby wanted killed.[35]

Philby's anti-Nazi work for the Allies was done with a clear eye on serving Moscow's interests, which envisaged a crushed Germany and most of Eastern Europe emerging from World War Two under communist rule. The Russian view in late 1943 and early 1944 shared common ground with that of hardliners in the UK and the US, who advocated Total War against Germany and its people, so as to reduce it to an economically and politically diminished agricultural society, leaving no room for a post-war settlement with any section of the German military or industry. The Morgenthau Plan, a memorandum signed by US Treasury secretary Henry

Morgenthau in September 1944, proposed exactly this.

In the words of Miguel Vermehren, a descendant of one of the anti-Nazi conspirators: 'the hard-line view was that there was no question of making peace with Hitler's generals however anti-Nazi they might be in principle. Best for the regime to implode from within, with rival generals shooting each other.'[36]

A US army intelligence report  from Allied occupied Germany of September 1945, four months after the unconditional surrender of the Germany military that followed Hitler's suicide,  noted:

> If the plot of 20 July had succeeded it would have undoubtedly saved the lives of thousands of Allied soldiers and the victors would have found Germany and Europe in a far better condition than it is now. On the other hand, the total defeat of Germany seems a far better guarantee for world security than might have been created by a peaceful entry of Allied armies into Germany in July or August 1944. As in 1919, a 'stab in the back' legend the famous 'Dolchstoss-Legende' would no doubt have sprung up again. Many Germans might have believed the German army really was not defeated and that surrender was only brought about because a clique of traitors sold the country out to the Allies. And Hitler would have been the great martyr. It would have been said, 'If the Fuehrer had not been murdered, we would have won after all.' Such an attitude on the part of a people not really convinced the war was lost might easily have given rise to still another nationalist movement, perhaps still another war, in a decade or more...

One unnamed Allied intelligence source quoted in the report called the men who planned the revolt against Hitler 'men of yesterday'. While the vast majority of them were 'honest, honourable and decent men', the report concluded, 'neither the world nor Germany would have found them imbued with a true democratic spirit or with the vitality and zeal which is the prerequisite for the leaders of a geographical centre of Europe in a democratic world.'[37]

Bell's wartime American colleague, the hardworking if also bon vivant aristocratic OSS London chief Bruce, was a real-life kindred spirit of the MI6 club coterie, who understood the Brits and felt at home in wartime London. While Bruce worked at the crossroads of the Anglo-American alliance figuring out its needs for intelligence, another of Bell's American friends, the OSS's man in Berne, Switzerland, Allen Dulles was left 'to wage almost his own private war at Hitler's doorstep, surrounded by enemy territory, left largely to his own devices to do what he thought an American spy should do'.[38]

As things turned out, Dulles, had he been British like Bell, might have been penned by John le Carré, trying to retain a sense of moral principle in a cynical world, as he struggled to pursue his links with anti-Hitler German conspirators, only to find that he lacked the political and military support, given a policy agreed by Churchill, Roosevelt, and Stalin of pushing for the total and unconditional surrender of all Germans.

A belief that much more could have been done to help the German conspirators succeed may have well weighed on Bell's conscience. It was a subject he did not talk about after the war, although his papers leave some clues as to what absorbed his mind. Bell kept among his most treasured articles a faded newspaper cutting of his friend and colleague Elizabeth Wiskemann's tribute to the courage of the German conspirators she had met, entitled *A Fact of History*.[39]

The full story of how plots against Hitler were handicapped by lack of Allied support at a political and secret intelligence level remains incomplete but we know enough to suggest that, in Bell's opinion, this was not one of MI6's finest hours. It was evidently a chapter in Bell's career he felt bound to keep secret. But among his personal papers a comment he made in a letter from the US to his mother on the outbreak of

World War Two sheds light on how he was opposed to political
expediency when it came to matters he believed required action
based on moral criteria. 'I have been saying all along that this
fiend [Hitler] should have been killed at the start,' Bell wrote.[40]
His plea went unheeded.

# 19
# The Russian Connection

Walter Bell's MI6 work in London between 1943 and the end of World War Two, and later in Washington, where he was posted from 1946 to 1948, had him meeting with three subsequently exposed notorious traitors, all members of the so-called Cambridge spy ring: Donald Maclean, Guy Burgess and Kim Philby.

One of the first of the Cambridge graduates to be recruited by the Russians in the early 1930s, Donald Maclean joined the Foreign Office, getting his first posting in the UK embassy in Paris in 1938 before returning to London after the Allied collapse in northern Europe and the German occupation of France in June 1940.

No evidence has emerged that Bell met Maclean during World War Two. Maclean's work during 1941–1944 has remained a mystery, with few clues to be found in Foreign Office files. According to his biographer Roland Philipps, Maclean was not a very active agent during this period, compared to his pre-war time in Paris and in the US after the war. Unlike Philby, Maclean was certainly not a recruiter, and operated very much as a lone wolf with his handlers. He didn't appear to know that another Foreign Office employee, John Cairncross, had become a Russian agent during the 1930s, and Moscow took good care to keep them apart – wisely, it turned out, as the Burgess–Philby friendship contributed to Philby's eventual exposure.[1]

Maclean was posted to the British embassy in Washington in May 1945 where he was to be joined in 1946 by Bell. The relations between the two men will be examined in a following chapter. Another Cambridge graduate recruited by the Russians, Guy Burgess, joined the BBC in 1936 before moving to MI6 in January 1939 in a new department handling propaganda and subversion. Bell met Burgess after he had been recruited by the Foreign Office news department, then based on the Ministry of Information which operated from the University of London's Senate House in June 1944.[2] Burgess, seemingly knowing from Philby of Bell's left-wing politics, invited Bell to a tour of some of the locations associated with Karl Marx when he lived in London between 1849 and his death in 1883.

Marx, in his early days in the English capital, drank in various pubs, got into arguments with locals, and on one occasion went running down the street smashing gas lamps.[3] The story would have been one close to Burgess's heart given the propensity he had for getting periodically drunk from his early days embracing communism while studying in Cambridge.

The 'tour' Burgess offered Bell began in Dean Street, Soho, where Marx wrote the first volume of *Das Kapital*, his seminal foundational treatise on materialistic philosophy and political economy, and ended in Belsize Park, north London, where Marx later lived and died. It promised visits to several surviving pubs known to Marx, along the Tottenham Court Road – the Jack Horner, the Rising Sun, the Fitzrovia Belle, the Court and the Northumberland Arms. If Burgess's intention was to trail Moscow's coats at Bell, he failed.[4] Bell managed two pubs then made his excuses and left, finding that Burgess, once drunk, became increasingly coarse and objectionable.[5]

The most famous of the Cambridge spies, Kim Philby, was recruited by the Russians before taking on the cover job as a *Times* correspondent covering the Spanish Civil War on Franco's side. Philby joined Section D, the sabotage section of MI6, in July 1940 when it was taken over by the newly created Special Operations Executive, becoming an instructor at the agents' school at Beaulieu, Hampshire. He was then given a job with MI6's counter-intelligence Section V, identifying enemy espionage operations as they originated in Spain and Portugal.

It was while Section V had its training operations at St Albans and later moved to Ryder Street near Piccadilly London that Philby developed his own relationship with his US counterparts, winning the trust of one of the young bloods of the OSS US intelligence agency, James Angleton, who Philby trained. Angleton later rose to be the head of counter-intelligence at the CIA. After the war, when Philby was posted to the British embassy in Washington as first secretary in 1949, he and Angleton shared long boozy lunches together, at which they traded the most intimate secrets.[6]

During World War Two Philby would attend social gatherings organised by the consummate social networker, MI5's Tommy Harris, whose well-appointed house in Chesterfield Gardens in Mayfair became a regular drinking haunt for an intimate coterie of off-duty MI5 and MI6 officers. Bell was not part of the group, nor did he have any inkling, until the fact was exposed years later, that Philby was working for the Russians. Bell recalled at least two meetings he had with Philby during World War Two when both worked for MI6 in London, although the precise dates remain unclear. The first took place after Philby had moved from Section V in Ryder Street to the MI6 HQ known as Broadway and was working under the same roof as Bell.

This was after September 1944 when Philby was posted to head up Section IX, which had been set up earlier in the year to deal with intelligence on communism and Soviet espionage. Bell's remit remained focused on liaison with the OSS. Both at the time worked out of the MI6 HQ on Broadway Buildings, across the street from St James's Park station in London, just a block away from where Bell had first been recruited in Queen Anne's Street in the mid-1930s.

One day Bell received a call from Philby addressing him on first name terms and inviting him to drop by his office for a friendly chat. He was greeted by Philby smoking a cigarette, tieless and with his feet up on the desk. By his desk and piled high were intelligence reports from field agents that he claimed his predecessor had been too lazy and incompetent to read through and follow up. Bell was impressed by Philby's youthful energy and professionalism.[7]

In fact, unknown to Bell and other colleagues, Philby had

gained access to MI6's document room and read the agency's secret files on its threadbare intelligence assets in Russia – reporting what he found to Moscow.

The second encounter with Philby that stuck in Bell's memory happened towards the end of World War Two. Bell had just lunched at his club, the Travellers, and was walking in the direction of Trafalgar Square past the Athenaeum, in the same block on Pall Mall, when he heard his colleague's familiar voice call out to him from its south-east-facing balcony overlooking Waterloo Place: 'Hey Walter, old man, why not come up and join me for a good vintage!' There was Philby, sitting on the edge of the balcony, with a bottle in one hand and glass in another, and with the smile of a rebel public school boy enjoying a bit of mischief.[8]

Bell was not unique in finding Philby affable and charismatic.[9] As Trevor-Roper wrote in his essay on Philby, later published in *The Secret World*, Philby was 'favoured by society, liberally educated, regarded by all who knew him as intelligent, sensitive, and transparently "sincere".'[10]

With the evidence of hindsight, Bell could hardly be blamed for not having been the first to blow the whistle on Philby. Personal and professional relations between the two between 1942 and 1946 were certainly never as close as those that Philby enjoyed with other MI6 colleagues, Tim Milne and Nicholas Elliott, and, to a lesser extent, with James Angleton, the OSS World War Two officer who went on work for the CIA post-war.

Philby nevertheless felt he knew enough about Bell to brief his masters in Moscow about him as to his potential as an agent of the KGB. As Philby secretly reported in 1943, 'Walter Bell is responsible for liaison with OSS (SI). He is extremely dissatisfied with his job as it offers little scope for originality. It has some compensations, however, in that it involves a certain amount of entertaining and Bell is a bit of a playboy. His political attitude however is Marxist.'[11]

Philby's report to Moscow on Bell was made two years

after Hitler unilaterally terminated his pact with Stalin on 22 June 1941 by launching Operation Barbarossa and the Soviet Union joined the Grand Alliance with Britain and the United Sates against the Axis powers. By 1943, Philby and Bell were working for MI6 in London and their paths crossed occasionally.

Far from recommending Bell for recruitment, Philby appears to have sent a veiled warning to his Russian masters that despite Bell's 'Marxist politics' there was nothing to suggest that he had the making of a double agent for his politics did not extend to unquestioning loyalty to the Soviet state. Nor, for that matter, did Philby feel threatened by Bell who at the time did not suspect him of being anything other than an MI6 officer who seemed professionally more competent and genial than many of his colleagues.

# 20
# Homer

Bell emerged from World War Two uncertain as to what the future held for him in post-war Britain. In September 1944 he had remained sidelined from the first stages of an internal reorganisation in MI6 that had seen Kim Philby successfully promoted above one of his senior officers, Felix Cowgill, and put in charge – irony of ironies – of a new section specifically tasked with tackling Soviet espionage.

By contrast to Philby, the end of the war found the loyal Bell up against a glass ceiling in MI6. The MI6 high command that Bell had served under Menzies and the two assistants Claude Dansey and Valentine Vivian was soon to be retired as the new Labour government of Clement Attlee put the agency under pressure to review post-war intelligence organisation and MI6's place in it.

The senior committee tasked by Menzies with post-war planning included four wartime colleagues Bell had also served with in different fields. Three were Maurice Jeffes, who had been appointed director of passport control in 1938; Dick Ellis, the wartime deputy of Bill Stephenson, the head of the British Security Coordination (BSC) in New York; and Bill Cordeaux, the wartime MI6 deputy director of navy-related matters. The fourth person on the committee, Kim Philby, was three years younger than Bell and was comparatively even younger blood than others within MI6, having joined the British secret service in September 1941, seven years after Bell.

One of the early post-war administrative measures brought into MI6 was the introduction in 1946 of annual reports for officers according to which each was matched up against various criteria such as 'general conduct', 'professional and intellectual ability', 'language qualifications', and whether they could be recommended for promotion.[1] Philby ticked all the right boxes, even if a closer exploration of his personal life would have disqualified any aspiring move up the career ladder.

By contrast Bell, as caricatured by Philby in his secret report three years earlier to his Russian masters, seemed ill-suited to take on a managerial role. Philby had reduced the complexity of Bell's character and typecast him as an armchair socialist who enjoyed his perks and socialising – in other words, ideologically frivolous and professionally suspect. Even if only a few of Bell's colleagues had been party to some of the left-wing views expressed in his private correspondence, they would have known Bell as much too much of a maverick to be promoted to a senior position requiring a safer pair of hands, with the pre-war organisational system of 'passport officers' who had joined MI6 in 1935 now considered well past its sell-by date.

The worldwide network of passport offices, like the one Bell had been posted to in New York, were established with both cover and revenue-generating purposes. But, as one intelligence historian put it, 'the revenue-generating part worked, but as a cover for an intelligence officer it stank. Soon every intelligence service worth its salt knew that to identify the local SIS (MI6) representatives all it needed to do was look up the roster for the British passport control office.'[2]

With the war over, the MI6 chief Menzies and his Whitehall advisers decided to phase out the old passport office cover entirely. MI6 officers would remain in post but would be listed as first, second or third secretaries, enjoying the social advantages of embassy life but given more operational responsibility and flexibility in recruiting agents, being more proactive spies outside the ambassadors' ambit of control.

In 1946, when Philby's job in MI6 and as a Soviet spy was secure, Bell certainly felt unfairly judged as well as poorly thanked for his years of loyal secret service in a challenging job. He saw himself as a victim of political and internal office manoeuvrings, although he could not identify who might be responsible. His sense of dislocation was fuelled by witnessing how some of the achievements of wartime intelligence cooperation and special operations seemed to be ignored when, on 20 September 1945, Roosevelt's successor as US president, Harry Truman, disbanded the Office of Strategic Services (OSS) with whom he had liaised on behalf of MI6 with a sincerely felt sense of mission and common purpose.

Bell's friend and colleague the wartime OSS chief in London David Bruce was among those who temporarily felt the future hidden from them. And yet within a year Bruce had joined a lobbying campaign with other OSS veterans to reconstitute a US foreign intelligence agency, which was to pave the way for the setting up of the CIA.[3]

Bell hoped for a similar revival to his career prospects and was thrown a new lifeline, partly because he still had influential friends who could come to the rescue and partly because he could use his pre-war and wartime experience of Anglo-American relations to advance into the uplands of Cold War foreign affairs.

His guardian angel came in the form of the Catholic author Christopher Sykes, whose network of friends included members of the aristocratic Lygon family into which Bell's sister Mary had married before the war. After an early career between the wars in the Foreign Office, with stints at the embassies in Berlin and Tehran, Sykes joined the Special Operations Executive (SOE) in June 1940, serving as personal assistant to its chief, Colonel Cudbert Thornhill, and had an eventful war.

In October 1941, Sykes was sent out to Tehran as deputy director of special propaganda (DDSP) under diplomatic cover (second secretary at the British Legation) in the aftermath of the Anglo Soviet invasion of Iran until November 1942 when he was transferred to Cairo. After returning to the UK, he spent the rest of World War Two with the Special Air Service (SAS) and liaised with the French Resistance. A year after the war was over, much to his chagrin, Sykes witnessed the disbanding of SOE and decided to dedicate himself to a life as a writer, but only after first recommending Bell for a posting that had come up in the British embassy in Washington – as private secretary to the incoming ambassador, Lord Inverchapel.[4]

Bell did not appear in the Foreign Office diplomatic lists as part of the Washington embassy staff, nor was he working any longer under his pre-war New York based cover as a passport officer attached to the British consulate. As far as his non-appearance in FO lists is concerned, it was not unheard for an ambassador's private secretary to be employed in a personal capacity separately from the normal diplomatic system.[5] Bell may have remained on the MI6 pay roll[6] although his official tasking as private secretary to the ambassador meant that he was not operating as an 'illegal' foreign agent, or proactive spy as far as the Americans were concerned.

Politics as well as his professional experience and friendships across agencies and government on both sides of the Atlantic favoured his appointment in the Washington embassy, as would later be the case with Kim Philby. The new UK government he was to serve under was that of the Labour Party, with whom Bell had sympathised since student days and where he had made friends.

In July 1945 Labour had won a majority in the first post-war election, defeating the Conservative Party led by Churchill, a hugely popular war leader but who large swathes of the working class and left-wing ideologues of Bell's generation and social background felt was unsuited for the social and economic transformation the post-war required.

During the 1930s Bell had befriended key Labour figures from left and right of the party, notably Harold Laski and Herbert Morrison, which made him comfortable with the new government. But the emerging story of the Great Terror, as the state repression carried out by Stalin during the 1930s and 1940s came to be known, together with his American friendships had meant that Bell had long lost his enthusiasm for the radical socialist ideology of Laski, his one-time university professor, a severance of ties that was confirmed when Bell returned to take up his new post in the US.

Laski was denounced by Churchill as the power behind an alleged revolutionary socialist bid for power as the chairman of the Labour Party during the 1945 election campaign. He was subsequently left out of the new post-war Labour government and became increasingly separate from it, opposing prime minister Clement Attlee's anti-Soviet policies in the emerging Cold War and becoming profoundly disillusioned with the anti-Soviet direction of American policy.[7]

By contrast Bell's friend Morrison, 'one of Labour's forgotten heroes ...the quintessential political organiser...' according to one of his followers,[8] had served in the wartime coalition government as a hardline home secretary during which he famously banned the British Communist Party's newspaper the *Daily Worker* for initially opposing the war with Germany.

While strongly supporting Labour's post-war nationalisations as leader of the House of Commons before serving briefly as foreign secretary, Morrison remained firmly anti-Soviet during the Cold War years and supported the intelligence and security services in their pursuit of suspect Russian agents. It was a world view that Bell was happy to embrace as he prepared to return to the US, and into the new order of post-war American leadership of the non-communist 'free world'.[9]

Bell's new boss, the British ambassador Sir Archibald Clark-Kerr, had been raised to the peerage by the new Labour government as Lord Inverchapel. In Inverchapel, the new foreign secretary, Ernest Bevin, saw not only someone who was respected within the Labour Party but a consummate professional whose reputation in high stakes diplomacy preceded him. Bevin entrusted him with the complex task of developing Britain's relationship with the US in the aftermath of World War Two.

It was an appointment that recognised Inverchapel's professional achievements but, given his troubled personal life, was not without its risks, as Bell became only too aware.

Inverchapel had distinguished himself in various overseas posts. After securing the prestigious appointment of ambassador to China during the Japanese occupation he moved to Moscow in 1942, where, as Bell later recalled, 'his sensitivity in gauging people's characters and reactions enabled him to establish a remarkable relationship with Stalin – and others in the Soviet Government'.[10]

Inverchapel experienced the German invasion of the Soviet Union, with his embassy evacuated from Moscow to Kuibyshev. He facilitated Anglo-Soviet diplomatic conferences during the final pivotal years of World War Two and attended summits involving Stalin, Roosevelt and Churchill in Tehran in 1943, and Yalta and Potsdam in 1945, which helped shape post-war Europe and the world. With the Cold War looming, such experience came to be thought useful in understanding the complexity of emerging geopolitics as viewed in Washington.

Bevin also admired Inverchapel's reputation for challenging the civil service with the periodic personal battles that he had waged with the Foreign Office during World War Two when he complained to Churchill about its lack of direction. Nonetheless, as Bell discovered, Inverchapel's complicated personal life – and the Russian butler he had brought with him from Moscow – made him a controversial selection. Inverchapel's much younger and tempestuous Chilean wife, María Teresa ('Tita') Díaz Salas left him during the posting in China and the couple later divorced in 1945, without children, only to remarry again two years later, by which time the ambassador was flaunting his bisexuality. 'He ignored her [Tita]. He preferred the company of young men which naturally gave way to gossip,' recalled Bell.[11]

What Bevin had not realised was that Inverchapel was physically and mentally nearing the end of his career. As Bell later recalled, he had just spent an exhausting ten weeks in the Dutch East Indies, where British troops from Admiral Mountbatten's South East Asia Command were stationed, trying to mediate between the Dutch government and the infant republic proclaimed by Sukarno. His mission had not succeeded in securing an agreement, with the new Labour government torn between loyalty to its Dutch ally and sympathy for the aspirations of a nationalist movement like those the British were coming to terms with in Burma and India.

Inverchapel emerged from the experience without the energy and motivation he had had while in Moscow, as Bell realised when he and Inverchapel travelled together to Washington from London in May 1946 to take up their respective new posts. Bell found the ambassador very depressed and daunted by the prospect of his new mission.

As for Bell, under his outwardly unemotional persona, born and bred in the village vicarage and educated at private schools, his feelings constrained by the nature of his work, lurked a complex character that refused to be boxed in by the establishment, struggled with the faith of his vicar father, and lived on his nerves, between periods of high excitement and intense depression, a condition he would later come to believe he had inherited from his father. As with many spies, his eyes seemed to oscillate between mischievous enquiry and resigned melancholy, a duality of expression and mood that deepened with the passing of the years.

Among the traits Bell shared with Her Majesty's Government's ambassador to the US, Lord Inverchapel, during the two years he served him as private secretary in Washington (1946–1948) was an instinctive rebelliousness not easily accommodated by the mainstream. He was certainly more patient and understanding than many of his peers of Inverchapel's self-indulgence – and suspected homosexuality – and irreverent sense of humour. Bell appears to have seen through Inverchapel's controversial eccentricity to the fragile humanity that lay behind it. Interestingly Inverchapel, the legendary senior diplomat in China and Moscow, who had become such a sad and lonely figure when Bell worked with him in Washington, was willing to share with his private secretary quite intimate details of his turbulent marriage. Divorced at the time he hired Bell, Inverchapel remarried his Chilean wife in 1947, but trailed a reputation for showing an attraction for well-built and handsome young men.

Inverchapel also had developed a mistrust for established authority in the intelligence world. Despite or perhaps because of knowing of Bell's background as a spy, the ambassador did not hide from him his lack of enthusiasm for the way he saw the secret services complicating when not undermining.

Bell found that when the MI5 chief Percy Sillitoe visited Washington in early 1948 he had 'some difficulty in making a suitable appointment' with the ambassador. Sillitoe, a former chief constable of Kent, had been controversially appointed as MI5's new director general in 1946 by the Labour prime minister Clement Attlee with the aim of keeping the British Security Service politically impartial.

Sillitoe made no secret of his distrust of intellectuals from privileged backgrounds and thought some of his more senior colleagues, despite their sense of entitlement and sharing similar clubs, lacked stature as well as intelligence experience. Nonetheless, Inverchapel told Bell that he could extend Sillitoe an invitation to lunch at the embassy as long as he agreed not to ask for any of his personal correspondence .[12]

Later circulating allegations – that Inverchapel had been implicated as a Russian agent in the Foreign Office by Walter Krivistky, the Soviet intelligence officer who defected to the West and was debriefed by MI5 – turned out to be unsubstantiated.[13]

And yet the MI5 director general Sir Percy Sillitoe's visit would be remembered by Bell mostly for the new step up in his career that it provided. For in a private conversation both men had, Sillitoe asked Bell if he would like to join MI5 once his job with the ambassador came to an end. Sillitoe explained that he was expanding MI5's operations overseas in the colonies and Commonwealth and was recruiting individuals who had experience of working abroad in intelligence. 'I was attracted by the offer because I had made many friends in MI5 during the War,' Bell later wrote.[14]

As his private secretary, whose responsibilities including drafting the ambassador's communications and speeches, Bell was to discover other controversial traits in Inverchapel. His indiscreet humour, for example, did not go down well among the more conservative elements of Washington society, not least seasoned former US ambassadors. Bell later recalled one particularly embarrassing evening when he accompanied Inverchapel to dinner at the home of the former ambassador to Sweden, Robert Woods Bliss. 'As we came into the drawing room, we were confronted by a signed photo of the Crown Prince of Sweden. Lord Inverchapel stopped at it and said, "Why on earth do you have a picture of the biggest bore in Europe on your table?" The Blisses were outraged!'[15]

One suspects that reports of such incidents, via Bell, would have found their way to MI6. The SIS, whose surviving wartime chief, Stewart Menzies, was no friend of Inverchapel's, must have read them with a certain degree of alarm. It was an extraordinary diplomatic appointment that Bell struggled to make sense of and serve loyally. 'He [Inverchapel] was a bad speaker with a rather inaudible delivery. He hated facts and figures – would leave noughts off or put them on – similarly he had no interest or understanding of economics. The American press were naturally deeply interested in such subjects, as they are now. Then, he was afraid of his tendency to shock.... He also complained all the time of being utterly bored– which was true,' noted Bell.[16]

Bell and Inverchapel arrived together in Washington at the end of May 1946, almost exactly two years after Donald Maclean had taken up a posting in the British embassy there as second secretary to Lord Halifax the wartime ambassador. Maclean and Halifax regularly played doubles tennis on the court of the impressive Lutyens-designed residence. Now Maclean was promoted to first secretary, with Inverchapel also taking a shine to him and declaring him a 'sweetie'.[17]

Bell's posting in Washington coincided with rising East–West tension over Berlin, with the Soviet Union in 1948 sparking a crisis in the city by cutting off land access between West Germany and West Berlin, necessitating a year-long airlift of supplies to the stranded citizens. Secretly ideologically opposed to the development of Britain's anti-communist alliance with the US, Maclean's main asset in intelligence terms was the special access he had, as the British representative of the American-British-Canadian Council on atomic secrets. The greatest intelligence 'treasure' he shared secretly with his Soviet masters was top secret information on the development and progress of the atomic bomb and the amount of plutonium available to the US.[18]

Inverchapel's embassy proved easy prey for the predatory instincts of Maclean, who had managed to infiltrate the Foreign Office as part of the Cambridge ring of Russian spies.

Maclean's access to official papers had him handing copious quantities of secret material to his Russian controller, including wartime correspondence between Churchill and Roosevelt. As a result the Soviet Union obtained secret information on two of the planners of the future map of the world, who were clearly mistrustful of the third.[19]

Maclean's double role and the pressures of keeping it secret would contribute to his increasing heavy drinking although his wife Melinda put it down to the long hours he worked on his official duties. His friends also passed it off as nothing they could be judgemental about.

When Melinda, having miscarried an earlier baby, became pregnant again and stayed in New York at her American mother's Park Avenue apartment, Maclean would visit her over several months while secretly meeting with his Russian handler. After the birth of their son in September 1944, Melinda joined Maclean in Washington. In January 1945 the Macleans moved from an apartment Donald had shared with a chain-smoking embassy colleague Michael Wright in Kalorama Road to 2710 55th Place in a more peaceful residential area of Washington DC.

The house, just a ten-minute walk away across Observatory Circle from the British embassy, had had as its previous tenant, one of Bell's World War Two intelligence colleagues in the British Security Coordination (BSC), and cousin of the Queen, David Bowes-Lyon.

When Bell, after his return to Washington in 1946, was invited to the Macleans' house, he knew it as an officially approved residence and found no reason not to trust its latest occupant. Bell and Maclean were both keen drinkers, affable and seemingly relaxed in each other's company.

Neither Bell nor anyone else in the embassy knew that Maclean was supplying top level intelligence to Moscow including information that passed between the ambassador and his private secretary. Even the Minister Plenipotentiary at the British embassy in Washington between 1945 and 1947 Roger Makins, who was close as anyone was to Maclean – they dined together, were the only two Brits on the top-secret atomic delegation, and both had American wives – didn't have a clue about Maclean's treachery.[20]

When Bell joined the embassy staff, Maclean went out of his way to make the new arrival feel welcome and comfortable in his new job, while avoiding doing anything that might raise suspicion about his work as a Soviet agent.[21]

Walter got on well with Maclean, regarding him as a friend and drinking partner as well as a good colleague whom he admired professionally. While both Bell and Maclean enjoyed their rounds of dry martinis and whiskeys in Washington, Maclean's drinking had not yet descended into the manic excess that was to become so apparent in his next posting in Cairo when he began to feel that he was under suspicion.[22]

Given the US sources and diplomatic experience Bell had developed during the 1930s and World War Two, Maclean may well have felt tempted at some point to mine him for intelligence. But if he did, no evidence has emerged in available files. Only a small part of Maclean's espionage was uncovered by the Venona decrypts, and he was never interviewed before he escaped to Russia in May 1951 so we can't be sure. Maclean arrived in Washington in the transition from World War Two to the Cold War and managed to serve a double term as one of the most senior diplomats in Washington, which made him a valuable asset of the Russians. But his biographer at least suspects that Maclean would never have let anyone else other than the Russians into his deception and did not work as part of a team.[23]

Maclean's skills in duplicity kept Inverchapel and Bell in the dark about the extent of his treachery, as they had done with embassy and other Foreign Office colleagues when he served under the previous ambassador to Washington Lord Halifax. As Bell recalled: 'Donald was obsessed with his work. No trouble was too much for him. When Philip Jordan, the Embassy press attaché who became quite a friend, arranged special background briefings for foreign correspondents, Maclean invariably enjoyed the business of parrying tough questions and giving as far as possible the reasons behind new policy decisions.'[24]

With some suspicions about the potential psychological flaws in Ambassador Inverchapel, but none about Maclean, Bell initially had taken to his post-war return to Washington like a duck to water. He was more than happy to escape from what he felt were the stifling bureaucracy and political machinations of Whitehall and find himself back in the political and diplomatic hub of the US – a country he knew well, had enjoyed living in during his early years as an MI6 officer, and where he had built up enduring friendships, some of which he now rekindled.

Bell's relationship with Inverchapel was dutiful and non-judgemental when it came to the ambassador's risqué sexual proclivities, even if he might have thought them a potential reputational risk increasing Inverchapel's vulnerability to blackmail.

Their posting got off to a good start when they discovered they were both pipe smokers. The ambassador showed his affection for Bell by giving him the gift of a family heirloom – a nineteenth- century silver snuff box dating back to an aristocratic ancestor and inscribed with the letter 'I'. But Bell's post-war appointment turned out to be a poisoned chalice, drawing him into a political and diplomatic minefield during a tense time in the developing post-war Atlantic relationship.

Soon after Bell and Inverchapel had arrived in Washington in May 1946, Congress had, after protracted negotiations, approved a US loan to Britain. A year later, in the last five months of 1947, Britain faced a severe financial and economic crisis. This situation brought out Bevin's sense of grievance regarding the US policies he believed were responsible, and his impatience with reports that the Americans were doubting Britain's own moral strength as a consequence of the problems they themselves had induced.

The crisis involved developing tensions between Bevin and the British embassy in Washington as Bevin lost trust in Inverchapel's ability to stand up to the Americans. As historian Martin Folly puts it:

> Inverchapel attempted to monitor the mood swings in Washington, and to influence them where he could. At the same time, he sought to explain them to Whitehall and to try to mould British actions so that they would play best in the Washington environment he observed. Bevin's responses to this particular style of reporting and policy recommendation, far from showing his sympathies with the sensitivities of parochial American opinion, evinced his impatience not only with it, but also with the Washington embassy for apparently endorsing rather than countering it. To Bevin, the embassy's task was to stand up for British interests and defend its viewpoints, and to build from there to persuade the Americans to take action. The embassy on the other hand, saw its job as primarily to 'get on the inside' and stay there, showing how close Britain was to American ways of doing things.[25]

During the two years he served as Inverchapel's assistant and speech writer, Bell worked on being an interpreter of American democratic values to the British, and of British ways to the Americans, at a time when the gulf in understanding was wide.'[26] In so doing he not only read his ambassador's mind but wrote it. Despite being the closest of allies, with shared values and language, attempts by the United Kingdom and the United States to reach accords on nuclear matters generated distrust and resentment.[27]

The early post-war years had Bell witnessing the end of nuclear cooperation that had developed during World War Two with legislation introduced by Senator Brien McMahon – the so-called McMahon Act of 1946, stipulating that the US would not share information concerning atomic weapons, which was signed into law by President Truman as the Atomic Energy Act (AEA) in August 1946. This was a bitter disappointment to the British government, and as a direct result Attlee's government initiated its own atomic weapons programme in January 1947.

On 10 March 1947 Inverchapel expressed his concerns about the latest manifestations of American misgivings regarding Britain and its Labour government in a letter that Bell helped draft and that went directly to Prime Minister Attlee, for Bevin was already in Moscow. The US Joint Chiefs of Staff, Inverchapel warned, were afraid that Great Britain and the rest of Western Europe would be unable to resist Soviet pressure. Moreover, Inverchapel felt that American caution about trusting Britain with atomic secrets was indicative of a broad trend in American opinion, as well as a specific response to the discovery in 1946 of the British physicist Alan Nunn May's nuclear espionage for the Soviet Union.[28]

By 1948, Inverchapel's time in Washington had come to an end with Bevin appointing Oliver Franks as his successor. Before his departure, Inverchapel wrote to the newly promoted Foreign Office's assistant under secretary of state, Sir Roger Makins, who had previously served with Maclean and Bell in the Washington embassy, sharing the high opinion he had of Bell, who 'had served me uncommonly well and has all the strings of his job tight in his hands. ...there should be no doubt in anybody's mind as to the satisfactory way in which he has carried out his work for me.'[29]

In his reply to Inverchapel, Makins made clear that he

shared a wider held view within the Foreign Office that the combination of Bell and Franks in Washington 'would not be a happy one. This a very personal matter, and Franks took his own decision'. He went on: 'This is of course no reflection whatever on Walter, whose merits are well known and appreciated by the Personnel Department and by all those who have recently served in Washington.'[30]

Bell had provided John ('Jock') Balfour, the deputy head of mission at the embassy in Washington who was overseeing the change in ambassadors, with an honest if blunt assessment outlining the private secretary's functions as he had experienced them.[31]

They ranged from expressing his firm conviction that most of the speeches drafted for the ambassador 'should be as practical as possible if they are to do any good' to the need to sift through incoming mail for the ambassador to save him from 'lunatics, cranks, and so forth'. 'There is a tendency for people to write to the present ambassador [Inverchapel] in incomprehensible Scottish. I confess that I am always in great difficulty to know what to answer. The cranks should be treated politely.'[32]

Bell evidently thought he had played a useful role as the ambassador's *eminence grise* as well as informal source of intelligence.

> There are all sorts of people who want to come to see the Ambassador whenever they visit Washington and with them, I think, the Private Secretary can do a useful job...I think it will be found that they are usually content to talk to the Private Secretary if he had made friends with them. I think I have succeeded in doing so with quite a large number of people from different parts of the country who come here from time to time. I find that it is most rewarding, not only because you find what they are thinking elsewhere, but also you can

call on them for help if the Ambassador is visiting their City or State, or indeed if other visitors from Britain want introductions.[33]

In another note to his friend Balfour, Bell made clear that he had felt rather more constrained in his job as a private secretary than in his previous assignment in the US when he had worked with some autonomy for MI6 in New York, Mexico City and Washington. As Bell wrote to Balfour:

> After having been here in this Embassy for two years, I am bound to say that one of the chief disappointments to me has been the difficulty of doing one's work in this building and at the same time 'living the United States'. When I worked in offices downtown, I used to lunch at restaurants, dropping in for a drink at the Mayflower Bar, or some place where people congregate, go to the Press Club, and generally live the life of any other person who might be working in an American government department or business office in Washington. I feel very strongly that the person who committed the folly of building this Embassy on Massachusetts Avenue did a great disservice.[34]

The reasoning behind Franks's appointment soon became apparent to Bell, as was the decision to not have Bell stay on in the Washington embassy. Transferred from academic life as a professor of moral philosophy in Glasgow to public service supervising British industry's support for the Allied war effort during World War Two, the intellectual Franks was cut from a different cloth to the eccentric career diplomat Inverchapel and certainly would not have relished the idea of inheriting as his private secretary a restless former MI6 officer who felt his wings had been clipped. Bell had hoped to remain in the Washington embassy, but his irascible and non-conformist personality was judged as a poor fit as private secretary to the incoming ambassador. Franks was a less eccentric character than his predecessor Inverchapel, even if as ambassador in Washington he waived his teetotal principles in the interests of diplomacy and drank martinis when the occasion required. Observers thought Franks aloof, and some saw him as intellectually exclusive.[35]

Working for Churchill's wartime coalition Franks had nonetheless earned a reputation as a steady pair of hands, a brilliant administrator and master of detail who showed himself capable of bringing together business and trade unions, and also managing to find a way through the rivalries of ministers with big egos such as Lord Beaverbrook (aircraft production) and Ernest Bevin (minister of labour).

It was Franks, as the epitome of the intelligent practical man, who applied his skills to diplomacy as head of the British mission negotiating Marshall Aid, reporting directly to Bevin. Franks's belief that Britain would become the US's 'shining example' of regeneration was eventually disproved, but it informed all his arbitration between the Foreign Office, the Economic Reconstruction Committee headed by Sir Richard Clarke, and the outside contenders, mainly the French and the authorities in Germany's Bizonia.

At the end of his period in the UK government Franks was appointed chairman of the OEEC (the Organization for European Economic Co-operation), the body that recommended the final divisioning of Marshall Aid and that also sought to establish a European customs union. This made him a natural choice as ambassador in Washington from 1948 to 1952 with Bevin trusting him to achieve British aims, which in the early Cold War period were not essentially at variance with America's.[36]

It was Bevin, as the first British foreign secretary of the Cold War, who decided that Franks was the ambassador who he wanted to have replace Inverchapel in Washington. As has been suggested by one of his historians, Bevin 'was not entirely comfortable with the approach the Foreign Office had evolved since 1944 of "steering the unwieldy barge" of US foreign policy by getting close to US policymakers.' Instead, he preferred 'a more robust policy of standing up for British viewpoints, defending them rather than either apologising for them or modifying them to meet US domestic political sensitivities'.[37]

By 1948 the Cold War was certainly already being played out in US politics with a Congressional witch-hunt against suspected communists, including some individuals who had been connected with the State Department and the OSS during World War Two. Among those investigated by The House Committee on Un-American Activities (HUAC) were two brothers, Alger and Donald Hiss, who worked in the State Department in the late 1930s and throughout World War Two.

That Bell might have known at least one of the Hiss brothers professionally and socially during his earlier assignment in US was suggested in a letter he received at the time from his friend Beatrice Phillips, whose father Willam Phillips, a senior US diplomat, had served as director of OSS in wartime London preceding David Bruce. 'Does the name of Donald Hiss mean anything to you? In addition to being a prominent government official and alleged communist underground agent he also graced the Washington "dancing classes" as I remember,' she wrote to Bell.[38]

Alger Hiss was subsequently convicted of lying to Congress after denying allegations by Whittaker Chambers, a former communist journalist and Soviet spy, that he had been part of a communist spy ring that sought to infiltrate the US government in the 1930s. Donald, who was named by Federal investigators as a member of the same apparatus, denied any Communist Party membership or associations for himself and testified on behalf of his brother. No charges were brought against him.

There is no evidence to suggest that Bell ever believed the Hiss brothers to have been part of a communist conspiracy. Phillips may have asked Bell about the Hiss brothers out of simple curiosity, or she may have been set up to ask it by the

FBI. The subject seemed an odd one to throw into a rather rambling letter otherwise devoted to news of a recently diseased mutual friend 'Harry', who had been swept overboard while sailing in a storm and the trials and joys of looking after two young nieces aged three and five.

By 1948 the hunt for suspect communists was being stepped up. The FBI was following up information about a US network of Russian agents provided by the double agent Elizabeth Bentley. The investigation developed from signals intelligence on Soviet spying provided by the US military's decryption project Venona which by August 1947 had identified a number of Russian agents in the US all referred to by their code names, among them 'Homer', which was traced to someone working in the British embassy in Washington from 1945 onwards.[39]

The FBI began focusing their investigation on the technical and support staff at the embassy rather than senior diplomats for the reason that 'since almost every American has relatives abroad…the loyalties of those people are divided between America and their historic homeland.'[40] Accordingly, the FBI initially did not scrutinise British staff members or even those with German antecedents (as wartime enemies of the Soviet Union) but concentrated on those with Eastern European or Soviet bloc origins. Nevertheless, even if the FBI was barking up the wrong tree, it was at least showing energy and a sense of direction that was lacking with any British investigation.[41]

The separate mole hunt carried out by the Foreign Office certainly proved time-consuming, being constantly distracted by false leads, given the necessity to trace and vet dozens of locally employed staff who had worked in the chancery or been employed in the cypher section.

It was only in December 1949, two years after Maclean's departure from Washington to a new posting in Cairo, that the Foreign Office considered for the first time a possible connection between the Washington leaks and information provided shortly before the outbreak of World War Two by the Russian defector,

Walter Krivitsky, that there was a Foreign Office source reporting regularly to Moscow in the 1930s. The head of security at the Foreign Office, George Carey Foster, settled on a list of six names of members of staff who had been in London in the late 1930s and then in Washington in 1945: John ('Jock') Balfour, Roger Makins, Robert Hadow, Michael Wright, Paul Gore-Booth and Donald Maclean.

In the end, the lack of evidence and refusal to believe that any of these high ups could even be considered as a traitor when there were so many junior staff to explore meant that the list did not get looked at again for some time, and the links between the six men and their subsequent Washington responsibilities not examined at all.[42]

There is certainly no evidence to suggest that either signal decrypts or the FBI investigation had any bearing on the Foreign Office's decision not to extend Bell's Washington posting under Inverchapel's replacement, Franks.

Among the reference letters written on Bell's behalf during his final days in Washington was one Inverchapel sent to his friend Sir Frederick Bain, President of the Federation of British Industries: 'He is efficient, adaptable, and an excellent mixer, and has travelled widely in North and South America, where he has contacts of every kind. I cannot help feeling that his excellent qualities and experience would be of great benefit to a business organisation, especially at a time when the drive for exports is so compelling.'[43]

Far from being left out in the cold, Bell returned to the UK to be offered a new job offer in the world of Cold War intelligence, this time with the British Security Service MI5. And by then he had found true love entering his adult life for the first time, in the form of an educated, self-assured, attractive and well-connected American woman, Katharine Spaatz. The daughter of one of the most celebrated wartime generals no less.

*Walter Bell's ancestor
John Bell, publisher.*

*Rev George Bell, WB's father.*

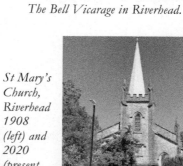

*The Bell Vicarage in Riverhead.*

*Walter's mother Muriel
(unsigned).*

*St Mary's
Church,
Riverhead
1908
(left) and
2020
(present
day).*

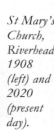

*Clockwise from top left: WB as his father's altar boy;*
*WB and his sister Mary Bell, 1914; WB, student and*
*part-time teacher, circa 1929; WB the young schoolboy,*
*circa 1916.*

*Tonbridge School, Kent.*

*The London School of Economics (LSE) during the inter-war years.*

*John Strachey, journalist and Labour Party politician (right).*

*Harold Laski, Marxist theorist, and one-time professor at the London of School of Economics.*

*Clockwise from top left: Mary Bell and the Hon. Reginald Lygon at their wedding 1930; William Lygon, 8th Earl Beauchamp; Reginald Fletcher, Labour MP; Herbert Morrison, Labour politician; Oliver Baldwin, Labour MP; Warden Chilcott, Conservative MP.*

*Clockwise from top left: WB's passport during his MI6 posting in New York; WB on a skiing holiday in US c.1938; Karen Blixen, author, 1930s friend of WB; Constance Cummings, 1930s actress, friend of WB.*

*Left: Beatrice Phillips, friend of WB and daughter of WW2 OSS officer and US diplomat William Phillips, 1948; Below: WB, still a bachelor on holiday with a friend in Sun Valley, Idaho, US, late 1930s.*

*Left: FBI Director J. Edgar Hoover;*
*Below: Hoover's letter to WB.*

JOHN EDGAR HOOVER
DIRECTOR

Federal Bureau of Investigation
United States Department of Justice
Washington, D. C.

*November 7, 1945*

Strictly Personal

Mr. Walter Bell
1106 Connecticut Avenue
Washington, D. C.

Dear Mr. Bell:

I have received your very gracious letter of
November 6th, and hasten to assure you that my inability
to arrange for a conference with you involved no personal
reason.

For the last several months I have been out of
Washington more than I have been in it, and for the last
week I have been confined to my home with a bad cold.
When I received word that you were leaving on the 6th
of November I did have hopes that I might be able to
get down to the office yesterday so as to say good-by
to you personally, but I was unable to leave my home.

I do want to take this opportunity, however, to
express to you my appreciation of your personal cooperation in all the matters of mutual interest. It is with
regret that I learn that you are returning to London,
but I hope that the separation will be but a physical
one and that our close official relationship will continue through Mr. Thurston of my office, who will shortly
arrive in London to be attached to our Embassy there.

With expressions of my very best regards and
highest esteem, I am

Sincerely,

J. Edgar Hoover

BRITISH SECURITY CO-ORDINATION

CIRCLE 5-5300

630, FIFTH AVENUE
(ROOM 3488)
NEW YORK 20, N. Y.

May 8th, 1945

My Dear Walter

Now that the war in Europe is over, the purpose for which
British Security Coordination was founded five years ago is virtually
fulfilled. On this day of victory, therefore, I am taking the
opportunity to thank those who have rendered the organization service
of particular value.

In terms of our own history you were here, of course, considerably before the beginning of time. You had experience of working
conditions and knowledge of essential details which you placed
unstintingly at my disposal, and on that account I feel personally
very much obligated to you.

However, while providing a link with the past, you were also
a pioneer of new and important activities. In October of 1940 you
undertook a job of reorganization in Mexico which produced results of
immediate value and has proved of lasting worth.

After your return to this country, you were entrusted with
various essential tasks both here in New York and in our Washington
Office. I cannot, within the limits of a letter, describe them in
detail or pay separate tribute to all your achievements. I would,
however, like to make especial mention of the very cordial relations
you developed with an American agency upon whose cooperation and
goodwill the success of our efforts has been largely dependent.

When you were recalled to London in November, 1942, I was

BRITISH SECURITY CO-ORDINATION

- 2 -

sorry to lose you and so were your many friends and associates throughout the organization. They would want to join me, I am sure, in this
brief expression of thanks and good wishes.

Yours sincerely,

W. S. Stephenson
Director

W. F. Bell, Esq.

*Letter from Bill Stephenson to WB on VE
Day.*

British Security Co-ordination

1940-1945

Certificate of Service

Walter Fancourt Bell

a member of British Security Co-ordination, has

performed valuable service of a confidential nature.

Wm Stephenson
Director

*Clockwise from top: WB's Certificate of Service with British Security Coordination (BSC); David Bruce, World War Two OSS chief, London;  Bill Stephenson, the head of BSC, receiving his Medal of Merit from OSS chief Bill Donovan, 1946.*

*Clockwise from top left: Tattie Spaatz as American Red Cross volunteer, in World War Two England; WB's father-in-law General Carl Spaatz; WB's passport during post-war Washington embassy posting; WB and ambassador Lord Inverchapel (both in pin-stripe suits) with visitors at the British embassy, Washington DC, 1946; Walter and Tattie cut their wedding cake.*

*Clockwise from top left: 1930s MI6 headquarters, Queen Anne's Gate; site of former MI6 building; Sir Stewart Menzies, MI6 World War Two chief; Sir Roger Hollis, director general of MI5; Sir Dick White, served as MI5 and MI6 chief; Guy Liddell, MI5 officer; Sir David Petrie, MI5 World War Two Chief.*

*The Soviet spies, clockwise from top left:*
*Donald Maclean, Kim Philby,*
*Anthony Blunt and Guy Burgess.*

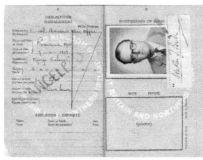

*Top: WB and Tattie sailing to Mombassa via Cairo; Centre: WB's passport during first Kenya posting; Bottom: Nairobi colonial staff meeting in the 1950s (WB is second on the left).*

*Jomo Kenyatta, anti-colonial activist who went on to serve as Kenya's prime minister and then president.*

*Julian Amery, Conservative MP, minister and friend.*

*A typical colonial residenc, Nairobie*

*Clockwise from top left: Bhola Nath Mullik, director of the Intelligence Bureau of India; Jawaharlal Nehru, anti-colonial nationalist and independent India's first prime minister; Louis Heren, The Times journalist; WB and Tattie with India's General Jayanto Nath Chaudhuri; the Bells on official reception duty.*

*C. L. R. James Trinidadian historian, journalist, and activist.*

*Chedi Jagantatt, Guyana's first elected prime minister.*

*Tattie and girlfriend with British officials (location and date unidentified).*

*Clockwise from top left: WB and Tattie in their early married years; WB and Tattie in England between postings; alleged KGB drop site, Pietà statue, London Oratory; Number 6, Onslow Square, WB's London Home (present day).*

# 21
# The General's Daughter

Donald Maclean was someone that General Carl ('Tooey') Spaatz had heard about before his daughter Katharine ('Tattie')'s marriage to Walter Bell. As Tattie herself recalled, it was after she met Bell but before she was married to him that she first heard about Maclean.

Her father received a complaint from a friend who was one of Maclean's neighbours about his heavy drinking as demonstrated by the large amounts of empty bottles that piled up regularly in the Englishman's backyard. 'Well, you should see the number of bottles in my backyard,' replied Spaatz, who was not exactly a teetotaller himself.[1]

Tattie was the oldest daughter – she was followed by two younger sisters – of General Spaatz, one of the most respected US generals of World War Two. When she and Walter met at a Georgetown cocktail party in 1946, 26-year-old Tattie's father was a well-known member of the Washington military–civilian political network, and she knew several of his American friends, just as she was soon to be introduced to Bell's British colleagues including Maclean and his American wife Melinda.

Tattie was eleven years younger than Walter. Well-educated, and brought up to be self-assured and, if needs be, discreet in diplomatic and government circles, she was a natural beauty, with a touch of Vivien Leigh – dark green eyes, pale skin, and a long and slender neck. She became attracted to the tall, suave Englishman with a dry sense of humour and a similar independence of mind who evidently liked and understood her country. Bell also shared her respect for her father as a result of his role in World War Two, during which Walter and Tattie pursued separate assignments on behalf of the Allied cause in the UK. When Bell had been secretly involved in British efforts to bring the US as an ally into World War Two, General Spaatz had helped counter the isolationism and defeatism of the then US ambassador to the UK Joe Kennedy by reporting, from a military perspective, on the superiority of the RAF.[2]

As befitting someone of his English upbringing and generation, Bell gave away few detailed secrets in his personal papers about his bachelor's life while in MI6, even if his reputation as a party goer was recognised by no more qualified observer than his colleague Kim Philby.[3] A few loose personal photographs he kept among his private papers suggest Walter was certainly not short of girlfriends, but no letters to any of them survive to suggest that he was serious enough to commit himself on a long-term basis.

By contrast by the time he began courting Tattie, he was thirty-seven years old and was ready to contemplate marriage if he came across a woman who could adapt to his complex personality while being supportive of his work. In Tattie he found what he had been looking for. Bell trusted the general's daughter, having her share in his interests in international politics and travel, without her seeking to probe too deeply into the true nature of his professional life or share it more widely with friends and family.

Although her father would have no doubt checked on his future son-in-law with his own sources and known about his work for British intelligence, Spaatz respected the undisclosed Anglo-American pact between agencies that protected the names of certain agents and officers from public disclosure on national security grounds.

Bell had a well-educated Englishman's accent, without coming across as a snob or with colonialist airs. Indeed, he could be irreverent of upper crust English pretensions, while highly social, at ease with Americans of most professions, and was a good dancer. When Walter proposed marriage, Tattie had no reason or inclination to press for details of his years serving the UK government although the fact that he had worked in a classified wartime role was not a secret between them.

Bell knew he had a tough act to follow in securing Tattie's

affections, for she venerated her father as an exemplary human being and legendary World War Two military leader. General Spaatz, as described by his biographer, had, along with a certain modesty and diffidence, a 'no-nonsense quality and an unmistakable professionalism'.[4] Any modern assessment of General Spaatz began with an understanding that he was 'his own man'. Among the military commanders of the twentieth century, neither Marshall nor Eisenhower, not even Churchill, overawed him; he regarded them unselfconsciously as his peers in the art of making war.[5]

General Spaatz was born Carl Spatz in Pennsylvania of Prussian ancestry, adding an 'a' to his name in 1937 to suggest Dutch rather than German origin. His war record, nonetheless, would fuel Hitler's racial anxiety that Americans of German descent had returned to confront the Fatherland in World War Two just as they had done in World War One.[6]

The man destined to lead the American air campaign against Hitler earned his wings as a loyal Allied fighter pilot fighting against the German Kaiser in World War One, subsequently finding himself promoted to Air Corps top commander in the 1920s, moving over to bomber command in the 1930s when modern long-range aircraft were coming into service.

Spaatz served at Langley Field, Virginia, on the staff of Major General Frank M. Andres, commander of General Headquarters Air Force until January 1939, when he returned to the office of the Chief of Air Corps at Washington as assistant executive director.

With war clouds gathering over Europe, Spaatz was assigned to the Plans D Division, later becoming the division chief. Before the US entry into World War Two, Spaatz, upon the formation of the Army Air Force (AAF) in June 1941, helped to plan and supervise the vast expansion of US military air power as first chief of the Air Staff.

Tattie, who in 1939 was finishing at Sweet Briar, the private women's liberal arts college in Virginia, had been planning to go to Europe that summer to begin a year of study at the Sorbonne university in Paris. She was ordered by her father to cancel the trip on the grounds that he thought the war in Europe was imminent and that her safety, in the event of Nazi occupation, could not be guaranteed.[7]

Spaatz would go on to launch bomber missions against targets in France, before being summoned by Eisenhower to the North African theatre to eventually command all Allied air power there. With her father destined for key military roles that were decisive to the outcome of the war, Tattie did not lose her determination to get to Europe where the war against Hitler would be decided. Once the US had entered the war, she persuaded her father to write to the US ambassador in London, John Winant, who had replaced Joe Kennedy, to see if there might be a job on the embassy staff or with the US military based in the UK.

An opportunity came up after May 1942 when Spaatz became commander of the Eighth Air Force as it transferred its headquarters to England in July. Aged twenty-one, Tattie followed her father to England as a volunteer with the American Red Cross, and remained there until after D Day, when she moved to mainland Europe with the American troops.

By a curious twist of fate, the Washington–London network that helped facilitate Tattie's job placement with the American Red Cross involved David Bruce, a friend of Walter Bell's, the man she would end up marrying after the war was over. Bruce had a great deal of influence with the US embassy, as the former head of the American Red Cross in wartime London, who had become the head of the OSS's European headquarters in the English capital.[8]

Bruce would have undoubtedly welcomed, if not encouraged, the propaganda opportunity of having General Spaatz's own daughter doing her bit for the Allied cause. A large morale-boosting photograph of the Spaatz reunion duly appeared in the US military magazine *Stars and Stripes* with father and daughter in an emotional embrace and captioned 'TATTIE SPAATZ GREETS POPS!'[9]

Tattie had joined a four-woman team attached to an American Red Cross mobile unit; part of a programme aimed at providing a recreational retreat for American servicemen stationed in various bases in the UK. The Clubmobiles, using vehicles loaned by London's Green Line Bus company, were an idea conceived by Harvey Gibson who succeeded David Bruce as head of the American Red Cross in wartime UK.[10]

The buses, each named after a US state (Tattie's unit was called The North Dakota) were modified into mobile kitchen units, with offside dispensing hatches and the rear easily converted into benches, and bunks if needed. With an on-board Victrola record player playing popular tunes from across the Atlantic, a built-in doughnut machine, a primus stove for making coffee, and magazines, cigarettes, candy and gum, the Clubmobiles brought the American military stationed in Europe a taste of home.

According to a US newspaper report published in September 1943, 'young, educated girls arriving from the US were sent to a basement of one of London's ancestral homes, in the heart of Mayfair where a doughnut school had been set up. There they learnt the art of turning out doughnuts for the troops at the rate of 840 an hour.'[11]

The morale-boosting qualities of Tattie's unit were already apparent months earlier when she and her three companions of the North Dakota Clubmobile were the subject of a propagandistic photographic report in *Life* magazine, which was headlined and prefaced, 'The Red Cross girls in England. Their job on the fighting front is romantic, but their days start at dawn and the work is never done.'[12] Photographs of the girls showed them with their faces discreetly made-up and dressed in stylish military jump suits. They were shown mixing the dough, with Tattie emerging from the club mobile with a rack full of the freshly made 'sinkers', accompanied by evidently appreciative American male ground and air personnel.

The location of the Clubmobile, one of fifty-one such mobile canteens operating in the British Isle, was vaguely described, for security reasons, as 'somewhere in England'. The Americans there included crews that flew B-17 Flying Fortresses on bombing raids in France and Germany under General Spaatz's command. Some of these planes were stationed at Snetterton airfield, in Norfolk.

As reported in *Life* magazine, 'at each stop, the girls are greeted with howls of delight, and the boys throng to the bus from runways, hangars and trucks, forming long queues all eager to get their coffee and doughnuts and a glimpse of an "All American Gal".'

'She's a perfect 42, fellas,' a mechanic is overheard teasing one of the other girls of the unit as his comrades in arms measure her waist. Tattie, the main focus of the report, is pictured deep in conversation with GIs – 'after many weeks of regular visits the girls are on first name terms with most of their customers, their slogan is doughnuts will win the war'.

Among the English towns Tattie visited with her unit was Cambridge, which during the war was populated by American military personnel from nearby bases with soldiers and airmen seemingly everywhere – in village shops, dance halls, and drinking dives, the Eagle Pub near King's College being a particular favourite with pilots. The American Red Cross service club at the Bull Hotel, next to St Catherine's College, was another popular haunt.[13]

Even the hallowed turf of Fenner's cricket ground (belonging to Cambridge University) was put at the disposal of the Americans, for a baseball match between two US Army teams, the Kentucky Rebels and the Yankee Eagles.

Among the Allied air crews based near Cambridge destined to achieve particular notoriety were those of the legendary Memphis Belle 'Flying Fortress' based in RAF Bassingbourn. Having completed twenty-five combat missions, the aircraft and crew were enlisted as part of a major propaganda campaign on their return to the US to sell war bonds and recruit for the RAF's Bomber Command.[14]

Once back in the base's Clubmobile in East Anglia with the US Army's 8th Air Force Tattie continued to hand out doughnuts that had been the rage in New York before the war and had become a special treat during it, while dancing with the soldiers of the infantry division on their last night before they headed for France.

When not with her mobile unit Tattie stayed in England, discreetly seeing her father with occasional weekend passes to London during the dark days of the winter of 1943–1944. It was a period during which her future husband Walter Bell had been relocated from the US to London to liaise secret intelligence between MI6 and the American OSS. Given the secret nature of Bell's work at the time, it is unlikely that he and Tattie would have met in wartime London, and no record survives that they did.

Tattie and her unit mates, Virginia Sherwood, 'Doolie' Townsend and Dorothy Myrick, stayed with the bomber groups until after the D-Day landings, and then accompanied the ground forces for the rest of the war,[15] through the Battle of The Bulge and onto Czechoslovakia, where Tattie celebrated VE Day in Prague, by which time her father had earned a reputation as a key Allied commander. After the war Eisenhower said that General Spaatz, along with General Omar Bradley, was one of the two American general officers who played the most important roles in World War Two.

In February 1946, General Spaatz was appointed commanding general of the (US) Army Air Forces and became the first chief of staff of the post-war United Sates Air Force the following year. Retiring from the military at the rank of general on 30 June 1948 he took the job of military editor at *Newsweek* magazine. By this time General Spaatz had hosted a visit to Fort Myer by the British ambassador Lord Inverchapel and his daughter Tattie was being courted by Walter after they had met formally at a British embassy function.

Tattie turned Walter down when he first proposed, because she suspected he would not be an easy man to live with and was reluctant to commit to a life that would be spent largely far away from her family and friends in the US. Whatever doubts she had, however, she quickly overcame them and said yes. Four months later, in September 1948, she and Walter tied the knot.[16]

At the time the old colonial house General Spaatz and his wife Ruth had moved into in Georgetown was still being restored so the family wedding took place instead at the home of close friends of the Spaatzes and Walter Bell, the well-connected journalist Lyle Wilson and his wife Connie.[17]

The first public announcement of the impending nuptials appeared in the society pages of the dominant Washington DC newspaper and one of the leading US media outlets at the time, the *Evening Star*.[18] Under the headline 'Katharine Spaatz to be Married', it reported two days ahead of the wedding that 'several parties had been arrranged'. However, since the engagement had been made known 'only yesterday', there was 'not much time for the usual round of entertainment'. Moreover 'Mr Bell', described only as 'secretary to former ambassador Inverchapel', had 'only just returned from England, having left Washington a month earlier to visit his parents'.

In fact Bell had been in London with the prime aim of securing a new job with MI5, knowing that his time in Washington was over and that his normal career with MI6 had already come to what he thought was a dead end, and yet details of his secret life had been carefully kept out of the pages of the American capital's most widely read newspaper.

Despite highlighting Tattie's well-known and respected parentage the single column item in the *Evening Star* noted that Mrs C. Wilson had invited only a few close friends of the bride-elect to cocktails that afternoon, and that she and 'Mr Bell' would share the honours at a party given by other well-known figures of the Washington DC social set. Those named by the newspaper included the distinguished World War Two journalists who had served in England and mainland Europe during the war, Helen Kirkpatrick and William Walton, and another World War Two veteran and rising star in the US air force, John White.[19]

The wedding itself in the Wilson house on Massachusetts

Avenue would be 'small', with only the Spaatz family and a 'few (unnamed) friends' present. The intimate nature of the occasion may have responded to Walter Bell's own preference to minimise publicity as he prepared to embark on a job move that required discretion. It is not clear the extent to which his closest sources in the America media knew about his secret life at the time, but Wilson by then was on a first-name basis with the FBI's enduring chief, J. Edgar Hoover and, like Bell, was favourably disposed towards the Bureau. Bell had been MI6's main link with the FBI while posted in New York.

Few of the UK embassy in Washington colleagues Bell might have invited to his wedding would subsequently achieve such notoriety as Donald Maclean. But less than a month before the Bell wedding Maclean, together with his American wife Melinda, cut short their US posting and boarded the *Queen Mary* back to England from New York, to take up the job of counsellor and head of chancery in the British embassy in Cairo, the strains of his double-life destined to weigh on him mentally and physically.[20]

The new posting, which Maclean was not particularly enthusiastic about, was nonetheless a promotion. He could have just as easily delayed his departure from the US with the valid excuse that his friend Bell's wedding was a social occasion that required his presence. Maclean did not as yet feel under any threat of exposure but was certainly feeling exhausted by the amount of duplicitous work he was doing. Perhaps he simply could not face the prospect of finding himself subject to scrutiny or indeed enquiry by some of the guests he knew would attend including those linked to the US and British intelligence and military community, particularly the host of the wedding party, Lyle Wilson, a good friend of the FBI supremo's, Hoover.

By the time he boarded the *Queen Mary* back to England at the end of August 1948, Maclean was feeling profoundly mixed emotions ranging from relief to a sense of achievement, but above all, 'exhaustion, laced with apprehension about what was to come in his espionage life'.[21]

# 22
# From Russia with Love

The newly married Bells left New York for Europe on 24 September 1948, aboard the MS *Sobieski*. The days of frequent transatlantic air travel were still to come and travelling by sea was something that Walter had, from his youthful travelling days, thought of as both adventurous and relaxing. After the rushed announcement and socialising of their marriage, the trip gave him and Tattie some quality time to prepare for the next challenge even, if it did fall short of the ideal honeymoon. The prospect was of a more colonial life on the other side of the Atlantic that would be very different to the modernity they had experienced as individuals in the US. They would be entering unchartered territory: British-ruled East Africa. Walter's new posting was as the head of the MI5 station in Nairobi, though this was still some months away.

The *Sobieski* would have appealed to Walter's sense of patriotism. It was a Polish passenger ship, named in memory of Poland's seventeenth-century century 'hero king' John III Sobieski, and had British links. Launched in the summer of 1938 from the Tyneside shipyard of Swan, Hunter & Wigham Richardson, it became a British and Polish troop carrier in World War Two and its route to Europe was now via the Canadian port of Halifax.[1] .

The new assignment taking Walter and his young American wife Tattie away from her family in the US would be overshadowed early on in Walter's new posting by personal tragedy, when Tattie suffered an ectopic pregnancy and had to have her ovaries removed. The experience, along with the realisation that she would not be able to biologically conceive a child at a time when the possible option of *in vitro* fertilisation was still decades away, was a terrible emotional blow to the newly-weds, but it forged the nature of their marriage from there on.

Tattie was happy to consider adoption and even started looking into getting a baby boy. Walter wasn't keen on this but didn't say no. However, she reluctantly came to accept that for Walter being a good father to his own child would have been a stretch, let alone being one to an adopted child. Walter became her child, endlessly fussed over, endlessly demanding, and quite content to be the centre of her universe.[2]

Bell was not an easy personality to manage. By the time of his marriage he had already developed a life-long habit of imbibing liberal quantities of dry martinis and gin and tonics – his nicknamed 'infuriators' because they had a habit of making him argumentative and sometimes morose. The dry martini was reputedly his wartime boss Bill Stephenson's preferred drink when he headed up the British intelligence operation in New York, the British Security Coordination (BSC). According to Ian Fleming, wartime naval intelligence officer and author of the James Bond 007 books, who visited Stephenson in the Rockefeller Center, the wartime intelligence chief mixed a powerful recipe of Booth's dry gin, high and dry, easy on the vermouth, shaken not stirred.[3]

Bell seemed to have less in him of the fictitious superspy Bond than of an amalgam of his real-life wartime faith-stirred MI6 colleague Graham Greene and the quintessential literary archetypal Cold War spy that John le Carré came to write about in fiction, a flawed individual trying to find meaning in a morally compromised world.

Like Nat, the main protagonist of le Carré's novel *Agent Running in the Field*, Bell seemed, on occasion, to suffer from what MI6 parlance referred to as 'camel's-back syndrome' – 'when the things you're not allowed to talk about suddenly outweigh the things that you are, and you go down temporarily under the strain.'[4]

He could be edgy, particularly when faced with policies he disagreed with and government colleagues who had been given posts of authority he thought they neither deserved nor were remotely suitable for. Tattie, who had a feisty spirit of her own, showed her enduring love for him by tolerating his occasional mood swings throughout their married life. She valued the better parts of him – his natural curiosity and openness to other cultures, his sense of humour, and lack of snobbery – and shared in his adventures, along with some of his secrets, however challenging.

\* \* \*

Bell's former boss Lord Inverchapel retired from government service before the end of 1948 after stepping down as ambassador, and provoking more criticism than admiration during his spell at the Washington embassy. With the passage of time, the history of the Washington embassy became overshadowed by the fact that it had been deeply penetrated by three of its staff – Donald Maclean, and later Kim Philby and Guy Burgess – who were working secretly for the Russians.

It was only after Maclean had left Washington in August 1948 for a new posting in Cairo that the FBI began to deepen its probe into intelligence leaks from the British embassy in Washington starting in 1944 – the year of Maclean's arrival – from a Russian spy code-named Homer.

It was while Maclean was in Cairo that Walter Bell, accompanied by Tattie, caught up with him and Melinda. Bell had decided he would drop in on his old Washington embassy colleague on his way on his new posting in Nairobi as the head of the MI5 station for East Africa in the spring of 1949.

Walter had obtained transit visas for Egypt for himself and Tattie prior to their departure from Port Said for Mombasa. By the time of the Bells' visit to Cairo, both MI5 and MI6 were aware that the FBI investigation into wartime leaks in the embassy in Washington was closing in on a prime suspect. Bell would have cleared his visit with his employers and in turn expected to report back on anything of potential interest. He would have certainly had sufficient elements to provide a disturbing eye-witness account of Maclean, under pressure because of his double life, and on the verge of a break down.[5]

Years later Tattie Bell recalled that while they were briefly in Cairo, she and Walter saw Maclean on one of his alcoholic binges, which, as they gathered from some of his colleagues in the diplomatic service once in Cairo, had become more frequent and destructive than any incident they could recall while in Washington.[6]

One evening the Bells and Macleans went to a drinks reception together and then on to dinner. Maclean drank heavily. But thanks to Tattie persuading Walter that they should both go to bed early to gather strength for their journey to Kenya, the Bells did not go on to follow Maclean in his post-dinner long journey into the night. Maclean's alcoholic binge took him to the flat of a junior official of the British embassy and ended in another flat in the same building belonging to a female librarian employed by the US embassy which he trashed in her absence, smashing the furniture, breaking up the bathroom, and throwing articles of underwear into the lavatory pan. The episode led to a formal complaint from the US ambassador and Maclean returned to London for a few weeks leave of absence.[7] He was accompanied by his wife Melinda who had loyally and protected her husband since their marriage and who stuck with him until finally separating twenty years later, following her affair with Philby.

It was the last the Bells would see of the Macleans. Bell would in time nurse a deep sense of betrayal by his one-time Washington colleague after Maclean had fled with Burgess to Moscow. Tattie would retain an enduring respect for Melinda, a fellow attractive American with a hidden resilience, even if she stuck with Maclean long after his treachery had been widely reported. Maclean's exposure as part of what subsequently became known as the Cambridge spy ring, and the witch hunt for moles among anyone linked in any way, as one of Bell's surviving relatives suggested 'must have been extremely uncomfortable' for Bell and his American wife.[8]

Tattie and Melinda were married to complex, unruly

Brits whose job was to represent their country in a third country. Melinda left Donald Maclean only when the marriage had long suffered irreparable damage. As Tattie recalled: 'Melinda may have looked soft and frail and helpless. Underneath, she was tough and adaptable and very shrewd.'9

Maclean together with Guy Burgess defected to Russia in 1951 just as British intelligence officers were about to interrogate them. By then Bell was well established as head of the MI5 station in Nairobi, having put his Washington days behind him, without any pending enquiry hanging over his career linking him to Maclean or his Soviet masters.

Inverchapel died that same year. The Cambridge spy affair would tarnish his legacy with rumoured communist sympathies that some of his detractors believed lay behind his reputation as an anti-establishment figure and the effectiveness or lack of it during his last posting in Washington. His friend and loyal private secretary Walter Bell did his best to defend Inverchapel's reputation, telling those who alleged he was a Soviet spy how way off the mark they were.

A more detailed exploration of Inverchapel's Washington embassy would take years to surface. Historians were given belated access to key Foreign Office files that had been previously been kept under official wraps which gave an insight into the early tension that developed between Inverchapel, the most senior UK professional diplomat at the time, and the foreign secretary who had appointed him to Washington, Ernest Bevin.

Both men disagreed over Inverchapel's early recommendation that Bevin should come to the US to win over American opinion. Bevin was also deeply embarrassed at having to be questioned in parliament in October 1946 about the Russian personal valet Evgeni Yost Inverchapel had brought with him to Washington as a 'gift' from Stalin. While Inverchapel told Bevin that he had no wish to embarrass him, the ambassador was, in the words of historian Martin Folly, 'exceedingly dilatory in arranging for Yost's departure from the embassy, showing a remarkably casual attitude to potential security implications and the bad publicity'.

It wasn't until January 1980, in the midst of the latest flurry of media fuelled espionage sensations alleging Russian moles, that *The Sunday Times* published what it claimed was the full story about Yost, who accompanied the ambassador to the British embassy in Washington after serving him in Moscow. It was titled *From Russia with Love*, like the Bond novel and film.[10]

The lengthy lead article in the newspaper's Review section was written by Frank Giles, then the deputy editor. It drew in part from Giles's own recollections of his time in Moscow as Inverchapel's private secretary, but also from conversations the diplomat turned journalist had much later with two key sources. One of them was Walter Bell, the second was Bell's friend Sir John 'Jock' Balfour', who served under Inverchapel as minister in Moscow and Washington as his deputy head of mission. Balfour, like Bell, was long retired from government service by the time *The Sunday Times* published its piece. Enduring friends, they were, in retirement, neighbours. Balfour and Bell and their respective wives lived in separate flats in Onslow Gardens, near South Kensington.

In addition to his two British sources Giles had managed to locate and get the cooperation of the Russian valet Yost, who by 1980 had been living many years out of the public eye in Scotland. Yost left Washington for the UK, in late 1947, a year after his arrival from Moscow to start a new life working at Inverchapel's Scottish home in Argyllshire. Yost continued to serve Inverchapel in the first years of the ambassador's retirement before branching out into a fish and chip business of his own with his Scottish wife. The article represented a major scoop for Giles, but it owed much to Bell's hidden hand.[11] Giles worked for Inverchapel in Moscow as private secretary for just four months before relinquishing his temporary foothold in public service for journalism. Bell served Inverchapel for two years in Washington. Without Bell's cooperation it would not have been possible for Giles to write the extraordinary story that was eventually published in *The Sunday Times*.

Despite its nod to James Bond with its title, Giles's article, the final pre-publication version of which was sent to Bell for his approval, dispelled the suggestion that Evgeni Yost was a Russian spy planted by Stalin even if his story cried out for a movie blockbuster that it never got turned into. 'Evgeni would play himself and central casting would surely turn up a likely candidate for the role of the despot in the Kremlin,' wrote Giles. 'But the star part would be Archie's [Inverchapel], whether bare-chested at a Moscow window or reading French novels in Java, or boasting to amazed Americans about his Russian slave…'

But after thirty-four years, Giles's verdict was the following: 'an extraordinary story, worth telling and re-telling whenever the talk turns to the bizarre footnotes of history; but it is not a story, or at least not a true story, of espionage or dark doings in high places'.[12]

The time had yet to come when Giles would be unceremoniously sacked as a scapegoat by his boss Rupert Murdoch after publishing what turned out to be the bogus Hitler diaries.[13]

But on the ambassador's valet story Giles stood to be vindicated, with Inverchapel cast, almost certainly fairly, as a more dutiful and sympathetic character than the rogue and traitor some of his early detractors caricatured him as.

While not uncritical of Inverchapel's long-term eccentricities and two-year spell in post-war Washington, Bell thought that the period, which he was in a unique position to witness intimately during his posting in Washington, was historic for reasons other than Maclean. It coincided with a turning point in Anglo-American relations and some of the credit for this should rest with the ambassador and his staff – a line followed later by Inverchapel's biographer Donald Gillies, who also played down the ambassador's pro-Soviet sympathies. Gillies also notes that the Foreign Office felt poorly informed by the embassy about the importance of developing US policy although Foreign Office documents  appear to support Bell's own view that this was not the case.[14]

Bell remembered how 'wisely and generously' Inverchapel behaved when the US under secretary of state Dean Acheson let the British embassy in Washington know about the altered US attitude to send aid to Europe – well before the US secretary of state George C. Marshall spoke about his eponymous plan in his famous and widely published speech at Harvard on 5 June 1947.[15]

Marshall's Harvard speech, offering to provide aid for European economic recovery if the Europeans themselves could work together in devising a plan, is considered by some historians as a watershed in post-war US foreign policy. Bell was not alone in getting advanced warning of the speech. Indeed, he had a discreet hand in ensuring that the British foreign secretary Ernest Bevin was well primed of its significance.

His friend and colleague 'Jock Balfour', the embassy's deputy head of mission, was briefed by Acheson on 22 May over an informal lunch and sent a detailed dispatch to London by diplomatic bag, on 3 June, which arrived on the day of Marshall's speech.

The day before the speech, three British journalists with World War Two experience in propaganda and secret intelligence were alerted by UK embassy sources of its importance before lunching with Acheson . They were Leonard Miall of the BBC, René MacColl of the *Daily Express* and Malcolm Muggeridge of the *Evening Standard* and *Daily Telegraph*.[16] As Acheson recalled, he told the journalists that Marshall was to deliver a speech of the utmost importance and hoped that 'they would not fool around with telegraphing the thing' but 'just give it over the phone and get it over to London at once'. They were to tell their editors to 'send it to Ernie Bevin and say that Dean Acheson wanted him to look at it'.[17]

While the Labour foreign secretary Ernest Bevin listened to Marshall's speech read over the BBC the next day, he was not taken by surprise.

'Bevin at once saw the importance of the altered policy

and was off to Paris to get things going...', recalled Bell in reference to Bevin heading off to confer with his French counterpart.[18]

The plan to help post-war Europe fight hunger, poverty, desperation and chaos, Marshall was to insist in his Harvard speech, was not directed against any country or doctrine. It would be up to the Europeans in a concerted action to decide how best to use the offer.[19] The resulting all-European conference met in Paris, with Stalin refusing to participate and blocking aid to his new Eastern European satellites.

Thanks to his pre-war and World War Two experience, Bell developed an enduring belief in the importance of Anglo-American cooperation and mutual understanding. The Special Relationship was destined to have its challenges during the Cold War, not least during Lord Inverchapel's relatively short two-year tenancy of the British embassy in Washington, leading to developing mistrust fuelled by the US's refusing to share with the British some of the details of its nuclear programme. One of Inverchapel's friends, the Conservative MP Robert Boothby, dismissed the ambassadorship as a 'great failure', adding that 'a glittering career ended in anti-climax', partly because Inverchapel 'was no good with the press and knew little about economics, both of which were vital for the American post'.[20]

Meanwhile Donald Gillies, his biographer, felt that 'Inverchapel's spell in Washington was not all it could have been.... He 'very soon became disillusioned and bored with Washington society', while his dislike of the telephone and preference for writing with a quill were only two of the eccentricities that led him to seem an anachronism in post-war America.[21]

Bell, drawing from his experience of working for Inverchapel in Washington, came to the view that if the ambassador had not had such a troubled marriage with his much younger Chilean wife Tita, he might have better controlled the homosexual tendencies that made him such as an easy target for the media, not least when they involved athletic-looking American youths and the Russian valet he had brought with him from Moscow.

As Bell later recalled, had it not been for Tita 'there would have been no youths from the mid-west included among his house guests, and that Soviet valet might also have never materialized and his relations with the big wigs of Washington, political and social, might also have been less listless than I believe them to have been while he was in Moscow.'[22]

# 23
# Medal of Freedom

On 16 April 1947 Bell should have received a letter from the US embassy in London saying that he had been awarded the Medal of Freedom, established by President Truman to highly honour civilians whose actions had aided the war efforts of the United States and its allies. He was still working in the UK embassy in Washington at the time and soon to be engaged to Tattie Spaatz, but the letter was misdirected to his father's address at the vicarage in Riverhead, Kent, and was not received by Bell until a few days later.

Bell received the written notice of his award from Colonel John B. Ackerman, a World War Two veteran who was then serving as the US air attaché in London (at 29 Davies Street, Mayfair). The full citation read:

*Walter F. Bell, British Civilian, for exceptionally meritorious achievement which aided the United States in the prosecution of the war against the enemy in Continental Europe, from 7th December 1941 to 8th May 1945. Throughout this period, he rendered inestimable service to the United Sates by directly supporting operations of a special unit in the European Theatre. Through his keen foresights, exceptional diplomacy, and outstanding devotion to his work the cooperation between English and American Services was highly productive and the operations developed produced results which contributed materially to the Allied invasion of the Continent and the defeat of the German Armies. His commendable achievements merit the highest praise and recognition of the United States.*[1]

Bell responded to Ackerman in a letter dated 29 April from Washington saying that he had only just received the letter that had been forwarded to him and apologised for not being able to attend the ceremony. He went on to say that since he was 'still a Foreign Office official' and a UK subject, he understood that he had in any case to seek permission before accepting a foreign honour.[2]

Bell wrote to Robert Dunbar CMG, MC, head of the Treaty Department at the Foreign Office that very same day, attaching the letter from Ackerman and saying 'My work during the war, both in the US and in London, was connected with American Intelligence, and it is for this that they have awarded it to me. Could you advise me whether I am allowed to accept it'?[3]

The award must have been a huge boost to Bell's self-esteem, a recognition of his below- the-public-radar intelligence work on behalf of the Allied cause, strengthening Anglo-American mutual understanding and cooperation. But it became subsumed in an extraordinary story of administrative incompetence.

Dunbar did not reply straight away. But Ackerman told Bell in a further letter that the award had been cleared with the Foreign Office[4] so Bell decided, out of courtesy to the Americans, to honour the rescheduled date they had set for June to pick up his medal. It was a low-key ceremony, kept out of the public eye and handled discreetly by a senior military intelligence officer in the US War Department in Washington. By contrast Bell's more publicity-seeking wartime boss at the British Security Coordination (BSC), Bill Stephenson, was photographed being handed his Medal for Merit seven months earlier, in November 1946 by his old friend and head of the wartime OSS Bill Donovan at a ceremony in Washington, photographed for posterity.

By 1947 the US War department was in charge of handling ex-personnel and documents related to the wartime OSS, which had been disbanded on 20 September 1945, prior to the foundation of the CIA in July 1948. During the transition period, Bell's award fell victim to poor departmental coordination between the wartime allies as well as within the Foreign Office.

It was only belatedly, on 3 September 1947, that Bell received a letter from the Foreign Office making the extraordinary claim that when the Americans had offered Bell the award 'it had entirely escaped the notice of all concerned at this end [London] that your [Bell's] services were rendered in a field that was to be covered by the general objections to the bestowal of Allied decorations upon persons serving under Foreign Office auspices.'[5]

So it was a cock-up not a conspiracy. Dunbar appears to have overlooked, or not been sufficiently informed about, Bell's wartime role of cooperating with the Americans in secret intelligence as an MI6 officer. There was an understanding rather than any cast-iron rule within Whitehall that it was generally not standard official policy for UK government service employees to receive decorations from foreign governments, and permission was needed and granted only in very exceptional circumstances.[6]

And yet Bell was not alone among the British intelligence community honoured for wartime service by the Americans. His own former boss, William ('Bill' Stephenson), was not only publicly honoured by the Americans, as we have seen, but also knighted by the British for his leadership of the British Co-Ordination Committee, headquartered in wartime New York, with MI6 approval. The Foreign Office claimed that, because of his seniority and the fact that he was Canadian, 'and for 'very special reasons that were held to apply in no other instance'' Stephenson's case was 'exceptional'. Details remain classified.[7]

Other British civilians in British government wartime service with intelligence links decorated by the Americans included the MI6 station chief in 1930s Vienna, Colonel Thomas Kendrick. He went on to serve as commandant of the Combined Services Detailed Interrogation Centre (CSDIC) for German prisoners of war in the UK, and was awarded the US Order of Merit,[8] the higher honour bestowed on Stephenson, as was the pioneer of radar technology Sir Robert Watson-Watt.

The wartime chief scientific adviser to the Ministry of Aircraft Production Sir Ben Lockspeiser was, like Bell, awarded the Medal of Freedom.[9]

Bell was among other distinguished company. Non-British national recipients of the US Medal of Freedom included Henriette 'Monique' Hanotte, one of the last surviving heroines of the fabled Comet Line, the Belgian Resistance network that helped hundreds of downed Allied airmen to safety across the Pyrenees onto neutral Spain in World War Two.

However, the situation was complicated in Bell's case by his employment status as a UK civil servant who was also working, with both the British and the Americans, in a clandestine capacity, details of which were classified and shared within government only on a restricted 'need to know' basis. This was bound to have caused problems, and general administrative confusion. He would not have appeared in any standard lists of overt government departments so it would have been difficult for other officials to check up on him.

The outcome was that Bell was asked to keep his award secret, with the Foreign Office deciding to minimise the diplomatic embarrassment of having his medal turned down, judging that his World War Two role as a spy remained too sensitive and that public exposure of any controversy over his award was a risk to national security. Bell wrote back to the Foreign Office, evidently piqued by its dysfunctionality, but resorting to wit as a way of lightening his displeasure. 'In case you are alarmed, I have not been disporting myself with it [the medal] at public functions, neither have I been wearing it on holidays or days of public rejoicing. I showed it once to my elderly mother who is in her 80th year. She shed tears of delight at the thought that my efforts to persuade elderly British officials to be moderately polite to their chiefest ally had been thus recognized.'[10]

In December 1947 another Foreign Office official wrote to Bell thanking him for his 'exhilarating' letter. It went on: 'Your discretion in keeping the gong in your handkerchief drawer is beyond praise, and I think the best solution for our problem will be for you to leave it there.'[11]

Bell was told he had been awarded the Medal of Freedom months before entering a new stage in his career that had opened up following Inverchapel's retirement in 1948 and may have thought it prudent not to ruffle official feathers more than he did.

On 17 August 1948, once the medal issue had been settled, Bell received a two-paragraph letter from the private secretary of the foreign secretary Ernest Bevin informing him that he had learnt with regret that he had relinquished his appointment under the Foreign Office. 'Mr Bevin desires me to convey to you an expression of his warm appreciation of the services you have rendered since joining the staff of His Majesty's Embassy, Washington in May 1946.'[12]

By now new avenues had opened up for Bell in the world of intelligence and security, with the support of his friend Guy Liddell, MI5's new deputy director general. In the early autumn of 1948, Bell received a letter from R. Hordocks from the Personnel department of Box 500 (MI5) confirming that the Security Service was offering him employment at an annual salary of £900 per annum raised by annual increments of £30 to £1080 and thence by increments of £35 to £1,220 per annum. 'Subject to satisfactory service,' Bell would be eligible for 'establishment as when vacancies occur, and this would entitle him to participation in MI5's Superannuation Scheme'.[13]

Interestingly, the initial offer suggested a step down for Bell in career terms but one he was prepared to take a risk on. Under the terms of his recruitment he was going from being an 'established' MI6 officer to being an 'unestablished' MI5 officer, potentially forfeiting the pension he had built up with MI6. It was a similar kind of contract to the one that would backfire many years in the case of Peter Wright, the MI5 officer whose disgruntlement over the loss of his pension rights motivated him to embarrass employers with the publication of his controversial autobiography *Spycatcher*.[14]

But while Wright claimed that MI5 expected its officers

to remain loyal unto the grave without necessarily offering loyalty in return, Bell would come to share no similar resentment towards his MI5 employers who within a short time of recruiting him gave him responsibility and additional tax-free perks, and an overseas posting based in Nairobi, as MI5's main officer in East Africa, with his pension rights restored.

On acceptance of the new job offer, Bell was asked to report for duty on 1 November 1948 at an MI5 building at 58 St James's Street and ask for a Colonel Spencer. Bell must have felt more than a touch of déja vue – a reminder of that day in 1935 when he had been recruited by a cigar-smoking Admiral Sinclair, the MI6 pre-war chief at the agency's HQ straddling the elegant Queen Anne's Gate and the functional Broadway Buildings near St James's, Westminister.

The letter of his new employment suggested that MI5 was still populated by Colonel Blimps – part Baden Powell, part Bulldog Drummond. In fact, the newly married Bell was entering a new post-imperial world and a fresh assignment that would demand the best he had to offer and test his ability to adapt to evolving circumstances, and different scenarios.

MI5's latest director general, appointed in the spring of 1946, was a former senior police officer, Sir Percy Sillitoe who the post-war Labour prime minister Clement Attlee had preferred over internal candidates and trusted to keep the Security Service, so far as possible, on the straight and narrow path of political impartiality.

One of the internal candidates who was passed over in favour of Sillitoe was Guy Liddell, who had been promoted during World War Two to head up MI5's counter-intelligence division. Liddell thought Sillitoe lacked sufficient stature in Whitehall to compensate for his lack of intelligence experience. He also felt that it was extremely discouraging for the younger members of the office and for others coming in to feel that the head of the office was likely to be appointed from outside.

Nonetheless as post-war deputy director general, Liddell was given a special responsibility for intelligence matters, including MI5's overseas operations, an area where he evidently rated the former MI6 officer Walter Bell who did not quite fit the prototype of 'Oxbridge types' and 'long-haired intellectuals' that Sillitoe mistrusted.

Bell's posting abroad by MI5 was jointly agreed by Liddell and Sillitoe at a meeting on 21 February 1949. A final decision to send Bell to East Africa as the head of station in Nairobi was taken by Liddell as a preferred alternative to the Ghanaian capital Accra 'owing to difficulties about accommodation' ill suiting Bell's requirements as a married man.[15]

The British prime minister Clement Attlee had intervened formally to strengthen the Security Service's role overseas and exclude MI6 from conducting clandestine operations in Commonwealth countries. An internal Whitehall note interpreting the so-called Attlee Directive reaffirmed MI5's lead intelligence role in the colonies and the Commonwealth, a prerogative it retained until the late 1960s when decolonisation was almost complete.

Things were looking up again for Bell. MI5 had made him an offer of a new posting abroad that combined security with secret intelligence, in a key British colony in the twilight of empire. It was a fresh opportunity that he embraced enthusiastically.

# 24
# Kenya, Part 1

Arriving in Nairobi in May 1949 with Tattie, Bell found that the MI5 station office in Kenya, responsible for the East African territories, had established an active if discreet presence in the post-war years. He inherited comprehensive files that had been built up on sources and suspects and no shortage of policy directives from London which he could draw on in order to better understand the local political and social landscape and key players. 'The records kept in the office seemed at the time almost too comprehensive, but there was considerable correspondence with London,' he noted.[1]

It wasn't until 2009, more than sixty years later, that declassified MI5 records were to reveal the extent to which British intelligence had, in the years leading up to and following Bell's posting, been monitoring the Kenyan nationalist leader, Jomo Kenyatta. Their checks were aimed at allaying the colonial authorities' fears about Kenyatta's alleged communist beliefs, which, in the words of Sir Evelyn Baring, the governor of Kenya between 1952 and 1959, made him the 'leader to darkness and death' of the Mau Mau insurgency that erupted in October 1952.[2]

Of the other territories he had to cover, Bell described Tanganyika 'a delight to visit' with the governor Sir Edward Twining 'conducting his affairs from a huge Moorish palace, with liberal quantities of gin'.[3] Bell found the security problems in Twining's fiefdom to be minimal, which he put down to the Germans largely destroying the tribal system when Tanganyika was their colony.

By contrast Uganda was a 'rich never land' at that time. It was, he reported, 'rich enough to maintain immaculate roads in particular. Revenues were derived from a prosperous cotton industry with a government monopoly of overseas sales. The only security problem was an intertribal rivalry which took over when independence was granted in the sixties, turning the country into the disaster it became'.[4]

As the Cold War set in and Britain's colonies pressed for independence, the situation in Kenya became a great deal more complex than that suggested by Twining, who asked Bell when they first met: 'how are you getting on in that superior little Hill station Nairobi?'[5]

The governor of Kenya when Bell was in Nairobi, Sir Philip Mitchell, was also less than diplomatic on occasions, with his colonial administration prone to pay little attention to the reports produced by MI5 until it was too late.[6] According to Bell, a senior colonial official wrote to Mitchell asking for advice about governing Somaliland. Mitchell replied that the only successful governor of that country had been 'the Mad Mullah[7] who had reduced the population by fifty per cent'.[8]

It was while in Kenya that Bell realised that the British colonial authorities were losing control and that no amount of intelligence that reached London seemed capable of impressing policy makers to come up with a solution that might avert an uprising. The in-built social inequalities and racism that prevailed in the last years of British colonialism when 30,000 settlers dominated over five million Africans would later be recalled by Sir Charles Markham, a Kenyan politician who was a member of the Legislative Council prior to independence. The native Kenyans 'had no status at all, they were laborers, they were servants, what have you'.[9]

A new radicalised movement had grown up among the youth of the leading Kikuyu tribe, who were prepared to use violence to press for independence and the recovery of land from which they had been displaced by White settlers. What became known as the Mau Mau rebellion, based on the taking of secret oaths, would awaken the deepest European fears of African savagery and would be met with brutal repression by the colonial authorities.

Reinforcing the growing Kikuyu hostility towards the colonial power, Bell would write, was the British failure to realise the impact that overseas service during the war had made on Kenyan African servicemen, who resented being released back into a tribal way of life when they returned home. According to Bell, it was the governor of Kenya between 1944 and 1952, Mitchell, who admitted this to him when it was too late to remedy.[10]

Quite apart from the dysfunctionality of colonial rule, Bell's posting in Kenya was further overshadowed, on the personal front, by a major family bereavement that deeply affected him. News reached him from England of the death of the woman he had loved and trusted as his confidante since childhood. On 8 June 1950 his mother Muriel died in a Sussex hospital after suffering from a respiratory attack and heart failure. She was aged eighty-two. Rather than be given compassionate leave and allowed to return to the UK for her funeral, Bell was asked by MI5's deputy director general Guy Liddell to go on a fact-finding mission to another politically volatile African colony.

Liddell was, at the time, developing the organisation's Cold War role, building MI5's relationships and operations overseas in ways that challenged MI6's previous dominance of intelligence matters and foreign links. In July 1950, by which time young radical Kikuyus had already founded the militant movement Mau Mau, inventing a new oath to incite a revolt against British rule, Liddell arranged for the French intelligence service, SDECE, to welcome and brief Bell on a visit to Madagascar about a controversial campaign to restore order.[11]

A nationalist uprising, fuelled by resentment that the island's veterans of the war had been less well treated by their French colonial masters than veterans from the metropolis, had been repressed with summary executions, torture, the burning of villages, and psychological warfare, aimed at terrorising villagers – among the tactics that the British would emulate in Kenya once colonial rule came under pressure there.

The British colonial authorities, while vaguely aware of Mau Mau when it was first formed, failed to assess the threat of an insurgency before brutally repressing it, Bell reflected years afterwards. 'Fortunately for me, I had left some months before the rebellion erupted' he recalled.[12] And yet the seeds of social injustice and resentment against the British had been sown prior to his arrival in Nairobi and the situation had deteriorated on his watch.

Long before his arrival, a certain aristocratic breed of mainly British White settlers in the area, often sent to Kenya as remittance men (receiving income from the UK) and located in and around the Wanjohi valley – the so-called Happy Valley set – had hardly covered themselves in glory during the 1920s and beyond. The subject of infamous scandals revolving around infidelity, cocaine, morphine, alcohol, and crimes of passion, as lurid newspaper articles, and eventually the book[13] and later film *White Mischief* would depict, it was a community characterised by privilege and decadence.

Bell and Tattie found more common ground between themselves as a couple in endeavouring to understand what motivated African nationalism. They developed a social conscience, sharing their admiration for the selfless educational and social work among the poor and marginalised native Kenyans by some of the Christian missionaries in Kenya. Their approach was in striking contrast to the self-indulgent lifestyle and racist attitudes of some of the White land settlers and colonial administrators.

As one of Bell's wartime MI6 colleagues Graham Greene was to discover when he reported for *The Sunday Times* on Kenya during the Mau Mau rebellion, as in countries under colonial rule such as Vietnam it was Catholic priests working with the poor that provided an alternative to the official narratives. The hardliners in the colonial administration, perhaps remembering the Irish uprising, distrusted Catholics, thinking they were assisting the insurgents.[14]

Bell, like Greene, undoubtedly would have found some of the Catholic missionaries useful sources of information. It was also Walter's rediscovery of his Christian faith that turned his contacts with missionaries in Kenya into something that he found inspirational. Bell was particularly impressed by the humanity and service to others of the Catholic Religious Missionary Congregation of the Holy Spirit (Spiritans), which ministered in remote poor native rural settlements. So impressed, in fact, that the experience helped erase his agnosticism and brought about his conversion to Roman Catholicism while in Kenya. His wife Tattie, who had not suffered her husband's strict Anglican upbringing, felt in no hurry to embrace religion until her later years, when she too became a Catholic.[15]

The Bells still formed part of a White settler and colonial service residential community in a Nairobi suburb, typically inhabiting a 'Surrey Tudor' style bungalow, with tiled rather than corrugated roof, comfortable rooms, a large veranda and a beautiful garden in colour the year round with well-watered native flowers. The furniture was hand-made by Indian craftsmen, and there was no shortage of domestic native staff, from kitchen 'totos' to garden boys.

Nonetheless the Catholic faith in action displayed by the missionaries, in solidarity with the grievances of the native Africans – a majority of whom lived in far poorer conditions that any White coloniser – spoke to Bell's social and political conscience, as well as search for God.[16]

As a couple the Bells managed to go some way towards dissenting from the popular self-interested 'White' depiction of British colonial rule in Kenya that would endure for many years: that it was both benevolent and necessary, bringing culture and civilisation to a people presumed to have neither.[17]

It was an image largely derived from the book *Out of Africa* published in 1937 whose author Karen Blixen a younger Bell had rather taken to when he met her on her visit to New York during his pre-war posting with MI6 there. As the historian Calder Walton puts it, 'Blixen presents Kenya as a kind of colonial Utopia…not only fertile, accommodating, and picturesque …also a place of racial harmony, where colonial settlers live happily and paternalistically with their Kikuyu laborers.'[18] While he may have easily found occasional solace in such a romantic notion, Bell's political antennae and professional experience soon disabused him of it, his work in Kenya posing even more of a challenge than he could have ever imagined.

The Bells enjoyed the comforts of colonial life in Nairobi, not least the temperate climate and colourful vegetation that flourished in their garden, and the stunning landscapes and wildlife beyond. They treated their African Kikuyu servants with decency and trust and made friends among the more civic-minded members of the white settler community. But Bell found his colonial bosses complacent and the colonial police in Kenya difficult to work with as they resented any criticism of the hard-line tactics they used against the native Kenyans. 'They tended to be rather stiff and always afraid that one was trying to interfere with what they considered their sole concern,' recalled Bell.[19]

While in Kenya, Bell's main assignment was to monitor the political movements and ambitions of Jomo Kenyatta, an African nationalist leader he felt unable to demonise, and indeed came to admire to the point of becoming a trusted adviser in later years. The background intelligence that Bell inherited and added to on becoming MI5's man in Nairobi suggested that Kenyatta had become disillusioned by the racism he encountered while studying in the Soviet Union and that his links with communist politics had been declining during World War Two. Indeed, in 1945 a previous MI5 liaison officer in East Africa had reported that while it was believed that Kenyatta had at one time been a communist, 'it was thought he had since quarrelled with the Party'.[20]

As far as Bell was concerned, to understand Kenyatta you had to go back to his African roots and the nature of British colonial rule as he lived it. Born in the late 1890s in the East African highlands southwest of Mount Kenya, Kenyatta spent his childhood there before any British government had been established in the area. As Bell later wrote: 'The only white men in the country were a few explorers, missionaries and surveyors for the railway that was to be built to Uganda. The Kikuyu were a people divided into clans ruled by councils of elders, fortified by their priests, who found out God's wishes by divination and interpreting omens'.[21]

Kenyatta was educated and employed by Scottish Presbyterian missionaries before he left for Nairobi and became an interpreter in the High Court. By this time the White settlers had arrived in his homeland in significant numbers and were in the process of carving it up into farms and coffee plantations, displacing a population that was growing in numbers after being stricken by epidemics of European contagious diseases. The seeds of social unrest and African nationalism had already been sown by the time Kenyatta moved to London to lobby for Kikuyu affairs. He studied at University College and the London School of Economics there before visiting Russia.

MI5 took an interest in Kenyatta's visit to Moscow, where he studied at the University of the Toilers of the East in the early 1930s under the alias James Joken. After he returned to the UK in 1933, a Special Branch informer claimed that Kenyatta had been approached to become a Soviet agent, an allegation that fuelled an enduring suspicion of the Kenyan that was to contribute to his becoming one of the most misunderstood leaders in the history of British Africa.[22]

When World War Two broke out, Kenyatta, at the request of the British colonial administration, was put under active surveillance as a suspect enemy agent. MI5's future director general Roger Hollis, head of the Security Service's F-Division at the time and responsible for identifying and tracking 'subversive activities', was put in charge of secretly monitoring him.[23]

In 1940 Kenyatta moved to Sussex, where he worked on a farm and four years later entered into a short-lived marriage to Edna Clarke, an English agricultural labourer. He was previously married to Grace Wahu, the mother of his first son and daughter. In 1946 he married his third wife, Grace Wanjiku, who died in 1951 after giving birth to a daughter.

Marital issues aside, as Kenyatta's political ties seemed to be dwindling, so MI5 became less suspicious of his alleged communist links. Bell later recalled nonetheless that while in England, Kenyatta had made many friends in the political and academic world. This deepened his political knowledge and outlook so that when he returned to Kenya in 1946 he was soon the acknowledged political leader. Bell later regretted that the colonial administration in those early post-war years was ill-equipped to deal, politically and diplomatically, with such a sophisticated leader of a nationalist movement and unable to see him as anything other than a suspect communist subversive and terrorist.

Colonial officials were mesmerised by Kenyatta, with his piercing eyes, the large ring he wore, and ornate ceremonial stick. A 'flamboyant bookmaker' was how a Kenya district commissioner Robin Wainwright described him. Terence Gavaghan, another Kenyan district officer recalled: 'He was totally informed about his people, their customs, and practices. He knew about Russia and Britain, a very broadly informed sort of man. I never felt other than dominated by his vibrant personality and hypnotic masculinity. One felt enveloped by his warmth, and at the same time slightly repelled by his menace.'[24] For years, instead of engaging with Kenyatta, the colonial authorities treated him like a pariah, blocking him from entering the Legislative Assembly.[25]

Bell came to the view that if Kenyatta was to lead his people, as he seemed destined to do, he was faced with no alternative than to adopt a militant line in recognition of the growing Kikuyu middle class and, even more importantly, hold out the prospect of satisfying the land hunger of the peasants, who were pressing even harder on the diminished land space that had been left to them after European settlement. The same considerations applied to other tribes who looked to Kenyatta to become their national leader even though they knew that his chief constituency was bound to be Kikuyu. 'In those days there was no other African who could in any way equal him,' wrote Bell. It was a view that was to inform his reports from Nairobi in the lead-up to the Mau Mau rebellion and his later personal dealings with Kenyatta as his adviser on intelligence and security matters during the transition to independence.[26]

Bell's reports, while ahead of their time, were destined to be ignored rather than acted upon. Accompanied by his wife Tattie, Walter would leave Nairobi in February 1952, ready for a new posting that he hoped would prove more productive, although frustrated at his inability to alter the descent into brutality and bloodshed in Kenya that unravelled within months of his departure from East Africa.

On 20 October 1952, amid reports of White settlers' farms coming under attack from Mau Mau rebels, and the fatal shooting of one of Kenya's most controversial chiefs, the pro-British Waruhiu wa Kung'u, the new governor in Kenya, declared a state of emergency, leading to increased violence as the British unleashed an aggressively fought counter-insurgency.

The colonial administration quickly held Kenyatta responsible as the alleged bloody cult leader. He was arrested and charged with instigating the uprising, and, despite protesting his innocence, was convicted along with five other defendants. It was later alleged by defence lawyers that the presiding magistrate Lansley Tucker had been bribed.[27] Sentenced to seven years' hard labour on 8 April 1953, Kenyatta was imprisoned in Lokitaung until 1959 and then exiled in Lodwar until 1961.

While many White settlers had little doubt that Kenyatta instigated the Mau Mau movement, the excesses for which it became notorious took place after the nationalist leader had been convicted of managing it and had been exiled to the Northern Frontier. Bell doubted that Kenyatta would have condoned the worst violence perpetrated on Africans and White settlers. This was a view that his successor at the MI5 station in Nairobi in 1952, C.R. Major, shared when he later reported to London that the colonial administration's decision led by the governor Sir Evelyn Baring to put Kenyatta on trial was motivated by political expediency and the need to find a culprit to placate the European settlers in the colony, a policy to which Major, like Bell, was opposed.

While there may have been consistency in some of their reporting the two MI5 officers were very different personalities – Bell by character and politics less pompous and officious than Major. This was reflected in an indiscreet letter Bell received from a friend, Joan Russell, who had stayed behind in Nairobi as a member of the colonial administrative staff. The gossipy missive was received by Bell in late September 1952, a month before the British clamp-down in Kenya and when he was already on a new posting, far from its impending East African turmoil. In it, Russell painted the life of the colonial administration and Major's involvement with it as a cross between an Ealing Comedy and a Somerset Maugham novella, poorly equipped for dealing with the rising social and political challenges:

> Major (I don't think we shall ever get on Christian name terms) is I think horrified at the idea of a one-man station here, he is so slow [underlined], and takes hours to read and assimilate anything…. He frequently comes in and says, 'Good morning, ladies.' We find it hard to compose our features suitably…somehow his humour is so forced as if he was trying to put over what a hell of a broadminded chap he was.[28]
> Major's wife fared no better and was easily caricatured by Ms. Russell's acerbic pen. 'Mrs. M. is of course deadly and so is the daughter, though I feel sorry for her, as Mama so obviously keeps her tied by her apron strings.' The letter was accompanied by a pencil drawing of a rather prim Mrs. M attending a cocktail party dressed in a 'dainty white spotted voile with while felt hat and shoes and flowers to match'.[29]

Russell painted a vivid picture of colonial life continuing in its own bubble of social privilege and complacency, with dry martinis and gin and tonics served at sundown in the exclusive Nairobi Club, and at the Police Ball in the Kenya regimental headquarters. Only once does her letter to Bell, halfway through, give a sense of any emergent crisis, suggesting that the media back home was somewhat overblowing things – although the situation remained unstable. 'Of course, everybody is writing from home in a frightful flap having read their Sunday Dispatches about the situation in Kenya,' Russell wrote.

> The English press of course vastly exaggerated the position, but all the same there are some very unpleasant things taking place here. The latest is, apart from murdering Mau Mau witnesses and tribal police, that they have brutally maimed and killed cattle and sheep in the Timau area.
> I do think that Michael O'Rourke[30] has been simply excellent in getting all the extra police organized and on to the job without loss of time. There can be absolutely no mercy for them now and as soon as a few of these vicious creatures are put to death, the better. Goodness, it makes one sick reading the false and ridiculous statements from our dear African politicians [sic]. We now have to have a permit from the police if we use certain roads out of Nairobi after dark, an excellent idea to limit all those spivs and things moving about the countryside.[31]

Joan Russell's letter provided Bell with razor-sharp information on the key characters involved in the last years of colonial rule in Kenya. Both chatty and confiding, it suggested that Bell could be good at personal relations, building trust and gaining sources.[32]

Bell was to develop a far more nuanced opinion about

Kenyatta than many colonial officials and White settlers, questioning the extent to which he was involved in the brutal rituals linked to the Mau Mau insurgency and concluding he was not responsible. As he wrote years later in a letter to his friend the Conservative Party politician Julian Amery: 'I think that his [Kenyatta's] Mau Mau exploits must be seen in the context of the time in which he engaged with it. He used it as a revolutionary weapon ready to hand. I wish that somebody would see the need to go very carefully over the evidence again to see whether he was really implicated in the "dirty' oaths. I am not convinced that he was.'[33]

Kenya proved a wake-up call in terms of Bell's political conscience. He discovered that the Kikuyu grievance that their land had been appropriated by White settlers at a time when their population had been decimated by disease was deep rooted and growing. The White, mainly English, settlers for the most part thought of the Africans as children they could dominate and exploit. They called the African men 'boys'. The British colonial authorities in Nairobi failed to realise that a growing number of educated and articulate individuals were having an increasing influence among the African population, particularly the Kikuyu in the central and western part of the country.[34]

It was in Kenya that Bell witnessed a protracted effort by die-hard British Tories to arrest the decline of empire, a policy he believed was doomed to fail but felt he should at least track. In August 1951, Julian Amery, a true God and Empire Tory, visited the country as part of his and his father Leo's attempts to shape defence policy from the early Cold War years, using the resurrected military study network dating from the 1930s called the Army League as a pressure group to influence government and public opinion.

Ignoring the roots and growing manifestations of an African nationalist conscience, the Amerys linked Kenya's future to colonial authorities making greater use of African manpower to create an 'Imperial Africa Army', and argued that the strategic needs of the Middle East, Far East and Africa could be met by utilising this great resource. There was nothing new in this idea, which had been a feature of the British manpower debate since the expansion of the Empire in the mid-nineteenth century, but the Amerys wanted to give it fresh impetus – and Julian felt he was well placed to have an impact on government policy.

Julian Amery had been elected to parliament a year earlier as an MP for Preston North and married Catherine, the daughter of the future prime minister Harold Macmillan. Before entering politics he had engaged in a series of colourful military adventures. As a young man he had volunteered on the Franco side in the Spanish Civil War as an observer attached to the Nationalist forces. During World War Two he initially served as an attaché in British missions to Belgrade, Ankara, Sofia and Bucharest. He went on to serve in special operations assisting partisans fighting against the Germans in the Balkans – his patriotic credentials contrasting with those of his brother John, the black sheep of the family, who ended up being executed for treason on account of his pro-Nazi sympathies.[35]

When they met in Kenya Bell counted the well-connected Amery as a useful contact and was on first name terms, as their correspondence from that time reveals. He shared a sense of camaraderie with Amery, a veteran of World War Two intelligence and special operations, even if he did not share his right-wing Tory views.

Bell wrote a personal letter to Amery suggesting they should meet away from his official programme of encounters with colonial officials and invited him to stay at the colonial residence he and Tattie lived in as a more comfortable option than a hotel. His tone suggested familiarity and invited intrigue. 'I hope that you will not be so immersed in official junketing as not to spend time to see us,' he wrote.[36] In the same letter Bell shared in the sad news of a mutual friend, the ambassador Lord Inverchapel who had died that summer, his reputation severely damaged but still respected by his former private secretary.

'I seem to be the only one of that Washington vintage who has not died or disappeared – although being here is almost tantamount to the latter,' he told Amery, which was not exactly true.[37] Maclean had defected to Moscow, and others who had served alongside Bell in the Washington embassy like John Balfour and Robert Cecil, were still in Foreign Office posts. Only to the extent that his MI5 role demanded greater discretion that any diplomatic post could Bell be said to have 'disappeared' in Kenya.

It was this discretion that led Amery, months after the two men had met in Kenya, to approach Bell on a matter that stirred up memories of wartime special operations and resistance while forming part of the intrigue of spies and agents that would characterise the Cold War.

In January 1952 Amery wrote to Bell introducing him to Colonel Zarko Popović, a shadowy character he had known and befriended during World War Two. The Serbian, a fluent Russian speaker, had worked for Yugoslav military intelligence in Italy, Moscow and the Middle East. Popović had moved to Nairobi a few months earlier from London and taken a job as an inspector with a South African insurance company. He was now, not for the first time, offering his services to the British. He told Amery he was open to employment of any kind, even as a clerk, or storekeeper if he could count on the recommendation of the Ministry of the Colonies.[38]

Amery described Popović's CV and qualifications as 'not unimpressive' in support of his letter to Bell recommending him for employment by MI5.[39] Amery may have thought Popović might be a useful agent or double agent given his early wartime collaboration with the Allies, his Russian expertise and intelligence background.

Bell was not convinced. His years in MI6 and the Washington embassy had made him weary of 'drop-ins', as the unexpected arrivals of suspected foreign agents offering information or other services were known in the world of intelligence. He distanced himself from any involvement, referring Popović 's case elsewhere and excusing himself from any further responsibility on the grounds that his own posting in Kenya was coming to an end. As he wrote to Amery after debriefing Popović : 'I have had some experience of trying to help people of this sort here and the difficulties are immense.'[40]

Popović  may have supported the British in World War Two and been a potential useful source in the Cold War, but he was considered an unreliable asset by the Foreign Office, and seemingly not trusted by MI5 and the colonial authorities. He may have boasted about his partisan adventures alongside SOE in the early days of World War Two, which had first brought him to Amery's attention, but Bell wisely thought it not a good enough reason to recruit him as the British Empire struggled to maintain its colonial grip on Kenya.

During the final days of Bell's first posting to Kenya, the main excitement and interest taking up the colonial authorities and the local expatriate community was the imminent arrival of Princess Elizabeth and her husband Philip the Duke of Edinburgh, which may have explained the reason for Bell being less than enthusiastic about helping on the Popović  case – he had other, more pressing, issues to deal with, including royal security.

On 31 January the royal couple had flown from Heathrow to Nairobi having been seen off by Elizabeth's father King George VI, who was too ill following surgery for lung cancer to make the tour himself. The young couple were staying at the isolated Treetops hotel in the heart of the Kenya forest when the king died in the early hours of 6 February 1952, although the news did not reach Princess Elizabeth until later in the day, by which time she had returned to a fishing lodge called Sagana, 20 miles away, which she had been given as a wedding present.

The Bells left Kenya the following month, with Walter suffering another family bereavement, that of his vicar father. George Bell died after having suffered from mental illness for many years. He had developed signs of serious mental disturbance after the end of World War Two with the temper that had characterised him from his early years turning into more extreme mood swings and hallucinations.

In 1948, just as his son Walter was being secretly recruited by MI5, matters had come to a head when, after months in which he was showing evident signings of losing concentration while celebrating church services, George told his wife Muriel that he must hand himself in to the police as he felt voices telling him there was someone he had to murder.[41]

After seeking urgent medical and psychiatric advice, Muriel gained the consent of her three children – St John, Mary and Walter – to have George admitted to the neurology hospital of Hurstwood Park in Haywards Heath, where he underwent a lobotomy. The aim was to 'cure' him of his moods and allow him to conduct fewer, if any, religious services as he had by then agreed to retire from his priestly duties in Riverhead, and move to a home for the aged in East Sussex.

George emerged from his surgery seemingly cured of his moods but with a much-diminished personality – a mere shadow physically of the imposing figure he had struck in his more active years of parish duties in Riverhead. After Muriel's death in June 1950, George was moved to another nursing home, Ruthven Lodge in Cuckfield where he developed increasing signs of senility. He died, aged seventy-seven, after slipping into a hot bath and scalding himself to death.[42]

A subsequent inquest failed to find conclusive evidence of any negligence on behalf of the staff or management of the nursing home, although the traumatic manner of his demise haunted members of his family for the rest of their lives, not least his son Walter, who spent his later years in dread of losing his own mind and fearing he might face a similar end to his life as his father.

George Bell's death and that of King George VI within a month of each other seemed to Walter to be dark omens, foretelling a time of great change and upheaval, not least in Kenya, where the African idyll soon became a nightmare from which the Bells were lucky to escape.

Bell was destined to be haunted by a feeling of guilt that he had failed to prevent the insurrection followed by repression in Kenya that unfolded once he had left. As the person in a key security and intelligence post during the build-up to the Mau Mau uprising, one of the bloodiest periods in British colonial history, he cannot be exonerated from blame for what followed. However, given that Bell's reports calling for a better understanding of the causes of the insurrection and the motivation of its leaders were being largely ignored, it is not the messenger that stands out as most culpable – but the nature of British colonial rule, and in particular the complacency of its governing powers and the brutal tactics they adopted to try and preserve it when it came under threat.

In the notes he later wrote on his period in Kenya, Bell accepted that  he was part of a collective failure both in intelligence and governance. 'It would probably seem that the SLO [Security Liaison Officer, MI5] job was useless...There were all sorts of ways in which we could have been helpful to the colonial government but looking back it is hard to see that we did anything substantial'.[43] He went on: 'Communist influence was almost non-existent although some people, particularly the Governor of British Somaliland expected me to ferret out communists from under thorn trees.'[44]

# 25
# India

On 24 April 1952 Bell and Tattie set sail from Tilbury for Walter's new posting in India, aboard the SS *Stratheden*, a P & O liner bound for the East. The 23,700-tonne steam turbine ocean liner was one of a fleet of four large passenger ships that had survived World War Two, serving as a troop carrier (eight others had been sunk by German torpedoes). The reconverted SS *Stratheden* carried over 1,000 passengers, the Bells being among a privileged minority, on a first-class ticket – in their case, presumably courtesy of Walter's employer. The passenger manifest identified Bell simply as a government official.[1]

The ship sailed to Bombay via the Suez Canal, and as the cold waters of the Bay of Biscay gave way to the temperate tranquillity of the Mediterranean, the Bells finally relaxed, for the first time since leaving Kenya. There was a mix of style and comfort on board, with fine dining, carpeted lounges and bedrooms, snug armchairs and sofas and solid-looking dark wood furniture – all in stark contrast to the canteen-style diner, wicker chairs and basic bunk beds of those who travelled in an upgraded steerage class. The Bells took the sun on the higher deck and occasionally took a dip in the soothing waters of the sea-water swimming pool. The leisurely three-week journey gave Bell plenty of time to reflect on times past and passing, and what awaited him in India.

Still close to Bell's heart was the memory of his beloved late mother Muriel, his enduring confidante and inspirer of adventures. In her twenties and still unmarried, she had sailed to India more than half a century earlier, failing to secure the husband her parents hoped she would find there before returning to England and writing a book of poems evoking the beauty of the Kashmir landscape.

Bell was now sailing in a more modern ship that boasted some notable clients from its pre-war days, including the author George Orwell, one of the writers Bell had found common cause with during the 1930s and into World War Two. Orwell had sailed second-class on the newly inaugurated SS *Stratheden* in September 1938, after being injured in the Spanish Civil War fighting 'for common decency' for the anti-Franco militia and suffering from weak lungs. Before disembarking in Morocco, Orwell, who had been born in Motihari, India, in 1903 during the British Raj, and served as a young recruit with the Indian Imperial Police force in Burma, would have had time to look on the colonials and their memsahibs heading onwards towards the East. They still very much belonged to an empire he had equated with class snobbery and racial prejudice. Their presence stirred up old memories and gave him ideas for new books.[2]

Bell had only recently had his own memories flooding back, not just of the death of his mother, but of his own pro-Republican stance during the Spanish Civil War, which had stirred his political consciousness during his first MI6 posting in New York in the 1930s.

A month before his departure for India, he had taken a short break and visited Spain for the first time. His old friend from post-war Washington days, the British diplomat Jock Balfour, had arrived a year earlier as the new British ambassador. Housed in the palatial ambassador's residence in central Madrid, Bell had looked forward to catching up on news about Franco's Spain and Balfour briefed him on its tense relations with the UK on the subject of the disputed sovereignty claim over Gibraltar. Another issue the old friends discussed was the British refusal to support Spanish entry into the United Nations and NATO. This was because of Franco's repression of political opponents, despite the fact that the US administration, as useful support for Washington's geopolitical Cold War power play, considered establishing military bases on the Spanish peninsula as a quid pro quo for accepting the dictator's virulent anti-communism – a trade-off both Bell and Balfour were less than happy about. Bell had planned to enjoy some of Madrid's cultural sights, too, but his trip was overshadowed by a near encounter with death when he narrowly escaped being crushed by a tram when crossing the Castellana avenue after being dazzled by a visit to the Prado museum.[3]

Shortly afterwards he returned to London in preparation for his new MI5 posting. His latest government-issued passport, one of several he would handle during a career under cover, gave him the deceptive professional title of 'civil assistant, War Office'.[4] This, along with his appointment as first secretary to the British High Commission New Delhi, was a cover for his role representing the British Security Service on his new foreign assignment.

As he sailed for India, Bell was aware of the very different challenges that awaited him on arrival. India was no longer under the Raj, and his fellow passengers were no longer almost exclusively colonials. They included other UK government civil servants on their way to remaining colonies in Southeast Asia such as Singapore and Malaysia, and Englishmen still involved in the lucrative tea trade. But many of the passengers, travelling in less comfort, had as their final onward destination Australia, part of a massive emigration from the UK by individuals escaping from the trauma of World War Two and the socio-economic changes that followed it, who sought a new life in a new continent.[5]

As the Cold War set in, Bell had left behind in Kenya the most valued of Britain's African colonies slipping from its grasp, the twilight of empire, with the British reverting, as a way of holding on to power, to the brutal repression of a native insurgency. He was now on his way to South Asia and would subsequently be visiting Southeast Asia, where repressive emergency powers had also been enacted, and with British forces and covert operations immersed since 1948 in countering a communist insurgency in Malaya. MI5 had officers based in the Malayan capital Kuala Lumpur and in Singapore among other locations in its remaining colonies.

In India the protracted efforts to retain the jewel of the British imperial crown, the 'last chukka of rule in the Raj', as one historian put it,[6] was effectively over by the time of Bell's arrival, although it had become clear towards the end of World War Two that the British administration was powerless to stem the tide of Indian nationalism.

As in Kenya, deep-seated grievances against colonial rule had spiralled bloodily out of control, but on a far greater scale, fuelled by religious prejudice. Despite the pleas for non-violent resistance from India's spiritual leader Mahatma Gandhi, Hindus and Muslims descended into violent rioting, leaving thousands of dead across several cities.

After the electoral victory of India's Congress Party in March 1946, Clement Attlee's Labour government took the decision to relinquish power. On 2 June 1947, the last Viceroy of India, Admiral Lord Louis Mountbatten, announced that the country should be divided into a mainly Hindu India and a mainly Muslim Pakistan, encompassing the geographically separate territories of West Pakistan (now Pakistan) and East Pakistan (now Bangladesh).

Britain's accelerated transfer of power and burial of the British Raj was a process 'drenched in bloodshed, accompanied by ethnic cleansing, mass population displacement and communal slaughter often on sadistic levels'.[7] And yet India and Pakistan both remained members of the Commonwealth, and the British government was able to maintain relatively close diplomatic relations with the two independent countries.

Crucially Bell's posting in India was to benefit from and build on the secret, and until recently undisclosed, close intelligence links that the British established with the new Indian independent government. His role was also better defined and made easier as by the time he arrived in New Delhi the old local problem of crosslines and competing fiefdoms in India affecting MI5 and MI6 – since both agencies were operating in Southeast Asia – had been largely settled. MI5 was now confirmed in its lead responsibility for security and counter-intelligence matters, and MI6 prevented from conducting clandestine operations in Commonwealth countries under an agreed secret UK government policy.

Before India's post-war independence, security and intelligence under British rule was controlled by a London-based government department called Indian Political Intelligence (IPI). Started in 1909, by World War Two the IPI had grown into a large organisation funded by the India Office and with strong links to MI5, its focus up until then being that of tracking the movements of suspect Indian nationalists.

Despite the transfer of power in India and Pakistan in 1947 and the significant reduction of non-Indians in their governing apparatus, the new independent states inherited the framework of the British Raj's civil service, with MI5 forming part of the new arrangements. Although not publicised at the time, MI5 played a critical role in Britain's transfer of power in India and in developing cooperation between London and the new post-independence Indian government.[8]

Senior British intelligence and security officials – led by Sir David Petrie, the director general of MI5, who had himself served as an intelligence officer based in Delhi prior to World War Two, his successor Sir Percy Sillitoe, and Sir Stewart Menzies, the head of MI6 during World War Two and its aftermath – had a series of meetings in 1946 and 1947 on the devolution of power in India. They decided to keep in place the British intelligence presence in India based around the Intelligence Bureau (IB), headquartered in Delhi, and the London-based IPI.

A watershed moment for the history of British intelligence in India came in the spring of 1947 when the outgoing head of the IB, the former police commissioner in Delhi, Norman Smith, was replaced in Nehru's interim government by an Indian, T.G. Sanjeev Pillai, the district superintendent from Madras. Pillai reported to the minister of the interior with responsibility for security matters, Saad Patel.

History had moved on since Bell's posting as an MI6 officer in the US during the late 1930s had involved him in keeping a watch on New York based Indian nationalists seeking independence. India was no longer under colonial rule but destined to be discreetly fought over by the spies of East and West as part of the Cold War.

The India Bell worked in as an MI5 officer had Jawaharlal Nehru as its first post-independence prime minister embarked on a declared mission of economic, social and political reform in the world's most populated nascent democracy. In contrast to his good personal relations with Mountbatten and his wife, Nehru's mistreatment before coming to power, including various jail sentences, at the hands of the British colonial authorities had left him suspicious of the British police and secret services.

Nevertheless, Nehru's influential security minister Patel was a committed anti-communist. MI5 happily cooperated with Patel when it came to the surveillance of extremist elements within the Congress Socialist Party (CSP), the socialist caucus of the Nehru-led Indian National Congress Party. The CSP fused in 1948 with the Bolshevik-Leninist Party of India, Ceylon and Burma (BLPI).

Despite Nehru's distrust of the British security apparatus, he did not get in the way of his government-in-waiting agreeing to a close liaison with British intelligence once independence had been achieved. The relationship was formalised when Guy Liddell, the then deputy director general of MI5, secured Nehru's agreement for an MI5 officer to be stationed in New Delhi after the end of British rule.

In August 1947 Nehru broadcast the historic announcement that India had been born as a newly independent nation and the world's largest democracy. In India, as in other colonies and newly independent Commonwealth countries, the presence of MI5's security liaison officer (SLO) became a significant if covert arrangement of the transfer of power.[9]

In 1948 Kenneth Bourne, who had served in wartime India in the Army Intelligence Corps before being recruited by

MI5, handed over to Bill Uren, a veteran of the colonial Indian police force from the war years who was then succeeded by another old Indian hand, Eric Kitchin, in 1950. That year Sanjeev Pillai, the head of the IB, India's domestic intelligence agency, held talks in London with Liddell on 'methods for purging the Civil Service of suspected elements and about security arrangements generally'. A few weeks later Nehru replaced Pillai with his deputy B.N. Mullik, a former police officer who was to remain in post for the next fourteen years as one of Nehru's most trusted advisers.[10]

Soon after independence MI5 became the sole channel by which the British were allowed to communicate on security and intelligence matters with the Indian government, so that Bell, when he was posted to New Delhi, was able to focus on developing MI5's cooperation with the post-independence Indian spy organisation, the IB.

Bell got on well personally and professionally with the Indian spy chief Mullik, cooperating in countering Soviet influence and sharing intelligence on suspected Indian communist 'subversives' in India and the UK. No sooner had Bell arrived in his new post in 1952 than he was encouraged by Mullik to visit the IB headquarters in New Delhi as well as its growing network of outstations in other Indian cities.

In return Mullik was received warmly in London a year later when he was met by the then deputy head of MI5 Roger Hollis, expressing satisfaction with the exchange of information on 'subversives' provided by MI5, and asking for more help from the British in the field of counter-espionage. In his memoirs Mullik noted that Nehru was 'only vaguely aware of how and to what extent intelligence functioned', and declared his personal appreciation for the support the Delhi Intelligence Bureau received from a 'friendly nation', i.e. Britain, for training in foreign intelligence.[11]

Declassified British security archives suggest a disconnect between Nehru's foreign relations and the MI5/Indian security and intelligence cooperation.[12] While Indian and British security and intelligence agencies focused on alleged communists, the visits of the Soviet premier Nikolai Bulganin and first secretary of the Communist Party Nikita Khrushchev to India, and Nehru's visit to the USSR heralded closer Indian-Soviet ties at government level in 1955.

A year later there was a further chill in UK diplomatic ties when British and French policy over Suez was condemned by Nehru, who by contrast did not condemn the Soviet suppression of the Hungarian uprising in the same year. And yet this had little impact on the security and intelligence cooperation Bell was involved in, with the sharing of information on Moscow's financial support for Indian communists. As Mullik wrote to Roger Hollis, the then deputy chief of MI5: 'I never felt I was dealing with any organisation that was not my own.'[13]

Mullik had in Walter Bell a British friend who both respected and trusted him, while Bell had in Mullik a key source at the heart of the Indian state. As Bell reported to his head office, Mullik was 'an exceptional man, both personally and in the position which he had, the fount of all knowledge that I wanted'.[14]

On a personal front, Walter and Tattie warmed to expatriate life in India. They were housed in a comfortable, well-staffed and comfortable residence from the days of British imperial rule, well insulated from the abject poverty that many Indians lived in. Bell nonetheless got to know India in its socio-economic, political and diplomatic complexity, not just in New Delhi, but travelling the country to other Indian cities for meetings with local sources and Indian security officials. A typical example was Calcutta, once considered the hotbed of Indian nationalism.

Walter and Tattie enjoyed the local hospitality provided by the Indian civil service and political and intellectual class. The Indians they befriended were always generous with food and never in a hurry. The Bells never tired of exploring the diverse geography as well as culinary delights of the country, along with its exuberant vegetation and its rich cultural history, architecture and iconography, from the mosques and forts of New Delhi to the ancient South India temples and grand ruins from the Mughal era.

Bell found Indians could be wonderfully indiscreet with their information, while Tattie later claimed that it was while living in India that she discovered she was a 'natural Hindu',[15] developing an enduring commitment to vegetarian food (and whenever possible a macrobiotic diet), and finding herself drawn to the tolerance implied in Hinduism's philosophy.

On the diplomatic, intelligence and military front, Bell's Indian posting included keeping abreast with regional tensions beyond India's borders, coinciding as it did with a key period of the Cold War years that saw the US's post-war emergence as a world power confronting the threat of two communist powers, the Soviet Union and China. Southeast Asia was embroiled in an enduring and unresolved struggle between great power ambitions, no more so than in Korea where, in June 1950, North Korea, supplied and advised by the Soviet Union and supported by China, invaded the South.

The United Nations, with the US as principal participant, joined the war on the side of South Korea, where a war lasting from 1950 to 1953 became part of a generations-long fight still haunting contemporary events and shaping modern America's relationship to the world. The Korean War was agitated on the US home front by the Wisconsin Republican senator Joseph McCarthy after blaming failures in American foreign policy on communist infiltration.[16]

While in India, Bell travelled discreetly to Singapore to what were almost certainly secret liaison meetings with other colleagues in the region. He also visited Thailand, where American friends were stepping up their propaganda efforts to publicise US accomplishments, emphasise communist threats, and draw in 'joint efforts' among its allies in the region to 'preserve freedom and cultural integrity'.[17]

After the Bells left New Delhi, Walter continued to keep in touch with his influential Indian friends. Among them was the Indian civil servant and high court judge Gopal Das Khosla, who believed the Americans should be more tolerant of Nehru's non-alignment. The Cambridge and Lincoln's Inn educated Khosla wrote to Bell in January 1956 claiming that the US was misreading India as pro-Soviet:

> We are not pro-communist in the sense that we embrace their ideology, or we would be prepared to toe the line with them. Unfortunately, the Americans think that if we are not with them 100 per cent, we are against them. You were long enough in India to see that the Hindu conception of life and our ethics are wholly opposed to communism. We cannot be so ruthless and restless as the Russians. We want peace not only for ourselves but for everyone. The welcome we gave the Russians would be given to the President of USA should he come here. No-one is more willing to make friends with the USA than Nehru, but why will the Americans make it a condition precedent that we become hostile to Russia?[18]

Bell also continued to correspond privately, years after he had left India, with his similarly anglophile friend General Jayanto Nath Chaudhuri, a recipient of the Order of the British Empire (OBE) award for his engagement in Anglo-Indian relations. Chaudhuri rose through the Indian military hierarchy under Nehru before being appointed chief of the army staff. He and Bell developed a shared interest in Cold War geopolitics, decolonisation and the fate of independent states that had been part of the British Empire.

Chaudhuri was happy to share his views about disputed territories with Bell. In a letter he wrote to Walter in 1965, he reported that the India–Pakistan hostilities over Kashmir – the result of the 'small war' between them – had unified and strengthened India while 'taking some of the bounce out of Pakistan'. China was 'knocking at our frontiers' which was 'irritating' and 'more to show that she can do it that for any more serious reason'. Meanwhile Africa looked as if it was going to be the new 'hot spot' because of Rhodesia's moves towards a unilateral declaration of independence and the growing democratic demands for power of the African majority in the colony.

Chaudhuri told Bell of his belief that Africans were 'trying to advance too fast' and this risked 'anarchy or military government'. He would have been aware that his spy friend might pass something of what he shared as information to the British government but had complete faith in him. He always signed his letters to Walter as 'Muchhu', the nickname he was given as a young trainee officer at Sandhurst owing to the moustache he sported throughout his military career. The scribbled signature was a sign of familiarity and trust.

Chaudhuri's private correspondence with Bell reflected the pro-Western sympathies of a professional soldier and a student of, as well a player in, the geopolitics of the Cold War. He proudly told Walter that on his appointment as army chief he was 'inundated with letters from British ex staff sergeants and NCOs to Generals, all of whom offered their services in defending India or building up the Indian Army'.[19] He counted on UK as well as US support, while still finding, as he put it, 'a good measure of friendship and understanding' in the Soviet Union as well. He continued to believe that India's interests during the Cold War were best served by a non-alignment policy.

Another enduring friendship Bell made in India was with Louis Heren, the London *Times* veteran foreign correspondent. Heren had joined the newspaper in the 1930s, aged fourteen, as a messenger boy and got his first reporting assignment for the paper in 1937 when he covered the street parties in the East End of his birthplace in celebration of the coronation of George VI.

Heren's experience of India dated from World War Two when he volunteered for the Royal Artillery and served there after France, Iceland and Greenland. After the war he returned to *The Times* as a reporter and in 1947 covered India's independence, Partition, and the savage riots that followed in the Punjab, during which he developed his critical view about the country's politics and the flawed nature of Indian democracy. In 1950 *The Times* correspondent Ian Morrison was killed in the Korean War, and Heren was sent out to replace him. He became the South Asia correspondent, based in Singapore, covering the Malayan emergency and the travails of collapsing imperialism in the Dutch East Indies, the Philippines and French Indochina, where he met Graham Greene and inspired passages in Greene's novel *The Quiet American*.[20]

Heren's second spell in India during 1953 to 1955 coincided with Bell's MI5 posting. An intrepid reporter, he was a rough diamond cast from a tough working-class East London childhood, a 'cockney radical' who had made his way in one of the leading newspapers in the world through sheer hard work and courage.[21] He was quick to identify Bell as a security and intelligence professional with a mind of his own, not afraid to share his criticism of policy and authority with those he felt would not betray him. Heren found little difficulty in winning Bell's trust, sharing his experience of India and tips from his sources while Bell reciprocated with background (strictly not for attribution) insights and information of his own.

Heren would later look back on the 1950s as the nascent Indian independent state's confident years, a brief golden age during which Nehru trod the national and international stage with elegance and assurance and the civil servants shared that assurance – and yet the society was deeply flawed. Alongside the embrace of the centralised bureaucracy run by officials who been sent to Moscow to learn the techniques of Gosplan (the agency responsible for central economic planning in the Soviet Union) lay a country of poverty-stricken peasants and naked fakirs, of technological backwardness and superstition. As Heren later recalled in his autobiography, his reporting of what he saw as the schizophrenia of becoming a member of both an elite and backward society unsurprisingly angered the Indian government.[22]

Bell was party to an incident illustrating the extent to which Heren's coverage of Indian politics was a matter of diplomatic concern. A transcript of a 'political' meeting chaired by Sir Alexander Clutterbuck, the British high commissioner in Delhi, and attended by Bell had Heren high on the agenda. The meeting heard a report of Heren's stormy relations with one of India's most prestigious and politically influential journalists, Prem Bhatia, who the English journalist had accused of being a lackey of the Nehru government and possibly a communist. The dispute was rustling government feathers. 'Prem Bhatia is upset because Louis Heren asked if he could see his [Communist]Party card – Bhatia may decide not to play in the cricket match on Sunday,' reported a minuted note of the meeting.[23]

The report seemed to reflect not just Heren's important status as *The Times* correspondent, but the growing political tensions provoked by Indian's strategic importance in the deepening Cold War. 'Not very encouraging, is it?' remarked the high commissioner, before asking Bell if he had anything further to report. 'No, my friends have said nothing this week,' Bell replied, with what one imagines was an undisguised touch of irony as the information about Bhatia had come from his friend Heren. [24]

Further postings awaited Bell before he and Heren converged again in London. Bell retained an enduring interest in the politics of India, a country he understood better than those who saw it simply as another battleground of the Cold War given the Soviet Union's growing military and trade links with the country. 'My years in India were something ... my wife and I liked the country and got to know a large circle of people with whom we have kept up since,' Bell wrote to a friend after his departure from New Delhi.[25]

# 26
# MI5 HQ

In early 1957, following his posting in India, Bell returned to London and served on a year's attachment as private secretary to Roger Hollis, who a year earlier had been appointed the new MI5 director general. Harold Macmillan had been appointed prime minister, and his son-in-law, Bell's old political contact Julian Amery, been given his first government post as under secretary of state for war.

In January 1957, in the aftermath of Anthony Eden's resignation over the Suez Crisis, Bell marked the occasion by writing a handwritten personal letter to Amery, the text of which suggested he had lost none of his ability to network at the heart of government. He seemed confident enough in his friendship with Amery to drop a jokey veiled reference about the minister's reputation for political outspokenness and how he might have to control it given his personal link to the prime minister though marriage to his daughter. 'This is just to offer congratulations from us both on your new appointment and to wish you every success. I hope that in time you will find it possible to temper your disapproval of my country-in-law [sic)]'[1] Within a year Amery had been made under secretary of state for the colonies as Bell moved to a new posting in the West Indies.

During Bell's time at MI5 headquarters, he and Tattie lived at Number 6 Onslow Square, the flat they had moved into between overseas postings to be closer to the Oratory, a very traditional Roman Catholic church that Walter began to frequent as a convert.

Family members who remained Anglican would struggle to come to terms with Bell's conversion to Rome and his apparent embracing of the most staunchly doctrinal 'papist' churches in the English capital. As his youngest and favourite nephew Jasper recalled many years later. 'Walter obviously had problems with his faith. The Anglican Church was a very broad one and as it turned out too much for Walter. He obviously became happier on joining the Roman Catholics.'[2]

Bell spent most of 1957 at the heart of the British security establishment at MI5's Mayfair headquarters, Leconfield House, just a short walk away from where MI6 was then located on Curzon Street and also within easy distance of the clubland where spies of his vintage networked. His appointment to MI5 HQ came at a time when Britain's perspective of herself and her place in the world had been deeply affected by the Suez Crisis,[3] which, with the added excuse of ill-health, had led to the resignation of Anthony Eden in early January 1957 and his replacement as prime minister by Harold Macmillan.

If the history of Britain's international relations since World War Two was essentially 'a story of inflated ambition and diminished circumstance', as argued by the *Financial Times* journalist Philip Stephens, then Suez was a moment of truth when it became painfully clear that Britain was no longer a world power that could afford to launch a major operation overseas to protect its vital interests against the will of the US. 'It also demonstrated the limits of the Commonwealth as a source of British power, when the majority of members, including India, opposed the UK over Suez at the United Nations.'[4] Nevertheless, the Cold War role of British secret security and intelligence emerged reinforced after the Suez Crisis, which unfolded as Soviet tanks rolled into Hungary in early November 1956 to crush an uprising against Moscow's domination.

Bell's time at Roger Hollis's side coincided with a period during which MI5 as an organisation was developing a focus on tracking potential communist threats within the UK. A recurring theme on the subject had been laid out in a secret MI5 memorandum circulated in the early summer of 1956 suggesting that the Communist Party of Great Britain (CPGB), supported by Moscow, had a strategy of using industrial strikes as a way of strengthening power and influence in the trade union movement. MI5's reporting was praised at the highest level of government, with Hollis being told that his organisation's reputation 'stood very high' within Whitehall.[5]

While MI5's star was on the rise, MI6 was in the government's bad books. The secret intelligence service had been deeply embarrassed by the bungled operation undertaken on its behalf by a Royal Navy lieutenant commander pioneer scuba diver and expert in the removal of underwater munition called Lionel ('Buster') Crabb, who is believed to have died – probably murdered by Russian frogmen – after diving to secretly inspect a Soviet warship in Portsmouth Harbour during the visit of the Soviet leaders Nikita Khrushchev and Nikolai Bulganin.[6]

Hollis, a former deputy director general, had been promoted after his chief Dick White was moved to head up MI6 with a brief to improve its operations after the Crabb debacle. White had originally chosen Hollis as his deputy at MI5, thanks to his reputation for having been foremost within the Security Service in foreseeing the post-war threat from Soviet espionage and communist subversion.[7]

Bell had forged a mutual professional respect as well as an enduring friendship with White as he had done with another senior MI5 official, Guy Liddell, who had taken early retirement from the service in 1953. Exactly why Bell came to be appointed as Personal Assistant (PADG) to Hollis remains unclear from available sources, but it is likely that it counted on White's blessing because of his record as an MI6 and MI5 officer.

Bell found Hollis more reserved and less clubbable than either White or Liddell, and also less intelligent.[8] As we shall see, when in later years Hollis and, separately Guy Liddell, emerged in newspaper reports and books as suspect Russian 'moles' Bell organised a campaign with White in their defence.

Bell emerged from his year working with Hollis without giving any cause for suspicion about his own loyalties. In December 1957, as he reached the end of a year in MI5 headquarters, he received a letter from his friend Bill Magan, one of MI5's most experienced and respected officers, congratulating him on his latest promotion. 'Your personality, stability, good humour, and sound sense have been a major influence for good both within the service and with many of our associates outside.... I am sure you will be carrying on the good work to excellent purpose in the Caribbean.'[9]

Bell's appointment to another overseas posting, this time in the British West Indies, had the full approval of the MI5 chief Hollis, who was to remain at the helm of the Security Service for another eight years, navigating turbulent waters. Hollis would impress Whitehall by sanctioning new electronic surveillance techniques although his tenure was overshadowed by various spy scandals compounded by the Profumo affair and allegations that MI5 had experienced hostile penetration.[10]

In 1963 Hollis authorised a secret investigation into his own deputy, Graham Mitchell, on what turned out to be an unfounded suspicion of being a Soviet agent. A series of inconclusive mole-hunting exercises covered a range of other possible culprits including Hollis himself although the claim that he was a Russian spy, while making front-page news in Britain, was never substantiated and was ultimately rejected.[11]

During the year he spent at his side, Bell formed his own view of Hollis as a plodding bureaucrat, less personable than other colleagues in MI6 and MI5 he knew, and a no better spy as a result of it. When, years later, he was asked over an informal lunch with close friends whether he thought Hollis might have worked for the Russians, Bell answered that he lacked the social and intellectual skills to be an efficient enemy agent.[12] Working closely with Hollis as his private secretary nonetheless did Walter Bell's career no harm, with his pension rights guaranteed as an established MI5 officer in Kenya and India.

Correspondence he had kept among his private papers with the US embassy and the Foreign Office relating to controversial circumstances of his award of the US Medal of Freedom were dutifully handed by Bell to John Marriott, MI5's head of personnel on 1 July 1957. They were returned to him by MI5, at his request, on the 18 August 1967 after Bell was appointed to the Most Distinguished Order of Saint Michael and Saint George (CMG), on his retirement from government service, with no apparent blemish on his record but rather given one of the highest honours for rendering extraordinary or important civilian service in a foreign country, and in relation to foreign and Commonwealth affairs.

In 1957 Bell was entering the final decade of his career in government service. Rather than being drawn further into head office management and Whitehall bureaucracy which ill-suited his restless personality, Bell had Hollis agreeing to cut him loose from MI5 HQ and trust him with a new assignment abroad with responsibility for MI5's operations in the Caribbean based initially in Kingston, Jamaica, and then in Trinidad. The posting was one that gave MI5 lead status over MI6 for security and intelligence, in a deceptively stable part of the fading British Empire.

# 27
# A Caribbean Assignment

During the years 1957–1960 Bell was appointed main liaison officer for MI5 in the West Indies, first with the government of Jamaica, then, from December 1957, in Trinidad with the governor general to the West Indies Federation.

The period of Bell's posting had him wrestling with the controversial creation of the ill-fated West Indies Federation, an internally federal state of ten island provinces, all British colonial colonies, including Jamaica, Trinidad, Tobago and Barbados. Bell had his work cut out as an informal intermediary with key political figures in a failed attempt to make the federation work as an alternative to direct colonial rule.

The new posting got off to an inauspicious start. 'We have been sweating in this exhausting place for two months…not that much has happened apart from droughts and railway accidents', he wrote.[1] Thus did he convey his first impressions of Kingston, Jamaica, an island that had achieved some political notoriety on 24 November 1956, the day British Prime Minister Sir Anthony Eden had arrived by air from London for a three-week holiday. As widely reported at the time Eden was doing so on the advice of his doctors as he was suffering from 'severe overstrain'. He was in the midst of a political crisis threatening the future of his Conservative government over Suez.

Looking somewhat drawn after the overnight trans-Atlantic flight, Eden was, along with his wife, met on arrival by Governor Sir Hugh Foot. 'The party left immediately for the Golden Eye resort where Eden will recuperate from the hectic months of the Suez crisis.'[2] Far from recovering, Eden would quit as prime minister just over a month later.

And yet Bell's Caribbean escape from his desk job in one of the inner sanctums of Whitehall (the MI5 director general's office) was to prove rather more enduring – a far from dull chapter in his career, with his intelligence and security work embroiling him in political intrigue under his diplomatic cover of 'liaison duties'.

The West Indian Federation was established in January 1958, just months after Bell's arrival, with the expressed intention of creating a political unit of all the British colonised islands in the region. The idea behind it was that the islands would become independent from Britain as a single state while still retaining strong links with their old colonial master. It was a test case of the review made by Harold Macmillan (Eden's successor) of Britain's position in the world, based, post-Suez, on 'soft power' rather than 'hard power' , on discreet persuasion rather than coercion or repression.[3] The residual colonialist federation project in the Caribbean was doomed by[4] political squabbling and collapsed in May 1962, over a year after Bell's departure.

As Bell reported, on arriving in the capital Kingston in late 1957, Jamaica was in a 'curious phase of development'. Many Jamaicans believed that the island could and should seek independence and Bell agreed with them. He was not best pleased with the comments that Sir Hugh Foot, one of Britain's senior colonial diplomats, had made to the local media, on ending his sixth post as governor in chief of Jamaica that year, when he said there was no racial discrimination on the island. 'He was talking nonsense…blind to realities', Bell noted.[5]

Two months into his own posting Bell had been made only too aware of the enduring racism that imbued certain colonial attitudes: 'The sort of White Jamaican women with red, kinky hair, reminded us of Kenya settlers. One should not exaggerate it, but it [racism] does exist, and I am sure that Norman Manley[6] and his like suffer a strong colour resentment.'[7] Bell thought there was no risk of serious political instability – 'the local communist movement is insignificant' – although he did not underestimate Jamaica's socio-economic problems. 'The worst feature of this island is the low calibre of labour and the general fickleness due, I suppose, to ignorance, poverty, under-employment, a very relaxing climate, and the tendency for the more energetic and enterprising to emigrate'.[8]

With an earlier history in the region linked to slavery, having been a sleepy colonial slum for a hundred years or so, Jamaica was rapidly turning into a rich man's holiday resort, with support for big investment to extract the large reserves of bauxite. There were fortunes to be made in property speculation and tourism as there was no tax on capital projects, as Bell discovered on a visit to Montego Bay. It was there that he met a talented young Jamaican by the name of John Pringle – 'by far the brightest person whom we have met so far'– who was extending the grounds of the lush tropical resort of Round Hill along a private bay of turquoise waters.[9] Early on in his posting, Bell had made contact and befriended one of the most influential and best-informed businessmen in the Caribbean.

John's grandfather had emigrated as a doctor from Scotland to the Caribbean and played a central role in the creation of Jamaica as a holiday destination in colonial times, initially as founder of the one of the great post-war hotels, Round Hill, and then as the country's director of tourism. The subsequent collapse of sugar prices and the squandering of family money on horse-racing threatened financial problems – but tourism provided a lifeline.

John Pringle was only thirty-one years old and well on his way to restoring his family fortune when Bell met him. The family-owned fashionable hotel drew celebrity friends such as the Duke of Sutherland and the jockey Steve Donoghue and served as a model for the young Pringle when, aged twenty-six, he began to plan his own establishment on the island's beautiful north shore.

A 110-acre private enclave with luxury cottages and a central hotel was destined to be one of the Caribbean's prime boutique destinations. As his newspaper obituary noted:

> Pringle proposed to sell the cottages to individual stakeholders, thus raising the money for their

construction. His first stroke of luck was to find himself next to Noël Coward on a flight to New York. Pringle pestered him with photographs until, in desperation, Coward grasped his knee and said: 'If you'll only stop boring me, I'll buy one of your effing cottages.' The next day Pringle sold a second to Adele Astaire.[10]

Opened by Coward in 1953, four years before Bell took up his post, Round Hill would play host to such celebrities as President John F. Kennedy, Grace Kelly, Alfred Hitchcock, Paul Newman and Clark Gable. Its many claims to fame included the facts that Cole Porter sang in the bar, and that Rodgers and Hammerstein worked on *The Sound of Music* there.[11]

Other visitors to Round Hill included Princess Margaret, whose reputation as a loose royal cannon struggling to break free from the steely self-discipline of the House of Windsor posed a potential problem that threatened to land in Bell's in-tray of potential storms that he might be expected to anticipate and, if possible, control. He took the prospect with a characteristic long-held irreverence towards the sense of entitlement he saw at the heart of the British establishment. When it came to commenting to colleagues on Her Royal Highness's reputation for attracting media interest, Bell was sardonic. 'Last time she [Princess Margaret] came to Barbados the police had an awful time trying to stop journalists from taking photographs of her in a bathing suit. They came around the corner in boats, in every sort of disguise and the police were nearly driven demented. I should have thought she looked all right in a bath-dress, but perhaps they thought that cameras contained concealed weapons,' he reported.[12]

By contrast Bell considered Pringle a source worth cultivating, a personable bon vivant who not only knew how to throw a good party but was also well informed on local politics and its main players. Pringle was a childhood friend of Michael Manley, scion of the Jamaican political dynasty who was destined to succeed his father Norman as the leader of the leftist People's National Party (PNP) and prime minister. He believed in foreign investment and the potential of White and Black working together as the best way of empowering Jamaica, as well an enriching himself. Pringle's services to British interests gained him a CBE in 1965 in addition to the Order of Jamaica.

Soon after arriving on the island Bell's MI5 work led him to an early meeting with Norman Manley, who had been appointed chief minister two years earlier. He was one of the local politicians who needed to be persuaded that the federation was going to work in Jamaica's best interests. 'I took a great liking to him, and I hope that he did not view me too dimly,' Bell reflected later.[13]

British interests lay in ensuring that Jamaica's politicians felt that the federation was a genuine step towards independence but in a loose association with its colonial master that would benefit it in socio-economic terms and minimise the risk of any radical rupture with London, let alone any violent outcome from its moves to self-government.

Bell thought Norman Manley – a left-wing socialist by conviction but not a communist – was someone who needed careful handling, a potential adversary who could become an ally in the strategic chess game of the Cold War and the twilight of the British Empire. 'My strong impression was that his one idea is to get rid of all Whitehall control as soon as possible – but he also talked of "Dominion" status and did not regard this as a term of inferiority as the Asians do'.[14] Drawing on his Indian experience where he had advised the former empire's most populated nascent democratic nascent independent state on security, Bell went on to define Manley as 'much the same as Nehru – a strong anti-Communist, a man who will respect your confidence, but be cooperative and friendly provided that the objective [of independence] is not questioned.'[15]

Bell had acute observational and analytical skills – the kind of qualities he put to good use in MI6 and MI5. His private papers show that he had little time for the enduring colonial dinosaurs who struggled to resist relinquishing imperial rule – 'a number of "Blimps" at the end of their service…thoroughly unsettled by the sundown', as he recorded privately.[16]

While in the Caribbean he nonetheless renewed contact with an old friend, the archetypal Conservative from the 'God and Empire' school, the soon-to-be-appointed cabinet minister Julian Amery. The two men exchanged intelligence on suspected communists in British Guiana (later Guyana) when Amery visited the British mainland West Indies on the north-east coast of South America as the newly appointed parliamentary under secretary of state at the British Colonial Office in June 1959.

British Guiana, once explored in the sixteenth century by Sir Walter Raleigh, was in its final years a potentially volatile outpost of disputed British colonial rule. The small state, which since the 1940s had been campaigning for self-government and ultimately independence, had been growing in geo-political significance, with the US pressuring the British to resist any communist influence there.

On Amery's return to London he received a letter marked 'secret and personal' from Bell on the subject of the colony's controversial politician Cheddi Jagan. The son of a foreman on a sugar-cane plantation, Jagan became a trade union activist after studying dentistry in the US and, with his American-born wife, established British Guiana's modern political party, the People's Progressive Party (PPP), becoming the country's first prime minister in 1953.

Inspired by Nehru's anti-colonial writings, both Jagan and his wife held openly Marxist views and appealed to the ethnic Indian community in British Guiana who made up half the population. Jagan introduced a radical socio-economic programme in the midst of strikes and popular demonstrations.[17]

Jagan's first term in office lasted a short time. Under pressure from Washington he was removed from power after the British suspended the constitution, declared a state of emergency, and intervened militarily, with the governor assuming direct rule, under the authority of the British Colonial Office. Winston Churchill, who was in his second period as prime minister, justified Jagan's overthrow by claiming, as did the CIA, that the PPP government had threatened to turn British Guiana into a 'Communist-dominated state'.[18]

In 1957 the PPP was elected to power again and Jagan pursued moderate policies of socio-economic reform as the new government's minister of trade and industry since there was no prime ministerial position. But fears of communist influences in the colony persisted within the British government and in Washington.[19]

Amery told Bell when they met up in the West Indies a year later that he believed Jagan (and by association also his US-born wife and close political ally Janet Rosenberg) was a 'Soviet agent' – a description that Bell, as MI5 head of station for the Caribbean, disputed. As Bell told Amery, the term 'agent' suggested that Jagan was in the service and pay of the Soviet Union or some other Iron Curtain source, which he believed was not the case. He wrote to Amery:

> It is more accurate to describe the Jagans as communists or communist sympathisers. 'Agent' means to me somebody who is under the control of a principle to whom he reports, and from whom he receives instructions. There is no evidence whatever that the Jagans are in this category. Like similar communist sympathisers in other parts of the world, they correspond with like-minded friends, they seek advice from people whom they feel would be able to help them in working out their local solutions, and they generally serve the communist cause as best they may. But to our knowledge, there is nobody who is telling them what to do.[20]

Bell went on to say there was no evidence that the Jagans were in receipt of any covert financial support from outside

British Guiana that Amery suspected came from Moscow. Instead, Bell reported, they were financing their activities by the 'ordinary methods' of party dues, and contributions from their ministerial salaries.

The Jagans had visited behind the Iron Curtain when first in power in the early 1950s. As Bell told Amery, there was strong evidence of communist sympathies, and yet he insisted that it 'would not be right to attach more significance to them than meets the eye'. As he put it: 'Naturally, it provided them [the Jagans]with a good opportunity to consort with birds of a like feather, but there has been no subsequent evidence that anything more sinister developed in consequence.'[21] Amery responded, reassuring Bell that there was no fundamental disagreement between them in terms of intelligence assessment. 'I do not think there is more between us than a mild difference in semantics, between a professional and a politician.'[22]

His comment was in fact an understatement of the wide gulf that existed between Amery and Bell in terms of how they perceived British Guiana's role in the Cold War. Amery remained convinced that the Jagans did correspond with individuals and organisations, more particularly in Britain and the US, which were communist, or communist infiltrated. 'Whether they receive more money that we know about it's hard to tell,' Amery told Bell, while adding that he thought the Jagans had at the very least built up a 'rudimentary network of contacts so that if for any reason they needed outside help or advice they would know who to turn to'.

Amery thought it best not to confront Bell further, judging – correctly, as it turned out – that it was the view of the politician not the spy that would prevail when it came to government policy. Instead, Amery signed off on a note of reassuring intimacy suggesting he valued his friendship with Bell and his wife Tattie: 'It was splendid seeing you both again. Do please say when you are back in London.'[23]

This exchange of letters, tucked away in Amery's personal papers held in the Churchill Archives Centre, provides a fascinating insight into the relationship between the two men and the politically controversial intelligence reporting of the Cold War which, in the case of British Guiana, struggled to prevail when it came to informing government action.

Bell was at odds with the American state department, the CIA and British officials within the Colonial Office on the issue of British Guiana. He was not a lone wolf in this, but very much reflecting intelligence that MI5 had developed since the late 1940s as a result of its surveillance of the British Communist Party and Jagan and his wife's contacts with it.

Walter's assessment was that although Jagan was certainly Marxist, and his wife was known to have been a member of the US Communist Party in her native Chicago, there was no hard evidence of affiliation with a communist state, let alone financing by one. [24] Jagan was, in Bell's view, 'above all a nationalist, albeit one who spoke in a Marxist language'. London and Washington ignored and sidelined MI5 and chose a less nuanced version of the facts that suited their political and strategic Cold War needs.[25]

Ignoring British intelligence and security assessments, the US State Department and the CIA launched a series of covert activities to destabilise Jagan after he had won the October 1961 elections leading to his replacement by Forbes Burnham, Washington's anti-communist protégé. Forbes Burnham went on to rule the independent Guyana for more than twenty years, during which he showed himself to be both corrupt and incompetent.[26]

In Port of Spain, the capital of Trinidad and Tobago, where Bell moved from Kingston, Jamaica, and based himself as MI5's security liaison officer (SLO) for the whole of the British West Indies, Bell reported that it had a reputation of being 'less relaxing than Jamaica – it could certainly not be more so'. He went on: 'I am told that in Trinidad it is one long cocktail party called a "jump up". We are all getting too old for that kind of thing, perhaps it can be tactfully avoided.'[27]

These views were contained in a long private memo Bell wrote to Patrick Buchan-Hepburn, 1st Baron Hailes, the governor general of the West Indies Federation who became a close friend of Bell's, considering him his eyes and ears, more in touch with local feeling than some of the colonial officials on his staff. Bell maintained a regular private correspondence with Buchan-Hepburn that was separate from official communications. In a letter of October 1958 he was full of admiration for what he saw as Buchan-Hepburn's diplomatic and political skills since he had taken on the post of governor general the previous January, in trying to overcome the 'stiff relationship between coloured and white people' which made it difficult for a newcomer to penetrate.

Bell believed that the federation offered an opportunity to overcome old barriers because it constituted a fresh start. 'But the opportunity had to be taken at once, and this, to me, is where Your Excellency has achieved a great triumph by the exercise of great imagination and also a display of genuine warmth towards West Indians which most British people find it hard to display, even if they entertain it.'[28]

Bell fed Buchan-Hepburn regular intelligence on local political leaders who the British had found it difficult to engage with on an official level. One of the more intriguing back-channels Bell maintained was with the influential Trinidadian socialist C. L. R. James. The two men met in Trinidad after October 1958, when James was appointed editor of *The Nation*, the pro-independence People's National Movement (PNM) newspaper, with the personal blessing of the PNM leader and chief minister Eric Williams. Both were advocates of the West Indies Federation but were destined to fall out as the project fell apart.

James was a radical bon vivant, a gifted author and historian with a background in revolutionary politics and an astute commentator on cricket[29] – a multifaceted personality of a kind that spies are trained to unpick. By the early years of the Cold War, and the anti-communist era of McCarthyism, James was suspected of being a subversive by the FBI. In the early summer of 1952, he had his application for citizenship rejected by the US immigration authorities and was detained in Ellis Island, with other communists, pending an appeal against deportation. In July 1953 he voluntarily decided to sail back to England, where he had lived during the 1930s. There he continued to lead a life of political activism and writing, not least on cricket which was his sporting passion.

Exactly when the British came to consider James an ally and potential agent of influence is not clear, but a significant gesture of engagement came in the spring of 1958, when he received a telegram from the governor general inviting him to Trinidad for the inauguration of the West Indies Federal Parliament.

James's return to his birthplace after a quarter of a century abroad mystified a majority of Trinidadians, and even the few who knew more about him considered him an enigma.

In his earlier days, James had taught Eric Williams, the future chief minister, history and English at the prestigious Queen's Royal College, the island's oldest non-Catholic secondary school in the 1920s. James was rumoured to be the *eminence grise* come home to advise his protégé.[30]

Walter Bell had first heard of James when they were both in New York in the late 1930s. He and other colleagues in MI5 had tracked his more recent movements in Africa. In 1957 James had travelled to the Gold Coast to celebrate the coming into existence of the new independent nation of Ghana under Kwame Nkrumah, whose ambition was to be the originator of a distinct Pan-African socialist political philosophy. Four years earlier, in 1953, the then deputy director general of MI5 Roger Hollis had submitted an overall assessment about communism in African colonies, reporting that the threat was not significant. In the case of the Gold Coast, MI5 persistently played down the communist threat posed by Nkrumah in Ghana and formulated a process of careful intelligence management as the colony moved towards independence and beyond.[31]

Bell had been part of a similar process in India and was now counting on James's support when he returned to Trinidad in the latest British attempt to control the process of decolonisation. With the support of Eric Williams, James was given an early political role, when he was made secretary of the West Indies Federal Labour Party (WILFP), a group of socialist parties across the West Indies islands.[32] The position had him visiting and meeting up with political contacts in various West Indies territories, which also fell under Bell's remit, including the politically controversial British Guiana. James spent three weeks there, during which he encouraged solidarity between Black and Indian citizens who he believed would benefit from the federation. Such visits increased James's value to the British as a well-informed source and someone they could trust politically.

The signs looked promising when James within weeks of his arrival had publicly toned down his radicalism, editing *The Nation* as a general interest rather than simply propagandist vehicle, while reigniting his literary interests and the West Indies' sense of cultural self-worth through fellow Trinidadians of international stature such as V.S. Naipaul.[33] But by the summer of 1959 the survival of the federation was being threatened by political rivalries. In one of their secret meetings James gave Bell detailed information of the personal conflict that was threatening the federation – that between Eric Williams and Sir Grantley Herbert Adams, the founder of the Barbados Labour Party, who had become the federation's first prime minister.

James warned Bell that Williams was under pressure from a growing section of their party, the PNM, to split from the federation and push for independence without deferring to the British. Although Williams was willing to consider serving in a federal government under Jamaica's chief minister Norman Manley, the federal ministers under Herbert Adams were 'clinging to the position at all costs because they know that if Trinidad and Jamaica get together their careers as important people would be finished'.[34]

In an attempt to try and find a solution James, with Buchan-Hepburn's blessing, arranged for Williams to have a follow up one-to one meeting with Bell over a private dinner at the MI5 officer's home. However, Bell found Williams in no mood to be persuaded to eat humble pie and engage constructively with Adams, his number one political enemy. He noted: 'I understood the importance from the West Indies point of view, and indeed the future of multi-racial societies, that everything should be done to try to salvage the Federation. He quite agreed but could not see how this could be effected.'[35]

Bell wanted to believe, as his friend James did, that the federation might in time grant powers of independent taxation and a genuine customs union in the region leading to a real West Indian nation, but he knew that he was trying to sell a project that had been badly executed and was politically unworkable.

Williams was viewed by the British as a troublesome politician with a chip on his shoulder – but part of the problem was the cautious attitude adopted by the colonial administration which they thought could accommodate their own inaction, much to Buchan-Hepburn's frustration. However hopeless his mission was, Bell tried his best to maintain a channel of communication with influential Jamaicans.

Bell had another source he got to know well in Theodore Sealy, the influential editor of Jamaica's leading daily newspaper *The Gleaner*. Over lunch early in December 1958, Bell shared with Sealy his belief that 'it would be a tragedy if the Federation failed because race relations in the West Indies compared so favourably with the United States and elsewhere.'[36]

A letter Buchan-Hepburn wrote to Bell in September 1960 after he had departed from the Caribbean – 'now that you have got out of this soggy climate, I am sure you will feel very ready for fresh fields' – showed just how much in his former adviser's debt the governor general felt. 'I do not know how to begin to thank you for all you did to help me, both with your friendship, and advice and support in official affairs. It is hard to put oneself back nearly three years, but I do know that when I was making my way, and not being helped very much by some, it just made the whole difference you being there,' Buchan-Hepburn wrote.[37]

The West Indies Federation came into existence in

January 1958 with the hope of a unified consensual approach to post-colonial arrangements. It fell apart because of constitutional and taxation disagreements, competing insular nationalisms and political feuds between influential local party leaders that Bell had anticipated but was unable to reconcile.

The federation proved a bold if short-lived constitutional experiment, effectively ending in late May 1962. By then C.L.R James's influence at the heart of Trinidadian politics had come to an end, with his 'protégé' Williams failing to support him when his rivals accused him of the alleged financial mismanagement of *The Nation* at the PNM's annual convention in March 1960 and a year later cast him aside. In April 1961 James and his wife Selma suffered a bad car accident during a lecture tour to Jamaica. They were offered all the care they needed by their old friend Norman Manley and remained in Jamaica until October to recuperate, long enough to see the ill-fated constitutional dream that was the federation crushed.

The federation's collapse followed a referendum in Jamaica that passed with 54 per cent of the vote in favour of political secession from the federation despite the opposition of Norman Manley, the province's premier at the time. Manley himself lost the subsequent island elections in April 1962, and Alexander Bustamante of the Democratic Labour Party became the first prime minister of an independent Jamaica on 6 August 1962. Two days later James and his wife Selma set sail for England, without waiting to see, two weeks later, Trinidad becoming independent from Britain under Eric Williams.

Bell returned to England and a new challenge. It involved a new posting abroad, back to Kenya, on a highly sensitive mission to ensure a peaceful transfer of power to a new government headed by the man once demonised by White settlers as a terrorist, Jomo Kenyatta.

# 28
# Kenya, Part 2

Bell's second posting in Kenya began in 1961 and elicited warm letters of congratulation led by two colleagues he had worked in different stages of his post-war career with MI5: the director general Roger Hollis and one of the agency's longest serving and most experienced operational directors, Bill Magan.

The following years would prove a challenging time reputationally for British intelligence with the fall-out from the defections of Burgess, Maclean, Philby and George Blake raising questions about the loyalties of MI5 and MI6 officers, and with Hollis the most senior British official to be publicly accused of being a traitor, a suspicion that lingered long after he died in 1971. Of Hollis and Magan, it was Magan who Bell always professionally respected the most, and enjoyed as better company, finding Hollis a grey and uninspiring character, who, he believed, had never betrayed his country and even if he had been a traitor, would have bungled it.

While Hollis was never much liked within MI5, Magan by contrast was not just popular, but considered a safe pair of hands who could be entrusted with the most delicate of assignments. Magan was a year younger than Bell, and five years Hollis's junior. He outlived all his contemporaries and died in January 2010, aged 101. He was remembered for a virtually unblemished record of heroic exploits in military intelligence in World War Two, and extensive security work in Palestine during the final days of the British mandate and other colonial hot spots such as Malaya, Kenya, Borneo, Aden and Cyprus, where he was personally involved in locating the likely hideout of the terrorist leader Col. Georgios Grivas.[1]

Hollis wrote to Bell: 'I am delighted by your promotion. You have a distinguished and exceptional career in your overseas postings. I have a feeling that your next one will not be without its difficulties, but I am sure that you will again make a thoroughly constructive contribution whenever there is even the hint of an opportunity to do so.'[2]

Magan wrote to Bell:

Your promotion is a source of great pleasure and satisfaction to me, as I have reason to be very well aware of the great value of the contribution you have been making over the years. I am only sorry that we are not going to have the benefit of your influence and the pleasure of your company in Head Office for a bit, but there can be no question of the importance of what lies ahead of you, or the rightness of you being asked to take it on, or of your ability to make a great success of it.[3]

Bell's second African assignment had him embroiled in the transfer of power to the new government of independent Kenya. The intervening years between Bell's earlier MI5 posting in Nairobi from 1949 to 1952 and his latest arrival had seen Kenya go through a period of unprecedented insurgency and repression leading to diplomatic moves aimed at setting in motion the transfer of power from colony to new independent nation.

Although a state of emergency continued until 1960, the Mau Mau rebellion had been effectively crushed by the autumn of 1955, with thousands detained and military operations effectively ceasing. The insurgency mobilised British colonialism behind an act of coordinated repression of the Mau Mau rebellion as senior colonial officials expressed concern that local political agitation was being inspired from outside Africa. In 1953 Jomo Kenyatta, who many White settlers saw as the African leader behind it all, was charged with the management of Mau Mau, and the Kenya African Union, which had been formed after World War Two to campaign for African independence and which some Mau Mau militants admitted to using as a cover, was banned.

During the four years of their counter-insurgency campaign in Kenya, British forces were estimated to have killed as many as 20,000 indigenous Africans – by contrast, just thirty-two colonial settlers lost their lives, fewer than the number of people killed in road accidents in Nairobi alone in the same period. An estimated 80,000 indigenous Africans were imprisoned, a higher proportion than in any other colony in the history of the British Empire. Thousands were held in detention camps in appalling conditions. They were kept behind barbed wire fences in a series of camps up and down the colony known as the Pipeline where they were subjected to a humiliating process of physical and mental degradation euphemistically called 'rehabilitation'.[4]

Many were subjected to brutal treatment authorised by Sir Jack Prendergast, who served as director of security and intelligence in Nairobi from 1955 to 1958 after an investigation into the state of security in Britain's colonies around the world had identified serious shortcomings in Kenya prior to the uprising. 'It is possible that, had our intelligence system been better, we might have been spared the emergency in Kenya....', stated Field Marshal Gerald Templer, Chief of the Imperial General Staff, after reading a report by Alec MacDonald, an MI5 officer seconded to the Colonial Office.[5] MacDonald was credited by some MI5 officers with the defeat of Mau Mau, but the repression would tarnish Britain's colonial human rights record.

A watershed moment for British rule in Kenya came in March 1959 when eleven inmates suspected of belonging to Mau Mau were beaten to death by their guards at Hola, a remote prison camp.[6] The Conservative politician Enoch Powell subsequently led British MPs in expressing moral outrage. Powell's career would later be overshadowed by his very contentious anti-immigration Rivers of Blood speech on 20 April 1968 to a meeting of the Conservative Political Centre in Birmingham, UK, which had him branded as a racist and ultimately got him sacked from the shadow cabinet as an old imperialist who was dangerous and unwelcome in modern Britain.

Powell made a very different speech on 27 July 1959 when he rose to criticise his own party for attempting to cover up the Hola Camp massacre. Although the speech was largely forgotten in subsequent years, it showed Powell in a sympathetic light, urging as he did the British colonial authorities to treat Africans with dignity and respect, a practice that was far from widespread at the time, and long before Mau Mau survivors of British detention camps in Kenya won reparations as victims of human rights violations from the UK government.[7]

Interestingly, one of Powell's unpublicised friendships during his parliamentary career was with Bell's sister Mary and her husband Reginald Lygon, with whom he regularly dined privately at the couple's residence in Embankment Gardens, Chelsea.

Mary and Reginald's good relations with Walter had them visiting him and Tattie on his overseas postings, first crossing the Atlantic as a newly married couple by ship to spend a short holiday with him during his MI6 days in mid-1930s New York. During the 1950s, despite a fear of flying, Mary braved turbulent skies to fly out to the Caribbean to stay with her brother Walter in Jamaica during his posting there.

It seems likely that Bell, either directly or through the backchannel of the Lygons, may have had a hand in providing Powell with information and views on Kenya that proved formative, not just for the MP but for British post-colonial policy towards Africa generally.[8]

After the controversial repressive tactics used by the colonial authorities, there was, in the words of the prime minister Harold Macmillan, a 'wind of change' sweeping through Britain's former empire that required a shift towards softer power politics, and discreet engagement.[9] World War Two had demonstrated that the empire was an expense, not a benefit. The 'wind of change' emanated from London with the understanding that it was necessary that colonies should feel that they had to some degree won their independence in order to also secure a good post-imperial relationship.

As an MI5 officer Bell had managed to manoeuvre the tricky waters of India's decolonisation and had played a constructive, if unpublicised, 'soft power' role in the Caribbean. He now seemed well placed to put his experience of Kenya to good use in support of engagement with Kenyatta, an African nationalist leader he claimed to understand and felt politically sympathetic towards.

Nearly two years earlier the first election in Kenya for domestic party leadership had ended in deadlock as had a second election in March 1959. Nine months later, in February 1960, the British government held the first of a series of constitutional talks in London about the future of Kenya during which the Macmillan government committed itself to African majority rule.

The Kenya African National Union led by Kenyatta's main political rival Oginga Odinga won a sweeping election victory in a general election held in February 1961 on a radical platform advocating confiscation of all White settler property, nationalisation and demands that Kenyatta be immediately freed.

Bell, accompanied by Tattie, returned to Nairobi in late May 1961. On their arrival they stayed for a week with the governor of Kenya Sir Patrick Renison[10] and his wife before reoccupying the spacious colonial bungalow they had lived in ten years earlier.[11] In what Bell would later describe as an extraordinary first two months, he visited the fledgling Kenyan Legislative Council, which he had been led to suppose was a 'bear garden' and was actually surprised that it was not. He credited Humphrey Slade, the speaker, as 'superb', and was impressed by the respect held by all for parliamentary debate and scrutiny even if some of the Kenyans lacked political sophistication.[12] As he wrote to his old friend Julian Amery in July 1961, 'the good humour which prevailed, and the general atmosphere was good. One or two of the speakers were incapable of saying anything in order, but after all they were beginners.'[13]

Amery had been promoted to secretary of state for air having served as under secretary for war (1957–1958) and under secretary for the colonies in 1958 to 1960, both government posts that involved close liaison with MI5. While Bell disagreed with some of his strongly anti-communist politics and his resistance to decolonisation and non-White immigration, Amery was a well-connected and influential politician and a helpful source on areas of mutual interest such as Africa.

Bell resumed contact with Amery a few weeks after another Conservative MP, Hugh Fraser, at the time a junior minister in the Colonial Office, had made a controversial trip to the African continent, accompanied by his then wife Antonia Fraser. The Frasers coincided with Bell while staying at Government House in Nairobi and met up with well-known members of the White settler community at the exclusive Muthaiga Country Club. Antonia Fraser would later recall her 'excitement' while at the club when she caught sight of the member of the 'Happy Valley', the personification of White Mischief herself, Diana Delamare, the notorious femme fatale in the unresolved murder of her aristocratic lover Josslyn Hay, Earl of Erroll, whose death scandalised colonial Kenya in January 1941. At independence the statue of Lord Delamere was removed from Delamere Avenue in Nairobi, when it was renamed after Kenyatta.

As Lady Antonia Fraser wrote to the writer Cyril Connolly, reminiscing about her visit in 1958 'and confessing that she had been always somewhat obsessed' by the case herself: 'Imagine my excitement on sitting at the Muthaiga Club…and seeing a leopard of a woman stalk by in pale gold jersey (everyone else in tatty cotton) with hair and skin the same colour, and even a fur coat on her arm (the temperature was about 75), and hearing a murmur, "Diana Delamere".'[14]

Bell found Hugh Fraser 'being battered by settlers et al' and a superficial observer might have concluded that all was dissolving into chaos.[15] The Bells attended a dinner for the Frasers at which other government officials, including the governor, Renison, and the chief secretary, Sir Walter Coutts, were present. Bell was appalled by the level and tone of conversation at table with 'African servants' in attendance. Coutts was vocal in his criticism of Kenyatta, against whom he harboured a long-term grudge, regarding him as a 'thorn in his side' when he had served as district commissioner twelve years earlier. 'What is the use of Coutts sitting at the Governor's table surrounded by African servants, boasting that he inspired that Church of Scotland churchman to attack Kenyatta at Edinburgh last week, all of which was full reported here and read by Kenyatta?', Bell wrote later.[16]

As for Renison, in Bell's view 'he knew nothing about Africa' and he was only capable of uttering 'banalities'. Even after Kenyatta's release from prison in 1961 after serving nine years on rigged charges of 'leading' Mau Mau, Renison persisted in claiming that Kenyatta was the leader of Mau Mau 'to darkness and to death'.[17] Bell also knew that Coutts and Renison objected to a request from Jack Morton, the MI5 officer with responsibility for relations with colonies and their transition to independence, that they facilitate Bell's re-entry into Kenya and accept his role as a key interlocutor with Kenyatta.

And yet Bell counted on powerful support from London. The government policy of accelerating Kenyan independence had been clearly signalled by the prime minister Harold Macmillan when he appointed Iain Macleod as secretary of state for the colonies. It was Macleod who told Macmillan in May 1959 that in Kenya, as elsewhere, 'the rights of the individual should be secured to him by virtue of his position as a citizen rather than the colour of his skin or his membership of a particular community'. In Kenya this meant an African majority in the elected councils. Macleod's vision of a Commonwealth underwritten by majority rule ensured a hastening of African independence, as well as a head-on collision with the right wing of the Conservative Party.[18]

Bell knew that Kenyatta had been running things from

his place of detention and doing it very skilfully. As he told Julian
Amery, three months after his arrival in Nairobi. 'I just do not
believe that he [Kenyatta]intends to play a tribal role when he
comes out, seeing that he has the opportunity to end his days as
a World figure.'[19] Bell went on to report how 'it is astonishing
how in six weeks or so the public attitude to Kenyatta has
changed, and even European business people hope he will be on
the scene before long.'[20]

Bell predicted that Kenya would follow the example of
the emerging independent state of Tanganyika, where MI5 was
presented by its overseas department director Alex Kellar to the
leader-in-waiting Julius Nyerere, as the link in a well-established
and mutually advantageous Commonwealth security network.[21]
As Bell told Amery, it was reasonable to expect that an African
government in Kenya would want British civil servants to stay
on with similar terms. 'Certainly, there is no air of panic among
the Civil Servants and there are many, particularly among the
younger ones who do not seem dismayed at working under an
African Minister. Almost everything depends on this as there is
no African Minister capable of running a ministry.'[22]

Bell reserved his most scathing criticism for a colonial
administrator, Anthony Swann, who served as provincial
commissioner and minister for defence and internal security in
Kenya. He was a 'lightweight with no political knowledge or
experience, dangerously placed in a key position demanding a
high degree of such knowledge combined with a calm and firm
disposition which he lacks.' He was critical too of Sir Edgeworth
David, the East Africa Commission's administrator of the
Central Legislative Assembly. According to Bell, David
represented the 'answer to Lord Hailes' term 'a Colonial Office
Ape'. Other members of the colonial team fared only slightly
better in Bell's irreverent roll call. Bell was more in step with the
Foreign Office, which always regarded itself as superior to the
Colonial Office and with superior people running it.

Such was the case of Hugh Herbert-Jones, the MI6 man
in Nairobi at the time reporting on 'third countries', in other

words drawing intelligence from neighbouring countries on the Russians in the region, who Bell described as – 'a dreadfully conceited know-all, as pleased with Herbert as he is with Jones, but withal doing a pretty good job, I should say…Incidentally, his papers are, at first, pretty good, and I am sure that the reports which stem from neighbouring countries are a real contribution.'[23]

Kenya was in transition from a British colony to an independent country, or a foreign territory within the Commonwealth, requiring a reassessment of the operational role and targets of British security and intelligence. In 1961 it was MI5, with Walter Bell in a trusted position, close to Kenyatta, that found itself very much in the driving seat in security and intelligence terms in Kenya, playing a key part in the transition to independent rule. As Bell reported to a senior MI5 colleague at the time, a radical rethink of British government attitudes towards Kenyatta was urgently needed in preparation for Kenyatta's release.

> He [Kenyatta]is in full possession of his faculties, and, indeed, a very healthy and vigorous man who has at least 10 years of public life left ahead of him. It is surely utter madness for these senior official representatives to engage in acrimonious debate with him at this late stage! That 'darkness and death' speech[24] was folly of the highest order. I tell you all this because it is our and my problem – ultimately yours of course, because presumably we shall have to go at Independence. Maybe R [Governor Renison] understands all this, but there is little indication that he does and to have spent ten days listening to the exchange of puerilities which would have not done credit to a gathering of preparatory schoolboys has been no mean strain.[25]

Bell's sympathetic views towards Kenyatta proved to be prophetic, and the issue of how the British should treat the emergent Kenyan leader turned out better than Bell, suffering one of his periodic Black Dog moods of despondency, predicted. As he later recalled, when Kenyatta was finally released from prison in August 1961after an apprehensive government decided to return him to Kikuyuland, 'he made a point of repeatedly reassuring white farmers – many of whom were leaving the country – that when he came to power, he would welcome all to stay who were prepared to live under an African regime to build a Kenyan nation. He was as good as his word: he saw Kenya becoming the Switzerland of Africa.'[26]

While the Swiss aspiration proved way off the mark, Kenyatta's reputation did undergo an extraordinary transformation in the eyes of the British,[27] from terrorist to collaborator, with Bell playing a discreet but important role in forging cooperative links between Kenyatta and the British security and intelligence authorities.

After Kenya was granted full internal self-government in late 1962, Kenyatta led a KANU (Kenyan African National Union) delegation to the latest set of constitutional talks in London. The African delegates were bugged by MI5.[28] The intelligence together with Bell's reporting from Nairobi allowed British officials to plot the diplomatic road map ahead.

In August 1963, during further talks at Lancaster House, Kenyatta met the director general of MI5 Roger Hollis at the Security Service's headquarters in Leconfield House, Mayfair. At the meeting Kenyatta told Hollis that he had developed a good entente with Bell in Nairobi and looked forward to building on the relationship. Bell's cooperation with Kenyatta included passing to Kenyan Special Branch intelligence information contacts of Kenyan politicians with the Communist Party of Great Britain (CPGB.)[29]

Bell worked hard on his personal links in Kenya, his personable outward-going American wife Tattie proving a helpful assistant. Together they developed a friendship with their neighbour, Kenyatta's daughter Margaret, from Kenyatta's first marriage to Grace Wahu.

Tattie won the trust of the politically active Margaret when she played a leading part in the Kenya African National Union women's branch by supporting Margaret's campaign to improve the lives and rights of African women. In May 1962 Tattie served as secretary as well as editorial coordinator of the first Kenya Women's Seminar to be chaired by Margaret Kenyatta in Nairobi. The seminars, which took place over a two-year period, brought together East African women leaders to discuss their role in the economic and political development of their nascent independent nations.[30]

In August 1962 Tattie developed further close ties with the Kenyan regime when she was appointed technical assistant to a five-day official The Kenya We Want convention in Nairobi, where supporters of Kenyatta featured among the most numerous and influential of the delegates drawn for their expertise on issues ranging from family planning and health education to citizen participation, and social and economic development.[31]

On his release from prison, Kenyatta became president of the Kenya African National Union (KANU) and led the party to victory in the 1963 general election, becoming president of the new independent republic of Kenya in 1964. 'This country [Kenya] has been disastrously mismanaged ever since the war, largely because British officials never came to terms with African nationalism, and never admitted that the Kenyan African was a human being who was potentially his equal and entitled to be treated with consideration and respect,' Bell wrote in early 1963.[32] Certainly by that January the British government had come to the conclusion that Governor Renison was too ill at ease with indigenous Africans and replaced him with Malcolm MacDonald, who was persuaded by Bell that Kenyatta was the wisest, strongest, and most popular prime minister of the independent nation to be.

Malcolm, son of Ramsay MacDonald, the British Labour Party's first prime minister, speeded up plans for Kenyan independence, believing, as advised by Bell, that the longer the wait, the greater the risk of radicalisation among African nationalists. Bell's careful personal nurturing of Jomo Kenyatta and his daughter Margaret produced its dividend when Bell was asked to stay on in Nairobi until 1967 to continue the good relations he had established with the African leader in a 'cover' role of counsellor, British High Commission.

The Bells enjoyed their extended Kenyan tour, leading a comfortable expatriate life as they had done on their first posting, the only difference being that the Africans they attended receptions and dinners with were now in government and VIPs. The country's beautiful landscape, vegetation and wildlife remained an enduring attraction that continued to draw regular visits by friends and family. It was in Kenya that Bell and Tattie showed 'great hospitality' to Walter's diehard Conservative insurance broker, Walter's older brother St John and wife Mildred.[33] And it was in Kenya that on another family visit Bell's father-in-law General ('Tooey') Spaatz and his wife Ruth Harrison fulfilled one of their retirement dream trips abroad and joined Walter and Tattie on a safari during which the wartime air force leader filled up a portfolio of stunning photographs.[34]

Outside their leisure time, the Bells continued to work discreetly as a very effective two-person team. Tattie, a spirited anti-racist and emancipated well-educated American woman, threw herself enthusiastically into discussions on Kenyan women issues. Walter carried on with work that by its very nature had to be kept from the public eye given its political sensitivity, as Kenyatta, just as he had promised the MI5 chief Roger Hollis, developed a close liaison with the British on security and intelligence issues.

As the Cold War began to dominate British security and intelligence tasking, the partnership deepened, with each side finding a mutual interest in dealing with the more radical Marxist threats to the new independent government posed by some of Kenyatta's political rivals.

In April 1965 the rumour of a potential Soviet-backed coup in Kenya by vice-president Oginga Odinga reached

British intelligence via secret sources, before surfacing publicly in the Kenyan parliament. A close ally of Kenyatta's, the Kenyan MP Thomas Malinda alleged that arms and ammunition were continuously being smuggled from communist and other foreign countries into or through Kenya for the purpose of staging an armed revolution to overthrow the government. Kenyatta, with Bell as a key conduit, secretly asked the British government for assistance in the form of military support if a coup was attempted, and the British government responded by making an extensive military plan to intervene, code-named Operation Binnacle.

The period 1964–1965 was a time of particular concern about Soviet and Chinese efforts to foment revolutions throughout sub-Saharan Africa, with Cold War fears triggered by internal military unrest in Kenya. Then the immediate British reaction was to suspect communist involvement and question whether what was being hatched was a more organised and widespread communist plot.[35]

At the time of the rumoured coup in April 1965 Bell reported that a 'determined and largely successful attempt' had been made to turn the Kenyan Government Information Services into a vehicle for communist influence and propaganda, with Soviet Bloc experts employed in the Kenya News Agency, and Kenyan students of journalism receiving training in communist countries. 'No impartial listener or viewer of radio and television could fail to detect the bias which has crept into an increasing extent during the past months and to be concerned at the influence that this must have on the general public,' he wrote in a wide-ranging report on post-colonial political issues in Africa.[36]

Bell noted the Kenyan trade union's movement's openness to subversion, and the fact that there were trained intelligence agents reporting to communist diplomatic missions in Nairobi, which posed a 'formidable threat' to political stability.

Despite the potential for destabilisation in the perceived communist threat, Bell's faith in Kenyatta at the time remained undimmed. 'Fortunately, Kenya possesses a sophisticated progressive government under the leadership of President Kenyatta, in spite of forces within it which look towards its disruption,' he wrote.[37] What his personal papers didn't reveal was the extent to which British security and intelligence officials including Bell were actively involved in shoring up the Kenyatta regime, by helping him monitor and disrupt his political rivals and thwart Somali incursions in the country's North-Eastern Province.[38]

As in Uganda and Tanzania, British troops were used to help Kenyatta suppress an army revolt, while MI6 provided intelligence on Somalian intentions. Bell respected and worked well and closely with the British high commissioner in Nairobi, Malcolm MacDonald, who in turn saw Bell as an experienced intelligence and security officer who had worked hard on winning the trust of Kenyatta and was well informed and prescient in his advice. When MacDonald arrived in Nairobi in 1963 as the final governor, he drew on Bell as his eyes and ears and a discreet negotiator who could help him keep Kenyatta on side.

In early April 1965 MacDonald, advised by Bell, telegrammed the Commonwealth Relations Office with a record of a conversation he had had with the Kenyan attorney general at which military assistance was requested although his telegram suggested perhaps some uncertainty about what form any action would take.[39]

MacDonald went to Kenya in 1963 as the final governor and became Kenya's only governor general and then high commissioner in 1964. He is widely credited, from the moment of his arrival, with having played a crucial role in reshaping perceptions in London about Kenya and Kenyatta. But behind MacDonald was the secret but no less important role played by Bell in moulding Kenyatta's security policy and making it more favourable to British interests. MacDonald's reputation endured, credited as the person who had rightly foreseen, in a way that previous colonial officials had been unable to, that

Kenyatta was someone with whom British governments should seek to cultivate a good relationship.

In 1965 Bell resumed contact with an old source with a shared interest in keeping an eye on how former colonies of the British Empire played out in the geopolitical context of the Cold War. The chief of staff of the Indian army General Chaudhuri wrote to Bell in February describing the appointment of MacDonald in Kenya as 'one of the wisest moves' made by the British government. 'With MacDonald as High Commissioner, I am sure a great deal of good sense will prevail and Jomo Kenyatta, will get the best advice available. He seems to show himself as being the most able of the African Premiers. It is wonderful what a little spell in jail will do for leaders seeking independence. It seems to give them a sense of maturity ...'[40]

In December Chaudhuri wrote again to Bell from New Delhi, predicting that a mutual source, Prem Bhatia – the Indian diplomat, hugely influential journalist, and friend of India's first post-independence prime minister Jawaharlal Nehru – would make a success of his appointment as high commissioner in Nairobi. He again referred to MacDonald in laudatory terms, knowing of his close links with Bell, as 'an excellent catalyst between East and West and South and North'.[41]

By 1967, Bell's last full year in post in Kenya, the ties between Kenyatta and MI5 had become even closer. Bell was given a formal post of secretary to the new Kenyan National Security Executive, Kenyatta's overarching law enforcement and intelligence arm, which reported directly to the president. By then, however, MI5's dominant role in the African continent was approaching its nadir, with MI6 set to overtake it with a reinforcement of its presence, pro-actively drawing intelligence on a new ideological battleground of the Cold War and seeking to retain the influence of newly independent states regarded as still within the British orbit, such as Kenya, in countering Soviet influence. In the following year, 1968, MI6 reinforced its presence in Nairobi, sending one of its new generation of recruits, untainted by the Philby affair, a 21-year-old

Cambridge graduate, Richard Dearlove, to Kenya.[42]

Bell's friend and colleague Dick White, who served as MI6 chief from 1956 to 1968 after being director general of MI5 in 1953 to 1956, retained a keen interest in Africa, to the point of being quite consumed by events on the continent.

In Kenya MI6, via its contacts with Bruce McKenzie, a White settler and confidant of Kenyatta, was involved in setting up the foreign intelligence aspects of the Kenyan National Security Executive.

By 1967, when he had reached the age of fifty-eight and was preparing to retire after thirty years in government service, Bell was finally given the public recognition he felt he deserved for his largely secret work in wartime and peace. He was appointed a CMG, or companion of the order of St Michael and St George – 'Call me God' in civil service jokey parlance – a diplomatic honour given by the recommendation of the Foreign Office to those who have given distinguished service overseas.

Senior figures in the world of intelligence were among the first to congratulate him.[43] They were led by Roger Hollis, who had retired two years earlier after serving as director general of MI5 during 1956-1965. Hollis's reputation was yet to be overshadowed by allegations, fuelled by disgruntled middle-ranking MI5 officers including Peter Wright, and a book written by the journalist Chapman Pincher, that he was a Soviet agent – a charge that Hollis denied till his death, and which MI5 as an organisation refuted as part of its official history.[44]

Hollis wrote to Bell in Nairobi, sending the letter via the 'secure' diplomatic bag, after passing through London on his way back to his country house in Wells, Somerset. He had just spent the weekend in Rye playing golf 'in bitter cold and utterly miserable conditions'. 'I am really delighted to see this distinguished recognition of the very distinguished service you are giving,' Hollis told Bell. 'I believe that the contribution to balanced and good relations which you and Tattie have made in Kenya, and earlier elsewhere, has been very significant, and all on the right side at a time when so many others have been doing so many stupid things.'[45] Particularly worthy of note is the special mention Hollis makes of Bell's wife Tattie, acknowledging the extent to which she proved a support not just to her husband but to MI5, an unusual official recognition of a spy's wife as dutiful in a professional as well as personal sense.

While his final posting in Kenya proved professionally rewarding, Bell's faith in Kenyatta would lead to disillusionment. When Kenyatta's fourteen-year presidency ended with his death in August 1978, Bell wrote a reflective article for the Catholic weekly *The Tablet* on his legacy, entitled 'The Wise Old Man'. After praising Kenyatta's contribution to Kenya's independence and his early years in government, Bell noted that in his final years old age had reduced him to being little more a figurehead. On his death Kenyatta had left Kenya facing an uncertain future with the problems of a growing population of rising discontents, the corruption of the Kenyatta family and Kikuyu politicians and continuing regional instability fuelled by the Cold War.

'All that can be said is that a chapter has been closed,' Bell concluded, 'and the one that is opening seems to hold increasing uncertainties.'[46]

# 29
# European Shadowlands

Bell spent the Cold War years as a discreet but active member of a network of World War Two veterans, his generation of intelligence and security officials. Some were promoted and endured in senior roles as paid members of the secret British civil service or, after retirement, drifted into the media, academia, and think-tanks, remaining in contact with an international network of former and serving spies engaging in Cold War anti-communist and pro-Western non-military psychological warfare, while continuing to meet with their closest friends in the gentleman's private clubs of Pall Mall, St James's, and Covent Garden.

After serving as an MI6 officer then working with MI5 and retiring from British government service in the late 1960s, Bell, with the blessing of his former employers, played a discreet role as a British liaison with a shadowy transnational research organisation involved in countering communist propaganda, which was conjured up by and involved Western European spies, operating in a murky realm between secret state and civil society.

The International Documentation and Information Centre (Interdoc), which also went by the name The East-West Institute, was headquartered in The Hague, where it operated during the 1960s and 1970s with a small administrative staff in a rented villa along a quiet street in the city's seaside suburb of Scheveningen.

Interdoc was founded in 1962 by Louis Einthoven who had retired the previous year as the head of the Dutch security and intelligence agency the Binnenlandse Veiligheidsdienst (BVD) but retained close ties with his former employers, as did Cornelis van den Heuvel, a one-time World War Two Resistance fighter and post-war Dutch intelligence officer specialising in psychological warfare, who became Interdoc's executive director.[1]

Funded privately by major Dutch companies, and covertly by the West German intelligence agency Bundesnachrichtendienst (BND),[2] Interdoc's origins were as a central clearing-house for distributing publications internationally as part of a form of defensive-offensive psychological warfare, raising awareness of the communist threat and projecting the Western values that best opposed it.

Interdoc supplied reports to selected journalists and think-tanks about Soviet ideological subversion and Soviet strategy towards the West. These were in fact based on selected facts and analysis gleaned from intelligence sources but appeared to come from independent analysts and institutions. Interdoc operations mirrored some of the CIA's Cold War propaganda operations as well as those of the Foreign Office's Information Research Department (IRD).[3]

During the 1960s Interdoc had discreet links with the CIA, IRD and MI6. Drawing on expert advice while at the same time fuelling a culture of intrigue and provoking internal political tensions, the involvement of secret intelligence in what purported to be a public information campaign proved a mixed blessing. According to an internal background paper penned by Bell, Interdoc was founded at a time when Western democratic governments were facing up to threat of the Warsaw Pact powers during the Cold War. 'Semi-private institutions were prepared to afford generous financial support...there was also subvention from institutions in the US over and above what was contributed by business in the Netherlands...'[4]

Interdoc coordinated diverse psychological warfare activities, from political, socio- economic and military studies to conferences and training university students on how the West should conduct its relations with Moscow. At the peak of its activity in 1970, its publications – which were intended for reprinting without attribution in newspapers all over the world – were being distributed across 119 countries via a contact list of over 2,000 potential opinion formers. While Interdoc's founding aim was to create an international network involving mainly West Germany, France, Britain and the US, it remained primarily Dutch-run and funded with the majority of the reports it disseminated put together by Dutch, West German, and French intelligence sources, and occasional conferences in mainland Europe and the UK.

The CIA director, World War Two veteran Allen Dulles, developed a good personal relationship with Louis Einthoven, the Dutch intelligence chief behind Interdoc's foundation. However, the CIA chose not to become more officially involved with what it saw as essentially an aspiring European public-private venture vulnerable to different political influences. The well-meaning Dutch struggled to develop a coherent strategy that did not run up against national self-interest among their main European 'associates', with the French foreign intelligence agency Service de Documentation Extérieure et de Contre-Espionnage (SDECE) acting more as rivals than allies at times, and the foreign intelligence agency of the West German government, the Bundesnachrichtendienst (BND), rocked in the early 1960s by scandals of KGB infiltration. The BND looked like badly damaged goods, and it is not surprising that there was hesitation on the part of the CIA to undertake a new cooperative venture at that time.[5]

American financial support proved at best elusive, which may have been a blessing in disguise as Interdoc avoided being caught up in the series of revelations about covert CIA funding of allegedly independent and private organisations and institutions published by the *New York Times* in 1967.[6]

MI6's relationship with Interdoc, of necessity very discreet, was both more complex and controversial, not least because British intelligence, while claiming a more special and privileged intelligence cooperation with the Americans than any other European country, suffered its own reputational damage as a result of revelations about the Cambridge circle's infiltration by the KGB.

When Bell was asked by British intelligence to serve as

their link with Interdoc towards the end of the 1960s it was done on the basis of great trust invested in him by his enduring friend Dick White, Britain's respected and experienced intelligence chief, the only person to have headed both MI5 and MI6 during the Cold War years.

Bell's predecessor in the role, in the early days of Interdoc's foundation was the reputationally tarnished Charles 'Dick' Ellis, a wartime colleague of Bell's who had served as deputy of the BSC in New York. Ellis entered the Interdoc network after the Dutch spy chief Einthoven had approached his British counterpart White to suggest who he might like MI6 to be represented by at an early planning conference for the fledgling documentation and research organisation.[7]

Ellis's European experience as an MI6 officer in Berlin in the 1920s, in Paris in the 1930s, and during World War Two, appears to have been behind White's recommendation of him as the most appropriate MI6 linkman with Interdoc during the early 1960s. Since retiring from MI6 and spending time in Australia, where he was involved in establishing the Australian Secret (Intelligence) Service, Ellis had remained in contact with colleagues in his old 'firm' although not all of them trusted him.

Ellis came under growing suspicion of being a Russian spy and was interrogated by MI6 and MI5 following Philby's defection in January 1963.[8] MI5 suspected Ellis of having betrayed his employers by trading wartime secrets with the Germans and the Russians. Although he was never charged, MI5 officers continued to insist that he had committed espionage for the Germans and been a long-term agent of the Russians, with the story publicly exposed by the journalist Chapman Pincher and 'Spycatcher' MI5 officer Peter Wright after Ellis died in 1975 after denying allegations against him of postwar espionage for the Russians. By then any role Ellis might have played on behalf of MI6 had been closed down.

The allegations surrounding Ellis of being a spy for both the Germans and the Russians did not initially seem to have affected his early involvement with Interdoc in any way, although he struggled to escape from the negative reputational cloud that built up around him. Ellis wrote to Interdoc director van den Heuvel at the end of 1967 defensively reassuring him of his integrity: 'I told [MI6] that I would stand no more nonsense about myself and demanded that they put their cards on the table or shut up. I have been told that "no action is contemplated"; they regret having embarrassed me (and others) but in view of the seriousness of the Philby and Blake cases (there is more to come!) they have to examine every possibility, however remote.'[9]

Van den Heuvel responded to the publication of *Spycatcher* in 1987, which alleged Ellis's treachery, by defending his former colleague: 'He (Ellis) perhaps went too far in his attempts to exchange information, which has therefore given a false impression. He was a remarkably active man. I have personally never doubted his loyalty.'[10] By contrast, doubts about Ellis within MI6 as well as MI5 went deeper than he claimed in his own defence and by the late 1960s he could no longer count on White's or the UK government's support, with Margaret Thatcher as prime minister in the 1980s resisting pressure from his family members to clear his name posthumously. Bell was among those who had by then long given up considering Ellis a reliable colleague. As he told a friend in the British intelligence service, he had found the Ellis affair deeply 'distressing' because of the emotional impact the public exposure of his alleged treachery had had on his unknowing wife Anne after he died and who Bell had helped resettle in New York away from media scrutiny. But as Bell confessed, he was in 'the difficult position of knowing quite a lot, but not enough' about her husband's activities.

Bell knew that Ellis was 'outraged and insulted at being sharply questioned by people who could have been his grandchildren' – a reference to his MI5 interrogators – and yet seemed to protest too much. As Bell put it, Ellis was 'terribly defensive and emotional, was not straight forward, and could be depended upon to make a bad case worse. His memory was poor. I am sure that he contradicted himself wholesale. I also strongly suspect he had acted thoughtlessly and possibly reckless at the time.'[11] It was a damning character reference from a long-term colleague which effectively undermined Ellis's credibility. Behind Bell's distrust of Ellis was the way he had breached confidentiality and tried to profit from revealing certain details about the BSC's wartime activities in a semi-fictitious book he had collaborated on with the author William Stevenson.[12]

Bell succeeded Ellis, who had retired officially for 'health reasons' as a UK liaison with Interdoc in October 1969. One of Interdoc's inner circle, the German assistant director Uwe Holl described Bell as an ideal 'softly-softly frontman' who 'made a living of keeping quiet'.[13] Bell distanced himself from Ellis and abandoned the rented central London office in Mayfair's Norfolk Street used by his predecessor, to work from his home in Onslow Square.[14]

Bell's involvement with Interdoc during the 1970s had him winning the enduring trust of his Dutch colleagues as a useful British representative who was an intelligence and security professional and networker with an unblemished record.[15] At the same time Bell almost certainly channelled information back to his friends in MI6 and MI5 about the intrigue and rivalries that bedevilled Western European attitudes towards the Soviet Union.

His initial involvement with Interdoc coincided with Ostpolitik, the policy of engagement with the then Soviet Union championed by the West German social democratic chancellor Willy Brandt and his foreign minister Egon Bahr. Launched in 1970, a year after Soviet tanks crushed the Prague Spring in Czechoslovakia, Ostpolitik's aim was to break down barriers with the Eastern Bloc through trade and diplomatic dialogue.

In 1971, with the help of his old friend Julian Amery, who was then serving in Edward Heath's government, Bell helped organise an Interdoc conference in the UK, under its other name The East-West Institute, at the Metropole Hotel in Brighton.[16] The conference included Dutch and West German speakers. The British headline speakers aimed to give a less conciliatory view on Russian affairs and the need for nuclear deterrence. Amery was a supporter of Britain's entry into the Common Market but was also part of the God and Empire school of UK politics and eventual patron of the Monday Club, the right wing and uncompromisingly anti-communist pressure group that was aligned with the Conservative Party.[17]

The keynote speech on NATO's policy towards the Soviet Union was made by Sir Bernard Burrows, a pillar of the British diplomatic and intelligence establishment who in Anthony Sampson's *Anatomy of Britain* (1965) was described as 'one of the five most powerful people in Whitehall'.[18] Another speaker invited by Bell was Brian Crozier, an 'intelligence expert' and ultimate Cold War warrior, a political vigilante who unashamedly cultivated a close, mutually beneficial, relationship with MI6, MI5 and the CIA. Crozier got on well with Bell, whom he trusted a great deal more than the Dutch and West Germans who were most active in Interdoc and who Crozier considered appeasers of Moscow, contrary to Western interests.[19]

In November 1972, Bell helped Interdoc set up its first major conference in the US with the presence of the secretary general of NATO, Joseph Lun, US administration officials and leading figures of the Atlantic Treaty Association in a bid to strengthen links with established transatlantic networks. Bell also helped bring in as a speaker Jeremy Russell of Shell UK, an expert on Eastern Europe, having seemingly convinced him of Interdoc's continuing relevance in international affairs.

The conference addressed the changing transatlantic relationship in an era of détente and US–China rapprochement. Long discussions centred on Soviet objectives in Europe, which were ranked from outright communisation as a maximum Soviet goal to 'Finlandisation' (making Western Europe neutral in the great power politics of East–West relations, as with Finland, which adopted a policy of neutrality during the Cold War as a minimum).

The East German state security service, the STASI, still keeping tabs on Interdoc after the withdrawal from direct involvement of the West German intelligence agency the BND, reported on the conference's message that 'the strength and unity of the Western alliance was a crucial prerequisite for successful negotiations with the East', an essential part of which was represented by the continuing presence of US forces in Western Europe.[20]

Some of Interdoc's publications espoused 'moderate' anti-communism, 'full of critical self-reflection about the imperfections of Western Democracy and anxious to promote social reform on both sides of the Iron Curtain.'[21] By contrast, one of Interdoc's main critics, Brian Crozier, a former journalist with the *Economist*, had in 1970 founded the brazenly anti-communist Institute for the Study of Conflict, with whom Bell would maintain an enduring link as an informal adviser with the blessing of MI5. As MI5's director general Michael Hanley made clear to Bell in a letter in June 1975, 'it is important that the Security Service agency is not associated publicly, this is not to say that we do not sympathise with what the Institute [for the Study of Conflict] is trying to do, and indeed we feel it necessary to keep in touch with them, if only to protect our own interests.'[22] Bell advised Crozier on the security of sensitive documents he had in his possession, warning that an unnamed 'KGB' person was 'sniffing around' and that he feared a 'sophisticated intelligence operation' was being planned aimed at undermining him and the Institute for the Study of Conflict.[23]

In a unique position of straddling both camps, by the mid-1970s Bell became well informed on the growing breakdown in the relationship between Crozier and Interdoc. While van den Heuvel may have had good reasons for considering Crozier's fanatical uncompromising anti-communism unhelpful in the era of Ospolitik and détente, Crozier felt that Interdoc, like the West German chancellor Willy Brandt, was becoming too gullible in its dealings with the Russians. In the autumn of 1976 Crozier accused Interdoc's van den Heuvel of going soft on communism as the reason why he could not belong to the circle of anti-communists to which the Dutchman belonged.[24]

Van den Huevel replied in a memo to Bell that Crozier's

accusations were 'unfounded, wrong and insulting'. He went on: 'In my own country, I had heard the same accusations. They come, however, from people who are regarded here as fanatics, whose judgement carried no weight in the discussion on East-West problems.' Van den Heuvel was furious. In November 1976 he had read a recent media report in *Izvestia*, the official newspaper of the Soviet government as published by the Presidium of the Supreme Soviet of the USSR, alleging a close relationship between Interdoc and the Institute for the Study of Conflict. He considered it harmful to his work, presumably because it risked drawing the attention of the KGB.[25]

If Interdoc's Dutch founders saw it as a bold attempt to build a West European 'strategic culture' in the fight against communist ideology away from the all-controlling activities of the US, as well as being a noteworthy project of intelligence liaison in the field of psychological warfare, Bell would come to see it as a failure in organisation and outcomes.

Interdoc's attempts to be more active and get more support in the UK never got off the ground after the 1971 conference in Brighton because British intelligence had no real interest in facilitating matters beyond their own immediate needs and had their doubts about the institute's efficacy and motivation, while of course wanting to keep tabs on what it was up to, from the inside – which is where Bell played his part.

By 1977 Bell had firmed up in his long-held view that it was the Soviet Union, not the West, that posed the greatest threat to world peace. At the time the US was engaged in a continuing policy of Henry Kissinger's détente, aimed at easing the geopolitical tensions between Moscow and Washington. Meanwhile van den Heuvel was pursuing his own version of it in a series of visits to Sofia, Warsaw and Moscow, which had his critics suggesting he was becoming not just too close to the Russians but might also be working for them. Bell, for his part, was openly confronting the then Catholic priest Bruce Kent, a leading British advocate of the Campaign for Nuclear Disarmament, for making 'no distinction between the total oppression of the communist states, and the cruelties in other parts of the world which the United States is supposed to stop... It is the Soviet Union that dashed all hope of the UN Security Council being the guarantee of peace post-WW2,' Bell wrote in response to a letter published by Kent in the British magazine *The Tablet*, 'by vetoing every resolution, after spewing vitriolic abuse on its fellow members.'

Bell added:

> On the Soviet side all is conducted in secrecy. A vast army of spies is employed to steal the secrets of Western methods and technology, largely because Soviet industry is incapable of developing its own systems; hence the Monsignor's[Kent's]impression that the Russians are always catching up. But what is the West supposed to do? Let the Soviet Union build up an overwhelming preponderance of forces and just trust to luck?[26]

The previous summer, in August 1976, ahead of an Interdoc conference in the Dutch town of Noordwijk that September, Bell told van den Heuvel in a briefing note that his organisation was struggling to define the scope and limits of its work, with the impact of communism on Western democratic society a more complicated subject than when the East–West Institute (Interdoc) was started at the height of the Cold War. 'It seems to be unlikely that there will support available from the type of sources which originally contributed so much to the Institute,' wrote Bell. [27]

In an analysis of the impact of communism on Western democratic society Bell noted that communist parties in Western Europe were 'rigorously asserting their independence from the imperialistic pressures and image of the USSR' while some Eastern European countries were cautiously showing 'some independence' although still being careful not to challenge the Brezhnev doctrine in too provocative a manner. In 1968 the Soviet leader Leonid Brezhnev had declared as foreign policy that the Soviet Union should intervene – including militarily – in countries where socialist rule was under threat. Bell warned against democratic governments adopting a 'feeble posture in relation to Soviet imperialism'.[28]

Bell quit Interdoc in 1977, anticipating the organisation's own demise in 1978 due to lack of funding, and internal political tensions, but kept in informal touch with van den Heuvel. Having been disowned by some of his closest European friends for adopting a too accommodating attitude towards Moscow, van den Heuvel had by the 1980s become actively engaged in the Paris-based Federation of European American Organisations, which sought to pursue good relations with the US under Ronald Reagan, while mobilising public support in the Netherlands for NATO's 'dual-track' missile deployments. Van den Heuvel continued to rely on Bell for developing his links with the British, including friends in the Special Forces Club in London.[29]

# 30
# Secrets and the Public Interest

When Bell wrote an article for the journal of international affairs *The Round Table* in July 1980, advocating a more open debate about intelligence matters and fair judgement of colleagues alleged to be Russian agents, there was still a year to go before the journalist Chapman Pincher published *Their Trade is Treachery*, his book about Soviet penetration of British intelligence that drew a *Daily Mail* front page headlining 'MI5 Chief was Russian Spy Suspect'.

The chief in question was Bell's former boss Roger Hollis (MI5 director general from 1956 to 1965). Both before and after his death in 1973, a dense web of conspiracy had been woven by a group of young virulently anti-communist intelligence officers who were recruited after World War Two and whose political views were coloured by the Cold War.

Faced with the advocates of maximum openness outside the secret service, those within it struggled to break with their self-protecting silo mentality and 'group think' that British spies were prone to, with MI6, in the words of Hugh Trevor-Roper, 'the most closely guarded citadel of the British bureaucracy'.[1] Given this context, Bell's *The Round Table* article was a courageous step by a former MI6 and MI5 officer to engage publicly in the tricky subject of how far the intelligence and security services should become more transparent and accountable in the public interest when having to deal with the fall-out of the widely publicised defection by British spies working for the Russians. The title of Bell's article, 'Treachery within the Establishment', was subtitled 'The Case for a More Open Approach to Security'.[2]

Most British intelligence and security records remained publicly unavailable with disclosure still restricted by legislation dating back to before World War One. The 1911 Official

Secrets Act, with its declared aim of protecting the UK against espionage and the leaking of sensitive government information, was still on the statute book. Offences covered by the act included spying and sabotage, but also the disclosure of sensitive information by employees and ex-employees of the security services. The criteria as to what could be justified as sensitive was arbitrarily set by the spy chiefs.

And yet the professional discretion and loyalty that had developed to an unusually high degree over the years was under severe strain by the late 1970s as British journalists successfully exploited the disgruntlement of a few veteran middle-ranking spies.

On 4 November 1979, a BBC radio editor, Andrew Boyle, published the first edition of his ground-breaking *Climate of Treason*, which led to the unmasking of Anthony Blunt as the fourth man in the Cambridge Soviet spy ring – the other three, by then already exposed, being Maclean, Burgess and Philby (the so-called 'third man'). On 15 November the prime minister Margaret Thatcher confirmed Blunt's guilt to an astonished House of Commons. Blunt's identity as the fourth man had been a long-kept secret with the agreement of Buckingham Palace and MI5, provoking a parliamentary and media outcry about the immunity deal that had been struck with the royal family's art adviser. Renewed allegations of a widespread penetration by the KGB and a key Soviet mole at the highest level of British intelligence fuelled a frenzied outpouring of articles.

In his article for *The Round Table* Bell noted that those of his generation who had betrayed their country had done so 'reacting in disgust against what they saw as a religion of bogus ideals and false values which had been exposed by Marx and other writers'.[3] And yet they were 'inexcusably blind to the horrors of Stalin's communism'. As he went on to point out, the Nazi-Soviet Pact signed by Hitler and Stalin early on in World War Two made the Germans and the Russians only temporary bedfellows, and when Germany attacked Russia in June 1941, the policy emphatically proclaimed by Churchill was that everything should be done to further Britain's alliance with Russia. 'There was neither time nor inclination to delve into the past of otherwise suitable recruits such as Philby – to recall whether they had been married some years before to a Communist long since divorced, or had joined a Jarrow March,' Bell recalled.[4]

And yet with the evidence of hindsight, Bell conceded that in the two or three years following the war, when Philby was appointed to head up the anti-Soviet section at MI6 and liaised with the CIA and FBI, there should have been a radical review of MI5 and MI6 employees as soon as it became clear that the main threat to national security would come from the Soviet Union and those with communist convictions. In fact, instead of war-time recruits who remained in the service having their records reviewed, an atmosphere of friendship and mutual trust, which had developed over the war years, prevailed. Philby got away with it thanks to his old boy and 'club' network with many of his colleagues taken in by his apparent professionalism. 'Even if Philby's earlier connection with Communism had been questioned, surely eleven years later and after outstanding war service for which he was awarded the OBE and promoted to high rank in his service, his reputation was unassailable,' wrote Bell.[5] As for the others, 'Blunt had left MI5 after the war, and Maclean worked for the Foreign Office who shouldered the responsibility having recruited him before the war, while Burgess's known failings at that time were 'drink, sex and general slovenliness; he had never been thought of as being a spy.'[6]

The Cambridge Spy ring affair, Bell wrote, produced two reactions often: 'On the one hand it was said that the Security Service had been lax and incompetent and covering up failings of their own; on the other, that an unaccountable body of inquisitors was engaged in relentless investigation of our private lives and interests – often, some think, to satisfy their salacious curiosity.'[7]

At the time of Bell's *Round Table* article in 1980, renewed media interest in intelligence 'history' had been stirred by the allegations that another colleague of Bell's, the former deputy chief of MI5 Guy Liddell, was a Soviet spy. Liddell had died in 1958. The allegation against him had first surfaced in an article in *Encounter* magazine in 1979 by the writer and diplomat Robert Cecil who had served with Bell, and two other Foreign Office colleagues John Balfour, and the Cambridge spy Donald Maclean, in the post-war British embassy in Washington during 1945–1948.

The former MI5 and MI6 chief Dick White, by then retired, was stung by the allegation as was his friend Bell. They both had worked with Liddell over many years and held similar personal and professional respect for him. White had been director general of MI5 when an internal investigation he had ordered and supervised had cleared Liddell.[8] He wrote privately to Bell from his house in Burpham, Sussex, recognising the complex networks in which both patriots and traitors might inadvertently mix while enlisting his support in refuting the allegations. 'It needs a comprehensive reply to be convincing and that in two points:

> First Guy [Liddell]was not a friend of Burgess although he was of course a close friend of Victor Rothschild[9] through whom he doubtless was introduced on not more than one or two occasions to Bentinck Street.[10] Moreover, it was Guy Liddell who effectively blocked a suggestion from Burgess to join MI5. All this I know but would find it difficult to say. The second point of the argument would therefore be rather thin. It would consist simply of saying that he retired normally at the age of 60, and here of course you and I know only too well he was the obvious man to succeed Petrie, but he was passed over for Sillitoe.[11] It's a very unhappy story – I rather doubt the advisability of trying to put it right without being able to say all. What do you think?[12]

White played a key role in in the development of the post-war British intelligence structure over the two decades leading to the disclosures of the so called Cambridge 'ring-of-five' – Burgess, Maclean, Philby, Blunt and Cairncross.[13] The letter is revealing to the extent that it shows White to be both calculating and also reliant on Bell's advice as to how best to defuse a controversy that threatened to expose skeletons the spy chief had hitherto kept firmly under lock and key.

Bell responded to White's call to arms by writing a letter to *Encounter* magazine, refuting the allegations made against Liddell by Cecil and obtaining a retraction. Cecil, who evidently had no wish to break ranks with old chums in the Foreign Office and the British intelligence community over claims of treachery he could not substantiate, wrote a letter to his senior colleague John Balfour, copying in Bell, 'in the best Whitehall tradition', presumably of collegiality as well as loyalty.

Cecil told Balfour:

> May I say from the start that I'm very sorry to have distressed you. There is, I think no doubt that the two Guys ([Liddell and Burgess)]were friendly, but this does not mean, of course, that they were engaged in similar activities. Nor was it my intention to imply this. After all, until 1951, I regarded myself as a friend of Donald's [Maclean]. However, I ought not to have repeated the comment that Guy Liddell lost his job on account of his connection with GB [Guy Burgess] without checking this statement, which I believed to be good authority...
>
> Walter Bell tells me he has had access to the facts and I'm glad that he should make the necessary correction. There seems to have some delay on the part of Encounter; but they will certainly publish the letter.[14]

Controversy and intrigue continued to embroil Bell and his friends in the intelligence community, however, as they tried to stem further reputational damage. The English spy supremo Dick White wrote to Bell suggesting that the obsessively anti-communist former CIA officer James Angleton was briefing journalists and stirring up a conspiracy of Russian penetration of the transatlantic intelligence relationship that had no foundation. 'My hunch is that Angleton is at the centre of a web of intrigue to advertise his own brilliance and the failures of the American and British Services.'[15]

In seeking to control disclosure and the pace of events, White continued to count on his friend Bell to help organise a coordinated damage limitation media campaign in defence of Guy Liddell. The campaign took a bold step towards a tactical engagement with allies in the media, when Bell persuaded a journalist friend at *The Times* he had befriended in his India days, Louis Heren, who was now deputy editor, to organise a private lunch at headquarters on 30 January 1980, with Dick White and the former Special Branch police officer turned MI5 interrogator Wiliam J. Skardon, both of whom had worked with Guy Liddell and were prepared to defend his and the Security Service's reputation. At the time such encounters in newspaper offices between senior spies and journalists were unheard of. But following the newspaper's interview with Blunt, Bell had successfully courted Heren's support for an encounter that was designed to influence coverage in support of White and his friends.

Much of the lunch was taken up by White being given full rein to argue the case for media and author restraint in reporting intelligence matters, stressing the need for a scrupulous regard for truth alongside the need to protect secret information that might come to MI6 about people, otherwise 'grave injustices and scandal would be rife'. According to notes taken by Bell during the lunch, White 'pointed out that there is a need for intelligence to be seen in proportion – i.e. it is but one part, and not necessarily a major part of the knowledge upon which a government has to make decisions'.[16]

White spoke very strongly about the 'iniquity' of the allegations against his friend Liddell without feeling the need to apologise for the organisational failure that had led to the Cambridge circle getting away with their treachery for so long. White, who had worked with Liddell in World War Two, said that 'he had never had the slightest doubt about his good faith' while Skardon said 'he was a wonderful man and any suggestion that he was a traitor is preposterous.'[17]

The campaign in defence of Liddell also involved a series of well-coordinated letters to the editor of *The Times*, signed by close friends, all with close links with wartime British intelligence, protesting his innocence. The most prominent letter was signed by a group of establishment names after they had been approached by Bell, showing that in retirement he had lost none of his ability to network in areas of influence. He worked closely with his neighbour in Onslow Square, the retired senior diplomat Sir John ( 'Jock') Balfour with whom he had coincided in the post-war British embassy in Washington. Balfour had served as deputy head of mission when Bell was private secretary to the ambassador Lord Inverchapel.

Apart from Balfour himself, the other signatories were Victor Cavendish-Bentinck (later 9th Duke of Portland),[18] who had served as the chairman of the Joint Intelligence Committee in World War Two, a retired senior diplomat, Sir Patrick Reilly, the former MI6 officer Hugh Trevor-Roper, who signed with his title as life peer Lord Dacre of Glanton, and Sir John Stephenson, a Lord Justice of Appeal and a member of the Privy Council. All had worked with Liddell or been a friend of his, describing him as having been a 'person of sterling worth and flawless integrity who deserves well of his country which in times of exceptional difficulty he served with loyalty, efficiency, devotion and distinction'.[19]

On 22 January 1980, the letter in defence of Liddell that Balfour and his friends had signed was published in *The Times*.[20] As part of a lobby campaign to clear his name that now straddled both sides of the Atlantic, Bell was happy to liaise and act as an effective post-box for his former boss Bill Stephenson, the former head of the wartime BSC in New York, who described Liddell as someone he had known for a long time and intimately 'as an able honourable and exceptionally outstanding leading member of the services'.[21]

After being briefed by Bell in a transatlantic telephone conversation, Stephenson agreed to send him his statement in the form of a personal telegram from his residence in Bermuda, authorising him to use his name to help counter the accusations against Liddell. Bell ensured that the telegram got to his friend Heren, and Stephenson's support for Liddell appeared in a story on the front page of *The Times* on 21 January 1980. It was accompanied by a supportive profile, written by the newspaper's reporter Stewart Tendler, crediting Liddell with 'holding together the disparate collection of gifted amateurs drafted in from universities as MI5 was enlarged during WW2'.[22]

The positive coverage did much to clear Liddell's name, although there was a limit to how much the media was prepared to be pressurised into whitewashing the failings of MI5, MI6 and the Foreign Office. A strong body of evidence had been building up since the end of World War Two that all three agencies had been infiltrated by the Russians from the 1930s onwards. No-one could easily shrug off the accusations that they had been shockingly complacent about the Cambridge spies, a story that no official history had been allowed to cover.

Meanwhile, on the other side of the Atlantic, as the US continued to impose itself as a global power in intelligence as well as military, diplomatic and economic terms, the perception endured that the Cambridge spy ring was a very English affair, the product of class and post-imperial networks that protected its kind simply because they shared a similar privileged education and spoke with the right accent or continued to meet up in their private clubs. As Bell was told by one of his CIA contacts Bronson Tweedy, the investigation into Philby was hampered by 'prejudices and reluctances, personal and professional'.[23]

Tweedy had served as CIA station chief in London during 1956–1959 before becoming deputy director of the agency during the late 1960s and early 1970s under Richard Helms. During the height of the Liddell controversy, Bell wrote to the by then retired Tweedy, trying to enlist his support in defence of his former MI5 colleague.[24]

In reply Tweedy told Bell that he discussed Liddell at some length with former CIA colleagues. While he had not found any evidence that he was suspected of being a Soviet spy, Tweedy believed that Liddell seemed to have shouldered some of the blame for not identifying earlier the 'serious cases' of betrayal – Burgess, Philby and Maclean – and thus a wider institutional failing. As Tweedy put it, regarding Burgess and Maclean: 'Apart from the obvious difficulty of spotting them as spies, their own personal conduct had for so long been so outrageous that it was a scandal they were allowed to remain in positions of sensitive responsibility.'[25]

Bell's campaign to enlist transatlantic support for his friend Liddell drew a more belated response from the controversial CIA officer James ('Jim') Angleton, who as a young 26-year-old Office of Strategic Services (OSS) officer during World War Two had been posted to the UK for training by MI6 officers including Philby as part of the cooperation agreement encouraged by the BSC's Bill Stephenson and the MI6 chief Stewart Menzies.

The shock that Angleton felt at Philby's betrayal may have tipped Angleton into believing that the British establishment as well as the CIA had allowed itself to be penetrated by the Soviet Union far more extensively than was officially recognised. Angleton belatedly acknowledged his British friend and mentor's treachery after Moscow triumphantly confirmed Philby's defection in July 1963. Bell and some of his friends were among certain US and British intelligence officers who came to believe that Angleton subsequently became mentally unstable, being driven half-mad by the Philby affair and its persistent cover-up by the British.

Angleton had been retired for five years and was living

relatively out of the public eye on both sides of the Atlantic when Bell contacted him in early 1980 over the Liddell affair. The American took several months to respond, seemingly in no hurry to get embroiled in the British campaign to vindicate one of its own top spies and revive the sense of humiliation he had suffered over the Philby affair. And yet when Angleton eventually wrote to Bell, he showed that although he had not abandoned his virulent anti-communism, he was no longer so obsessed as to want to point an accusing finger at Liddell against whom there was no evidence. 'I have never heard of the allegation that the CIA had any question regarding Guy [Liddell] At least if there had been a problem of that sort, I certainly would have known and remembered it,' Angleton wrote in his letter to Bell dated 6 July 1980. 'I remember Guy as being greatly respected for his professional reputation.'[26]

In his letter Angleton claimed to sympathise with how frustrated and angry Bell and other friends of Liddell's felt by the media allegations against him, suggesting that here indeed was a case of irresponsible journalists willingly duped by mischievous sources, and that the Soviets were deliberately using disinformation as a tactic to disarm the west by discrediting the reputation of respected individuals. As Angleton went on: 'I fear that it [the media reporting] will continue unabated simply because a service cannot defend itself. More important is the general ignorance of significant and influential personages in the media regarding the history of opposition services and the inherent difficulties of attempting to penetrate and contain agents from a totalitarian regime with its unlimited resources and unwavering political objectives.'[27]

There was no love lost between Angleton and the media, nor was he supportive of political moves to make the intelligence world more accountable as Bell had argued for in his *Round Table* article. The ex-CIA officer drew on deep-rooted prejudice fuelled by personal experience. He had resigned from the CIA amid growing criticism in the media and Congress about his failed mole hunts and his pursuit of anti-war protesters and other domestic dissident organisations he regarded as being communist subversives. He believed that his friends in the UK intelligence world were facing a similar potentially hugely damaging onslaught. 'I perceive the British Press is in the process of destroying the Official Secrets Act as part of their common objectives to seek some kind of parliamentary oversight to render the Service "accountable". If that should come to pass, I doubt whether any professional can carry on with the protection of sources,' he wrote to Bell.[28]

Angleton, unlike Stephenson, had written to Bell on the understanding that his comments would not be made public since he believed 'it would be improper to become involved with internal matters in the UK'.[29] The sense of betrayal Angleton blamed his one-time friend Philby for, however, evidently still haunted him seventeen years after his defection. 'I have turned down several interviewers who are bent on pursuing Philby and co. I, for one, believe his ability to harm has been underestimated.'[30] He went on to refer to a recent interview given by Graham Greene, in which the author mentioned that he had received a teasing postcard on the subject from Havana signed 'Philby', which he suspected was a deliberate spoof from Philip Agee, a former CIA case officer who worked for the Cuban communist regime. 'As I understand, the nonaligned conference meetings were underway there. Of interest also was the active presence of Agee,' wrote Angleton.

In the conspiratorial world in which Angleton had immersed himself, the obsessively anti-communist and patriotic CIA veteran could barely hide his dislike of the three individuals mentioned – Philby, Greene and Agee – all of whom were anti-American and, in Philby's and Agee's case, traitors, who had defected to the communist cause. In his extraordinary letter to Bell, Agee's name is highlighted in capital letters, presumably as Angleton considered his 'betrayal' not only the most current at the time but also the most despicable given that it concerned a former CIA officer.

While Philby's treachery as a Soviet spy was well known, the other two also held pride of place in Angleton's black book of rogues. Greene, who had worked for MI6 in World War Two and retained friendships with some of his former colleagues, had written a sympathetic preface to Philby's memoirs equating his faith in communism to his own Catholic faith and had increasingly become critical of American post-war imperialism from Vietnam to Central America.[31]

As for Philip Agee, the CIA officer turned whistle-blower, Angleton would never forgive him for having penned a very critical book about the agency published in 1975, *Inside the Company*.[32] Angleton was part of a campaign aimed at discrediting Agee's reputation. This partly succeeded in painting Agee as a Cuban asset which, given the repressive nature of the regime in Cuba, where Agee chose to live in exile, countered his self-projected image as a principled defender of liberty.[33]

The campaign Bell helped orchestrate in defence of Liddell achieved some success in limiting further reputational damage to British intelligence even if the Cambridge spy ring and its ramifications continued to remain a media and literary obsession for many years. Bell was acutely aware of the lessons that could and should have been drawn earlier by the intelligence services from the media probe of alleged moles that developed in the 1970s, often aided by frustrated one-time agents and officers. In his seminal article for *The Round Table* in 1980, he conceded that thanks to the exposure of the Cambridge spies, 'old assumptions were shattered, and loyalty was no longer assumed, no matter who presented themselves for recruitment in government service'. The background checks on recruits to sensitive areas in Whitehall were intensified. And yet as he wrote, 'there remained a very proper resistance to over assiduous policing and prying into the views and convictions of the citizens of a free society', and the spy world struggled to strike a balance between the need to safeguard secrets and the necessity for accountability and the duty of a free media to probe failings or actions that were judged contrary to the public interest.[34]

Bell showed himself well ahead of his generation of spies,

recruited in the 1930s, by arguing that the security and intelligence services should explain their duties more clearly and engage in a reasonable public discussion about their role – even if his defence of Liddell showed the intelligence community determined to protect the reputation of one of their own when they perceived it to be unfairly attacked.

While never betraying his country or his colleagues and prepared to defend the reputation of those he felt unfairly accused of treachery, Bell felt that the failings as well as achievements of the intelligence community should be the subject of proper scrutiny, and that excessive defensiveness had its risks. As he went on to argue: 'There is surely no inherent reason why the duties of the Security and Intelligence Services should not be explained more clearly than they are. Mystery-making invites curiosity and provokes derogatory criticism. There is the further complication that people who spend their working lives in secrecy may develop their own paranoia which impairs their judgement and outlook.'[35] Bell may have had James Angleton in his sights here, for his CIA friend came to personify the obsession of seeing a communist subversive under every media, congressional, and whistleblower bed.

Bell concluded that while he did not dispute the contention that the detailed activities of the intelligence agencies must be kept secret for them to be effective, this did not preclude a reasonable public discussion of their role. A workable compromise would be difficult to achieve but it had to be sought. As he would go on to write: 'Not only because accountability of public servants is a basic principle in a democratic society, but also because people should understand that the effective operations of Security and Intelligence Services is an essential defence against the country's enemies whether they are a menace from abroad or conspire within.'[36]

# 31
# A Very Catholic Spy

In an article published in the international Catholic weekly *The Tablet* in December 2019, a year before John le Carré died, the Church historian Massimo Faggioli analysed one of the spy author's most celebrated characters and found in le Carré's imperturbable intelligence officer George Smiley an example of how fidelity and commitment can survive betrayal and disenchantment.[1] Just a few months earlier a former MI6 chief Sir Richard Dearlove in a Hinsley memorial lecture delivered in Cambridge University had criticised le Carré for painting an unfairly negative picture of British intelligence.[2] Walter Bell's true-life story suggests that Faggioli is not wide of the mark, in that we might indeed have something to learn from spies – real ones as well as their literary constructs – from both their mistakes and their redemptive incisiveness. They are human, after all.

As Faggioli points out, overt religion is almost absent from le Carré's stories, and the same holds true for George Smiley, le Carré's best-known character and perhaps his greatest fictional creation. Smiley, as the author defined his fictional character, was an amalgam who sprang from a much deeper imaginative well than any of his apparent counterparts in real life but was nonetheless drawn from a real world in which few great novelists were more rooted. Le Carré drew from his experience of intelligence services and the extraordinary cast of characters he encountered as a young intelligence officer under the real-life name he had been recruited under, David Cornwell.[3] He worked for MI5 and MI6 during the 1950s and 1960s, when both services were led by the older generation of World War Two veterans which Bell belonged to, along with some of the other real-life characters who have made an appearance in this account of his life and times.

While researching Bell's biography, it occurred to me that le Carré and Bell shared similar misgivings about the shadowlands they inhabited, and that the paths of spy turned author and the spy who was always a spy might have crossed. They certainly shared some common friends. During one of his first postings at the British embassy in Bonn in the early 1960s, le Carré worked and formed an enduring friendship with David Goodall, one of his Oxford contemporaries, who, together with Bell, went on to form part of an English Catholic network of former senior civil servants, politicians, journalists, publishers and spies.

Short of stature, shrewd, monkish and slightly owlish in appearance, the Benedictine Ampleforth-educated Goodall had joined the Foreign Office in 1956 after a short-term commission in the army had taken him to Kenya as well as Cyprus.[4] He knew Bell from his Kenya days. Both men came to form part of a network of clubbable Roman Catholics and in retirement became contributors to and supporters of *The Tablet*, which had earned a reputation as a relatively small circulation but influential international Catholic magazine that punched well above its weight.

Faith, if not Belief, ran deep in Bell's life even if he struggled with both. While one line of his ancestry led back to the most unreligious *News of the World*, he was also born into a vicarage where his father was a deeply religious and ritualistic High Church Anglo-Catholic priest who set high standards of morality.

Walter's formal conversion to the Roman Catholic Church took place at some point during his first MI5 Kenya posting (1949–1952) when he was in his mid-forties. There is no surviving record of the exact date, but the recollections of family members suggest there was no single moment, no Damascene revelation. Having been partly traumatised as a child by his father's overzealous priesthood, Bell spent his student days rebelling against the past, flirting with Marxist political economic theory and rebelling against the establishment while also befriending some of its members.

His choice of a career in MI6 and MI5 had him escaping as far away as possible from the picture postcard Kent village vicarage he had been born in and into the futuristic landscape of New York and a world of secrets and intrigue across the old empire. But he could never bring himself to break from his upbringing and, in the darkness of the build-up to World War Two, sought light in the writings of Roman Catholic scholars such as Christopher Dawson and Jacques Maritain, who seemed receptive to the challenges of the times and offered a reinvigorated Christian alternative to atheism. For Bell, both Marxism and Catholic theology fuelled his belief that repression, war, injustice, and totalitarianism, as expressions of evil, could be defeated.

And yet, like W.H. Auden, one of the poets of his generation, Bell would also migrate to the US in search of necessary space, have his humanism tested by the Spanish Civil War, and his views on communism by Stalin, while World War Two brought home the full dehumanised horror of Nazism as the polar opposite of Christianity.[5]

If Bell was to later draw inspiration from the selfless sense of service to the poor of Catholic missionaries in Kenya, as with Auden his life-long exploration of various traditions and anti-traditions led him to the conclusion that he needed God. And if he struggled to the end of his life to believe, navigating through periods of doubt, in his later years he found a sort of coming home in the sacramental ritual of Roman Catholicism, in liturgical tradition – something he could feel emotionally involved in, leading him back to the faith he was born into, that of a God worth worshipping.

In retirement Bell returned to his ancestral roots in newspaper publishing – not to the redtop *News of the World* his family had once owned, but rather to writing articles and book reviews for *The Tablet*, when not writing occasional letters to *The Times*.

Parish accounts show that Walter contributed to the fund-raising campaign for the Church of England parish church of St

Mary's at Riverhead during all the years his father, George, was a vicar there. After his father died he tried to ensure that his grave was regularly cleaned and maintained to acknowledge his service to the parish church he had served for forty-two years.

According to George's expressed wishes, he was buried not in the main cemetery but in a lone grave bordering the east wall of the church, with the apparent aim of preventing any encroachment on the interior by any further architectural addition to the historic late Georgian styled building that had been consecrated in 1831 and its late Victorian extension. For George the church had reached the limit of its restoration by human hand. It was a sacred place and was to be for ever preserved as such.

It was among the humble missionaries in Kenya that Bell came across a different kind of church, closer to the Gospel story and often at odds with the established order of colonial authority and settlement, not part of it. Up to that point his 'priesthood', like Smiley's priesthood, belonged to a particular kind of dying Church, a post-war Britain overseeing the disintegration of its empire. As Smiley's retired colleague Connie Sachs tells Smiley: 'Poor loves. Trained to Empire, trained to rule the waves … You're the last, George, you and Bill.'[6]

As a student Bell briefly sold copies of the *Daily Worker* at the door of the London School of Economics, befriended radical Labour MPs and fellow travellers and included a member of the American Communist Party in his contacts list. His career had him working in peacetime and war, World War Two and the Cold War, with British colleagues who were later discovered to be Russian spies (Maclean and Philby) and serving and defending the reputation of two others who were suspected of betrayal, but against whom the allegation of treachery was never proven (Roger Hollis and Guy Liddell).

If Bell saw no need to become a public campaigner in his anti-communism, it is because he was both a professional spy and a man guided by private conscience, not ideology. He was a youthful socialist supporter of the British Labour Party and his personal papers since the late 1930s show him to have been critical of Stalinism, and to have believed that his work in MI6 and MI5 was always firmly in the best interests of the West. He never had any wish to join the Communist Party or betray his country – unlike Smiley's nemesis in *Tinker, Tailor, Soldier, Spy* Bill Haydon, whom le Carré based loosely on Philby. During his retirement years, Bell moderated his politics, and went public with them, in 1981 signing up as one of the founding members of the British Social Democratic Party, a moderate centre-left breakaway from the then socialist Labour Party.[7]

Bell was by that time disillusioned with Britain's traditional party system, largely inspired by one of the new party's Gang of Four founders, the Catholic MP Shirley Williams who, in 1987, following the annulment of her first marriage to the moral philosopher Bernard Williams, married Richard Neustadt, the Harvard professor, historian and adviser to several US presidents. Having served under both Harold Wilson and Jim Callaghan's premiership, Williams split from Labour as it lurched to the left under the leadership of Michael Foot. She later supported the SDP's merger with the Liberal Party that formed the Liberal Democrats.

Bell respected Williams's razor-sharp political mind and personal warmth, her commitment to social justice and internationalism, her support for European integration and special interest and respect for the democratic politics of the US to which she was linked, as Bell was, was by work, study, and marriage. With its progressive but undogmatic nature and its clear opposition to communism and fascism, Williams's world view was one that Bell identified with politically.

Crucially, perhaps, Bell was honoured on both sides of the Atlantic – with the US Medal of Freedom during his World War Two service, and with the British Order of St Michael and St George for his security and intelligence work during the Cold War and twilight of empire. And no one ever found a reason for taking away such recognition.

In retirement Bell became involved in a carefully orchestrated campaign in defence of colleagues he believed had been unfairly and inaccurately alleged to have been Russian agents after being cleared by internal investigations. As with so many of his generation, Bell's career was overshadowed by the betrayal of the Cambridge Five, which raised what he felt was legitimate scepticism about the ability and willingness of the clubbable intelligence establishment to allow itself to be accountable to the media and the law. He remained faithful to the values of Western democracy on both sides of the Atlantic and tried his best to conduct himself professionally in a way that was reasonable and non-fanatical, showing great understanding for those who sought independence from British colonialism. Bell, as Faggioli wrote of Smiley in *The Tablet*, 'knows which side he is on, but he recognizes the crooked timber of humanity on both the Soviet and the "free world" side of the Berlin Wall. He is a warning against the myth of easy dualism …. the unalloyed bad and the unalloyed good.'[8]

After retiring officially from government service, Bell did not manage, as some other colleagues would, to carve out a bigger salary in the private sector, whose doors did not open to him even if he did approach some leading US entities for a job after leaving MI5.

After his final overseas posting in Kenya, he gave some serious thought to seeking more lucrative employment in the US, a country where he had built his career and been honoured as wartime intelligence officer, where he had made enduring friends, and where his wife 'Tattie' Spaatz could count on a closely knit family network. He was encouraged by an old New York friend, Professor William ('Bill') Hansberry, who had founded the post-war influential African-American Institute, one of numerous foundations that secretly benefited from CIA support during the Cold War years.[9]

Hoping for a job in strategic or security advice, Bell approached Lehman Brothers and Chase Manhattan without success. He met several similar cul-de-sacs at IBM, Time Inc., and Morgan Guarantee. He also failed to strike lucky with Pan American Airways, whose vice-president Laurence S. Kuter, a retired US air force general, had served Bell's father-in-law

General Spaatz. None of them apparently had an available slot that could draw on his expertise.[10] Bell's papers provide few clues as to whether there might have been any other reasons and none have come to light. One can only speculate that the Cambridge spy ring affair had cast a long shadow across the Atlantic, undermining the reputation of British intelligence because of the extent it had been penetrated by Soviet intelligence through betrayal and institutional failure.

Undaunted, however, he devoted the last twenty years of his life to reflecting on and sharing the lessons drawn from his time in active service, occasionally lecturing and writing articles and letters. Settled in their comfortable flat overlooking the private Onslow Gardens, which as a keen gardener Bell helped preserve, he and his enduringly loyal wife and companion Tattie enjoyed playing convivial hosts to a circle of friends – 'cocktails and laughter', as one regular attendee recalled[11] – drawn from the world of diplomacy, secret intelligence and journalism.

In Kenya he had converted to Roman Catholicism and would refer disparagingly to the colonial days when the governor's sabre was placed on the altar of Nairobi's Anglican Cathedral in an annual ceremony. His Catholic faith later became an absorbing concern to him, perhaps because the moment of revelation in times of dislocation and darkness fascinated him as did the poetry of T.S. Eliot. As he struggled with his dark moods of depression, and occasionally raged against those he had to keep secrets for, Bell seemed to follow in the steps of the Magi in T.S. Eliot's poem 'Journey of the Magi', who, once they had embarked on a difficult journey, required a different course to be taken. The 'old dispensation', as Eliot, put it, wouldn't do any more. Bell's private papers articulate the shifting sands of human experience, which continued long after he left government service.[12]

# 32
# Brothers in Arms

The personal archive Walter Bell built up during his lifetime included the correspondence he maintained with his friend Dick White, who served as head of both MI5 and MI6 during the Cold War years and whom he outlived by twelve years. The spy writer Andrew Boyle described White as 'one of the best and most gifted men in the secret world...a remarkable survivor and a lasting inspiration to all who knew him.'[1] White was a 'self-effacing, intelligent and honest patriot'[2] who dominated the British intelligence services for thirty-five years.

Dick White was born in Tonbridge, near where Bell was born, although the two only met for the first time in adulthood and did not belong to the same old boy network. White was educated at Bishop's Stortford School and Christ Church, Oxford, Bell at Tonbridge School and the London School of Economics.

White was three years older than Bell and became a much better known and prominent figure in both agencies. Before he died in 1993, he wrote to Bell, thanking his enduring friend and colleague, who had managed to stay below the radar of public notoriety and scandal more successfully than less patriotic spies of their generation. Bell would outlive White by eleven years:

> I am very glad that in old age you and Tattie and Katie (White) and I have grown close. I always thought of you in the office as a friend of Guy (Liddell) who shared many of his admirably relaxed, tolerant, and wise qualities. You have them in even greater measure now and at greater depth because you have allowed yourself time to reflect, helped I expect by your Catholic way of life and the blessing of your marriage. Tattie is such a constant

figure.[3]

Prior to his death from cancer, White corresponded regularly with Bell from the modern timber-framed house in Burpham, on the Duke of Norfolk's Arundel estate in Sussex, that he had moved into after his retirement in 1972, when not meeting up for lunch in London at one or other of their beloved clubs. Their subjects of shared interest and concern ranged from the world of intelligence and its relationship with the media to US politics and, increasingly, matters of faith. White enjoyed conversation and friendships, 'quietly convinced that eventually history would acknowledge the value of an honest intelligence service to the nation's government'.[4]

While Bell deferred to White as the colleague who had reached the high echelons of government service, uniquely heading up MI5 and MI6 in different stages of his career, their correspondence suggests that the professional respect was mutual and their friendship, based on genuine trust, long-lasting. As White told Bell, 'I always enjoy the news from Onslow Square.[5] You sit there scanning the world of metaphysical and political ideas and invariably come up with something of special interest to me.'[6]

On a matter that had taken up much of their covert plotting and lobbying in later years – the relationship between the media and secret intelligence – one letter referred to an article on the case of the spy Michael Bettaney by the former MI5 officer Miranda Ingram published in *New Society* on 31 June 1984. White disagreed with Ingram, a former colleague, who wrote that the core of MI5's philosophy and working conditions was the British class system, which made the British security fertile ground for communist infiltration. 'In my time I knew many Labour voters in MI5 (I was at the time one myself) and quite a number of officers of humble social origin. The service was far less class-ridden than the next at Whitehall,' White told Bell.[7]

Both men had served in MI5 and MI6 (the 'next' at

Whitehall referred to by White) in different stages of their careers, and thus knew well the different identities and characters in each organisation, and the tensions and betrayals that this provoked among some of their colleagues. Both White and Bell had also lived and worked in the US and had a shared interest in American politics and the various permutations of the World War Two and Cold War transatlantic relationship. In retirement they had come to find relaxation in each other's company, often forming a convivial foursome lunching after a long walk in the Sussex Downs with their respective spouses, the English novelist Kathleen Bellamy, and the US general's daughter Tattie, both vegetarians and strong women in their own right, who had the true measure of their respective husbands, and also got on well with each other.

As the Cold War reached its final stage, the two veteran spies discussed the nature of Reaganism and Thatcherism. White wrote to Bell in 1984 arguing that the ground-breaking decision taken by the liberal judicial activist chief justice Earl Warren's Supreme Court in support of civil liberties and civil rights had let loose the 'formidable decadence' of the 1970s, which in turn had found its rival in 'the moral majority' behind Reagan. 'I would have thought the "formidable decadence" was mostly the product of the pop culture of the "60's", a phenomenon evident in other western countries and much subscribed to here in England', White wrote.[8] For White, as he told Bell, the more important 'decadent' feature of those years was 'the extent that the so-called "liberal consensus" blamed America rather than Russia for the tensions of the times and influenced movements like the campaign for nuclear disarmament, CND.'[9]

White took particular satisfaction in witnessing the collapse of communism with Glasnost. By contrast Bell declared himself less than enamoured with the world leaders who were subsequently empowered, along with the free-market economics they championed, Reagan and Thatcher.

Bell wrote to White commenting that Washington DC was 'awash in seriousness' after media reports had surfaced that the US CIA director turned President George Bush had overlooked the Panamanian military leader General Noriega's illegal activities because of his cooperation with American intelligence and his willingness to permit the American military extensive leeway to operate in Panama.[10] 'I have little to say that could be of interest to such experts on the city (Washington DC) as you and Tattie. Bush certainly does not impress,' responded White.[11]

If Walter Bell had from an early age sought to cut loose from the conformity of the High Anglican vicarage into which he was born, it was faith nonetheless where he was destined to continue to search for a new meaning in life. In the late 1970s Walter became a trustee of the Catholic weekly *The Tablet*, where the clubbable and well-connected editor and author's father Tom Burns's[12] networks of friends straddled the ecclesiastical and secular world.

Some of the friends Burns made before and during World War Two when he worked in propaganda and intelligence in the British embassy in Madrid served as spies in the Cold War and he maintained a secret informal relationship with members of British and US intelligence during his post-war years as a publisher and journalist.[13]

When on the advisery board of *The Tablet* Bell found himself in influential company, a sample of English Roman Catholics with distinguished careers, including his friend the spy chief Dick White's landlord Miles Fitzalan-Howard, Duke of Norfolk (White's cottage was located in Norfolk's Arundel estate), the cabinet secretary Sir John Hunt, the novelist Graham Greene, the editor of *The Times* William Rees-Mogg, and the director general of the BBC, Charles Curran.

In time they would be joined by Sir Michael Quinlan, another senior mandarin from Bell's network of Catholic friends, who had gained a reputation as the leading civilian thinker in Whitehall on defence policy and as a strong believer in the value of deterrence from the 1970s to the 1990s.

Politically *The Tablet* tended towards the centre ground,

as vocal in its denunciation of Soviet Communism as of South American dictatorships, with its letters' pages reflecting an openness to different views on ethical issues from nuclear deterrence to birth control. Both as an adviser and an occasional contributor to its pages, Bell felt theologically stimulated by a magazine that espoused the teaching of the reformist and ecumenical Second Vatican Council of the 1960s. He regarded its pages as very much concerned about the Catholic Church's integrity and missionary mandate, while also creating an environment of dialogue, engaged in all the forces of the modern world.

Dick White became a supporter of *The Tablet*, gladly accepting a gift subscription from Bell, even though, as a life-long member of the Church of England, he resisted conversion to the Roman Catholic Church. During the early 1980s of the Thatcher premiership and the Reagan presidency leading to the collapse of the Soviet Union, White became an enthusiast of the magazine as an informative and well-informed weekly read that seemed to him reassuringly less radical in its coverage of the secular world than in its broad ecumenical and theological outlook.

As White made clear in a letter to Bell, the magazine was very much on message, as far as he, an old Cold War warrior, was concerned:

> I know that you have a part to play in the management of *The Tablet* and may therefore possibly be interested in the effect it has upon an English 'heretic'. I very much like its openness and generally liberal and ecumenical outlook. It confronts the modern world of changing values in a critical rather than a doctrinaire manner and it is persuasive rather than authoritarian. It can only be a help to all of us in our confusions, whatever the Church we may belong to or none, ....so thank you dear Walter.[14] . . . Even if it does not convert me, it will surely improve my mind and open my heart. As

I see things, conversion is not all that important…
You can today even be an agnostic Christian still
tied emotionally to the English Church flying at his
turret the flag of St George.[15]

Unlike White, Bell nonetheless was a man of doubt, for
whom a search for a Christian God became something of an
obsession in his later years. He saw no contradiction in warming
to the liberal utterances emerging from the Catholic Church's
Second Vatican Council, while wanting to deepen the
experience of contemplative prayer and the eucharistic ritual of
his childhood. He began to frequent the nearest Roman
Catholic church to where he lived in South Kensington – the
very traditionalist London Oratory, built in the second half of
the nineteenth century and dedicated to the sixteenth-century
Roman priest Saint Philip Neri and the memory of the most
revered of Anglican converts to the Roman Catholic faith, John
Henry Newman.

Only years later did Bell and others in British intelligence
discover a curious allegation about the church's secret history in
the Cold War years, which its reverend fathers and congregation
were also unaware of. If the memory of a KGB defector can be
relied upon, this was his extraordinary claim: on the grounds
that it was a Roman Catholic Church and not state-run, the
London Oratory was chosen by the KGB as a sufficiently secure
place for a 'dead-drop' (the spy trade craft of passing items of
secret information between agent and 'handler', avoiding direct
meetings with the aim of maintaining operational security) by
Soviet spies between 1975 and 1985, in the decade which
culminated in the rise to power of Mikhail Gorbachev.[16]

The alleged dead-drop location was the church's ornate
World War One memorial, just on the right of its front door
when you stepped in from the outside. Outside service times,
when the church was largely empty, documents were apparently
hidden by the KGB contact near a Pietà statue that lies beneath
a relief of folded flags and a wreath with crossed guns, set in a

large golden arched and ruby red mottled marble alcove with the Latin inscription from the poet Horace, *Dulce et decorum est. Pro patria mori*, which translated to English means '*It is sweet and fitting to die for one's country*'. Thus had the London Oratory, for a brief period in its history, become a theatrical hiding place for top secrets. The KGB agent runner allegedly chose it because people went in and out of it all day, and no one paid any attention to them. As he put it, 'the church is not "state property"' so 'there are no people keeping a round-the-clock watch on it.' The trained Russian Cold War spy was inclined to think that there was no safer place in central London to deliver his secret post.[17]

However true or false the story of the dead-drop, Bell's motivation for frequenting the church in his retirement years was certainly spiritual. In the robust structure of the imposing neoclassical building and the rituals performed within it he sought a unity of architecture and faith, a sacred place of enduring Christianity, a comfort zone amidst his inner doubts and the tensions and fleeting materialisms of the secular world. He attended the church every morning of the week while in London, to hear mass in Latin and with the priest celebrating the sacramental mystery of transubstantiation. Bell seems to have been drawn to the Oratory not in pursuit of any KGB papers or agent, but because of his friendship with one of its most legendary and eccentric priests, Monsignor Alfred Gilbey, a fellow member and resident of The Travellers Club.

When not spending his leisure hours in the club's library, Gilbey went to great care to celebrate the pre-Pius XII's rites of the Tridentine (or traditional Latin) mass with a small, yet very loyal congregation. His lengthy 1983 paraphrase of the old 'penny' catechism – *We Believe: Commentary on the Catechism of Christian Doctrine*, based on the 'truths of the Faith' – which Gilbey considered his proudest achievement., became a bestseller among traditionalists. Yet Gilbey was sometimes more liberal in private than in public, saying different things to different people, not by way of being duplicitous, but in tailoring what he said to the hearer, engaging with rather than confronting doubt despite always defending doctrine.[18]

This was why Bell enjoyed his conversations with Gilbey whenever they met at the Travellers Club, which the priest would attend in his shovel hat, and dressed in his monsignor cassock with colourful silk cincture, piping and embellishments. It must have seemed to Bell, if only subconsciously at times, that he was in the presence of a ghost of his vicar father, even if in caricature. When robed in the sanctuary for mass Gilbey wore watered-silk purple soutane, tasselled cape and a purple pompon biretta. This was as much a manifestation of his Victorian outlook and ultra-montane Catholicism (advocating strong papal authority and centralisation of Roman Catholicism) as a mere question of sartorial preference.[19] Gilbey was not quite Bell's idea of God's messenger, but almost.

Bell's conversion to Roman Catholicism defied an element of religious prejudice within the British intelligence world that had its roots in the Reformation. MI6 and MI5 recruits of Bell's generation were still given a history lesson that began with the first popular spymaster, Sir Francis Walsingham, who pursued alleged Catholic traitors as Queen Elizabeth I's principal secretary, invoking his legendary mantra 'There is less danger in fearing too much than too little.'[20]

Bell stuck to the key 'truth' of the church he had converted to, the belief in the sacramental consecration of the body and blood of Christ at mass, but also believed, as *The Tablet* did, that Catholicism could be a broad if ultimately loyal church, respectful of papal authority but not uncritically so, accommodating conscience as something fluid and instilled with Cristian historical optimism, not static.

Walter was instinctively in favour of a church that drew on tradition but was open to the world. His faith was neither sectarian nor fundamentalist. On one occasion his friend, the editor of *The Tablet* Tom Burns, was refused communion in the hand as opposed to the most traditional form on the tongue, at a requiem in the London Oratory for his predecessor, the uncompromisingly ultra-montane Roman Catholic Douglas

Woodruff. Bell, suspecting an act of Inquisitorial retribution against a 'heretic', wrote an outraged letter to Fr Ignatius Harrison, the London Oratory's provost, demanding an explanation. Harrison wrote back excusing the oversight by claiming that that Holy Communion had been distributed by a visiting priest over whom he had no authority. The editor of *The Tablet* ended up getting a letter of apology from Fr Ignatius.[21]

Thanks to a close association with *The Tablet* during Burns's editorship, and that of his successor, fellow convert John Wilkins, Bell became strengthened in his view that his life as a Catholic provided a better understanding of, and reconciliation with, the world. It helped him engage with humanity's smooth as well as rougher edges and hang on to the ideal of a society serving the common good.

Next to matters of faith, power politics and international affairs were also of enduring interest to Bell. In 'One Man's View of the American Century', a talk he gave to military historians and strategist members of the London-based Military Commentators Circle in 1979, Bell spoke eloquently about the dualities and contradictions running through American history – its early slavery, the liberal ideals of its founding fathers, its periods of engagement with the world and yet America First isolationism, its tolerance and prejudices, its shining light to the free world and yet its equal disservice, at times, to the cause of human solidarity when tackling poverty or injustice in the developing world.[22]

For all his dalliance with Marxism during his student days, Bell had no love lost for communism and mistrusted the Soviet Union. Thus, in his talk to the Circle he noted how Americans, initially supportive of the UN, became 'justifiably aroused by the maddening Soviet obstruction, and the clear Soviet intention to use it only for their own ideological ends. Americans realized that they had been deceived by an ally and made to look foolish; this was unforgiveable.'[23]

He recalled how, while posted in the British embassy in Washington from 1946 to 1948, he had watched the American government gradually come to realise that there was absolutely no way of reaching a peaceful understanding with the Soviet Union. There was a sudden realisation that the Soviet system, expanding outside its old boundaries, challenged everything that Americans cherished and believed in – 'liberty in all its aspects and particularly, the right to enjoy the result of hard work and endeavour'.[24]

> Americans saw themselves being threatened with the prospect of living in a society totally controlled by a dictatorial government infinitely worse than what grandpa and grandma had fled from two generations before. [25]
> And so, with the 'idle, incompetent, snobbish British' no longer capable of fulfilling their old role of contending with these forces, the United States had to lead a crusade against the new and fearful menace whenever it presented itself.[26]

Bell would take issue with what he saw as the anti-US bias of campaigners for nuclear disarmament, contrasting the Americans publicly debating foreign and military affairs with the Soviet side 'where all is conducted in secrecy', and 'a vast array of spies is employed to steal the secrets of Western methods and technology'.[27] At the same time he was only too conscious of the ethos of US isolationism that had survived two world wars. The word 'Europe' meant everything to the descendants of immigrants who formed a majority of the American population – everything their forefathers had escaped from after getting sucked into the 'old quarrels between emperors and kings'; and facing the 'terrible voyage across the ocean to an unknown future'.[28] 'In his farewell address, the first President of the United Sates (George Washington) warned Americans against being drawn into European disputes. So, the whole tradition is one of aversion to the old continent-tempered by the natural compulsion to enquire about and visit the places whence their forebears came.'[29]

But he also regretted that the Cold War had made Americans angry, with an emerging tendency 'to turn on those who were suspected of being sympathetically lukewarm regarding Soviet ambitions or the Communist philosophy generally'. In Bell's view McCarthyism was a dark hour which did 'untold harm to democracy'. It 'confused and dismayed many of those who would otherwise have been admirers and friends of the United Sates. It certainly made things much easier for Communists in the Third World.'[30]

A year after his talk to the Military Circle, Bell penned a long letter to *The Tablet* criticising the Catholic peer Lord Longford's welcome to ex-President Nixon to London as part of the promotion of Nixon's book *The Real War*, analysing US strategic shortcomings and tracing the Western struggle against Russian ambition to the rise of Muscovite power under Ivan I in AD 1325.[31]

If he despaired of the intrinsic intolerance of the Soviet Union, Bell was no admirer of Nixon, his reputation irrevocably blackened by Watergate. As Bell wrote, 'After the Vietnam disaster America needed inspired leadership to recover her traditional optimism and sense of purpose. Instead by Nixon and his minions, America was served with meanness, dishonesty and chicanery which came near to destroying the Republic.'[32] As for Ronald Reagan, Bell predicted on 22 September 1984 that it was almost certain that he would be re-elected for a second term – as indeed he was. 'The United States under President Reagan will pursue a course which will provide for much conspicuous consumption by the fortunate, but quite large, minority who stand to benefit from it.'[33]

Eight years later, on 4 July 1992, in another letter penned for *The Tablet*, Bell delivered an acerbic political critique of Reagan's legacy in which he argued that society needed its defences fortified against the ever-seductive appeal of individualism. 'No cheer from the other side of the Atlantic: where unemployment steadily rises and mountainous debt, both public and private, caused by the profligacy of the Reagan bonanza prevents his bewildered and floundering successors from taking any of the formerly accepted steps to ease the problem...' Bell wrote.

He lamented the difficulties of countering tendencies that seemed so entrenched in the 'system'. .'At least in the 1920's and 1930's of this awful century there were the serene voices of people such as John Strachey and Harold Laski and still more Maynard Keynes to analyse a faltering economic and social system...we are rapidly getting back to the old days, but even worse: with nationalism, stimulated by the most lethal weaponry bidding fair to push over our over-fed complacent world of individual self-indulgence into a terrifying anarchy.'[34]

Thus did Bell seem to articulate a sense of drawing lessons as well as faith from history, a continuum that led from his early gurus of the 1930s – the liberal Marxist friends Harold Laski and John Strachey and 'New Deal' John Maynard Keynes – to his conversion to Roman Catholicism, and social democracy.

All the while the issue of secret intelligence remained a subject he could never get away from because it was the life he had signed up to. A review he wrote for *The Tablet*, entitled 'Intelligence Chief Extraordinary', of Patrick Howarth's biography of Bell's niece Barbara's father-in-law, Victor Cavendish-Bentinck, the chair of the World War Two Joint Intelligence Committee, drew on what he had learnt about the subject from his own wartime experiences as an intelligence officer. 'A shrewd and tolerant character, with a firmness enlivened by humour, and an experienced diplomatist, he [Cavendish-Bentinck] developed the JIC of the chiefs of staff, which made a crucial contribution to the successful conduct of the Second World War, providing indispensable facts and projections on which to base decisions.'

Bell went on to note the tensions that had nonetheless arisen between MI6, charged with employing agents in enemy territory –and who needed quiet and secrecy – and the newly established Special Operations Executive tasked with sabotage and causing maximum disruption of communications. 'This inevitably provoked harsh enemy reaction, which increased the perils of the secret service agents,' wrote Bell.[35]

But it was in a tribute he paid to his old friend Christopher Sykes when he died in December 1986, that Bell provided a veiled public hint of his wartime involvement with the anti-Hitler German conspirators, shielding the sense of guilt he must have felt for not being able to support them sufficiently. It was Sykes who, after serving special operations in World War Two, pursued a life as an author and wrote a biography of Adam von Trott, one of the leading anti-Hitler conspirators who ended up being executed. Bell said of him: 'Christopher saw religion in black and white. He had a deep love of German music, particularly Bach, Mozart and Wagner. Hitler brought Götterdämmerung to the Germany Sykes loved and understood. He thought Hitler was the ultimate evil and had destroyed the soul of Europe.'[36]

*Tattie and WB in retirement, on a Spanish holiday.*

*WB & Jimmy Burns at a private reception in London, 1994*
*(Tattie Bell in the background)*

# 33
# A Last Awakening

Despite Bell being my senior by forty-four years, I developed a friendship with the old spy during his long twilight years after he had retired. We first met in early 1986 when he invited me to lunch at his club The Travellers thanks to an introduction from my father, Tom Burns, an old friend of his. Bell wanted to hear all I could tell him about Argentina, where I had just ended a posting with the *Financial Times* that had begun in December 1981, three months before the Falklands War. He generously encouraged my becoming a member of the club, introducing me to several eminent and influential members.

When not at the Travellers, we would meet occasionally at his flat in Onslow Square, where his engaging, if increasingly healthy-diet-obsessed wife Tattie would insist on feeding us spartan meals of salads and nuts and seeds, reducing Walter and I to almost liquid lunches of dry martinis and claret. Walter and I found we were not short of topics to converse about.

As the twentieth century drew to a close, the intelligence world was set to change, but in ways that many spies and journalists failed to predict. The 1990s, after the collapse of the Berlin Wall in 1989, saw the end of the Soviet Union and of the IRA military campaign.

It was a period of unprecedented recalibration of British intelligence priorities that left MI5 and MI6 struggling to come to terms with an unsettled new world order and trying to identify an enemy as a new millennium approached. 9/11, the misuse of false intelligence of alleged weapons of mass destruction to justify the war with Saddam's Iraq and the war on terror were yet to come as was the threat of a new Cold War under Putin following the Russian invasion of Ukraine.

Encouraged by Bell, I attended two 'intelligence' conferences during the 1990s – one at Ditchley Park, in Oxfordshire, the other at St Antony's College in Oxford – on the future challenges facing the world of intelligence in the new century. The mood among the intelligence 'experts' gathered there was on the whole relaxed and, as it turned out, complacent.

There is a saying that dates back from the days of the Cambridge Five that speaks of the English playing their game of spies while playing billiards in the club. It was at a Ditchley Park conference that I came across a variation on the theme. The scene I was a witness to involved a delegation from the CIA enjoying themselves after the main dinner. I watched them take over the use of the billiards table from the MI6 contingent and their leader telling the Brits he would teach them how to play 'Alberta Crud'. The CIA team proceeded to vigorously throw white balls by hand across the table to knock out the reds, engulfing the room with their raucous laughter, like cowboys in a saloon. The MI6 officers looked on aghast.

As I later discovered, at the time MI6, which for years had struggled to come to terms with its loss of global clout to the US, was particularly proud of having beaten not just the Americans but also their French and German counterparts in a bid to train some of the intelligence services in emerging democratic Eastern European states liberated from Soviet rule.

One such contract was with Czechoslovakia, as I was told in the early 1990s. I was in St Antony's Oxford attending a weekend conference on the changing post-Cold War intelligence landscape when a friend suggested there was someone among the foreign delegates I might be interested in meeting in a more relaxed atmosphere. That Saturday evening I made my way to one of the town's quieter pubs to find my friend having a pint with a casually dressed man in his forties. His foreign 'guest' was bespectacled, had a thick moustache and longish dishevelled hair, and was smoking a pipe. He greeted me with a warm handshake and a mischievous glint in his eye. Had he been alone or with some students, I could have easily mistaken him for a somewhat eccentric Oxford don. But the presence of a retired MI6 officer at his side suggested a more intriguing possibility, and I was not disappointed.

It turned out that the 'foreign guest' was the anglophile Oldrich Cerny, the newly appointed head of Czech intelligence, who was at the time being trained and advised by MI6. (The British had won a contract against strong competition from the CIA, the Germans and the French.)

The genial Czech told me that he had been a barman in Newcastle, UK, while studying English. During the 1980s he had worked for the anti-communist dissident Charter 77 movement while employed as a lowly technician in a film studio dubbing foreign films. It was when his country was still behind the Iron Curtain and the work proved perfect cover for exchanging information with fellow dissidents and maintaining contact with helpful foreign friends.

Not long after that, in 1993, Václav Havel, the leader of the 'velvet revolution', became the founding president of what is now the Czech Republic. Havel then offered our 'guest' an appointment as his country's head spook. 'I told Vaclav that I had no experience of working in an intelligence agency – to which he replied, "That is why I want you to be the head: you have to clean out the organization from top to bottom as I can't trust anyone else to do the job."'

I never met Cerny again. I would later come to wonder how this spy who came in from the cold got on as the end of the Cold War gave way to an international environment motivated by self-interest and opportunism rather than ideology, and where the intelligence services of democratic states became increasingly drawn into the questionable practices of the US-led 'war on terror' after 9/11.

The answer came when I read one of several tributes to Cerny when he died, aged sixty-five, after a long illness fighting lung cancer, in the spring of 2012. It was noted that his passionate dedication to peace and freedom had continued after leaving the intelligence world, heading up Forum 2000, a discussion platform founded by Havel and the Romanian-born American writer and Nobel Peace Prize laureate Elie Wiesel to explore ways of preventing the escalation of conflicts that have religion, culture or ethnicity as their primary components. Cerny had also set up the Prague Security Studies Institute to help safeguard and strengthen individual freedoms and democratic institutions of the countries in Central and Eastern Europe and beyond.[1]

Part of me later wished Bell had joined me round the pool table in Ditchley and at the pub in Oxford with the Czech spy. I suspect that on both occasions he too would have proved an interesting interlocutor – the old spy with his renewed faith confronting a new generation of spooks justifying their existence in a morally shifting and conflictive world but finding much common ethical and ideological ground with Oldrich Cerny.

It was around that time that the Bells, long retired, went on one of their increasingly infrequent holidays abroad to visit their friends, my British father Tom and Spanish mother Mabel, at their beach home in southwest Spain. It was there that Walter managed to deal with his life-long struggle with depression. After attending a daily local mass in the local village chapel and busying himself pruning and weeding plants in the garden of our family home, he would join my father on a balcony facing the Atlantic Ocean, for a discussion about common friends and world affairs that lasted late into the night.

My father Tom had worked for intelligence and propaganda in the British embassy in Madrid during World War Two. Post-war, he had re-entered the world of publishing. Despite his liberal Catholicism, he was a political conservative and his network of friends with whom he often met in the Garrick, where he was a long-term member, included senior members of the civil service, MPs, writers, journalists, and retired intelligence contacts.

Along with Bell and Graham Greene, my father's enduring post-war friendships in the world of intelligence included Archie Roosevelt, who served as CIA station chief in London in the 1960s during the Profumo affair, and the MI6 officer Peter Lunn, whose expertise in tapping Soviet communications was made much use of in post-war Vienna and subsequently East Berlin before he worked in Northern Ireland.

While Bell shared other common friends with Burns on both sides of the Atlantic, he confessed to having a more critical view of the excesses of US power, Tory Party politics and certain Foreign Office initiatives which he considered still suffered from a colonialist post-imperial mentality when it came to Europe and the developing world. The discussion reached its peak close to midnight one evening they shared together in Spain in their final years, with Burns driven to expostulate: 'Walter, you are no better than a communist'.[2] The next morning before the Bells had joined my parents for breakfast my mother Mabel, who had supported Franco in the Civil War, asked my father whether he thought Walter was a communist. 'I would have been told if he was,' came back the reply.

Before he died, Walter Bell told a friend half-jokingly one day that perhaps the attribute Freedom Fighter might be inscribed on his gravestone. It never was of course although the comment prevailed in an unsigned diary tribute in *The Tablet*[3] on the occasion of Bell's requiem mass held at London's Brompton Oratory in February 2004. As the comment went on to note, although Bell's work brought him into close contact with the establishment, he was a 'radical at heart'.[4]

In his formative years in MI6, Bell was as horrified by the rise of Hitler's Third Reich and Stalin's purges and the enduring Cold War repression of freedoms by the Soviet State, as he was impressed by F.D. Roosevelt's New Deal. He understood and admired US democracy when based on freedom and justice and interpreted these values to the British.

Walter Bell died on 23 January 2004, aged ninety-four, with Tattie at his bedside. A small group of former colleagues and relatives from both sides of the Atlantic later gathered for his requiem mass at Brompton Oratory where he had become a regular parishioner in his retirement years.. Tattie and Walter's niece, Barbara Lygon, helped organise the service as best they could. They did so out of respect for Walter's faith and love of ritual. A grand-niece Rose de Wend Fenton, daughter of Barbara's sister Mary, read from Isaiah 11:90 'They shall not hurt or destroy in all my holy mountain; for the earth shall be full of the knowledge of the Lord as the waters cover the sea…' .Another grand-niece Hanna O'Hara sang Schubert's *Ave Maria*.

The service ended with a prayer from John Donne, a poet born into a recusant family who became an Anglican cleric.

> *Bring us, O Lord God, at our last awakening into the house and gate of heaven, to enter into that gate and dwell in that house, where there shall be no darkness nor dazzling, but one equal light; no noise nor silence, but one equal music; no fears nor hopes, but one equal possession; no ends nor beginnings, but one equal eternity; in the habitation of thy glory and dominion, world without end. Amen.*

In later years a legend developed among some members of Walter's English family that his ashes were scattered over the Sussex South Downs in memory of one of his favourite walks, not because he wished in any way to emulate Anthony Blunt, the Cambridge spy who asked that his ashes be scattered across the Marlborough Downs.[5]

But a different story later emerged among those in the family who were most closely involved with the post-death arrangements for Walter, and later Tattie. Walter's ashes were not scattered on the Downs. Perhaps that was his wish and/or Tattie's intention, but she never got around to it. Tattie temporally stored the little wooden casket containing his ashes in the basement of 6 Onslow Square where the Bells had their London flat. Tattie's American niece Ruth Thomas found the small ornamental box when she was going through her aunt's belongings after her funeral in 2005, as if Tattie had been waiting for the time to join her beloved Walter. Thus, this story goes, were Tattie and Walter reunited, their ashes scattered in the London garden they both loved.

Walter Bell's spirit was finally freed after struggling with debilitating mental and physical health problems, accompanied to the end by his enduring American-born companion and wife of fifty-six years, Tattie Spaatz. who survived him by just over a year.

While a heavy drinker, Bell suffered from no addictions, and managed to hold together his marriage in a mutually sustaining and for the most part enduring loving relationship. He was betrayed by some colleagues, but friendships with those who deserved his respect, also endured. He was true to his conscience and followed a moral compass, which is more than can be said of some of the characters in the murky world he inhabited.

Walter Bell was an interesting man in important times. While intelligence history and popular spy literature in recent decades has been overshadowed if not dominated by the themes of amorality and betrayal, and the self-justification of those who put ideology or simple self-interest before country, and their apologists, Bell's story is about finding faith in God and country.

He remained a patriot in World War Two and during the Cold War, forging genuine friendships and professional links with his American friends, and dutifully, although not uncritically, serving the last bastions of colonial power in Africa, India and the Caribbean in the twilight of empire, when the UK had lost its status as a global power.

It was Bell's view that his World War Two boss in New York, the head of MI6's British Security Coordination, William Stephenson, should have had himself written about by a serious scholar who should have been left to make his own enquiries and assessments – but that was not Stephenson's way. 'He had his tycoon, Hollywood, Daily Express side which craved notoriety after a career of exaggerated anonymity – and then he had his stroke …'[6]

Bell's concern for Stephenson was typical. He was critical of institutional cover-ups and enduring class-based social prejudices that infected government policy, personalities, and actions in the covert world. His papers are infused with a candour and independence of mind when commenting on the inner tensions of the secret world he inhabited, and the challenges faced by those who worked in it.

One is left wondering what Walter Bell would have made of the world as it made its way into the second decade of the twenty-first century drawing from his experience of the twentieth century. I suspect he would have been disillusioned about the reports of flawed intelligence used to justify the invasion of Iraq in 2003, and been as outraged by the Trump presidency as he was by Putin's invasion of Ukraine in 2022, though his enduring Catholicism may well have embraced a glimmer of light in a troubled and insecure world.

Rose Fenton, one of his beloved great nieces who survived him told me:

> He would have been appalled and extremely worried on so many fronts: the age of cyber warfare, AI, and of fake news; the undermining of democracies and rise of the right; the threats posed by China and Russia; and of course the ecological and climate emergency which ushered in so many terrifying scenarios – failure of crops; mass migration, wars over scant resources, hunger, civil unrest – which threatened to pave the way for ever more autocratic repressive governments across the world. Walter was critical quite a lot of the time![7]

Like so many in secret intelligence, Bell was a complex, ambiguous character, and could be elusive, with motives that were not always quite what they seemed. He was no knight in shining armour and was prone to human and professional failings, as identified in these pages. But he had integrity. A man of faith with a strong moral of sense of justice and a belief in democracy, he still found space for nuance and irony, for a lightness that contrasted with the heaviness of ideology that turned some of his generation towards extremes of intolerance, and even betrayal. Not that betrayal would ever have been an option for Walter Fancourt Bell. Loyal to his church, friends, family, colleagues, king and country, he was a truly faithful spy.

# Epilogue to the Paperback Edition

Publication of a book about a spy whose career remained a well-kept secret during his lifetime, but details of which were made possible thanks to the personal papers that came into the author's possession, has fuelled some further information which I now include in this paperback edition.

There seems little doubt that the project always risked ruffling a few feathers in the intelligence world as some academics and fellow authors, who had sight of an early draft, warned the author of *A Faithful Spy*.

Former MI6 chief Sir Richard Dearlove thought that the subject Walter Bell, having worked for MI6 and MI5, 'stretched the rules'[1] on official secrecy by keeping his personal archive rather than destroying it or handing it to his employers before ensuring that it was handed to his friend, the author, by his widow.

Thankfully, Sir Richard conceded that a public interest case for stopping publication after Bell's death would have been too weak to withstand challenge, before sharing some further helpful insights when reviewing the book.

Bell may well have never held high office, but he was a well-respected intelligence professional, both loyal and patriotic. As Dearlove noted, 'unauthorised disclosures generally issue from the poisoned pens of the disillusioned and the dissatisfied, but this story has a very different feel to it and stands as a tribute to a devoted secret servant of the state, covering from 1939 to the Cold War and touching on many of the themes, character and events that define 20th Century intelligence history.'[2]

Dearlove, born in 1945, drew on institutional memory, to provide context for and affirmation of much of what Bell - born 1909 - covered in his papers. Dearlove joined MI6 as a young university graduate in 1966 before being posted to Nairobi in 1968, just as Bell was leaving Kenya and back to retirement in London.

Bell, as Dearlove noted, like every other intelligence officer of his generation, could not escape the shadow cast by Soviet penetration of the British intelligence and foreign policy establishment, given that he had worked and socialised with three of the Cambridge five - Maclean, Burgess and Philby.

Bell's papers show the extent to which a sense of natural justice led him to defend with determination some of his colleagues wrongly accused of being Soviet 'moles'.

And yet while Dearlove suggests that Bell's lack of career experience of the Soviet Union might have detracted from his ability to exercise real influence in these matters, Bell showed 'skill, empathy and good judgement'[3] in his overseas postings, not least Kenya, where he was one of the first to recognise Jomo Kenyatta, otherwise written off as a *Mau Mau* terrorist, as a future African leader - an 'astute assessment' given Kenyatta's subsequent importance as a bastion against early Communist Chinese and Soviet influence in newly independent Africa.

Among the additional information that has surfaced on Bell's story, I am indebted to Daniel Payne, Curator for Politics and International Relations at the LSE Library of the London School of Economics. He has shed light on the somewhat unclear narrative that Bell left in his papers about his student days.

Payne helped uncover Bell's student file which had languished unseen for years among thousands of documents held by the university in an off-site storage.

According to the file, Bell in 1926 passed the School Certificate Examination of the Oxford and Cambridge Joint Board with credits in Latin, Elementary, Mathematics, History, English & Scripture during his last year at Tonbridge School - but was unable to go to Oxford or Cambridge owing to his parents' financial difficulties at the time.

So he went to teach for five years in private schools, at the same time as reading for the Bar where he networked with senior barristers, among them Alexander Fachiri, the New York born international law expert.

Bell applied to study economics at the LSE in the summer of 1934. He was initially told that he would have to sit again for an examination as the university did not recognise his Oxford & Cambridge certificate. However, Bell managed to overcome administrative bureaucracy thanks to a glowing reference from his old school headmaster, and crucially the support of Fachiri, a widely respected and influential lawyer, who acted as his mentor.

The headmaster of Tonbridge H. H. P. Sloman (MA Oxon) described Bell as having had an "excellent character at school, showing good ability and industry. I recommend him very strongly to read in the School of Economics, a subject in which has a real interest and unusual qualification."[4]

Bell began his undergraduate studies at LSE in the autumn of 1934 before secretly being interviewed by MI6. By December he had been recruited to the Passport Control Office in New York, the cover post for the MI6 station, ostensibly on the grounds of his legal skills. He wrote a curt letter to the LSE principal who had initially blocked his application after sitting successfully for his entry examination. Bell wrote that his university life had 'in a sense all been rather abortive as I have been appointed to a post in the Passport Control Office in New York which means I shall be leaving for America in January.'[5]

In his first and only university term, he had attended lectures on economics, the growth of English industry British Constitution as well as German for beginners and French intermediate.

LSE historian Professor Michael Cox told the author that he thought likely that Bell began his friendship with the Marxist Professor Harold Laski while at LSE, as the Professor 'had a reputation for developing good relationships with his students.'[6]

As intriguingly, Bell coincided at LSE with Jomo Kenyatta. Although no firm evidence had yet to emerge of this among existing documentation, Cox thought it at least a possible that Bell might have met the future Kenyan president, while

Kenyatta was studying anthropology at the LSE under the social anthropologist Bronislaw Malinowski in the late 1930's and when the student population of the university was much smaller and personally interactive than what it became in the 21st century.

Certainly, as Cox points out, Bell's papers indicate that 'Bell knew a lot more about Kenyatta when it came to Kenyan affairs than his colonial masters.'[7]

The LSE trail led me to further research on Kenyatta's student days undertaken by the academic Victoria de Menil. (*Once upon a time... when Jomo Kenyatta was a student*, LSE August 18th, 2018)

According to de Menil, Kenyatta began attending seminars at LSE in 1934, at the age of 43, arriving during the soviet famine by way of Moscow State University – 'a bastion of Communism and an unusual feeder school to LSE.' Kenyatta had been involved with the International Trade Union Committee of Negro Workers in Moscow, under the influence of his friend and pan-Africanist George Padmore.

Kenyatta's LSE masters' studies thesis was published as the book *Facing Mount Kenya: The Tribal Life of the Gikuyu*, an ethnography of Kenya's largest ethnic group, the *Kikuyu*. Kenyatta's dedicated the book: 'To ... all the dispossessed youth of Africa: for perpetuation of communion with ancestral spirits through the fight for African Freedom, and the firm faith that the dead, the living, and the unborn will unite to rebuild the destroyed shrines.'

As de Menil points out, the book is 'suffused with politics', in particular the politics of land return and the question of female circumcision, which Kenyatta was in favour of.

'Studying at LSE enabled him to master the language of the oppressor so as better to fight it,' writes de Menil[8].

After publishing the book, Kenyatta went on to continue lobbying on behalf of the Kikuyu in London, and later organised the 5th Pan-African Congress in Manchester. He returned to his native British East Africa in 1946, where he quickly re-entered local politics, joining and ultimately presiding over the Kenya

Africa Union, focused on campaigning for independence when he came under Bell's radar during the spy's two posting to Nairobi.

I am indebted to Rupert Allason, for correcting or clarifying some names mentioned in the first edition of this book which I have now incorporated. I also acknowledge some additional bibliographical  material which I had overlooked. Allason's book *A Matter of Trust* (Weidenfeld & Nicholson, 1982) on the history of MI5 from 1909-1972 published under his pseudonym Nigel West, notes that Bell's appointment as private secretary to the controversial MI5 chief Sir Roger Hollis, after his first posting in Kenya and in India,  caused a furore inside the service because Bell had been expected to return to Washington given his previous US experience, as the security adviser of the British embassy, but a soviet expert within the service was sent to the US instead .

It was around this time that MI5 received information from a Polish defector that the KGB was operating a spy in the British Admiralty, what subsequently was uncovered as the 'Portland spy ring' which in 1961 involved the arrest, trial, and conviction of five Soviet spies, three of whom had been living as 'illegals' living in London under cover. MI5 considered this one of the Service's most significant post-war counter-espionage successes.

When the theory that Hollis was suspected of being a Soviet spy was splashed across the *Sunday Times* in 1985, Bell and his wife Tattie happened to be having lunch, as guests of his old friend from Delhi days, the veteran *Times* man Louis Heren, and his son Patrick, who was also a journalist. As Patrick recalled: 'Conversation danced unavailingly around the Hollis question, until I asked:

"So, Walter, was he?"

He gave me a solemn, melancholy look.

"Was who what?"

"Was Hollis a Russian spy?"

"I don't think so."

"Why not?"

"I worked closely with him and knew him pretty well. I don't think it would have been possible for a man so stupid to have carried off such a deception for so many years."[9]

A brilliant reply: the lunch party was convulsed in fits of laughter, and of course it was impossible to press the question any further. That was typical of Walter in his later years. He remained discreet about intelligence matters, but he was prepared in some circumstances to let in a little light on the mystery because he knew that his old services needed to be understood by British society, and especially by the media. He did this through personal contacts, and through forums such as The Tablet Table, an influential talking shop convened by the liberal Catholic weekly.

Walter Bell was a much more typical British intelligence officer than the dramatic, often violent image promulgated by the media. His work was important but low key. He thought deeply – sometimes agonised – about that work, and its moral underpinning.' (*The Article* March 21, 2024).

I have chosen to keep to the spelling of Tattie that Walter Bell and his British friends used and which she herself adopted after the war, as preference to the 'Tatty' her American family had called her from childhood which in English spoken by the British is used to describe something thought untidy, rather dirty and which looks uncared for - which could not be a more inaccurate description of the woman of style, natural beauty, as well strong and courageous personality that Tattie became in adulthood.

The final addition to this paperback issue is the most extensive and revealing, justifying an expanded presence of Katherine ('Tattie') Spaatz in the story of her husband Walter Bell.

The diary extract by the oldest daughter of the WW2 US Air Force lead commander General Carl Spaatz, is based on her letters to her mother Ruth Harrison[10]. They provide a colourful and insightful account of the two years Tattie spent as a volunteer with American Red Cross mobile unit, mixing with

American troops, pilots, and their commanders as they fought back against and defeated the Nazis, a heroic story, also filled with scenes of high risk, loss and devastation, and occasional interludes of love affairs and parties.

It shows how the war forged and framed her character, expanding her life-experience beyond the comfort zone of her privileged education and upbringing, preparing her post-war role not just as a dutiful, occasionally suffering wife of a British spy, but his unrivalled confidante and ally, across continents, fearlessly sharing in his challenging covert and diplomatic work.

According to Patrick Heren, Bell owed much to *Tattie* Spaatz, the intelligent and independent young woman the spy married in 1948 after serving two years as private secretary to the British ambassador in Washington Lord Inverchapel. 'Without Tattie, it is doubtful that Walter would have risen as far as he did, beset as he was by doubt and depression.' wrote Heren.[11]

It was thanks to a surviving close friend of the Bells, Katherine MacLean, that I obtained further details of Tattie's WW2 experience whose role serving doughnuts, coffee, candy and gum to US troops and pilots stationed in England and mainland Europe forms only part of the unique real human drama she was part of.

The new information reached me in early 2024, just as *Apple TV* began streaming *Masters of the Air*, an American WW2 drama following the actions of the 100th Bomb Group, a B-17 Flying Fortess heavy bomber unit in the Eight Air Force based in England.

An actress playing Tattie, identified as General Spaatz's daughter, makes a very short appearance in one episode at a dance organised by US airmen who had returned safely from a mission. She had clearly caught the eye of at least two of the airmen, but nothing develops beyond that, at least on screen in a series that focuses on the heroics of men rather than women.

In Tattie's wartime account, one can get a clearer sense of her strong personality, her character forged by the challenges she faced. She tries as best she can to keep up the spirits of the

American soldiers and pilots, serving them a taste of home, but also determined to follow them to war, despite fears that the Germans might kill or take her hostage as a key US General's daughter, as she accompanied the American military through France, Belgium, Germany, and finally liberated Czechoslovakia.

Tattie's WW2 experience began in June 1943 when at an unidentified location in the US, she walked five blocks in the midday sun wearing a gas mask, part of her basic training, while praying 'that the Germans won't use it (the gas).'

She seemed more oblivious to the clear and present danger of a German U-boat sending her to the bottom on the ocean when days later she sailed from New York aboard a packed US troop carrier bound for England. She and the other females on board - Red Cross volunteers and a huge number of army nurses - were treated to comfortable cabins which made the whole voyage 'a luxury cruise for us' while the troops were jammed in, sleeping all over every inch of the outside, or stacked in the lower decks.

Tattie and the girls had two good meals a day, at nine and seven - then spent the rest of the time lounging on the sun-deck - the only place they had access to - except for the large lounge, the dining room and their cabins, where there were men aplenty.

'There was a continuous chorus of young returning RAFers around the piano signing *Jolly Sixpence* and *Bless 'Em All*', they were a very cute lot…' Other males included a raft of fellow Americans - Army Air Force engineers commanded by Brigadier General Stuart Godfrey, some Air Corps boys, and the enormous staff for the ship and the troops.

Tattie with four other girls shared a cabin that swam with the fumes from the cologne *Aphrodesia* they poured on themselves from head to foot.

Tattie found two of the girls quite sweet. The other two were not. One called herself 'Dolly Reckless' was referred to by her colleagues as '*Hey Sexless.*' The other sang torrid Spanish love songs. A third, by the name of Josephine, read the *Republic of*

*Plato* and snatches of Anatole France most mornings as she lay in bed.

The fourth girl had been advised not to take a sea voyage for three months by her best and favourite soothsayer who warned that the boat she travelled on would be torpedoed and she would be the 'Human Albatross'. 'The poor girl stayed in her bunk, shaking with fear all the way across.

The cruise for a while that summer in 1943 turned into an English idyll as the Red Cross girls were assigned to *Clubmobile* duties at various air force bases.

Tattie had hoped to be assigned to the OSS London office headed up by David Bruce, but was given only a vague promise that this would happen if and when allied troops landed in France.

Instead Tattie focused on her training making doughnuts while leading an active social life given  her status as Spaatz's daughter, including grand balls in the company of the Eagle squadron base commander Genera Ross Hoyt, weekend stays with Sir John Slessor, the British Assistant Chief of the Air Staff, his wife Lady Slessor and older daughter Pamela and night outs in the popular *Cote d'Azur* club in the company of fun-loving war correspondent Bob Considine on occasional visits to London.

Tattie and her first club mobile team '*West Virginia*' were billeted in a four hundred year old thatched roof cottage in the Cambridgeshire village of Glatton, just four miles from one of the major bases used by the Americans, built by the 809th Engineer Battalion (Aviation) of the US army in the last months of 1942.

Tattie wrote fondly of her time at Glatton, being taken care of by the two grand lanky and handsome English gentlewomen, and sharing the cottage also with a three-year-old evacuee girl and three Pekinese dogs. Now and then some of the Americans from the nearest base came over and sat around the small open fire in the living room, and played swing records.

By September 1943, Tattie was with the 96th Bomb Group that were flying B-17 missions over France and into Germany. Her team leader was Ginny Sherwood, niece of

Robert Sherwood, the Pulitzer winning playwriter and speech writer for President Roosevelt.

One of the problems Tattie and Ginny faced as they carried out their duties was dealing with the tensions that developed between the GI's and the 'officer class' of pilots with which the well healed Red Cross girls felt socially drawn to.

It was the pilots who endeared themselves to Tattie, setting off as they did on their high-risk missions, knowing that some would be killed or shot down to be taken prisoners of war. Tattie felt that unless a guy was in combat, she was not prepared to waste on him any of her supply of energy and what verve and spirit there was left after a day of doughnut making.

Among those Tattie befriended was the bomber pilot John Winant JR, son of the US ambassador in London who in October 1943 was shot down and taken prisoner by the Germans and sent to Colditz, from where he was released in April 1945. He was luckier than her favourite crew at the 351$^{st}$, Major Shaw, Harvey Wallace and Harry Morse who were killed after being shot down during a terrific raid that same month.

Among the survivors that autumn was another pilot 'Hoss' with whom Tattie spent a day and night out in London, lunching on fine oysters at *The Mirabel* and wondering around Mayfair where she had several drinks at *Shepherds* and got mixed up with an attractive Irish Wing Commander, Bob Foster.

After the bar closed, Tattie and her pilot friends headed for a little hole in the wall called the *New Yorker Club* on Piccadilly for more drinking, and light gambling. They played a 'foolish game' called *Oppsie-Oppsie* - guessing the total number of coins they all held in clenched fists. Then they went for an evening of Chinese food and dancing at *Maxim's* into the early hours of the morning when Tattie returned to base on a morning train.

Days later one of the clubmobiles, driven by a GI called Mike, nearly collided on the base runway with a landing B-17. Otherwise, it was a good day. A great number of doughnuts were produced for the base, and a mission entrusted to the 96$^{th}$, sent up the greatest number of planes, all returned to base in an orderly fashion completely unharmed.

Weeks later, just after Christmas 1943, Tattie witnessed the 'most beautiful crash landing' by a B-17 that was unable to get its landing gear down and had to slide on its belly including the belly turret. Tattie received a belated Christmas present when she was reunited with her father General Spaatz who had arrived in the UK, fresh from Italy to take up his new post as head of US Strategic Air Forces in Europe.

The General on arrival was honoured by an unpublicised reception of the allied air force and intelligence community at Widewing, the US air base in Bushy Park. Attendees included General Ira Eaker the head of the 8th Bomber Command in England, the RAF's Air Marshal Elwell, another key US air force commander General Pete Quesada, and David Bruce, who headed up the OSS in London. Days later, the photograph immortalising the welcoming hug that Tattie gave her father, appeared in the GI paper *Stars & Stripes* under the caption '*Tatty Spaatz Greets Pops*'. When copies of the paper began to circulate in US bases, a group of GI's, came storming around whining 'We want to see the General's daughter', they shouted. Tattie was down on her knees washing cups. She felt like a stag at bay. Thankfully they drifted away.

From then on, when any of the GI's checked her name and asked if she was related to the General, she replied: 'Of course - his daughter I am'. At which point they all just shrieked with laughter and pounded her on the back like it was a big joke.

Tattie was soon assigned to a new Clubmobile unit named the *North Dakota* - newly repainted and shiny. That January 1944, she introduced her father to her 'young man', Hoss a pilot with the 303rd squadron, with whom she had earlier visited Madame Tussaud's wax works in London. She had been told it was something to experience. But Tattie found it rather dreary, just a collection of old English murderers and murderesses.

Days later, *Life Magazine* arrived to take pictures of Tattie and her crew as part of a morale uplifting story aimed at raising funds for the US Red Cross. The photographer was Bob Landry, who had been with the 8th Army and the assault troops in Sicily, and was in England 'marking time' prior to the Normandy landings.

One of several photographs he took of Tattie had her 'looking soulful and Madonna-like', clutching a tray of doughnuts. Landry told her, jokingly, 'that's perfect - we'll call it 'Virgin with Doughnuts.''

Tattie was not best pleased with the outcome. The photographs were developed dark and grey like the weather they were taken in, and 'lacked the friendliness of sunny pictures'. Everything looked stark and hardlined, not least herself, she thought.

Nonetheless, Tattie was not short of suitors. 'Nobody ever propositions me anymore - they all want to marry me. Maybe it's being Daddy's daughter again.'

In early June 1944, as D-Day approached, censorship was stepped up restricting what Tattie could write about but her letters convey the sense of preparation for the invasion. She was now assigned to the 363rd Fighter Group of the 9th Air Force, with additional duties, caring for Wing Headquarters, a Service Group, and various ordnance, anti-aircraft and signal corps units.

On June 27th Tattie was reassigned to the 1st Infantry Division. Her new invasion doughnut wagon was called '*Sitting Bull*'- one of eight Clubmobilers attached to each unit as well as numerous supply trucks, generators and water trailers.

Her next letter, three days later, was written from 'somewhere in France', reporting on her final days in wartime England celebrating with her father his 53rd birthday on 28th June, 'taking a train out of London packed with the old and young - the wretched and hysterical getting out and away from the buzz bombs'.

Her doughnut unit was one of the last to be loaded before their sea transport crossed the Channel, the smoothest boat run

Tattie had ever known, not a ripple in the water. The convoy of doughnut units, supply trucks, and five Hillmans - 'a small British vehicle that goes sideways' - the next morning made its way up to Cherbourg.

Tattie followed the American forces as they overcame stiff resistance from the Germans. The coast towns that they drove through were completed shattered - 'it was like a bad dream' - hard to understand how the French people could laugh and wave, throwing flowers and screaming '*Les Americains*'. At the Red Cross headquarters in Cherbourg, Tattie was met by the war correspondent Helen Kirkpatrick who took her away to a chateau that the press had acquired for themselves.

Tattie had her first bath since leaving London and lunched on fresh artichokes. Then she spent the afternoon lying in the garden in the sun with a 'fine group of newspaper guys', Bill Walton of *Time*, Al Newman of *Newsweek*, and Dave Sherman of *Life*. They dined on rare steak, and drank *Calvados* 'during a long, funny evening', in the garden by the fountain. 'It was the most completely unreal day,' wrote Tattie.

Seven weeks after the D-Day landings, Tattie caught up with 'Papa Tooey' the familiar family name she used for her father General Spaatz, who was at the front coordinating US air support for *Operation Cobra*, a breakthrough offensive launched by the First United States Army under the command of Lieutenant General Omar Bradley.

The intention was to take advantage of the distraction of the Germans by the British and Canadian attacks around Caen, break through the German defences that were penning their forces, and advance into Brittany. *Operation Cobra* began on 25th July with a concentrated aerial bombardment from thousands of Allied aircraft.

'The big push is now over here (in France) ...do hope that the war ends soon - then Daddy and I can be home for Christmas with our family,' Tattie wrote that July. There were months to go yet of war.

Attached to the US Army Fifth Corps, made up of survivors since D-Day, she found herself among Texans 'sporting great shaggy beards'. *G* company had a rodeo going, 'GI's careering around on poor tired old French farm horses in black fedoras they had lifted from some Normandy shack.'

General George Hays, commander of the 2nd Infantry Division's artillery on Omaha Beach during the Normandy landings, dropped in for dinner, 'another wiry fighting guy, who apparently spends his time in his jeep looking for dead Germans and gazing upon them and rubbing his hands with glee.'

In early August Tattie moved with the US troops to *Cerisy-la*-Forêt, a commune in the Manche department of Normandy in north-western France, reaching Lieutenant General Brereton's garish modern chateau 'for a lovely hot bath and shoeshine before Daddy and the rest of the boys came back to dinner.' Tattie's quarters were in nearby Campeux, in a four-room bungalow which she shared with five other girls, serving doughnuts and gallons of coffee to the 3rd Battalion of 116th Regiment, and also helping them drink some champagne cider that they had unearthed.

On August 21st, 1944, onwards to Sées. It was the first French town Tattie had encountered which was completely undamaged and operating normal civilian life. She was now with the 90th Division's Cavalry Recon Troop, which counted a collection of French resistance fighters     and anti-Franco Spanish veterans of the Spanish Civil War among their number.

Tattie was with the troops that filled Paris following its liberation on August 25th, 1944. She got there on the Monday after the Saturday it had officially fallen to the Allies - and joined the American soldiers, who went on a spending spree with their vast numbers and deep pockets. At *Aux Trois Quartiers*, the city's glamorous department store, she bought herself two bottles of French perfume *Messager* and *Je Reviens*, some pure silk lingerie, bobby pins and 'everything impossible to get in England and the US. Paris will probably be cleaned out soon with all the mad Yank buying going on,' she wrote.

After visiting Colonel George Wertenbaker of the 48th Fighting Group at the Ritz and dining at the Hotel Lancaster, Tattie was billeted in a wing of a wounded veterans' home at Mousy Le Viex, fourteen miles outside Paris, with 'lots of good GI friends to keep us company', and French children attending a summer school, who walked around in columns, singing patriotic songs all day.

Tattie then moved into Belgium, with the 5th Armoured before receiving the news in early October that she and her group were to report to Paris for reassignment to the 9th Air Force before moving towards Germany.

'All the way through France we have run into German camouflage and always the hideous German road signs of an odious yellow with dirty black lettering and the buildings used by the Germans with all the windows painted a harsh dull blue - but it was counteracted by the natives putting out all the flags, especially the charming handmade American ones... Now we are in a province which is German, though it now belongs to Belgium, and things get ugly - though the people are all right, just dull country louts - but not a flag,' Tattie wrote on October 16th, 1944.

By the New Year, the German counter-offensive was being stepped up, and concern for Tattie's safety had her back in Paris. She was only too aware, however much she wished against it, that being General Spaatz's daughter required careful handling.

As she wrote in a letter to her mother Ruth on January 7th, 1945, every member of the American Red Cross was aware that the reason for pushing around of *Sitting Bull* (Tattie's latest mobile unit) was to keep to keep the General's daughter safe and out of Germany for as long as possible.

In Belgium, Tattie and her mobile unit spent a day in Aachen with the 5th Armoured, the 34th Tank Battalion and a company of the 2nd Ranger Battalion before joining the press corps attached to the 1st Army in Spa, on the borders of the Ardennes massif. Among the journalists was Ernest Hemingway. 'All the younger newspaper gents were sitting in the bar around Mr Hemingway like a chorus saying: 'Yes, Mr.H. - and what do you think Mr.H?'

From there to Eupen, fifteen kilometres from the German border and another unnamed town, 'jammed full of (American)troops, just like Normandy - everybody stacked up - very exciting - all waiting to go across the Rhine.'

On March 20th, 1945, Tattie wrote of the a 'terrific looting' that was going as the German homes were 'full of loot' from France and Holland that the Nazis took out of the conquered territories.

She noted there was a black platoon with the battalion of the 38th. The Commanding Officer had asked them to think up a name for themselves. 'The fighting black panthers with a knot in their tail,' they replied.

Days later Tattie returned to Paris where there was assembled 'the latest collection of generals I had ever seen', among them her father, General Spaatz.

Together they flew to the Supreme Headquarters Allied Expeditionary Force (SHAEF) in Reims where Spaatz got Eisenhower's permission for his daughter to continue with the allied advance into Germany, as long as it was with the rear corps, that ran no risk of her being killed or captured as a hostage by retreating German troops.

On March 28, 1945, Tattie found herself in a 'nasty, unnamed, little German town that had been untouched by the war (that is by the aerial war) and was crawling with stupid Germans.'

'The Germans are licked but there doesn't seem to be any responsible person to make the surrender - we will apparently have to take every single inch of the Third Reich.'

The roads nearby were filled with hundreds of refugees, Russian, Polish, Italian and French laborers streaming past, pushing carts and on foot.

Days later, driving from Waldeck to Wolfhagen, a 2nd IV reconnaissance jeep stopped Tattie and her team of girls just in time as they were heading towards a German army pocket where later in the day the 2nd took 800 prisoners.

Tattie then managed to wrangle a short leave for her and three of her colleagues to the South of France, aboard a C-45 transport from Giessen, arranged by her father.

In Cannes, they stayed for a week in the Hotel Martinez, 'just like we were crown princesses....so perfect and dreamlike.' The week's leave included a visit to Eden Rock, the former luxurious bathing club which had been fixed to accommodate 2,000 American troops, a shopping spree at Juan-les-Pins, and an evening of drinking and dancing with young fighter pilots back in the Hotel.

In Nice, Tattie met up with her father and dined in a chateau that had been requisitioned for military use. 'Never had Daddy paid so much attention to me - we had a long sad conversation about how hard it is going to be for us to go back in the style to which we are accustomed -very funny.'

At about two o'clock that night, the phone rang and General Spaatz was told that President Roosevelt had died. 'We were all horrified and some terrified at the prospect of life under Truman - but maybe he will delegate all authority to good substantial people, if there is any spring to his side - we hope. Still hard to believe,' Tattie wrote.

Tattie remained only too conscious that she was General Spaatz's daughter and the extent to which this conditioned her war time experience. The problem of her moving with the troops into Germany, as Hitler urged all Germans to fight a desperate rear 'total war' defence of the fatherland, was not that she might risk getting sniped at or killed but that she might be captured and hauled off as a political prisoner which 'would have been very nasty.' But now that her unit was so heavily guarded and German action seemed to have fallen apart, she had been given the go-ahead. 'I can hardly wait to get out of this evil country, but there was lots I wouldn't have known about if I hadn't stayed on.'

She was driven towards Naumberg in central Germany after it was taken by American troops on April 12th. The clubmobiles were stationed in a huge barracks, only recently occupied by German troops. Right across the street was a

German military hospital full of patients and medics busy giving the Nazi salute until they were slapped into a prisoner of war cage, 'Damdest war and Americans mixed up in this welter of fear and hate and horror make it even stranger,' she wrote.

On April 23rd, under the orders of General Clarence Huebner, commanding General of the First Infantry Division, she went through the Buchenwald concentration camp which had been liberated twelve days earlier by a detachment of troops from the US 9th Armoured Infantry Battalion.

The morning she spent there 'made the most violent and desperate impression' on her, 'all the remaining youth and bounce of Tatty has left.'

'This damned accursed country and its foul people - all the German citizens that are being shown through the camp cry and snivel that they knew nothing of the situation, the dirty fearful skin savers. Made me so mad at the whole world - I've known people who were no damn good, but now it is so irrevocably confirmed. And the Russians will now do exactly the same things to forced German labour, which I suppose is justice of a kind - but it makes for a horrible eternal cycle of terror. Christ, what a world so hopeless and lost. Feel lonesome and desperate for all the dispossessed millions of Europe, the survivors - nobody in the world has a home or place except Americans and some of the members of the British Empire.'

On May 4th, 1945, Tattie wrote: 'Now I suppose the war is over and De Valera (*Note: Éamon de Valera, Irish prime minister*) makes a condolence call on the German minister on the death of Hitler.'

She had heard that Hoss, the American pilot she had befriended when she was based in England, had gone missing in action a month and half earlier while flying with the 8th Air Force. Days later she heard via Bob Kimmel that another pilot, Ed Snyder, had told him that he was flying on Hoss's wing and that had gone down under control. 'So pray that he is all right - probably sitting back in Georgia now with his shoes off,' she wrote on May 19th from Pilsen in Czechoslovakia. She had arrived there on VE-Day, joining the American troops. 'The

Czechs really loathe the Germans - extra guards have to be put on the prisoners to keep the Czechs from tearing the Germans to pieces.'

For days Tattie and her unit found themselves making doughnuts more constantly that at any time since she had left England, serving a battalion every afternoon and evening, with dance parties every night, 'really very gay except for not feeling very gay.'

She was tired of doughnut making and weary of being in the company of American GI's with their 'tendency to be very rude and often foul-mouthed' now replacing their 'fine combat character and humour and reticence'.

But then she was flown to Paris in a B-25 to catch up with her father who had asked to see her. From there she flew to England for word had reached her via her father that Hoss had survived. His had gone down on March 30th - two of his engines knocked out by flak and a third went out when he had almost reached the Canadian lines. He had landed in no-man's land but the Germans got to him first and marched him back to Stettin (Szczecin) in North-West Poland where there were several Air Force prisoner of war camps.

After the Russians had moved in, the 1st Bomber Division flew in in and took the American POW's back to England.

Hoss was in for a 16-day quarantine that all ex-POWs had to sit through, somewhere in the peaceful English countryside where Tattie used to take doughnuts twice a week prior to the Normandy landings. He was waiting to be assigned back to combat duties in the Pacific. He had at least missed the terrible ordeal of administrative chaos at Camp Lucky Strike at St. Valery, France, 45 miles from the port of Le Havre, where nearly 60,000 troops had impatiently awaited transportation home after VE-Day.

Tattie wrote her last letter to her mother from Europe before flying home on June 2nd, 1945, two years after she had first taken up her doughnut duties. It was datelined Pilsen, where she had caught up with her father after visiting Paris, and Hoss in England.

'Victorious celebrations have subsided - and the wild exchange parties with the Russians…when we go out of the town, we run into roadblocks with large signs saying, '*Limit of Allied Advance.*'

A new post-war Europe, divided between East and West, was emerging, one which Tattie Spaatz was destined to experience, at the side of Walter Bell.

London, April 2024.

# Notes

**Preface**
[1] *The Times,* 4 March 2004.
[2] Peter Hennessy's Hinsley lecture, 24 October 2005: 'The Last Customer: British Intelligence and the British Historian'.
[3] Sir Richard Dearlove's Hinsley lecture, 13 November 2019: 'The Secret Intelligence Service and Its History'.

**1 Rites of Passage**
[1] Bell papers, Author's Archives ('AA').
[2] Walter Bell ('WB') to Anthony Hartley, 1 April 1994, AA. The county of Kent, known as the Garden of England with its hop gardens, oast houses, and orchards, became also the setting from the 1920's for a growing mining community that felt excluded and discriminated against. See Peter Williams, *In Black & White, The History of the Kent Coalfield* (PWTV,2019).
[3] John Ranelagh to author, AA.
[4] WB's letter to Anthony Hartley, AA.
[5] Keith Jeffery, *MI6: The History of the Secret Intelligence Service 1909–1949* (London: Bloomsbury, 2010).
[6] Bell papers, AA.
[7] Walter Bell unpublished memoir, AA.
[8] Keith Jeffery, *MI6* op.cit.
[9] John Ranelagh to author, AA.
[10] WB unpublished memoir, AA.
[11] ibid.
[12] An extensive bibliography over the years on Philby 'includes Philip Knightley, *The Master Spy* (New York: Alfred A. Knopf, Inc., 1989), Philby's autobiography, *My Silent War* (New York: Modern Library, Inc., 1968) and Ben Macintyre, A Spy Among Friends (London: Bloomsbury, 2016). For Blake, see Simon Kuper, The *Happy Traitor: Spies, Lies and Exile in Russia:*

*The Extraordinary Story of George Blake* (London: Profile Books, 2021 ).

[13] WB unpublished memoir, AA.

[14] ibid.

[15] ibid.

[16] ibid.

[17] WB's letter to Anthony Hartley, AA.


## 2 A Family of Influence

[1] St Mary's Riverhead Parish newsletter, November 1909, church archive.

[2] For details on Bell ancestry in books and newspapers, I am indebted to James Mussell, *The Foundation and Early Years of the News of the World: 'Capacious Double Sheets'* (White Rose Research Online, University of Leeds, 2016).

[3] Mussell, op.cit.

[4] Also, Laurel Brake, Chandrika Kaul and Mark W. Turner (eds.) Also, *The News of the World and the British Press, 1843–2011 Journalism for the Rich, Journalism for the Poor* (London: Palgrave Macmillan, 2015).

[5] Mussell, op.cit.

[6] Roy Greenslade, 'The News of the World: The Good, the Bad and the Ugly', *Guardian*, 2 December 2015.

[7] ibid.

[8] *In Memoriam* Riverhead Parish magazine, 1952. Also Jasper Bell to author.

[9] Jasper Bell's letter to author 26 November 2021.

[10] St Mary's Riverhead Parish newsletter July 1910, church archive.

[11] For Bell ancestry information and family background I am indebted to Jasper Bell (Bell & Backhouse family album.)

[12] Lorna Sage, *Bad Blood* (London: HarperCollins, 2001).

[13] Walter Bell personal memorandum, *An Anglican Upbringing*, Bell papers, AA.


## 3 The Vicar's Son

[1] Walter Bell personal memorandum, op.cit.

[2] ibid.

[3] ibid.

[4] WB's letter to Paul Sieghart, AA.
[5] WB, personal memorandum, op.cit., AA.
[6] ibid.
[7] ibid.
[8] ibid.
[9] ibid.

**4 Lest We Forget…**
[1] Record of a 1920 minute relating to St John Bell, Corpus Christi College, Cambridge.
[2] 'Notes on the English Character', first published in the American journal *Atlantic Monthly* in 1926 and reprinted as the opening essay in the 1936 collection *Abinger Harvest*. Quoted in Laura Marcus, 'E.M.Forster and the Character of "Character",' *The Cambridge Quarterly*, Volume 50, Issue 2, June 2021,
[3] Heather Rossiter, *Lady Spy, Gentleman Explorer: The Life of Herbert Dyce Murphy* (Random House Australia, 2001).
[4] In 1974 Walter Bell introduced his niece-in-law, Ruth Thomas, then a student at Oxford, to Professor Zaehner when he was teaching Eastern religions and ethics. Ruth Thomas to author 28 November 2021.
[5] Danby Bloch, *Prof RC Zahner: academic, eccentric, spy* (Tonbridge Society, 6 February 2020).
[6] Andrew Lycett, *Conan Doyle: The Man Who Created Sherlock Holmes* (London: Orion, 2008).
[7] See Conan Doyle's letters held at the Norrish Central Library, Portsmouth.
[8] Tonbridge School archive.
[9] WB's letter to Anthony Hartley 1 April 1994, AA.
[10] WB's letter to Mary Lygon 8 August 1937 (Rose Fenton private archive).

**5 Making a Living**
[1] WB's letter to Muriel Bell 7 January 1927, AA.
[2] Ben Macintyre, *A Spy Among Friends*, op.cit.
[3] WB's letters from Jersey to Muriel Bell 7 and 14 November 1927, AA.
[4] ibid.
[5] WB's letter from Jersey to Muriel Bell 21 July 1928, AA.

[6] WB's letter from Paris to Muriel Bell 21 August 1928, AA.

[7] WB's letters from Jersey to Muriel Bell 8 and 20 October 1928, AA.

[8] WB's letter from Reading to Muriel Bell 15 November 1928, AA.

[9] WB's letters from Reading to Muriel Bell 11 January and 8 February 1929, AA.

[10] WB's letter to Muriel Bell 11 January 1929, AA.

[11] Mary Lyon diary entry 23 April 1929 (Rose Fenton private archive).

[12] WB's letter to Muriel Bell 27 May 1929, AA.

[13] I am indebted to information provided by Dr Peter Martland & David Liebler, biographers of Sir Samuel Hoare.

[14] Selina Hastings, *Evelyn Waugh: A Biography* (London: Sinclair-Stevenson, 1994); Philip Eade, *A Life Revisited* (London:Picador 2017).

[15] WB unpublished memoir, op. cit.

[16] Mary Lygon diary (Rose Fenton private archive).

[17] WB's letter to Muriel Bell 22 October 1929, AA.

[18] WB's letter to Muriel Bell 14 November 1929, AA.

[19] Barbara Lygon Langrishe to author, AA.

## 6 Political Networks

[1] Christopher J.Walker, *Oliver Baldwin: A Life of Dissent* (London: Arcadia, 2003).

[2] *Financial Times*, 19 February 2021.

[3] E.M. Forster, *Maurice* (London: Penguin Books, 2009); see also article by Kate Symondson, *EM Forster's Gay Fiction* (London: British Library, 2016).

[4] WB's letter to Muriel Bell 15 February 1930, AA.

[5] WB's letter to Muriel Bell 18 July 1930, AA.

[6] WB's letter to Muriel Bell 1 August 1930, AA.

[7] WB's letter to Muriel Bell 10 October 1930, AA.

[8] Dr Peter Martland to author.

[9] Richard Griffiths, *An Intelligent Person's Guide to Fascism* (London:Bloomsbury 2006).

[10] Andrew Cook, *Cash for Honours* (Stroud: History Press, 2008).

[11] Michael Veste, 'Honours and Rebels', *Spectator,* 22 April 2006.

[12] ibid.

[13] Christopher Andrew, *The Defence of the Realm* (London: Allen Lane, 2009).

[14] WB's letter  to Muriel Bell 14 March 1931, AA.

[15] WB's letter to Muriel Bell 1 September 1931, AA.

[16] WB's letter to Muriel Bell 20 October 1931, AA.

[17] WB's letter to Muriel Bell 7 November 1931, AA.

[18] Quoted in Kingsley Martin, *Harold Laski* (New York:The Viking Press, 1953).

[19] Keith Jeffery, *MI6*, op.cit.

[20] WB's letter to Muriel Bell 10 April 1932, AA.

[21] Ruth Thomas to author 28 November 2021.

[22] Peter Wright, *Spycatcher* (Australia: Heinemann, 1987).

[23] WB's letter to Muriel Bell 8 August 1932, AA.

[24] WB's letter to Muriel Bell 13 November 1933, AA.

[25] WB's letter to Muriel Bell 22 November 1933, AA.

[26] WB's letter to Muriel Bell 22 November 1933, AA .

## 7 The Curious Traveller

[1] WB's  letter to Muriel Bell 1 March 1934, AA.

[2] WB's  letters to Muriel Bell 3  and 10 March 1934, AA.

[3] Ben Macintyre *A Spy Among Friends,* op.cit.

[4] Tim Milne, *Kim Philby* (London: Biteback, 2014).

[5] Obituary of Baron Clement von Franckenstein, *The Times,* 11 June 2019.

[6] For Frankenstein family history, I am indebted to Felix Von Moreau. See also WB's letters to Muriel Bell July (undated) 1934, 20 January    1939 and 2 February 1939). Baron Konrad Franckenstein died in 1938. He was survived by his wife Anne-Marie who died in 1968.

[7] WB's letter to George Bell (undated) July 1934, AA.

[8] Helen Fry, *SpyMaster* (Yale, New Haven and London, 2021).

[9] WB's letter to George Bell July (undated) 1934, AA.

[10] WB's letter to Muriel Bell 5 August 1934, AA.

[11] ibid, AA.

[12] Walter Bell unpublished memoir, op.cit., AA.

## 8 An Englishman in New York

[1] WB unpublished memoir, op.cit., AA.

[2] Andrew Lownie, *Stalin's Englishman* (Hodder & Stoughton, 2015).

[3] Nigel West: *MI6, British Secret Intelligence Service Operations 1909-1945* (Frontline Books, 2019).

[4] ibid.

[5] Jeffery, *MI6*,op.cit.

[6] West, *MI6*, op cit.

[7] Kenneth Benton memoir, 'The ISOS years, *Journal of Contemporary History*, vol.30, no.3 (July 1995)

[8] ibid.

[9] Christopher Andrew Cambridge Intelligence Seminar 11 February 2022.

[10] WB's letter  to Muriel Bell 13 March 1935, AA.

[11] WB unpublished memoir, op.cit, AA.

[12] WB's letter  to Muriel Bell 26  March  1935, AA.

[13] WB's letter to Mary Lygon 22 August 1935, AA.

[14] WB's letter to Mary Lygon 20 August 1935, AA.

[15] WB's letter to Muriel Bell 26 August 1935, AA.

[16] Bell papers, AA.

[17] ibid.

[18] WB's letter to Muriel Bell 10 August 1935, AA.

## 9 Matters of Faith

[1] WB's letter to Muriel Bell 11 July 1935, AA.

[2] Hansard, 24 October 1935, vol. 305, cc 357-69.

[3] Jeffery, *MI6*, op.cit.

[4] WB's letter to Muriel Bell 26 September 1935, AA.

[5] WB's letter to Reginal Lygon 10 April 1935, AA.

[6] WB's letters to Fletcher  27 October  1938 and 27 June 1939, AA.

[7] WB's letter to Muriel Bell 21 April 1936, AA.

[8] WB to Muriel Bell 21 April 1936, AA.

[9] WB to Muriel Bell 8 April and 21April 1936, AA.

[10] WB's letter to Muriel Bell 21 April 1936.

[11] Ayn Rand, *The Fountainhead* (New York/London: Penguin Books, 2007);

David Harriman (ed.),*The Journals of Ayn Rand* (New York/London: Penguin  Publishing Group, 1999).

[12] WB unpublished memoir,  op.cit.

[13] WB personal memoir, op.cit.

[14] John Strachey, *The Coming Struggle for Power* (London: Victor Gollancz, 1933).

[15] Kingsley Martin, *Laski*, op.cit.

[16] WB's letter to Mrs Norris Darrell 6 July 1968, AA.

[17] J. William Galbraith, *John Buchan: Model Governor General* (Toronto: Dundurn, 2013).

[18] WB's letter to George Bell , 4 January 1939. MI5 files declassified in 2001 reveal British suspicions about Danylo's father Pavlo's links with the Nazi regime while living in Germany through the 1930s and World War Two. By contrast British intelligence during World War Two and in the early years of the Cold War deepened their contacts with Danylo, once he had moved from Germany and spent most of 1938 in the US and Canada, before moving to England in 1939. MI5 were initially suspicious because of his family's German connections but came to consider him less as a security risk than as someone who could be useful to UK interests (see KV-2-661 and KV-2-662 files at the National Archives, Kew).

After World War Two, Danylo became one of the founders of the Association of Ukrainians in Great Britain (AUGB). In April 1956, he signed a memorandum to the UK government condemning the USSR's totalitarian regime and arguing for self-determination for the Ukrainian people and organised protests against Soviet leader Nikita Khrushchev's visit to Britain. Less than a year later, on 22 February 1957, after dining at his favourite restaurant in London, he felt sick and went home where he lost consciousness. That night he was taken to hospital and died the next morning. The inscription on his tombstone read: 'I am building Ukraine for all and with all.' Rumour had it that he was killed by a KGB agent named Sergei, who allegedly followed him during the last days of his life. See Serhii Plokhy's book, *The Man with the Poisoned Gun* (London: Oneworld Publications 2016).

[19] Bell papers, AA.

[20] Bell papers, AA.

## 10 Social Networks

[1] WB's letter to Muriel Bell 26 February 1936, AA.

[2] John Ranelegh to author. For Roosevelt's speech, see Josh Zeitz, 'The Speech that Set Off the Debate about America's Role in the World,' *Politico* magazine, 29 December 2015.

[3] WB's letter to his sister Mary 14 November 1935.

[4] For Leslie Howard's recruitment by the Ministry of Information see Jimmy Burns's *Papa Spy*. Also Matthew Sweet's profile of Alexander Korda: *Producer, Director, Exile, Spy* (BBC Radio 3 24 July 2020).

[5] WB's letter to Muriel Bell 18 August 1936, AA.

[6] Bell papers, AA.

[7] WB's letter to Muriel Bell 4 September 1936, AA.

[8] WB's letter to Muriel Bell 20 October 1936, AA.

[9] WB's letter to Muriel Bell 27 October 1936.

[10] WB's letter to Muriel Bell 6 April 1937, AA.

[11] WB's letter to Muriel Bell  20 April 1937, AA.

[12] ibid.

[13] Jeffery, *MI6*, op.cit.

[14] When Samuel Hoare died in 1959 without an heir, his country estate Templewood House was inherited by his nephew Paul Paget, the son of his sister Elmer and the Bishop Henry Page. (Peter Martland to author.)

[15] Nigel West, *MI6*, op.cit.

[16] WB's letter to Muriel Bell 14 October 1937, AA.

[17] Christopher Andrew, *The Defence of the Realm*, op.cit.

[18] WB's letter to Muriel Bell  14 October 1937, AA.

[19] WB's letter to Muriel Bell 26  October 1937, AA.

[20] ibid.

[21] WB's letter to George Bell 21 December 1937, AA.

## 11 The Gathering Storm

[1] WB 's letter to Mary Lygon 2 August 1938, AA.

[2] ibid.

[3] WB's letter to Mary Lygon 26 January 1938, AA.

[4] Rhodri Jeffreys-Jones, *Ring of Spies* (Cheltenham:The History Press, 2020).

[5] FBI historian Ray Batvinis letter to author 26 May  2021.

[6] 'A Byte Out of History: Spies Caught, Spies Lost, Lessons Learned' FBI archives official history 12 December 2007.

[7] Dr Peter Martland to author.

[8] Raymond  Batvinis's letter to author, AA.

[9] Raymond J.Batvinis, FBI Studies 22 February  2020. See also Peter Duffy, *Double Agent* (New York: Scribner Book Company; illustrated edition,  2015).

[10] WB's letter  to Muriel Bell 24 April 1938, AA.

[11] WB's letter  to Mary Lygon 16 September 1937, AA.

[12] WB's letter to Mary Lygon 5 October 5th 1937, AA

[13] WB's letter  to Muriel Bell 10 May 1938, AA.

[14] WB's letter to George Bell 24 May 1938, AA.

[15] WB's letter to Muriel Bell 27 October  1938, AA.

[16] ibid.

[17] Jane Mulvagh, *Madresfield, The Real Brideshead* (London: Black Swan, 2009).

[18] WB's letter to Muriel Bell 18 November, 1938, AA.

[19] WB's letter to Muriel Bell 2 December 1938, AA.

[20] WB's letter to George Bell 4 January 1939, AA. Bell  was photographed by the fashion photographer Toni Frissell in the 1 April 1939 issue of the American *Vogue* magazine, along with a group of New York socialite friends, including Frissell's husband McNeil Bacon, and wealthy married women such as  Mrs Drayton Cochran and Mrs Sheffield  Cowles, who Bell went skiing with earlier that year  in Sun Valley. ('Skiing in the Spring', *Vogue* 1 April 1939, *Vogue* archive.)

[21] While Lunn and Bell's postings as MI6 officers are thought never to have coincided and they ended up working for different agencies when Bell moved to MI5, they shared in common some Catholic friends in the intelligence world including the author's father Tom Burns. See Jimmy Burns, *Papa Spy* (London: Bloomsbury, 2010).

## 12 Seeking Allies

[1] Helen Fry, *Spymaster* (London: Yale University Press, 2021).

[2] WB's letter to Muriel Bell 20 January 1939, AA.

[3] WB's letter to Muriel Bell  27 June 1939, AA.

[4] Marya Mannes's obituary published in the *New York Times*, 15 September 1990.

Ruth Thomas to author email 24 February 2022.

[5] WB's letter to Muriel Bell 23 March 1939, AA.

[6] *Never Give In! The Best of Winston Churchill's Speeches* (New York: Hyperion Books, 2004), p.108.

[7] WB's letter to Muriel Bell 6 April 1939, AA.

[8] WB's letter to Muriel Bell 19 April 1939, AA.

[9] WB's letter to Muriel Bell 26 September 1939, AA.

[10] ibid.

[11] Nicholas J. Cull, *Selling War, The British Propaganda Campaign* (Oxford: OUP, 1997). See also Henry Hemming, *Our Man in New York* (London: Quercus, 2019).

[12] WB's letter to Muriel Bell 15 November 1939, AA.

[13] ibid.

[14] ibid.

[15] WB unpublished memoir, op.cit.

[16] ibid.

[17] WB's letter to Mary Lygon 4 March 1940, AA.

[18] Seidl: www.fdrlibrary.org/ Frank Roosevelt Library & Museum.

[19] WB's letter to Muriel Bell 21 April 1940, AA.

## 13 The East River Club

[1] *New York Times*, 6 November 2013.

[2] WB's letter to Muriel Bell 3 September 1939, AA.

[3] See Raymond R.Batvinis: *The Origins of FBI Counter Intelligence* (Lawrence: University Press of Kansas, 2007).

[4] Astor to Roosevelt 18 April 1940, Roosevelt Library (Copy enclosed in letter from Thomas F.Troy to WB 23 June 1983, AA) Troy (1919–2008) was a career CIA officer, US intelligence historian and the author of *Donovan and the CIA: A History of the Establishment of the CIA* (1981).

[5] Ray Batvinis to author.

[6] Astor to Roosevelt, op.cit.

[7] Nelson D.Lankford, *The Last American Aristocrat* (New York: Little, Brown, 1996); Nelson D.Lankford (ed.): *OSS Against the Reich: The World War Two Diaries of Colonel David K.E.Bruce* (Ohio: Kent State University Press, 1991).
Further notes from email conversation between Nelson D.Lankford and author.
See also Nelson MacPherson, *American Intelligence in War-Time London, The Story of the OSS* (London: Routledge, 2003).

[8] David Bruce told the CIA historian Thomas F. Troy that he was instructed in espionage tradecraft by Bell's MI6's colleague Dick Ellis. (Troy interview with Bruce 30 December 1972: Troy Papers RG, NARA quoted by Macpherson).

[9] Duncan M. Spencer unpublished memoir, Leslie Spencer archive.

[10] J. William Galbraith, *John Buchan: Model Governor General* (Dundurn, 2013).

[11] ibid.See also Ursula Buchan, *Beyond the Thirty Nine Steps*, *A Life of John Buchan* (London: Bloomsbury, 2019).

[12] Leslie Spencer to author.

[13] ibid.

[14] Duncan M. Spencer unpublished memoir Leslie Spencer archive

[15] www.jpmorganchase.com/news-stories/advancingcities-paris 5 November 2018.

[16] Ursula Buchan to author 8 July 2020. John Buchan's diary at the National Library of Scotland Special Collections.

[17] John Buchan's diary.

[18] Duncan M.Spencer unpublished memoir, Leslie Spencer archive.

[19] ibid.

[20] ibid.

## 14 To War

[1] WB's letter to Muriel Bell January (undated) 1940.

[2] WB's letter to Muriel 26 September 1939.

[3] H. Montgomery Hyde, *The Quiet Canadian* (London: Hamish Hamilton, 1962).

[4] John Colville, *The Churchillians* (Weidenfeld & Nicholson, 1981).FBI historian Ray Batvinis wrote of Stevenson's *A Man Called Intrepid.* 'Avoid any reference to it like the plague. It has been thoroughly discredited.' British Foreign Office historian Gill Bennett considered Stephenson an 'unreliable narrator' (separate email correspondence with author).

[5] Australian-born Charles Howard 'Dick' Ellis, a World War One veteran, who was recruited by MI6 and posted to Berlin in 1923. During World War Two, he served as Bill Stephenson's deputy in the British Security Coordination (BSC) and was subsequently embroiled in allegations that he had passed secrets to the Nazis and the Russians.

[6] Copy of WB's letter to James Fulton 12 October 1982, AA.

[7] Gill Bennett in correspondence with the author.

[8] Jennet Conant, *The Irregulars* (London: Simon & Schuster 2009.)

[9] Nigel West, op.cit.

[10] ibid.

[11] Jeffery, *MI6*, op.cit.

[12] Gill Bennett, *Churchill's Man of Mystery: Desmond Moreton and The World of Intelligence* (Abingdon: Routledge, 2007).

[13] Gill Bennett to author.

[14] For an interesting re-examination of Stephenson's clouded early life see Bill Macdonald's *The True Intrepid: Sir William Stephenson and the Unknown Agents* (Vancouver: Raincoat Books, 2001).

[15] WB's letter to Muriel Bell 2 June 1940.

16 Bell papers, AA.

17 Hemming: *Our Man in New York*, op.cit.

18 WB's letter to Muriel Bell (undated) January 1940, AA.

19 Bill Macdonald, *The True Intrepid*, op.cit.

20 Leslie Spencer to author.

21 Grace Old to author.

22 ibid.

23 ibid.

## 15 South of the Border

1 Nicholas Reynolds, *Need to Know: World War II and the Rise of American Intelligence* (Boston: Mariner Books, 2022).

2 Nigel West (introduction) *The Secret History of British Intelligence in the Americas, 1940-45* (London: St Ermin's Press,1999)

3 Robert J.Cressman, *The Official Chronology of the US Navy in World War 11* (Naval Historical Centre, 1999).

4 Bell papers, AA.

5 Hemming, op.cit.

6 ibid. See also Mark Weber, Roosevelt's 'Secret Map' speech: Institute for Historical Research.

7 William Boyd, 'The Secret Persuaders' *Guardian*, 19 August 2006.

8 Montgomery Hyde: *Secret Intelligence Agent: British Espionage in America and the Creation of the OSS* (London: Constable, 1982).

9 Bell papers, AA

10 Bell memorandum 23 March 1975, AA.

11 Barbara Lygon to author.

12 Selina Hastings, *Evelyn Waugh* (London: Capuchin Classics, 2013); www.bbc.co.uk/history/ww2peopleswar/stories

14 Barbara Lygon to author.

15 Riverhead Parish magazine, 1952.

16 Margaret Nicholas to author.

17 ibid.

18 Sir Oswald Mosley, founder and leader of the British Union of Fascists. Harry Pollitt served as the general secretary of the Communist Party of Great Britain from 1929 to September 1939 and again from 1941 until his death in 1960.

19 WB's letter to Muriel Bell 1941 (undated) AA.

## 16 Pearl Harbor

1 WB to Muriel Bell 1941 (undated) Bell papers, AA.

[2] Susan A. Brewer, *To Win the Peace: Propaganda and the United States during WW2* (New York: Cornell University Press, 1997).

[3] Jeffery, *MI6*, op. cit. See also Douglas Clarke. 'Before the Colonel Arrived: Hoover, Donovan, Roosevelt, and the Origins of American Central Intelligence 1940-41', *Intelligence & National Security*, volume 20, 2005, issue 2 .

[4] Bell papers, AA. Another colleague Bell admired was John Foster, whom he knew from his student days studying law when Foster was called to the Bar in 1927 (Inner Temple) . Foster was appointed legal adviser and first secretary to the British embassy in Washington in early World War Two . 'It is such a relief to have someone about who is not (Civil) 'Service' – and has the same attitude towards everything as oneself.' (WB to his father in 7 December 1939). In the spring of 1942, Bell enjoyed a 'few evenings' in Washington with a fellow MI6 recruit who spent part of World War Two writing film scripts, the World War One veteran, journalist and author Valentine Williams. He described Williams as 'very good company.' (WB to his father 8 March 1942).

[5] Andrew Roberts, *The Holy Fox: The Life of Lord Halifax* (London: Head of Zeus, 2015).

[6] ibid.

[7] Nelson Lankford, op. cit.

[8] Bell papers, AA.

[9] ibid.

[10] ibid.

[11] Roberts, op.cit.

[12] WB's letter to George Bell 29 March 1941.

[13] Katharine Sanson, *Memoir Sir George Sanson* (Diplomatic Private Research, 1972).

[14] ibid.

[15] Nicholas Reynolds, op.cit.

[16] John Costello, *Days of Infamy* (New York: Pocket Books, 1994).

[17] Jeffery MI6, op.cit.

[18] H.Montgomery Hyde, *The Quiet Canadian* (London: Hamish Hamilton, 1962); *Room 3603* (London: Mayflower, 1964).

[19] Bell papers, AA.

[20] Sanson memoir, op.cit.

[21] *Finest Hour Journal*, vol.138, Spring 2008 (International Churchill Society).

[22] Larry Loftis, *Into the Lion's Mouth: The True Story of Dusko Popov* (New York: Berkley, 2016); West, *MI6*, op.cit.; Hervie Haufler, *The Spies Who Never Were* (New York: Open Road Media, 2006); Dusko Popov autobiography, *Spy/Counterspy* (New York: Grosset & Dunlop, 1974). The name originally given by Popov as an FBI agent has been corrected to Charles Lanman.

[23] Nigel West, *Historical Dictionary of British Intelligence* (Lanham: Scarecrow Books, 2005; Ben Macintyre, *Double Cross* (London: Bloomsbury, 2012).

[24] Ray Batvinis, *The Origins of FBI Counter-Intelligence*, FBI Studies.com.

[25] Thomas F. Troy, 'The British Assault on J.Edgar Hoover', *International Journal of Intelligence & Counter Intelligence*, vol. 3, 1989.

[26] Mark Riebling, *The Wedge: From Pearl Harbor to 9/11* (Chicago: Touchstone, 2002).

[27] Loftis, op.cit.

[28] WB's letter to Walter Summers 27 April 1989, AA. See Anthony Summers's Hoover biography, *Official and Confidential – The Secret Life of J.Edgar Hoover* (London: Ebury Press, 2020).

[29] Nicholas E.Reynolds to author.

[30] WB's letter to Muriel Bell 5 December 1941.

## 17 Making Friends with the FBI

[1] Hoover to WB, Bell papers, AA.

[2] Bell papers, AA.

[3] ibid.

[4] ibid.

[5] Ray Batvinis: A Thorough Competent Operator, FBI Studies.

[6] Walter Bell memorandum 23 March 1975, AA.

[7] Bell papers, AA.

[8] Nicholas Reynolds, *Need to Know*, op.cit.

[9] FBI historian Raymond J.Batvinis letter to author 26 May 2021.

[10] Bell papers, AA.

[11] Jeffery: *MI6*, op.cit.

[12] Bell papers, AA.

[13] ibid.

[14] Nigel West (ed.) *The Guy Liddell Diaries Vol 1* (New York/London: Routledge, 2009).

[15] ibid.

[16] ibid.

[17] ibid.

[18] Hoover's justified complaint against the British Security Coordination (BSC) was Stephenson's broken promise not to spy in Washington against the Spanish and French (Vichy) embassies. Nigel West(Rupert Allason) to author .

[19] ibid.

[20] ibid.

[21] ibid.

[22] ibid.

[23] Batvinis's letter to author 26 May 2021.

[24] West, *Liddell Diaries*, op.cit.

[25] ibid.

[26] FBI historian Ray J.Batvinis letter to author 26 May 2021.

[27] Memorandum from WB 23 March 1975, AA. Copy of version believed to have been shared at the time with Professor Harry Hinsley, but never published.

[28] Bell memorandum. In September 1941 the influential secretary of state for Latin America Adolf Berle warned President Roosevelt that the growing organisation of British Security Co-ordination employing its own secret agents and informers was a potential violation of US law involving a foreign power. See Henry Hemming, op.cit.

[29] Raymond J.Batvinis to author.

[30] Bell memorandum, op.cit.

[31] Hoover's letter to WB 7 November 1942, Bell papers, AA.

[32] Jeffery, *MI6* , op.cit.

[33] MacPherson, op.cit., Batvinis's letter to author 26 May 2021.

[34] ibid. Batvinis.

[35] ibid. Batvinis.

[36] Philby, *My Silent War*, op. cit.

[37] Jeffery, *MI6*, op.cit.

[38] ibid.

[39] Cedric Belfrage's brother Bruce was a BBC newsreader during World War Two. He was reading the news when Broadcasting House was bombed during the Blitz on 15 October 1940 and lived to tell the story www.bbc.com/historyofthebbc/100-voices/ww2/bh-bombs/

[40] KV 2.4004 National Archives Kew. See also Sam Jones in the *Financial Times* and BBC report ('The Hollywood Spy' https://www.bbc.co.uk/news/uk)

[41] Sally Belfrage, *When it was fun to be red: UN-American Activities, A memoir* (New York: Harper Collins, 1994).

[42] Belfrage was questioned by the FBI in 1947 about his involvement with the Communist Party. The interview covered his relations with the general secretary of the Communist Party of the US (CPUSA) Earl Browder, Jacob Golos, V.J.Jerome, and documents about Scotland Yard surveillance techniques and the Vichy government. Elizabeth Bentley recounted Belfrage's interaction with Golos in her 1951 memoir *Out of Bondage* (Whitefish:Literary Licensing LLC).

[43] John Earl Haynes and Harvey Klehr, *Venona, Decoding Soviet Espionage in America* (Yale: Yale University Press, 2000).

[44] ibid.

[45] Cedric Belfrage, *The Frightened Giant: My Unfinished Affair with America* and *The American Inquisition, 1945-1960* (London: Secker & Warburg, 1957).

[46] For the alleged wartime Soviet penetration of the BSC see Nigel West, *Cold War Spymaster* (Barnsley: Frontline, 2018) and Roland Philipps, *A Spy Named Orphan: The Enigma of Donald Maclean* (London: Vintage, 2019).

## 18 Plotting Against Hitler

[1] Danny Orbach, *The Plots Against Hitler* (London: Head of Zeus, 2018).

[2] P.R.J.Winter, 'British Intelligence and the July Bomb Plot of 1944: A Reappraisal' (*War in History*, vol.13, no.4 October 2006).

[3] Peter Hoffmann (ed.), *Behind Valkyrie: German Resistance to Hitler Documents* (Kingston, Canada: McGill-Queen's University Press, 2011).

[4] Max Hastings, 'Plotting to Assassinate Putin is Beneath us', *The Times*, 24 March 2022.

[5] Orbach, op.cit.

[6] Philip Knightley, 'The Spy Files', *Independent*, 17 November 2006); Tim Milne, *Kim Philby: The Unknoan Story of the KGB's Master Spy* (London: Biteback, 2015).

[7] P.R.J.Winter, op.cit.

[8] Lankford, op.cit.; Anthony Cave Brown, *The Secret Life of Sir Stewart Menzies* (London: Macmillan, 1987); Bill Macdonald, *Intrepid's Last Secrets* (Canada: Friesen Press, 2009).

[9] Letter and photograph Beatrice Drayton Phillips 6 August 1948, AA.

[10] Thomas Troy interview with Bruce, 30 December 1972, Troy papers; Nelson MacPherson, op.cit. See also the late wartime OSS Fisher Howe's review of Nelson's MacPherson's book on OSS in London (2008), published online by The OSS Society.

[11] MacPherson, op.cit.

[12] ibid.

[13] Bill Macdonald, *The True Intrepid* , op.cit.

[14] Nelson D.Lankford (ed.), *Diaries of Colonel David K.E.Bruce,* op.cit.

[15] Cave Brown, op.cit.

[16] MacPherson, op.cit.

[17] ibid.

[18] Cave Brown, op.cit.

[19] Greg Bradsher, 'A Time to Act: The Beginning of the Fritz Kolbe Story 1900-1947' *Prologue* magazine, National Archives, spring 2002.

[20] P.R.J. Winter, op.cit.

[21] Guy Liddell Diaries, KV 4/191 National Archives, Kew,

[22] Ben McIntyre, A *Spy Among Friends: Kim Philby and the Great Betrayal* (London: Bloomsbury, 2014).

[23] David Astor, newspaper publisher. His links with British intelligence during World War Two had him serving in naval intelligence and with the Special Operations Executive (SOE) .

[24] Christopher Sykes, *Troubled Loyalty: The Story of a German Aristocrat Who Defied Hitler* (London: Collins 1968).

[25] ibid.

[26] *The Times*, 30 November 1968.

[27] Miguel Vermerhen interview with the author.

[28] Richard Bassett, *Hitler's Spy Chief* (London, W & N, 2005).

[29] Michael Howard, *British Intelligence in the Second World War* (London: Stationery Office Books, 1990).

[30] G-2 Intelligence Report, Cave Brown papers.

[31] Tom Bower, *The Perfect English Spy: Sir Dick White and the Secret War* (London: St Martin's Press, 1995).

[32] Jimmy Burns, *Papa Spy* (London: Bloomsbury, 2009).

[33] US State Department history papers history.state.gov/milestones/1937-1945/Casablanca

[34] Orbach, op.cit.

[35]Putlitz's memoir, the Putlitz Dossier was published in January 1957 (London). For Philby and Canaris see Richard Greene, *Russian Roulette, The Life & Times of Graham Greene* (London: Little, Brown, 2020).

[36] Michael Vermehren to author.

[37] G-2 Intelligence Report, Cave Brown papers.

[38] Reynolds, op. cit.

[39] Bell papers, AA.

[40] WB's letter to Muriel Bell September 1939, Bell papers, AA.

## 19 The Russian Connection

[1] Roland Philipps, op.cit.

[2] Tattie Bell to author.

[3] www.londonist.com/london/drink/do-the-karl-marx-pub-crawl

[4] On insights into the Cambridge Five, I am indebted to George Carey, documentary director of *The Spy Who Went Into the Cold* (BBC 2013) and *Toffs, Queers, and Traitors* (BBC 2017).

[5] Tattie Bell to author.

[6] Phillip Knightley, *Philby*: *KGB Masterspy* (op.cit.); Tom Mangold, *Cold Warrior* (London: Simon & Schuster 1991); Jefferson Morley, *The Ghost: The Secret Life of CIA Spymaster James Jesus Angleton* (London: St Martin's Griffin, 2017)

[7] Tattie Bell to author.

[8] Tattie Bell to author.

[9] MI6 World War Two chief Menzies was among those who clung to the forlorn hope of Philby's innocence and reportedly felt crushed when the spy's betrayal was later proved beyond all doubt. See Tom Bower, *The Perfect English Spy*, op. cit; Phillip Knightley, *Philby KGB Masterspy*, op.cit.

[10] Hugh Trevor-Roper, E.D. Harrison(ed.), *The Secret World* (London: IB Tauris, 2014)

[11] KGB archive report in Nigel West and Oleg Tsarev, *The Crown Jewels: The British Secrets at the Heart of the KGB* (London: Yale University Press, 1999).

## 20 Homer

[1] Jeffery, *MI6*, op.cit.

[2] Paddy Hayes, *Queen of Spies* (NewYork/London: Duckworth, 2016).

[3] Lankford, op.cit.

[4] Bell papers and Tattie Bell to author.

[5] Gill Bennett to author.

[6] On his retirement in the late 1960s Bell drew on government pensionable pay from 1942 , the year he returned to the UK from his years of untaxed service in the US.

[7] Martin, *Laski*, op.cit.

[8] Peter Mandelson preface to Bernard Donoghue and George Jones, *Herbert Morrison: Portrait of a Politician* (London: W& N, 2001.)

[9] Bernard Donoghue & George Jones, *Herbert Morrison*, op.cit.

[10] WB's letter to Donald Gillies, Inverchapel's biographer, 25 July 1991 (copy in Bell papers, AA).

[11] ibid.

[12] Bell papers, AA.

[13] Richard M.Bennett (Espionage: *Encyclopedia of Spies & Secrets* [London: Diane Pub. Co, 2002]) writes that a Soviet agent in the Foreign Office described by Krivitsky as a 'Scotsman with bohemian tastes' was not Maclean but 'more likely' Inverchapel. See Christopher Andrew, *The Defence of the Realm*, on Krivitsky's 'inability to provide clear leads during his debriefing to any current Soviet agents or intelligence personnel in Britain'.

[14] Bell papers, AA.

[15] WB's letter to Gillies, op.cit.

[16] ibid.

[17] Ronald Philipps, op.cit.

[18] Robert J.Lamphere and Tom Shachtman, *The FBI-KGB War: A Special Agent's Story* (New York: Mercer University Press, 1986); Allen Weinstein and Alexander Vassiliev, *The Haunted Wood: Soviet Espionage in America – The Stalin Era* (New York: Random House, Inc. 1998); also Gillies, op.cit. on Maclean and Makin's relationship.

[19] Roland Philipps, op.cit.

[20] Roland Philipps to author.

[21] ibid., Tattie Bell to author.

[22] ibid.

[23] Philipps to author, John Earl Haynes, *Venona*, op.cit.

[24] ibid., Andrew Boyle, The *Climate of Treason* (London: Coronet, 1979).

[25] Martin J. Folly, *Journal of Transatlantic Studies*, vol.10 2012, issue 2.

[26] *The Times*, 4 March 2004.

[27] See Andrew Brown contribution to US-UK Nuclear Cooperation after 50 years (Centre for Strategic and International Studies, Washington July 2008).

[28] Folly, op.cit. The British nuclear physicist Alan Nunn May was a a Soviet spy who supplied British and US atomic secret to the Soviet Union during World War Two. He was arrested and, having confessed to espionage, was sentenced to ten years' hard labour in May 1946.

[29] Inverchapel's letter to Makins 29 March 1948, Bell papers, AA.

[30] Makins's letter to Inverchapel 8 April 1948, Bell papers, AA.

[31] WB to Balfour memorandum and follow up advisery, 2 March 1948, Bell papers, AA.

[32] WB to Balfour memorandum.

[33] ibid.

[34] ibid.

[35] Keith Middlemas, obituary of Franks, *Independent*, 16 October 1992.

[36] ibid.

[37] Folly, op.cit.

[38] Beatrice Stephens's letter to WB 6 August 1948.

[39] Robert J.Lamphere and Shachtman, op.cit.; Weinstein and Vassiliev, op.cit.

[40] Philipps, op.cit.

[41] ibid.

[42] ibid.

[43] Inverchapel's letter to Sir Frederick Bain 23 April 1948, Bell papers, AA.

## 21 The General's Daughter

[1] Tattie to author.

[2] 'Stephenson (British Security Co-ordination chief) achieved much in the early days before the US entered the war. He got Donovan (Founder of the OSS) the VIP treatment in 1940 so that Donovan convinced Roosevelt that Kennedy was forming a wrong judgement and should be replaced. My father-in-law contributed to this separately by reporting on the superiority of the RAF.' WB's letter to James Fulton 12 October 1982, Bell papers, AA.

[3] West and Tsarev, op.cit.

[4] David R. Mets, *Master of Airpower: General Carl A. Spaatz* (San Francisco: Presidio Press, 1988).

[5] Michael Carver, *The Warlords* (London: Leo Cooper, 2005).

[6] The suggestion that Spaatz dropped an 'a' to make his surname sound less German made in Brendan Simms's book *Hitler* (London 2020) is disputed by one of his granddaughters Ruth Thomas. 'The change of the spelling of Spatz to Spaatz had nothing to do with wanting it to look more Dutch than German. It was a futile attempt to get people to stop pronouncing it 'spats'. My grandfather didn't much care, but my grandmother absolutely hated it. Someone in the Spatz family told her there was a branch that spelled the name with an extra 'a' and she seized on that to press the case for making the change. As I said, it did no good. Most people still say 'spats'. (Ruth Thomas email to author 28 November 2021).

[7] Mets, op.cit.

[8] Lankford, op.cit. biography of David Bruce

[9] Mets, op.cit.

[10] Women in Wartime: ARC Clubmobile. The Butterfly Balcony blog post 31 October 2014.

[11] *Milwaukee Journal* 21 September 1943.

[12] *Life* magazine February 1943.

[13] Dr Peter Martland to author on World War Two Cambridge archives.

[14] The first major American movie star to enlist in the US military in World War Two and to be based in England was James ('Jimmy') Stewart. He trained as a pilot, and in August 1943 was assigned to the 445th Bomb Group, first as operations officer of the 703rd Bomb Squadron and then as its commander, at the rank of captain. In December the 445th Bomb Group transferred to the Allied air force base in Tibenham, Norfolk, and immediately began combat operations. www.norfolksamericanconnections.com/people-u-z/james-jimmy-stewart/

[15] By early April 1945, Tattie Spaatz had moved from England to liberated France, and was based near a villa in Cannes overlooking the French Riviera which was being used by the US military as a rest and recuperation centre. The American army general Henry (Hap) Arnold had flown in to meet with other senior commanders. It was 'one of the perks' of being the daughter of General Spaatz who was the highest-ranking air force officer based in Europe. Arnold recorded in his diary being joined at an *al fresco* breakfast by Tattie coming to the villa 'with three other Red Cross girls and three aviators to swim and enjoy the sunshine'. (Bill Yenne, *Hit The Target* (Dutton Caliber, 2016).

[16] Ruth Thomas email to author 24 February 2022.

[17] Mets, op.cit.Lyle C.Wilson served in the US army in the last stages of World War One  and was a member of the American League, the veterans' association. As a war correspondent with United Press International he reported from England and mainland Europe during World War Two. Prior to his death in 1967, Wilson's career with UPI spanned 42 wars including 37 years in Washington, where he was one of the most distinguished figures in the capital's journalism and became UPI's vice president. The FBI file held on him was disclosed as a result of a Freedom of Information Act (FOIA) request submitted  by the late American FBI historian Professsor Athan Theomaris after Wilson had died and is deposited in the archives of Marquette University where Theomaris taught. (Series 38, Box 1, Folder 1 File No. 94-42524, #1-88, 5 November 1941-23 May 1967). I am indebted to the university library's special collections archivist Amy Kerry for facilitating access. The files show that Wilson, who after World War Two became a Cold War virulent anti-communist, enjoyed a close friendship with the FBI's powerful director J.Edgar Hoover, director from 1941 (coincidentally around the time Walter Bell was developing his links with the FBI) and into the 1960s, defending the reputation of the Bureau's long-serving chief through various controversies, while enjoying privileged access to senior FBI sources.

[18] Report published on Thursday, 16 September  1948. The *Star*, founded in 1852, was the most financially successful newspaper in Washington DC and among the top ten in the US until its decline in the 1970s. See also Faye Haskins, *The Evening Star, The Rise and Fall of a Great Washington Newspaper* (Washington DC, 2019).

[19] Helen Kirkpatrick of the *Chicago Daily News*; William Walton, *Time* magazine, briefly editor in 1948 of the *New Republic*, and a friend of journalist and author Ernest Hemingway; John White graduated from West Point, the US military Academy, in the inter-war years. After serving as a bombing training instructor in World War Two  he was deployed on the staff of the United States Air Forces in Europe (USAFE). In the summer prior to the Bells' wedding, he was involved with  the US and British combined Berlin Airlift before being appointed in July 1948 to the newly formed United States Air Force (USAF) , following his promotion to the rank of lieutenant colonel.

[20] Roland Philipps, op.cit.

[21] ibid.

## 22 From Russia with Love

[1] The ship was sold to Russia in 1950 and renamed *Gruziya* (Soviet Georgia).

[2] Ruth Thomas email to author 27 December 2021.

[3] Hemming, op.cit.

[4] John le Carré, *Agent Running In The Field* (London: Penguin Books, 2019).

[5] Despite his misbehaviour in Cairo, Maclean had yet to be identified as a Russian spy, and in 1950 was in London having been promoted to head of the American Department in the Foreign Office, which allowed him to continue to keep Moscow informed about Anglo-American relations and planning. He defected to Moscow on 25 May 1951, with the Soviets planning his escape from England so that he would not break under interrogation by MI5.

[6] Tattie Bell to author.

[7] ibid.  See also account in Andrew Boyle, op.cit.

[8] WB's niece Hannah O'Hara to author.

[9] Quoted by Andrew Boyle, op.cit.

[10] Frank Giles's *The Sunday Times* article entitled 'From Russia with Love'.

[11] Bell papers, AA.

[12] Giles's *Sunday Times* article, op.cit.

[13] In 1983, *The Sunday Times*, under Frank Giles's editorship, claimed to have Hitler's diaries, written in the Führer's own hand. They were first authenticated and then disowned as false by Bell's wartime colleague, the former MI6 intelligence officer, Oxford historian Hugh Trevor-Roper, Lord Dacre, then Master of Peterhouse, Cambridge, whose earlier investigation into the last days of Hitler was published to great acclaim.

As the *New York Times* later reported in an obituary about Giles, *The Sunday Times*'s top editors discovered the truth at the last minute and tried to stop their publication. 'But the paper's owner, Rupert Murdoch, dismissed their concerns and ordered that the presses roll, leaving The Sunday Times, one of the world's great news organizations, with serious egg on its face. The editor of the paper, the mild-mannered, urbane Frank Giles, took the fall and was fired,

bringing a distinguished career to an abrupt and ignominious end.'
Katharine Q. Seelye, *New York Times*, 12 November 2019.

[14] Donald Gillies, *Radical Diplomat* (New York: Bloomsbury, 1999).

[15] Bell papers, AA .

[16] During World War Two, Leonard Miall served in the Political
Warfare Executive in psychological warfare in New York and San
Francisco; René MacColl was head of press and radio at the British
Information Service in New York, and Michael Muggeridge served
in the intelligence corps and then in MI6.

[17] James Chace, *Acheson: The Secretary of State Who Created the American
World* (New York: Simon & Schuster, 1988); see also Elizabeth
Barker, *The British Between the Superpowers* (Toronto: Palgrave
Macmillan, 1983).

[18] Tattie Bell to author.

[19] For text and recording of the speech on 5 June 1947 The George
C.Marshall Foundation.

[20] Martin Folly chapter on Inverchapel in *The Washington Embassy*
(London, 2009)

[21] Gillies, *Sunday Times*, op.cit.

[22] Bell papers, AA.

### 23 Medal of Freedom

[1] Ackerman's letter to WB 16 April 1947, AA.

[2] WB's letter to Ackerman 29 April 1947, AA.

[3] WB's letter to Dunbar 29 April 1947, AA.

[4] Ackerman's letter to WB 2 June 1947, AA.

[5] Foreign Office (E.W.Light) to Bell 3 September 1947, AA.

[6] Gill Bennet email to author 3 March 2022.

[7] ibid.

[8] Helen Fry, *The Walls Have Ears* (London: Yale University Press,
2020).

[9] Montgomery Hyde papers, WCA.

[10] ibid.

[11] ibid.

[12] Bevin's letter to WB 17August 1948, AA.

[13] Bell papers, AA.

[14] *Spycatcher* was published in 1987. As one commentator at the time
put it, 'Writing his book was an act of revenge, summed up by
Wright in one sentence: "I learned a lesson I never forgot -- that MI5
expects its officers to remain loyal unto the grave without necessarily

offering loyalty in return." This is a reference to the time when MI5 persuaded Wright to give up 15 years of his pension rights with the Admiralty and to join MI5 with the promise that it would compensate him for them. But when he retired, MI5 did not live up to this promise. *Spycatcher* is therefore above all a brazen and unscrupulous attempt to recoup the lost pension.' Henry Brandon, *The Washington Post*, 9 August 1987.

[15] West, *Guy Liddell's Cold War MI5 Diaries*, op.cit., volume 2.

## 24 Kenya, Part 1

[1] Bell papers, AA.

[2] The National Archives (TNA) KV (MI5) files 2/1787-1788 See also Christopher Andrew, op.cit. *and Calder Walton, Empire of Secrets: British Intelligence, the Cold War and the Twilight of Empire (London: Harper Press, 2013)*

[3] Bell papers, AA.

[4] ibid.

[5] ibid.

[6] Calder Walton, op.cit.

[7] The Somaliland campaign, also known as the Dervish War (1899–1920), had the Salihiyya Sufi Muslim militant leader Mohammed Abdullah Hassan opposing the British protectorate agreement between the British and Somali Sultans.

[8] Bell papers, AA.

[9] *End of Empire*, 1985 Granada Television series written and produced by Brian Lapping and Norma Percy.

[10] Bell papers, AA.

[11] Nigel West, *Liddlell's Diaries* vol.2, op.cit.

[12] Bell papers, AA.

[13] James Fox, *White Mischief* (London: Penguin Books, 1982).

[14] Richard Greene, op.cit.

[15] Tattie's father General Spaatz was raised as a Lutheran but had no interest in organised religion when he grew up. The Spaatzes' Washington DC house on 5 Grafton Street was across the road from an Episcopalian church, and every Sunday General Spaatz would look out the front door and call to his wife, Ruth, and say, 'Ruth, the damn bible thumpers are blocking the driveway again.' As for Spaatz's wife, 'she used to go to Christmas and Easter services at that church, but that was about it.' It's not clear they even had their children baptised. Certainly, one of Tattie's sisters wasn't baptised

until she was about 10 and that was due to a family friend who was appalled to learn it had never been done. What Tattie used to say about her own religious orientation was that she was a natural Hindu. (Tattie's niece Ruth Thomas in email to author 27 December 2021).

[16] Despite her Lutheran family ancestry and her dislike of some Catholic priests, Tattie Bell converted to Catholicism prior to her death, on 25 February 2005 (aged 83). It was marked by a requiem in the Roman Catholic church of The Oratory, the setting for her husband's funeral service a year earlier, and where she had been 'instructed' in the fundamentals of the Catholic faith by the celebrant priest, a member of the traditional Oratorian order.

[17] Calder Walton, op.cit.

[18] ibid.

[19] Bell papers, AA.

[20] The National Archives, Kew, (TNA) KV (MI5) file 2/1788

[21] Bell papers, AA.

[22] Andrew, op.cit.

[23] Walton, op.cit. d

[24] *End of Empire*, Granada TV, op.cit.

[25] *The Tablet* 2 September 1978. Bell, as well as contributor, also served as Trustee of the International Catholic weekly.

[26] Bell papers, AA.

[27] According to American historian Caroline Elkins (*Imperial Reckoning: The Untold Story of Britain's Gulag in Kenya)*, Thacker was bribed £20,000 (Sh2.8 million) by the colonial government to find Kenyatta and co. guilty.

[28] Bell papers, AA.

[29] ibid.

[30] Police commissioner in Kenya during Mau Mau.

[31] Bell papers, AA.

[32] Hannah O'Hara to author.

[33] WB's letter to Julian Amery 17 July 1961, Amery papers, Churchill Archives. See also Mickie Mwanzia Koster, *The Power of the Oath: Mau Mau Nationalism in Kenya, 1952–1960* (New York: University of Rochester Press, 2016).

[34] Bell papers, AA.

[35] See Julian Amery, *Approach March: A Venture in Autobiography* (London: Hutchinson, 1973) Also Jimmy Burns, op.cit.

[36] WB 's letter to Amery 17 July 1951, Amery papers, Churchill archives.

[37] ibid.

[38] Popović is mentioned in Amery papers, Churchill archives.

[39] Amery's letter to WB, 19 January 1952, Amery papers, Churchill archives.

[40] WB's letter to Amery, 1 February 1952.

[41] Jasper Bell to author.

[42] ibid.

[43] Bell papers, AA.

[44] ibid.

## 25 India

[1] P & O Outward Bound Passenger lists London–Bombay. The National Archives, Kew (TNA) For information on *SS Stratheden* www.pandosnco.co.uk/stratheden.html

[2] Bernard Crick, *George Orwell: A Life* (London: Penguin Books, 1980).

[3] WB to author.

[4] The War Office was publicly identified as a department of the British government responsible for the administration of the British Army between 1857 and 1964, when its functions were transferred to the new Ministry of Defence. It was also used by MI5 as a suitable cover government department name for some of its officers and external communications.

[5] Between 1947 and 1972 over one million people paid a fare of £10 for passage to Australia, earning them the nickname 'Ten Pound Poms', and the majority of these travelled with P & O. See history of cruising www.cruisedialysis.co.uk

[6] Walton, op.cit.

[7] Walton, op.cit.

[8] ibid. See also Andrew, op.cit.

[9] MI5 officers posted from New Delhi to Hong Kong reported to Britain's inter-service -agency in the Far East, Security Intelligence Far East (SIFE) founded in 1946. Its headquarters for gathering and disseminating intelligence assessments was within the offices of the commissioner general of Southeast Asia in Singapore. The National Archives, Kew (TNA) KV files 4/421.

[10] Walton, op.cit.

[11] B.N. Mullik, *My Years with Nehru: The Chinese Betrayal 1948-64.* (New York: Allied Publishers, 1972).

[12] Report on declassified MI5 archives in *The Times of India*, 12 April 2015.

[13] Andrew, op.cit.

[14] MI5 archives See also Andrew ibid.

[15] Ruth Thomas email to author 27 December 2021.

[16] Bruce Cumings, *The Korean War: A History* (New York: Random House, 2010).

[17] Declassified telegram from US embassy in Bangkok to US State Department, 9 December 1953, Office of the Historian, US State Department papers.

[18] Gopal Das Khosla's letter to WB 5 January 1956. Khosla was one of the judges in the trial of the assassins of Mahatma Ghandi on 30 January 1948, Bell papers, AA.

[19] General J.N. Chaudhuri letters to WB 23 February 1965, and 14 December 1965 when Bell was on his second posting in Nairobi, Bell papers, AA.

[20] Louis's son Patrick Heren to author: 'He spoke to me at length several times about their jaunt round Indochina. We have a photo of Greene wearing a sarong and sitting down in a tropical garden which I guess is at our house in Kampong Loyang.
They spent a couple of weeks together, and some of the episodes in *The Quiet American* have their origins in those two weeks. Louis complained (good-naturedly) that Greene had stolen some good phrases from him. A mass of rotting bodies in a canal looking like Irish stew, for instance. So why wouldn't Louis have written about Greene in his memoirs? He didn't much like *The Quiet American*. Especially he didn't like the way Greene makes Fowler take sides in the end. There is no doubt that my father Louis's strongly held view that reporters should report and not get involved in what they are reporting is reflected in the character of Fowler, until he commits himself near the end. He also did not like Greene's growing anti-Americanism.'

[21] Louis Heren, *Growing Up On The Times* (London: Hamish Hamilton, 1978).

[22] ibid.

[23] Bell papers, AA.

[24] ibid.

[25] ibid.

## 26 MI5 HQ

[1] Amery's letter to WB, Julian Amery papers, Churchill archives.

[2] Jasper Bell's letter to author 26 November 2021.

[3] In July 1956, Egypt's nationalist president Gamal Abdel Nasser nationalised the Suez Canal. On 29 October 1956, Israeli armed forces pushed into Egypt with French and British troops, as part of a secret deal struck by the UK with Israel and France. Britain's military action was condemned by the US and Commonwealth countries,and a special emergency session of the UN General Assembly. Huge pressure by the US forced Eden to seek a ceasefire. British and French forces withdrew by December, followed by Israel relinquishing control over the canal to Egypt, which reopened the Suez Canal in March 1957. 'The British government was left alienated and humiliated, its international reputation in tatters.' (Walton, *Empire of Secrets*.op.cit.).

[4] Philip Stephens, *Britain Alone: The Path from Suez to Brexit* (London: Faber and Faber, 2021). See also Helene von Bismarck's review in the *Financial Times*, 5 February 2021.

[5] Andrew, *Defence of the Realm*, op.cit.

[6] Nigel West, *Historical Dictionary of British Intelligence*, op.cit. See also *Portsmouth News* (19 April 2016) on the sixtieth anniversary of 'Buster' Crabb's 'disappearance' during a diving mission. Later the authorities announced his headless body had been washed up in Chichester Harbour. But conspiracy theories continued as to whether he had been discovered by the Russians and killed at the scene or imprisoned and taken to the Soviet Union. Others say he probably died as a result of equipment failure.

[7] Andrew, op.cit.

[8] Private information.

[9] Bell papers, AA.

[10] John Profumo resigned from parliament and the cabinet as secretary of state for war on 5 June 1963 having been discovered to have lied to parliament about a sexual relationship that was considered to have possibly endangered national security.

[11] For allegations against Hollis that he was a top-level Soviet spy see Chapman Pincher and Peter Wright. Both Hollis and Liddell were cleared by internal enquiries and no substantiating evidence has come to light. In March 1981 Prime Minister Margaret Thatcher told parliament that two earlier enquiries had concluded that Hollis was not a Soviet agent. According to MI5's historian Christopher

Andrew, the Russian defector Oleg Gordievsky confirmed what an earlier MI5 investigation had already shown – that the allegations that Hollis had worked for Moscow were 'nonsense'. See also Ben Macintyre, *Agent Sonya: Moscow's Most Daring Wartime Spy* (London: Crown 2020). Sonya was the code name of the Russian spy Ursula Kuczynski Burton who was recruited in the 1930s. 'Proof that Russia ran a British traitor inside MI5 that was never caught would be a publicity coup of immense value to Moscow…if the head of MI5 *had* been a Soviet super-mole, Putin would be unable to resist boasting about it.'
[12] Louis Heren's son Patrick Heren to author.

### 27 A Caribbean Assignment
[1] Bell papers, AA.
[2] *New York Times*, 22 November 1956; also *Madera Tribune* (California) 24 November 1956. University of California newspaper digital collection.
[3] Walton, op.cit.
[4] Bell papers, AA.
[5] ibid.
[6] Chief minister of Jamaica who became the island's prime minister in 1959.
[7] Bell papers, AA.
[8] ibid.
[9] ibid.
[10] See obituary *Daily Telegraph* 27 January 2007.
[11] ibid.
[12] Bell papers, AA.
[13] Bell papers, AA.
[14] ibid.
[15] ibid.
[16] ibid. Bell's impressions of members of the colonial service, some of whom were recruited by MI5 from the late 1950s and rose to senior positions, would anticipate those of a later recruit in the late 1960s who would go on to become MI5's first female director general, Stella Rimington. She would recall her own career rise in what was definitely a man's world inhabited by a minority of dinosaurs who 'seemed to do very little at all, and there was a lot of heavy drinking'. Stella Rimington, *Open Secret: The Autobiography of the Former Director-General of MI5* (London: Arrow, 2022).

[17] Walton, op.cit.

[18] ibid.

[19] Talk by Clem Seecharam. The National Archives, Kew, 7 June 2013.

[20] WB's letter to Julian Amery 11 June 1959, Amery papers, Churchill College archives.

[21] ibid.

[22] Julian Amery's letter to WB 19 June 1959, Amery papers, Churchill College archives.

[23] ibid.

[24] Walton, op.cit.

[25] ibid.

[26] CIA Covert Operations –1964. Overthrow of Cheddi Jagan in British Guiana, Digital National Archive, Archive website, nsaarchive@gwu.edu posted 6 April 2020.

[27] Bell papers, AA.

[28] WB's letter to Patrick Buchan-Hepburg, October 1958, Bell papers, AA.

[29] See Clive Davis, 'The Trotskyite who Loved Test Cricket, *The Times*, 19 March 2022.

[30] John L. Williams, *CLR James: A Life Beyond the Boundaries* (London: Constable, 2022).

[31] TNA CAB158/16 Chiefs of Staff. Joint Intelligence committee (JIC) and other documents referenced by Walton, *Empire of Secrets*, op. cit.

[32] John Williams, op.cit.

[33] ibid.

[34] Bell papers, AA.

[35] ibid.

[36] WB's letter to Patrick Buchan-Hepburg 10 December 1958. Buchan-Hepburg papers, Churchill College archives.

[37] Bell papers, AA.

## 28 Kenya, Part 2

[1] See obituary 'MI5 Spymaster and Soldier of the Raj Who Was Born in Ireland', *Irish Times*, 27 March 2010.

[2] Roger Hollis's letter to WB 11 January 1961.

[3] Bill Magan 's letter to WB 8 January 1961.

[4] Walton op.cit.

[5] Glenmore S.Trenear-Harvey, *Historical Dictionary of Intelligence Failures* (Maryland: Rowman and Littlefield, 2014).

[6] Bell papers, AA.

[7] Hansard House of Comms report 27 July 1959; also *New Statesman* 4 February 2010.

[8] Mary and Reginald Lygon's daughter Barbara in conversation with author, August 2020.

[9] The 'wind of change' speech was made by Macmillan to the Parliament of South Africa on 3 February 1960 in Cape Town, after a month visiting a number of remaining British colonies, The speech signalled clearly that his government would not block independence in many of its territories − a shift from the policy adopted by Conservative governments from 1951 onwards who had halted the process of de-colonisation initiated by the Labour government after winning the first elections after the end of World War Two.

[10] A graduate from Corpus Christi College, Cambridge, Renison was governor in the West Indies (1952−1958), first in British Honduras and then in British Guiana, the West Indies, before his Kenyan appointment. In a speech in 1960 he described Kenyatta as 'the African leader to darkness and death'.

[11] See Anais Angelo, *Power and Presidency in Kenya* (Cambridge: Cambridge University Press, 2019).

[12] WB's letter to Julian Amery, 17 July 1961, Amery papers, Churchill College archives.

[13] ibid.

[14] Quoted in James Fox, *White Mischief* , op.cit.

[15] WB's letter  to Julian Amery 17 July 1961, Amery papers, Churchill archives

[16] Bell papers, AA.

[17] Walton, op.cit.

[18] Macleod's letter to Macmillan 25 May 1959 Prem 11/2583. See also Hilda Missimi, 'Mau Mau and the Decolonisation of Kenya', *Journal of Military and Strategic Studies*, spring 2006, vol., 8, issue 3.

[19] WB's letter to Julian Amery 17 July 1961, op.cit.

[20] ibid.

[21] ibid. For Kellar role, see Walton, op.cit.

[22] WB to Amery. ibid.

[23] Bell papers, AA.

[24] The governor of Kenya, Patrick Renison, persisted in claiming that Kenyatta was the leader of Mau Mau 'to darkness and death'.

[25] Bell papers, AA.

[26] *The Tablet*, ibid.

[27] Walton, *Empire of Secrets*, op.cit.

[28] Peter Wright, *Spycatcher*, op.cit.

[29] Files on organisation of Intelligence Services in Kenya CO 1035/187 National Archives, Kew.

[30] Bell papers, AA.

[31] ibid.

[32] ibid.

[33] Jasper Bell's letter to author 26 November 2021.

[34] Mets, *Master of Airpower*, op.cit.

[35] CRO to Dar es Salaam, Kampala and Nairobi, TNA DO 213/54/1 National Archives Kew. See also Poppy Cullen, 'Operation Binnacle: British plans for military intervention against a 1965 coup in Kenya', *The International History Review*, vol. 39, 2017, issue 5, 28 January 1964.

[36] Bell papers, AA.

[37] ibid.

[38] Walton, *Empire of Secrets*, op.cit.

[39] Cullen, op.cit.

[40] Chaudhuri's letter to WB 23 February 1965, Bell papers, AA.

[41] Chaudhuri's letter to Bell 16 December 1965.

[42] Sir Richard Dearlove , MI6 chief 1999–2004.

[43] Bell papers, AA.

[44] Andrew, *In Defence*, op.cit.

[45] Bell papers, AA.

[46] *The Tablet*.

## 29 European Shadowlands

[1] Giles Scott-Smith *Western Anti-Communism and the Interdoc Network: Cold War Internationale* (London: Palgrave Macmillan, 2012.)

[2] See Giles Scott-Smith, op.cit. The BND channelled payments via a German study institute based in the quiet resident Munich suburb of Pullach. The BND's psychological warfare chief Rolf Geyer sent deputies to The Hague with briefcases full of cash.

[3] Rory Cormac, *How to Stage a Coup: And Ten Other Lessons from the World of Secret Statecraft* (London: Atlantic Books, 2022).

[4] Note by WB for the Noordwijk Conference 17 September 1976. Bell papers, AA.

[5] Scott-Smith, *Western Anti-Communism*, op. cit.

[6] Tity de Vries, 'The 1967 Central Intelligence Scandal', *Journal of American History*, vol.98 no. 4 March 2012.

[7] Scott-Smith, *Western Anti-Communism*, op. cit.

[8] Nigel West, *At Her Majesty's Secret Service* (London, 2006); Peter Wright *Spycatcher,* op.cit.

[9] Scott-Smith, *Western Anti-Communism*, op. cit.

[10] ibid.

[11] Walter Bell's letter to 'Bill' 22 September 1983, Bell papers, AA.

[12] William Stevenson, *A Man Called Intrepid* (London: Lyons Press, 2000). First published in 1976, the book, whose factual content remains questioned by official historians on both sides of the Atlantic, includes a 'historical note' by Ellis in which he describes himself as one of the historians of the British Security Co-Ordination who readily placed his own papers at the disposal of the author. Ellis claims, somewhat disingenuously, that he did so as a way of countering any disclosure of BSC activities surfacing as a result of information provided to the Russians by Kim Philby. 'In 1972, we knew that the Russians had learned rather more (about BSC) and might use information to bludgeon our friends, to distort history, and to hurt United States and Canadian relations with Britain. Full disclosure at least was the answer to the threat and to the demands of history. Hence this book.'

[13] Scott-Smith, *Western Anti-Communism*, op. cit.

[14] ibid.

[15] Bell maintained a personal correspondence with Cornelis van den Heuvel long after Interdoc's demise. In 1984 van den Heuvel wrote to Bell as the Dutch member of the Atlantist Paris-based Federation of European American Organisations representing voluntary organisations in Europe seeking to promote good relations with the US – a 'body in which I am actively engaged, and which does not have a British member-organisation'. Den Heuvel thanked Bell for sending him a paper entitled 'Diminishing the Nuclear Threat' and continuing to facilitate British contacts including 'friends in the Special Forces Club in London'. Van den Heuvel's letter to WB 15 March 1984 ), Bell papers, AA.

[16] WB's letter to Julian Amery 12 August 1971, Amery papers, Churchill College archives.

[17] Bell papers, AA.

[18] 'Masterly British Diplomat at the Centre of World Crises and Spy Scandals', *Guardian* 16 May 2002.

Also, programme of International Interdoc Conference Hotel
Metropole, 'The Policies of Western Europe and North America
Towards The Soviet Union' Brighton, 17-18 September 1971, Bell
papers, AA.

[19] 'Intelligence Expert who Formed His Own Organisation to
Counter Communist Propaganda', *Guardian* 9 April 2012.

[20] Scott-Smith, *Western Anti-Communism*, op. cit.

[21] See William Glenn Gray, *Journal of Modern History*, vol. 86, no. 4
(University of Chicago Journals).

[22] Michael Manley's letter to WB 18 June 1975, Bell papers, AA.

[23] WB's letter to Brian Crozier 3 October 1974, Bell papers, AA.

[24] Van den Heuvel's letter to WB 30 November 1976, Bell papers,
AA.

[25] Bell papers, AA.

[26] WB's letter to *The Tablet* 9 January 1977, Bell papers, AA.

[27] Note by WB for the Noordwijk Conference 17 September 1976,
Bell papers, AA.

[28] ibid.

[29] Van den Heuvel's letter to WB 15 March 1984.

## 30 Secrets and the Public Interest

[1] Hugh Trevor-Roper, *The Secret World*, op.cit.

[2] 'Treachery within the Establishment: The Case for a More Open
Approach to Security,' *Round Table 1980*, Bell papers, AA.

[3] Bell papers, AA.

[4] ibid.

[5] ibid.

[6] ibid.

[7] 'Treachery within the Establishment', op.cit.

[8] See Tom Bower's *The Perfect English Spy*, op.cit. White was 'stung'
by the allegation made to Andrew Boyle by Goronwy Rees, while the
Welsh academic and journalist lay dying in Charing Cross Hospital,
that Liddell 'was a traitor' and had had a homosexual relationship
with Guy Burgess. In 1999 the KGB defector Vasili Mitrokhin
published the Mitrokhin archives, based on a collection of
handwritten notes he had made secretly during his thirty years as a
KGB archivist. They included a file on Rees, documenting his
recruitment by Burgess during the mid-1930s. The file, however,
noted that Rees supplied no information to the Soviets of any value
and that he had abandoned his communist affiliation at the outbreak

of World War Two. (See The *Mitrokhin Archive: The KGB in Europe and the West* by Christopher Andrew and Vasili Mitrokhin).

[9] Lord Victor Rothschild, the banker, was recruited by MI5 in World War Two after studying at Cambridge during the 1930s where he became a member of the Cambridge Apostles, the intellectual society with Marxist leanings, and befriended Burgess, Blunt and Philby. During the Cold War years he was embroiled in various reported conspiracies of alleged Soviet penetration of the highest levels of British intelligence. He encouraged the retired MI5 officer Peter Wright and the journalist Chapman Pincher to publish allegations against the spy chief Sir Roger Hollis 'of whose innocence he had no doubt', writes Christopher Andrew in *Defence of the Realm*, perhaps having concluded that this 'would distract attention from the innuendoes accusing him of involvement with the KGB, with which he had become obsessed'.

[10] Number 5 Bentinck Street was the Marylebone London house made notorious by Guy Burgess. The property was owned at the time by Victor Rothschild.

[11] Sir David Petrie, MI5 director general (1941–1946); Sir Percy Sillitoe, MI5 director general (1946-1953). Guy Liddell was head of MI5's B Division (intelligence) when Sillitoe was made DG. Liddell was appointed deputy to the DG, a post he held until 1953, when he left MI5 and became security adviser to the Atomic Energy Authority.

[12] Dick White's letter to WB 24 April 1978, Bell papers, AA. Number 5 Bentinck Street, off Oxford Sreet, was leased by Victor Rothschild in October 1940 to his assistant at MI5 and future wife Tess Mayor and her friend Patricia Rawdon-Smith. Anthony Blunt joined to help with costs, and Guy Burgess would sleep over. (Andrew Lownie *Stalin's Englishman*, op.cit.)

[13] Nigel West's postscript to Guy Liddell's *Cold War MI5 Diaries*.

[14] Copy of Robert Cecil's letter to Sir John Balfour 12 June 1978, Bell papers, AA.

[15] Dick White's letter to Walter Bell 5 June 1979, Bell papers, AA.

[16] Bell papers, AA.

[17] Bell papers, AA.

[18] The Duke of Portland's son James Cavendish-Bentinck married Walter Bell's niece Barbara Lygon in 1960. The couple divorced in 1965 but Barbara and Walter remained on good terms with the Duke of Portland after James died in 1966.

[19] Letter to *The Times* 20 January 1980.

[20] ibid.

[21] Copy of telegram from William Stephenson to WB 19 January 1980, Bell papers, AA.

[22] *The Times* 21 January 1980.

[23] Copy of Bronson Tweedy letter to Walter Bell 16 January 1980, Bell papers, AA.

[24] ibid.

[25] ibid.

[26] Jim Angleton's letter to WB 6 July 1980, Bell papers, AA.

[27] ibid.

[28] ibid.

[29] ibid.

[30] ibid.

[31] Kim Philby, *My Silent War*, op.cit.

[32] Philip Agee, *Inside the Company* (New York: Bantam Books, 1981).

[33] See 'Do Whistleblowers Damage National Security?', a review by Justin Vogt in the *New York Times* 21 May 2021 of Jonathan Stevenson's biography of Agee, *A Drop of Treason* (Chicago: University of Chicago Press, 2021).

[34] Walter Bell, 'Treachery within the Establishment', op.cit.

[35] ibid.

[36] ibid.

## 31 A Very Catholic Spy

[1] Massimo Faggioli, 'Smiley's Priestly People', *The Tablet*, 17 December 2019.

[2] The Hinsley Memorial Lecture 2019: 'The Secret Intelligence Service and its History' 13 November 2019, op.cit.

[3] Faggioli, op.cit. See also John Sisman's biography of Le Carré, *John Le Carré: The Biography* (London: Bloomsbury, 2016).

[4] 'Word from the Cloisters' *The Tablet*, 17 December 2020.

[5] For an insight on how W.H. Auden explored various traditions and anti-traditions before a final conclusion 'I need God', see Tim Stanley, *Whatever Happened to Tradition?* (London: Bloomsbury Continuum, 2021). Also *The Tablet* interview with Stanley by Peter Stanford in *The Tablet* 4 December 2021.

[6] John le Carré, *Tinker, Tailor, Soldier, Spy* (London: Sceptre, 1974).

[7] Bell's SDP membership declaration (Bell papers, AA) .The SDP's founding leadership were four leading Labour Party moderates, Roy

Jenkins, David Owen, Bill Rodgers and Shirley Williams, the so-called Gang of Four. They supported electoral reform, European integration and a decentralised state while rejecting the excessive influence on Labour politics of trade unions.

[8] Faggioli, op.cit.

[9] Hansberry correspondence, Bell papers, AA. 'You are certainly not ready to "retire" in the usual sense and if Foundation "air" does not prove possible or acceptable there may well be opportunities in the private sector,' Hansberry wrote to Bell in January 1967. For CIA links, see *New York Times* 26 December 1977.

[10] Bell papers, AA. Pan American Airways' VP Kuter wrote to Bell in June 1968 that while 'your extraordinary high-level associations in areas of importance to the company was appreciated', there was 'no requirement in the company at all commensurate your own stature and your high qualifications'.

[11] Private information.

[12] On T.S. Eliot, I am indebted to the Catholic writer Catherine Pepinster's reflection on The *Magi* as shared in a BBC Radio 4, *Thought For the Day*.

## 32 Brothers in Arms

[1] *Independent* 23 February 1993.

[2] Bower, op.cit.

[3] Dick White's letter to WB 26 June 1984, Bell papers, AA.

[4] Bower, op.cit.

[5] Onslow Square was the location of Bell's London flat at Number 6.

[6] Dick White's letter to WB, Bell papers, AA.

[7] White's letter to Bell 6 July 1984, Bell papers, AA. Bettaney was convicted under the Official Secrets Act at the Old Bailey in 1984 for photographing secret documents for the KGB. He was jailed for 23 years in 1984 and released on parole in 1998.

[8] WB's letter to White, Bell papers, AA.

[9] White's letter to WBl, Bell papers, AA.

[10] For Bush's relationship with Noriega see Peter Eisner, 'Manuel Noriega , the Invasion of Panama and How George H.W Bush Misled America', *Newsweek* magazine 758, 18 March 2017.

[11] White & Bell correspondence when the US media exposed Noriega's illegal activities. See Seymour Hersh. 'Panama Strongman Said to Trade in Drugs, Arms and Illicit Money' the *New York Times* 12 June 1986.

[12] Tom Burns was editor of *The Tablet* 1967 to 1982.

[13] Jimmy Burns, *Papa Spy* , op.cit.

[14] White's letter to WB 16 January 1984, Bell papers, AA.

[15] ibid.

[16] Christopher Andrew & Gordievsky, op.cit.

[17] Christopher Andrew & Gordievsky, op.cit.

[18] See David Watkin, *Alfred Gilbey: A Memoir by Some Friends* (London: Michael Russell Ltd, 2001).

[19] See Gilbey's obituary in the *Independent* 28 March 1998.

[20] Roche, Jonathan *God's spies: the Spanish Elizabethans and intelligence during the Anglo-Spanish War,* PhD thesis, University of Nottingham, 2020.

[21] Correspondence between Walter Bell and Fr Ignatius, Bell papers, AA.

[22] 'One Man's View of the American Century'. Talk given by Walter Bell to the Military Commentators' Circle in London 14 August 1979, Bell papers, AA.

[23] Bell papers, AA.

[24] ibid.

[25] ibid.

[26] ibid.

[27] ibid.

[28] ibid.

[29] ibid.

[30] ibid.

[31] *The Tablet* 22 September 1984.

[32] ibid.

[33] ibid.

[34] ibid.

[35] *The Tablet* archives.

[36] ibid. 'Götterdämmerung' comes from the final part of Adolf Hitler's favourite Richard Wagner opera *Der Ring des Nibellungen,* which ends in mass destruction. It is the name given to the last days in Hitler's bunker during the Battle for Berlin, and before the surrender to the Soviet forces. In his book about the last days of Hitler, the historian Hugh Trevor-Roper, a wartime MI6 officer, described the world Hitler lived in as 'cloud cuckoo-land'.

### 33 A Last Awakening

[1] Henry Porter, 'Oldrich Cerny: a farewell salute to my old friend – the perfect spy,' *Guardian* 8 April 2012.

[2] Mabel Burns to author.

[3] *The Tablet* archives.

[4] *The Tablet* archives.

[5] During his retirement years, Bell often went to the South Downs to visit his old spy friend Dick White, or his nephew Jasper Bell.

[6] WB's letter to James Fulton 12 October 1982.

[7] Rose Fenton to author 18 July 2023.

### Epilogue to the paperback edition

[1] The Garrick Club newsletter March 2024

[2] Ibid.

[3] Ibid.

[4] Walter Bell LSE personal file, LSE archives.

[5] Ibid.

[6] Michel Cox email to author 27/02/2024

[7] Ibid.

[8] Victoria de Menil , *Once upon a time…when Jomo Kenyatta was a student* (LSE online)

[9] Patrick Heren , *The Article*, March 21, 2024

[10] I am indebted to Katherine Maclean , for sharing Tattie Spaatz Bell's Red Cross Clubmobile Chronicle based on letters to her mother, Ruth Harrison Spaatz, (June 1943-June 1945)

[11] Heren, opp.cit.

# Sources

This book is based on a large collection of Walter Bell's unpublished personal papers (AA-author's archive) covering a lifetime of more than nine decades spanning the twentieth century and the early part of the new millennium, working for the British intelligence and security services, MI6 and MI5, and collaborating with US agencies. The papers were made available to me by Bell's widow, Katharine Spaatz.

In addition, the book draws on interviews with family members, former intelligence officers, and other private, academic and intelligence archive records. On the whole the book has relied on written rather than oral material including a select bibliography to provide context and supportive evidence.

## Newspapers, periodicals, academic papers, online, personal & printed sources

*The Times*
*The Sunday Times*
*Financial Times*
*New York Times*
*Guardian*
*Daily Telegraph*
*The Tablet*
*The Spectator*
*The Irish Times*
BBC Radio & Website
Hinsley Lectures, Cambridge University (2003 and 2019)
Corpus Christi College, Cambridge Chapter Book
Tonbridge School Archives
FBI vault
FBI records, Lyle C.Wilson papers, Marquette University
Pat Spencer personal papers
The National Archives, Kew, MI5 files

Churchill College, Cambridge, Archives
Riverhead Parish Church records
Georgetown University Library
Author's Archive (AA)

## Images

Personal images are from the Walter Bell archive. Other images are available in the public domain with the exception of the photograph of Oliver Baldwin (SuperStock / Alamy Stock Photo).

## Books

Andrew, Christopher and Gordievsky, Oleg, *Instructions from the Centre: Top Secret Files on KGB Operations, 1975–85* ( London, 1991)

Andrew, Christopher, *The Defence of the Realm: The Authorized History of MI5* (London, 2009)

Andrew, Christopher and Green, Julius, *Stars and Spies: The Astonishing Story of Espionage and Show Business* (London, 2022)

Bower, Tom, *The Perfect English Spy*: Sir Dick White and the Secret War 1935–90 (London, 1995)

Boyle, Andrew, *The Climate of Treason*, (London, 1979)

Brake, Laurel, Kaul, Chandrika, Turner, Mark W. (eds), *The News of the World and The British Press, 1843–2011* (London, 2015)

Buchan, Ursula, *Beyond the Thirty-Nine Steps: A Life of John Buchan* (London, 2019)

Burns, Jimmy, *Papa Spy* (London, 2010)

Cook, Andrew, *Cash for Honours: The True Life of Maundy Gregory* (Stroud, 2008)

Cormac, Rory, *How to Stage a Coup: And Ten Other Lessons from the World of Secret Statecraft* (London, 2022)

Costello, John, *Days of Infamy: Macarthur, Roosevelt, Churchill – The Shocking Truth Revealed* (New York, 1994)

Donoughue, Bernard and Jones, G.W., *Herbert Morrison: Portrait of a Politician* (London, 2001)

Eade, Philip, *Evelyn Waugh: A Life Revisited* (London, 2017)

Fry, Helen, *Spymaster: The Man Who Saved MI6* (Yale, 2021)

Galbraith, J. William, *John Buchan: Model Governor General* (Toronto, 2013)

Gibbs, David, *In Search of Nathaniel Woodard: Victorian Founder of Schools* (Cheltenham, 2011)

Greene, Richard, *Russian Roulette: The Life and Times of Graham Greene* (London, 2020)

Griffiths, Richard, *An Intelligent Person's Guide to Fascism* (London, 2006)

Hayes, Paddy, *Queen of Spies: Daphne Park, Britain's Cold War Spymaster* (New York/London, 2025)

Hayne, John Earl and Klehr, Harvey, *Venona: Decoding Soviet Espionage in America* (Yale, 1999)

Hemming, Henry, *Our Man in New York: The British Plot to Bring America into the Second World War* (London, 2019)

Heren, Louis, *Growing Up on 'The Times'* (London, 1978)

Hopkins, Michael F., Kelly, Saul and Young, John W., *The Washington Embassy: British Ambassadors to the United States, 1939–77* (London, 2009)

Jeffery, Keith, MI6: *The History of the Secret Intelligence Service 1909–1949* (London, 2010)

Knightley, Phillip, *Philby: KGB Masterspy* (London, 1988)

*The Second Oldest Profession: Spies and Spying in the Twentieth Century* (London, 1987)

Kuper, Simon, *The Happy Traitor: Spies, Lies and Exile in Russia* (London, 2021)

Lamphere, Robert J. and Schachtman, Tom, *The FBI-KGB War: A Special Agent's Story* (New York, 1986)

Lankford, Nelson D.( ed.) and Bruce, David, *OSS Against The Reich: the World War II Diaries of Colonel David K.E. Bruce* (Kent, Ohio,1991)

—*The Last American Aristocrat: The Biography of David K.E. Bruce*( New York, 1996)

Laski, Harold, *The American Democracy* (New York, 1948)

Lownie, Andrew, *Stalin's Englishman: The Lives of Guy Burgess*

(London, 2016)

Lycett, Andrew, *Conan Doyle: The Man Who Created Sherlock Holmes* (London, 2008)

Macdonald, Bill, *The True Intrepid: Sir William Stephenson and the Unknown Agents* (Vancouver, 2001)

McDonald, Iverach, *The History of the Times* (London, 1984)

Macintyre, Ben, *Agent Sonya: Moscow's Most Daring Wartime Spy* (London, 2020)

—*A Spy Among Friends: Kim Philby and the Great Betrayal* (London, 2014)

MacPherson, Nelson, *American Intelligence in War-time London: The Story of the OSS* (Abingdon-on-Thames, UK, 2003)

Martin, Kingsley, *Harold Laski: A Biography* (New York, 1953)

Mets, David R., *Master of Airpower: General Carl A. Spaatz* (Novato, 1988)

Milne, Tim, *Kim Philby: The Unknown Story of the KGB's Master -Spy* (London, 2014)

Mulvagh, Jane, *Madresfield: One House, One Family, One Thousand Years* (London, 2009)

Norton-Taylor, Richard, *The State of Secrecy: Spies and the Media in Britain* (London, 2020)

Page, Bruce, Leitch, David and Knightley, Phillip, *The Philby Conspiracy* (London, 1968)

Philby, Kim, *My Silent War: The Autobiography of A Spy* (New York, 2003)

Philipps, Roland, *A Spy Named Orphan: The Enigma of Donald Maclean* (London, 2019)

Pincher, Chapman, *Their Trade is Treachery* (London, 1986)

Rand, Ayn, *The Fountainhead* (New York/London, 2007)

Rees, Goronwy, *A Chapter of Accidents* (New York, 1972)

Reynolds, Nicholas, *Need to Know: World War II and the Rise of American Intelligence* (Mariner, 2022)

Roberts, Andrew, *The Holy Fox: The Life of Lord Halifax* (London, 1991)

Rossiter, Heather *Lady Spy, Gentleman Explorer: The Life of Herbert Dyce Murphy* (Sydney, 2001)

Scott-Smith, Giles, *Western Anti-Communism and the Interdoc*

*Network: Cold War Internationale* (London, 2012)

Simms, Brendan, *Hitler: A Global Biography* (London, 2020)

Stephens, Philip, *Britain Alone: The Path from Suez to Brexit* (London, 2021)

Stevenson, William, *A Man Called Intrepid* (New York, 2000)

Strachey, John, *The Coming Struggle for Power* (London, 1933)

Sykes, Christopher, *Tormented Loyalty: The Story of a German Aristocrat Who Defied Hitler* (New York, 1969)

Symondson, Kay, *EM Forster's Gay Fiction* (London, 2016)

Verrier, Anthony, *The Road to Zimbabwe 1890–1980* (London, 1986)

Walker, Christopher J., *Oliver Baldwin: A Life of Dissent* (London, 2003)

Walton, Calder, *Empire of Secrets: British Intelligence, the Cold War and the Twilight of Empire* (London, 2013)

Weinstein, Allen and & Alexander Vassiliev, Alexander, *The Haunted Wood: Soviet Espionage in America –The Stalin Era* (New York, 1998)

West, Nigel, *Historical Dictionary of British Intelligence* (Plymouth, 2014)

—*MI6* : British Secret Intelligence Operations (London, 1983)

—(with Tsarev, Oleg) *The Crown Jewels* (London, 1999)

—(ed.) *Guy Liddell Diaries Volumes 1,2, & 3* (London/New York 2009)

—(ed.).*The Secret History of British Intelligence in the Americas, 1940-1945* (New York, 1999)

Whitwell, John, *British Agent* (London, 1966)

Williams, John L., *CLR James: A Life Beyond the Boundaries* (London, 2022)

Williams, Peter, *In Black & White* (Peter Williams Television PWTV, 2019)

Wright, Peter, *Spycatcher* (New York, 1987)

Yenne, Bill, *Hit the Target* (New York, 2016)

# Acknowledgements

While the various individuals who helped with this project in some way are too numerous to mention, and some would prefer to remain anonymous, I would like to extend a special thanks to the following:

Rupert Allason; Christopher Andrew; Richard Bassett; Raymond Batvinis; Dominic Bell; Jasper Bell; Gill Bennett; Robert Brinkley; Lisa & David Buchan; Ursula Buchan; George Carey; Amy Cooper Cary; Sir Richard Dearlove; John de St.Jorre; Catherine Edis; Nick Elwood; Rose Fenton; Helen Fry; David Gioe; Roger Golland; Richard Gompertz; Robert Graham; Peter Hennessy; Patrick Heren; Michael Hodges; Claire Huffman; Nelson D.Lankford; Fr Julian Large; David Liebler; Andrew Lownie; Barbara Lygon; Peter Martland; Beverley Matthews; Fr Shaun Middleton; Margaret Nicholas; James Naughtie; Hannah O'Hara; Allen Packwood; Hayden Peake; Michael Phelan; Roland Philipps; Penny Phillips; Charles Pinck; John Ranelagh; Nicholas Reynolds; Andrew Riley; Giles Scott-Smith; Brendan Simms; Duncan M.Spencer; Leslie Spencer; Scott S.Taylor; Stewart Tendler; Carla Thomas; Jean Thomas; Ruth Thomas; Felix Von Moreau; Calder Walton; Ben Welch; Rachel Wigley; Heather Williams; Philip Wright.

Thanks too to my publisher, Stuart Leasor, and editor, Miren Lopategui, for bringing this to fruition.

# Index

# H

# I

# X

# Y

# Z